CHILDREN'S RIGHTS IN AFRICA

Children's Rights in Africa
A Legal Perspective

Edited by

JULIA SLOTH-NIELSEN
University of the Western Cape, South Africa

ASHGATE

Published by
Ashgate Publishing Limited
Gower House
Croft Road
Aldershot
Hampshire GU11 3HR
England

Ashgate Publishing Company
Suite 420
101 Cherry Street
Burlington, VT 05401-4405
USA

www.ashgate.com

British Library Cataloguing in Publication Data
Children's rights in Africa : a legal perspective
   1. Children's rights - Africa 2. Children - Africa - Social
   conditions
   I. Sloth-Nielsen, Julia
   323.3'52'096

Library of Congress Cataloging-in-Publication Data
Children's rights in Africa, a legal perspective / edited by Julia Sloth-Nielsen.
       p. cm.
    Includes index.
    ISBN 978-0-7546-4887-1
   1. Children--Legal status, laws, etc.--Africa. 2. Children's rights--Africa. 3. Child welfare--Africa. I. Sloth-Nielsen, Julia.

    KQC145.M55C48 2008
    342.608'772--dc22

                                                                    2008017518

ISBN 978 0 7546 4887 1

Mixed Sources
Product group from well-managed
forests and other controlled sources
www.fsc.org Cert no. SA-COC-1565
© 1996 Forest Stewardship Council

Printed and bound in Great Britain by
MPG Books Ltd, Bodmin, Cornwall.

Contents

Preface

This volume was born from the experience of more than a decade of teaching a LLM module on 'Children's rights and the law in African context'. This programme has since inception enabled access to groups of students from throughout Africa, who have participated annually as part of the LLM (Human Rights and Democracy in Africa) programme established by the Centre for Human Rights at the University of Pretoria. Many have continued to further law studies, amongst them some who have pursued doctoral studies in the children's rights sphere. This book is dedicated first to the many past students in the course whose insights, practical and theoretical knowledge of African human rights issues, and ability to deepen current discourses have enriched both teaching and classroom debates. They form, in the main, the contributors to this volume.

Next, thanks to the Community Law Centre staff and colleagues – Jacqui Gallinetti and Daksha Kassan of the Children's Rights Project and Helene Combrinck of the Gender Project, who have all found time in their busy schedules to write chapters to further the cause of children's rights. Stalwarts Jill Claassen (documentalist), and Trudi Fortuin, Virginia Brookes and Janine Demas deserve special mention, especially in meeting the needs of our LLM and LLD students. To the other authors whose work is featured here, I express my heartfelt thanks and appreciation. With one exception, all the authors are of African origin, and all committed to developing an African human rights – and child rights – agenda.

I would like to acknowledge all the wonderful child rights activists I have met during various projects in Africa – Itumeleng, Ricardo, Gabi, Seamus, my dear friend Belinda, Anna, Akur, Judge Twea, and staff from the African Child Policy Forum, to mention but a few. It is their passion and understanding that is laying the basis for Africa's renaissance in the children's rights sphere.

Appreciation must be expressed to the National Research Foundation of South Africa for supporting research on the themes addressed in this book, as well as to the Ford Foundation, who provide core funding to the Community Law Centre's Children's Rights Project. The views expressed in this volume are, however, those of the authors.

Last, a very special word of thanks to Benyam D. Mezmur, who has given indefatigably of his advice, assistance and labour in the editing process. Without his dedication and commitment, this work would not have come to fruition.

Julia Sloth-Nielsen
University of the Western Cape
February 2008

List of Abbreviations

ACERWC	African Committee of Experts on the Rights and Welfare of the Child
ACHPR	African Charter on Human and Peoples' Rights
ACRWC	African Charter on the Rights and Welfare of the Child; a.k.a. African Children's Charter
ANPPCAN	African Network for the Prevention and Protection against Child Abuse and Neglect
APRM	African Peer Review Mechanism
AU	African Union
AWP	Protocol to the African Charter on Human and Peoples' Rights on the Rights of Women; a.k.a. African Women's Protocol
BLNS	Botswana, Lesotho, Namibia and Swaziland
CEDAW	Convention on the Elimination of All Forms of Discrimination Against Women
CESCR	Committee on Economic, Social and Cultural Rights
CLC	Community Law Centre (University of the Western Cape, South Africa)
CLPA	Child Labour Programme of Action (South Africa)
CRC	Convention on the Rights of the Child
CSO	civil society organization
DAC	Day of the African Child
DDR	disarmament, demobilization and reintegration
DRC	Democratic Republic of Congo
ECOWAS	Economic Community of West African States
EFA	Education for All
FAWE	Forum for African Women Educationalists
FGM	female genital mutilation
FPE	Free Primary Education
HSIC	Heads of State and Government Implementation Committee
ICC	International Criminal Court
ICCPR	International Covenant on Civil and Political Rights
ICERD	International Convention on the Elimination of all Forms of Racial Discrimination
ICESCR	International Covenant on Economic, Social and Cultural Rights
ICRC	International Committee of the Red Cross
ICTR	International Criminal Tribunal for Rwanda
ICTY	International Criminal Tribunal for the former Yugoslavia
IDP	internally displaced person
IHRDA	Institute for Human Rights and Development in Africa
ILO	International Labour Organization

IOM	International Organization for Migration
IPEC	International Programme on the Elimination of Child Labour
LLRC	Lesotho Law Reform Commission
LRA	Lord's Resistance Army
LSAC	Labour and Social Affairs Commission
LSAD	Labour and Social Affairs Directorate
MDG	Millennium Development Goal
MTCT	mother-to-child-transmission
NEPAD	New Partnership for Africa's Development
NGO	non-governmental organization
NICRO	National Institute for Crime Prevention and the Reintegration of Offenders
OAU	Organization of African Unity
OVC	orphaned and vulnerable child
RAPCAN	Resources Aimed at the Prevention of Child Abuse and Neglect
RUF	Revolutionary United Front
SALRC	South African Law Reform Commission
SCSL	Special Court for Sierra Leone
TECL	Towards the Elimination of the worst forms of Child Labour
TRC	truth and reconciliation commission
UDHR	Universal Declaration of Human Rights
UNAIDS	Joint United Nations Programme on HIV/AIDS
UNDP	United Nations Development Programme
UNESCO	United Nations Educational, Scientific, and Cultural Organization
UNFPA	United Nations Fund for Population Activities; a.k.a. United Nations Population Fund
UNGASSoC	United Nations General Assembly Special Session on Children
UNHCR	United Nations High Commissioner for Refugees
UNICEF	United Nations Children's Fund
UNICT	United Nations Information and Communication Technologies
UN JDL	United Nations Rules for the Protection of Juveniles Deprived of their Liberty
UNODC	United Nations Office on Drugs and Crime
UNSC	United Nations Security Council
USAID	United States Agency for International Development
UTREL	Unidade Técnica da Reforma Legal (office in the Ministry of Justice responsible for law reform in Mozambique)
WFP	World Food Programme
WHO	World Health Organization

PART I

Chapter 1

Children's Rights and the Law in African Context: An Introduction

Julia Sloth-Nielsen

As Murray points out, the notion of the protection of children and fulfilment of their rights is not new on the African continent, the first Declaration on the Rights and Welfare of the Child having been adopted by the Assembly of Heads of State and Government in 1979 (Murray 2004, 165). Furthermore there have been a number of Declarations and Resolutions adopted by OAU/AU (Organization of African Unity/African Union) organs concerning children, primarily related to development, health and children affected by armed conflict. The pride of place, however, is occupied by the regional treaty, the African Charter on the Rights and Welfare of the Child (ACRWC), which was adopted in 1990, and which entered into force shortly before the dawn of the new millennium in 1999 at about the same time that much of Africa and her children were emerging from the devastating impact and economic consequences of Structural Adjustment Programmes. Lloyd has previously noted:

> The African children's charter prides itself on its African perspective on rights, yet was inspired by the trends evident in the UN system. It was intended to be a complementary mechanism to that of the UN in order to enhance the enjoyment of the rights of children in Africa. (Lloyd 2002, 182)

From the outset, it must be granted that many a reader will be familiar with the tales of Africa's misery and woe that constantly feature in popular media, in hard-hitting research reports and in global debates about the continent's future (both from an economic and from a human rights perspective). As Viljoen, writing in 2000, pointed out:

> In many respects, children are more likely to be victims of human rights violations than adults, and African children are more likely to be victims than children on other continents. Causes of human rights violations in Africa, such as poverty, HIV/Aids, warfare, famine and harmful cultural practices have a disproportionate impact on the continent's children. (Viljoen 2000)

It cannot be gainsaid that serious underdevelopment, prevalent violations of children's basic rights, war, famine and disaster, not to mention the devastating impact that is being wrought by HIV/Aids in sub-Saharan Africa, commonly tarnish the idea that African children may benefit positively through conferring human rights-compliant legal rights upon them. However, as the chapters in this volume spell out, considerable progress has been made towards making children's rights visible in a variety of domains on the continent since the entry into force of the ACRWC.

This volume of essays is anchored in an African conception of children's rights and the law, and reflects contemporary discourses taking place in the region in the children's rights sphere. In focusing on child rights issues which have particular resonance on the continent, the chapters span themes which are both broad and narrow; they contain subject matter which is both theoretical and illuminated by practice; the pan-African focus has been fostered by the existence of a growing network of collaboration and information dissemination amongst lawyers, academe and policy makers in this region (African Child Policy Forum 2007b). The central objective of all the contributions, however, is to profile recent developments and experiences in furthering children's legal rights in the African context, and to distil from these future trends for Africa's child rights environment, and the specific role that the law can play in this.

The chapters in Part I of this volume are general in nature. The regional human rights architecture is characterized by an overarching treaty providing for the human rights of African peoples (the African Charter on Human and Peoples' Rights – ACHPR). The ACHPR has recently been elaborated with the addition of an optional protocol on women's rights (Protocol to the African Charter on Human and Peoples' Rights on the Rights of Women – AWP), and in July 2004, the statute for the establishment of an African Court on Human Rights came into operation. Setting the scene for ensuing chapters by elaborating this architecture for the protection of human rights in the African regional system is Olowu in Chapter 2, who additionally charts the restructuring of political governance at the regional level that has taken place in recent times. He describes the demise of the OAU, and the birth of the AU, the development of the New Partnership for Africa's Development (NEPAD), Africa's commitment to immediate action for the creation of a climate conducive to sustainable economic development, and its internal self-review mechanism, the African Peer Review Mechanism (APRM), which has attracted international interest and support (see too, Chirwa, Chapter 6). Seen together, it is arguable that these treaties and the concrete commitments recently put in place by NEPAD and the APRM already go some way to providing the basis for a more optimistic outlook regarding the future implementation of children's rights in Africa.

The regional body tasked with oversight of the ACRWC, the African Committee of Experts on the Rights and Welfare of the Child (ACERWC) is, at the time of writing, poised to consider the first four country reports received. The key features of the ACRWC and the achievements and challenges faced by the ACERWC form the subject matter of Chapter 3 authored by Lloyd, and the normative framework of the substantive provisions of the African Children's Charter also underpin the analyses in subsequent thematic chapters.

Chapter 4 (Sloth-Nielsen) documents the ongoing project of domestication of children's rights across the continent. Commencing with an overview of the elaboration of children's rights in African constitutions, particular attention is paid to the impact of South Africa's constitutional clause pertaining to children's rights, adopted a decade ago and hailed as the most extensive constitutional protection for children anywhere. The fact that the constitutional rights enumerated therein are justiciable, including the socio-economic rights accorded to children, has led to an evolving jurisprudence which has attracted international repute (Innocenti Centre 2008; Sloth-Nielsen 2002; Sloth-Nielsen and Mezmur 2007b).

This chapter also reviews the domestication processes and law reform initiatives that have been taking place on the continent since the adoption of the first comprehensive children's act, that of Uganda in 1996. These endeavours have the aim of reshaping the colonial heritage, of modernizing and synthesizing child law, and of domesticating international human and child rights standards, and of targeting especially vulnerable groups of children for enhanced legal protection. The law reform processes in each of the examples have followed different trajectories, have involved a variety of stakeholders and partners, and are currently at various stages of completion. Some are still being drafted, others have been enacted, whilst a third group await introduction to, or passage through, parliament.

It has been pointed out that considerable regional sharing of ideas and proposed provisions has occurred, and that in many ways indigenous innovation has been fostered. This cross-border fertilization has arguably been the most extensive in the field of child justice, both from the programmatic and from the legislative points of view. Since the mid-1990s, South African NGOs have provided diversion programme training in Zambia, Kenya, Malawi and Lesotho, to name a few examples (Gallinetti and Sloth-Nielsen 2004; Sloth-Nielsen 2006). There is clearly a need for an expanded focus on children and access to justice in Africa more broadly, beyond the sub-Saharan countries that have thus far benefited from regional collaboration.

It can be suggested, too, that the benefits of these legal processes are not simply confined to the realm of law, rights and forms of adjudication: there have been economic spin offs, enhanced public awareness of children's rights through participative exercises that accompanied the law reform processes (also discussed by Ehlers and Franks in Chapter 7), and concerted examination of the structures and resources necessary for the fulfilment of children's rights at a more practical level.

Himonga (Chapter 5) situates a changing perspective on the role of culture and customary law – and hence the place of children in African society at large – within the context of a shifting socio-political environment, brought about, amongst other reasons, by altered family and kinship structures. She highlights the intersections between customary law and children's rights, pointing to the cultural sensitivity of recent statutory legal reforms and their dispute resolution mechanisms which attempt to harness traditional structures to the benefit of children. Concluding that African customary child law is increasingly acquiring a new face, she situates this in the intersection brought about by new children's legislation and living customary law systems.

As Chirwa notes in Chapter 6, Africa is currently experiencing a wave of democratization, and a raft of new constitutions have shepherded in fragile, but fledgling, democracies. Further to this, though, economic indicators appear to be improving, and there is globally and on the continent a great degree of consensus concerning at least some of the goals of economic recovery via, for instance, the Millennium Development Goals. Chirwa situates his discussion about socio-economic rights in the context of the general neglect of this group of rights in African constitutions, and their under-protection at the domestic level, even where they do enjoy constitutional protection. He argues for more targeted measures to ensure the fulfilment of children's socio-economic rights, and that they be accorded priority status in all development endeavours.

The past decade has undeniably seen the traditional invisibility of the African child dissipate, in favour of rights-based approaches and a more prominent societal role being accorded to children who, in most African countries, constitute fully 50 per cent of the population. In customary and traditional African society, children occupied a silent space in the kinship structure, depending on adult intervention for a voice. However, African children's voices are increasingly being heard in matters which concern them; they have achieved heightened prominence in processes ranging from the quasi-political (through children's parliaments for example), to the fiscal and economic terrain (Barberton 2006; Innocenti Centre 2007), and extending to the legal and jurisprudential terrains (Sloth-Nielsen and Mezmur 2007b).

The more general chapters in Part I set the scene for the consideration of the individual themes dealt with in Part II. This second section of the book deals with selected individual topics, ranging from inter-country adoption, to the rights of children with disabilities, to child soldiers and refugee and migrant children. The themes forming the topics of each chapter in Part II are of critical significance to Africa as a whole and were selected for that reason. The authors use the matrix of the legal aspects of children's rights in African context as the lens through which their analysis is presented. As a general proposition, the view is propounded that child law – international law and national law – is providing a useful tool for the advancement of children's rights at a practical level, and that further development of a regional child rights jurisprudence is warranted (Skelton, Chapter 8 and Odongo, Chapter 9, for instance).

The first chapter in Part II, Chapter 7 (Ehlers and Franks), deals with child participation in African law reform processes, amongst others, and reflects on the extent to which authentic voices of children have been captured and integrated in the processes they have chosen to profile. Child participation in the recent Global Study on Violence in various regions on the continent has revealed the rich contribution that children's voices can make in researching children's rights and remedies, and above all, the child participation processes that were part of the Global Study have definitively placed the African child on the centre stage in debates that affect them (see also Chapter 10 [Kassan] for a discussion of African children's voices in relation to the UN Violence Study).

Children in conflict with the law feature in both Chapters 8 and 9. Successful juvenile justice reforms have been introduced in a number of jurisdictions in Africa, with a growing continental emphasis on diversion and alternative programmatic responses to children in conflict with the law, approaches which at the same time overcome the resource constraints that prevail in African context. Some relevant initiatives are detailed in Skelton's chapter on restorative justice and children's rights in African context (Chapter 8), others appear in the study of law reform in six African countries in the child justice sphere by Odongo (Chapter 9). Skelton cites positive examples of indigenous approaches (in countries such as Uganda, Namibia and Lesotho) to harness beneficial customary structures and traditions to support children's rights (Sloth-Nielsen 2006). Both chapters also demonstrate how regional skills transfer is occurring to develop human resource capacity and locally appropriate solutions.

Chapter 10 (The Protection of Children from All Forms of Violence – African Experiences) updates continental developments that have occurred especially in the build up to the UN Study on Violence against Children, although the point is clearly made that corporal punishment is regarded as being culturally acceptable on a pervasive basis, to the extent that only in the recent Interim Constitution of Southern Sudan has a prohibition on parental physical punishment been provided for. It is testimony to the resilience of beliefs about the practice that even in the South African law reform process that is described in detail in several chapters in this volume, a legislative ban on parental corporal punishment has not, at the time of writing, successfully passed parliamentary muster.

In Chapter 11, titled 'The Protection of Refugee Children under the African Human Rights System: Finding Durable Solutions in International Law', Kaime reviews the applicable legal context with the specifics of the problems facing migrant and refugee children on the African continent. In this regard, the provisions of the African Children's Charter are particularly nuanced towards the effective promotion of the rights of displaced children. The quest for durable solutions may be described as an endeavour towards normalcy, entailing that all the rights to be afforded to refugee children are taken into account by states parties, onerous though these might be.

In Chapter 12, Mezmur reviews the applicable international legal framework addressing various aspects relevant to child soldiers, an enduring feature of regional conflicts in places such as Chad, the Democratic Republic of the Congo (DRC), Congo-Brazzaville and Sudan. He reviews recent literature illustrating the variety of roles in which children play a role in armed conflicts, and how this has affected the contemporary legal framework, with emphasis on the Optional Protocol to the Convention on the Rights of the Child (CRC) dedicated to the issue of child soldiers and the new safeguards it employs. The review also addresses novel provisions enshrined in the Optional Protocol regarding post-conflict issues, including demobilization and reintegration of child soldiers, but at the same time laments the lack of specific legal provisions catering for the needs of girl soldiers. Noting that ending a culture of impunity for the recruitment of child soldiers remains a key issue related to enforcement; recent prosecutions for the act of recruiting child soldiers or 'bush wives' is a welcome development in the further fight against the use of children in war.

Implementation of the right to universal free primary education and the concomitant increase in access to education has been underway since the turn of the millennium in a number of countries (Lesotho, Kenya, Ethiopia, Mozambique, Uganda, to name a few) with notable advances recorded (Tomasevski 2006). Mwambene, in Chapter 13, discusses positive developments in furthering the right to education of the African girl child, insofar as significantly gendered existing school attendance figures are a key indicator of the extent of the implementation gap concerning the right to access education in most parts of the continent. She examines efforts being undertaken to improve girl's access to education in laws and policies generally before proceeding to examine some of the difficulties and challenges, especially those related to education in conflict areas or in relation to refugee children. Some of the issues that have emerged in the era of free primary education – such as 'access shock' (Tomasevski 2006) – are also reviewed.

Chapter 14 deals with the highly problematic topic of trafficking in children, an area in which there has been considerable regional activity on the African continent of late, and in which promising successes at the legal, policy and practical level can be recorded in reducing the incidence of this scourge. Gallinetti and Kassan review the applicable legal framework, notably the UN Convention Against Transnational Organized Crime of 2000 and its Optional Protocol to Prevent, Suppress and Punish Trafficking in Persons, Especially Women and Children (the Palermo Protocol) with its comprehensive definition of trafficking. The contribution of the international community (International Labour Organization – ILO; International Programme on the Elimination of Child Labour – IPEC) to programme development to combat trafficking is discussed, and the chapter further illustrates a series of concerted efforts underway at regional and country level to reduce children's exposure to this harmful practice.

Intercountry adoption, with African states overwhelmingly featuring as countries of origin (or sending countries), is a topic of some contemporary relevance, given recent dramatic events involving figures of fame (Madonna, Angelina Jolie) and high-profile arrests and criminal prosecutions (notably the Zoe's Ark saga relating to children removed from Chad). It can be suggested that a sound international framework for co-operation on intercountry adoption matters exists, one which was developed to promote the best interests of the prospective adoptive child, in the form of provisions of the CRC, the ACRWC, and the more detailed Hague Convention on Intercountry Adoption of 1993, with provisions for central authorities to oversee and monitor adoption processes and their follow-up. However, one key area of concern has been the low number of African signatories to this Convention. The recent international publicity may change this state of affairs, though, and there are, in addition, welcome signs of domestication of intercountry adoption protections in several pending law reform processes. Davel discusses aspects of intercountry adoption from the perspective of the African context in Chapter 15.

HIV/Aids has been described as the most significant threat to the child rights gains that have been made in sub-Saharan Africa. The tentacles of this disease challenge our assumptions about childhood, as children are of necessity being required to make important decisions (concerning access to information about their HIV status, for instance) or to head households at an age when they must still enjoy the protections that the status of childhood should confer. Nor is it as yet clear how the law should respond to the impact of HIV/Aids upon children, although the first tentative steps are being taken in this regard in several countries. These initiatives form the basis of the chapter by Sloth-Nielsen and Mezmur, Chapter 16, which concludes with an assessment of some paradoxical benefits regarding the implementation of children's rights to which the HIV pandemic has arguably given rise.

Chapter 17, authored by Combrinck, concerns the plight of children with disabilities in Africa, and the applicable legal framework within which to promote fulfilment of their rights. Written as the African Decade of Disability is underway, this chapter is centred around the social model of disability now enshrined in the UN Convention on the Rights of People with Disabilities (2006), which at the time of writing had received 17 of the required 20 ratifications necessary for its entry into force. From a child rights perspective, of no less import is the CRC Committee's

General Comment no. 9 on the rights of children with disabilities. The author suggests, though, that this sound rights-based framework notwithstanding, there is a significant implementation gap on the African continent, and that efforts must be targeted at approaching the education of disabled African children with urgency.

In the sphere of child labour, Gallinetti (Chapter 18) refers to a concerted effort to put mechanisms and action plans in place in several African countries to reduce the involvement of children in the worst forms of child labour, again signalling progress in the protection of children's rights. Here ILO Convention 182 on the Elimination of the Worst Forms of Child Labour (1999) is accorded a signal role in spurring programme development, new policies and, increasingly, legal reform. This chapter breaks new ground in its consideration of implementation aspects of ILO Convention 182, of special relevance to children on the African continent.

In sum, an overly pathological focus on the violations of rights experienced by African's children masks some important constructive developments, encouraging initiatives and, ultimately, important steps forward that are being made towards achieving the fulfilment of the rights of children in Africa. The contributors to this volume are realistic about Africa's challenges, underdevelopment, and the litany of children's rights violations that can be catalogued, but, at the same time, have profiled positive practices and examples related to the fulfilment of children's legal rights that support the proposition that some progress is indeed being made, or, at least, that the legal architecture for change to occur is largely in place. An example is the concerted international attention focused on the plight of child soldiers, and the utilization of legal means to bring perpetrators who recruit child soldiers to book of late. Further, there is thus considerable support for the assertion that the African child is now, despite cultural norms that still pertain, to a far lesser degree than was the case in the past, 'seen and not heard'. And, as is argued below, a child rights-centric awareness of the challenges of engaging with children in research that has been brought about by the HIV/Aids crisis breaks new ground in childhood studies. Many advances in overhauling and updating child-related laws at national levels are recorded in this volume, and children's visibility in governance structures via such innovations as children's parliaments, co-ordinating committees or commissions, or ministries specifically tasked with children's rights implementation has increased markedly (African Child Policy Forum 2007a). Implementation of free primary education policies, since the turn of the millennium in particular, have seen children flood into schools, and the beginnings of economic growth trends in many countries has brought with it possibilities of more widespread poverty alleviation programmes to benefit children (such as cash transfers, social grants targeting children, bursaries and the like [African Child Policy Forum 2007a]).

Ultimately, the inspiration for promoting the children's rights agenda in African context must lie within these territorial confines: ideally, African solutions must be developed and fostered, and an indigenous jurisprudence and normative approach built upon. Documenting this should fall to scholars with hands-on knowledge of the African context, its particular challenges and its rich possibilities. As Zeleza points out, trading, sharing, and incorporating human rights experiences, practices and symbols across culture and the enduring West-East and North-South divide can assist in the development of a truly universal human rights discourse, which at the moment does not yet exist. (Zeleza 2004, 43)

He continues to urge those making assertions about African human rights to immerse themselves in African history and philosophy, to which possibly be can be added jurisprudence. At present, there is a dearth of accessible writing on children's legal rights and their role in development in Africa, one of the key reasons being the inaccessibility of resource material. It is difficult, hence, to obtain a cohesive picture of what good practices exist and how they can be replicated. It could also be asserted that the development of an African child rights jurisprudence is still in its infancy, and clearly calls for more attention. This collection of essays on children's rights and the law in African context represents a modest attempt to embark on that mission.

References

Articles, Books and Chapters in Books

Davel, C. (ed.) (2000), *Introduction to Child Law in South Africa* (Cape Town: Juta and Co.).

Gallinetti, J. and Sloth-Nielsen, J. (eds) (2004), *Child Justice in Africa: A Guide to Good Practice* (Cape Town: Children's Rights Project, Community Law Centre).

Heyns, C. and Stefiszyn, K. (eds) (2006), *Human Rights, Peace and Justice in Africa: A Reader* (Pretoria: Pretoria University Law Press).

Lloyd, A. (2002), 'Evolution of the African Charter on the Rights and Welfare of the Child and the African Committee of Experts: Raising the Gauntlet', *International Journal of Children's Rights* 10, 179–98.

Murray, R. (2004), *Human Rights in Africa* (Cambridge: Cambridge University Press).

Tomasevski, K. (2006), *Human Rights Obligations in Education: The '4-A' Scheme* (Nijmegan: Wolf Legal Publishers).

Viljoen, F. (2000), 'The African Charter on the Rights and Welfare of the Child', in Davel, C. (ed.).

Zeleza, P.T. (2004), 'The Struggle for Human Rights in Africa', in Heyns, C. and Stefiszyn, K. (eds).

General Comments, Unpublished Papers, Treaties, Declarations and Reports

African Child Policy Forum (2007a), 'Child-friendly Laws and Policies in Africa' (draft report) (Addis Ababa: African Child Policy Forum).

African Child Policy Forum (2007b), *Realising their Rights: Harmonization of Law for Children in Eastern and Southern Africa* (Addis Ababa: African Child Policy Forum).

Barberton, C. (2006), *The Cost of the Children's Bill: Estimates of the Cost to Government of the Services Envisaged by the Comprehensive Children's Bill 2005–2010* (available from the National Department of Social Development, South Africa).

Innocenti Centre (2007), *Reforming Child Law in South Africa: Budgeting and Implementation Planning*, <www.unicef-irc.org/publications> (accessed 12 November 2007).

Innocenti Centre (2008), *Law Reform and Implementation of the Convention on the Rights of the Child*, <www.unicef-irc.org/publications> (accessed 12 January 2008).

Sloth-Nielsen, J. (2002), 'Children's Rights in South African Courts: An Overview since Ratification of the UN Convention on the Rights of the Child', *International Journal on Children's Rights* 10:2, 137–56.

Sloth-Nielsen, J. (2006), 'Best Practice: Law Reform in Lesotho' (unpublished paper prepared for the African Child Policy Forum, Addis Ababa).

Sloth-Nielsen, J. and Mezmur, B.D. (2007a), 'Surveying the Research Landscape to Promote Children's Legal Rights in an African context', *African Human Rights Law Journal* 7:2, 330–53.

Sloth-Nielsen, J. and Mezmur, B.D. (2007b), '2 + 2 =5? Exploring the Domestication of the CRC in South African Jurisprudence 2002–2006', paper delivered at the International Conference on the Rights of the Child, Ottawa, Canada, 15–17 March 2007. Also published in *International Journal on Children's Rights* 1 (2008), 1–28.

UN Convention on the Rights of People with Disabilities (GA RES A/61/611 dated 6 December 2006).

Chapter 2

The Regional System of Protection of Human Rights in Africa

'Dejo Olowu

Introduction

When, at the very end of the last millennium, Professors Steiner and Alston described the African regional human rights system as 'the newest, the least developed or effective ... the most distinctive and the most controversial' (2000, 920), they must have had at the back of their minds the picture of an unsteady regional arrangement, of the helplessness of human rights standards to tame the vicious spirit of *génocidaires*, irrepressible rebels, warlords and brutal dictators. To these must be added the unmistakable pangs of human misery, on a continent replete with manifest contradictions between human rights norms and effective human rights protection.

There have indeed been many volumes of scholarly works on the subject of human rights in Africa ranging from the philosophical, the conceptual and the historical, to the epistemological, the empirical and the semantic. It has been an engaging endeavour for scholars to contend about the remoteness of universalism to indigenous 'human rights' thinking in Africa (see, for instance, Shivji 1989; Cobbah 1987; Howard 1986; Busia Jr 1994); and the weaknesses, ambivalence or Utopian goals of the African regional human rights system (see, for instance, Udombana 1999; Baah 2000, 39–41; Bondzie-Simpson 1988; Murray 2001; Gutto 2001, 181–5). While some authors have engaged the impracticability of certain categories of human rights in and for Africa and the mass of impediments to human rights protection in African states (see, for instance, Busia Jr 1994; Eze 1984; Donnelly 1984; El-Obaid et al. 1996; Eze 1990; Doebbler 2003; Murray 2004), others have concentrated on documenting the history and spate of state-sponsored violations of human rights particularly as they relate to democratization, electioneering and the political process (Gutto 1993, 47–9; Udombana 2003).

The historical dimensions of human rights violations and the continuing scepticism about the efficacy of human rights in Africa are, however, at variance with the essence of this chapter. This chapter is forward-looking in all its ramifications and its focus involves: presenting a general overview of the African regional human rights system; an assessment of the importance of this system in the overall development of the African continent; and an insight into the prospects of strengthening the system. This chapter therefore analyses some of the significant normative and institutional aspects of the African regional human rights system and accentuates the unique and emergent features of the system and their capacity to sustain a vibrant and integrative human rights culture in Africa. In this regard, this chapter adopts a descriptive approach in its presentation of the African regional human rights system, highlighting the capabilities of its normative frameworks and institutional mechanisms.

An Overview of the African Regional Human Rights System

By 'African regional human rights system', is meant the past, present and ongoing collective or concerted efforts by African peoples and states to secure human rights and freedoms for all peoples under a coherent arrangement. This system revolves around diverse institutions and normative frameworks. Like the other existing regional human rights arrangements, namely those of Europe and the Americas, the African regional human rights system is based on treaties that are elaborated and explained by other non-binding documents, such as resolutions, declarations and guidelines. The most significant treaties that enunciate the African regional human rights system are:

- the African Charter Governing Specific Aspects of the Refugee Problem in Africa, 1969, which entered into force in 1974;
- the African Charter on Human and Peoples' Rights, 1981, (ACHPR) which entered into force in 1986;
- the African Charter on the Rights and Welfare of the Child, 1990, (ACRWC) which entered into force in 1999;
- the Protocol to the African Charter on Human and Peoples' Rights Establishing the African Court on Human and Peoples' Rights, 1998, which entered into force in 2004;
- the Protocol to the African Charter on Human and Peoples' Rights on the Rights of Women, 2003, (AWP) which entered into force in 2005.

These essential documents serve as common standards to guide African member states on their obligation to protect and promote human rights within their respective jurisdictions. The mechanisms for enforcing such human rights obligations vary within the institutions established by the African regional human rights system as well as among African states.

Prominent among the institutions directly dealing with the African regional human rights system are:

- the African Union (AU), the Pan-African organization that succeeded the defunct Organization of African Unity (OAU) in 2001;
- the African Commission on Human and Peoples' Rights (the African Commission);
- the African Court on Human and Peoples' Rights (the African Court); and
- the African Committee of Experts on the Rights and Welfare of the Child.

Apart from the bodies mentioned above, there exist a number of specialized agencies or personnel whose mandates are specifically aimed at human rights protection and promotion in Africa. Among these are:

- the Special Rapporteur on Arbitrary, Summary and Extra-Judicial Killings;
- the Special Rapporteur on Prisons and Conditions of Detention in Africa;
- the Special Rapporteur on Women's Rights in Africa;
- the Special Rapporteur on Human Rights Defenders in Africa;
- the Special Rapporteur on Refugees and Internally Displaced Persons in Africa;
- the Chairperson of the Follow-Up Committee on the Guidelines and Measures for the Prohibition and Prevention of Torture, Cruel, Inhuman or Degrading Treatment or Punishment in Africa; and
- the Working Group on Indigenous Populations and Communities.

Some reflections on these institutions and mechanisms are provided below.

Establishment of the African Regional Human Rights System

Regional human rights mechanisms are commonly thought to be potentially more effective than UN human rights mechanisms, because they are able to take better account of regional conditions (Shelton 1999). In another significant way, the UN itself has always encouraged the creation of regional mechanisms to deal with security and human rights, which should complement UN mechanisms (Weston et al. 1987).

The Charter of the defunct OAU entrenched the fundamental objective of regional solidarity for purposes of decolonization and self-determination for all African peoples. The OAU Charter contained no provision on human rights and thus, it can be said that at that stage, African human rights thinking had not proceeded beyond political independence (Evans and Murray 2002; Murray 2004). However, although human rights were not on the front burner of the African regional integration agenda, the steady pace of decolonization of the 1960s followed by the escalating atrocities of neocolonial tyrants like Bokassa in the Central African Republic, Idi Amin in Uganda, and Mobutu Sese Seko in former Zaire had ignited agitation among key African nationalists for a coherent human rights policy within the OAU (Udombana 2002a; Heyns 2004; Shivji 1989). In order to demonstrate a stronger commitment to human rights on the African continent, therefore, the Assembly of Heads of State and Government of the OAU (the Assembly) created a normative and institutional system for the guarantee of human rights in Africa. The Assembly proposed the ACHPR, which was adopted on 27 June 1981, and entered into force on 21 October 1986. Today, all the 53 member states of the AU are parties to the ACHPR.[1]

At the zenith of the institutional arrangements for the African regional human rights system was the Assembly of Heads of State and Government of the OAU, now replaced by the Assembly of Heads of State and Government of the AU. The AU succeeded the OAU as the Pan-African regional organization with a more comprehensive agenda than the OAU, and with the broad objectives of promoting peace, security, stability, democratic principles, popular participation and good

---

1 Morocco is the only African country not a member state of the AU, as it pulled out of the defunct OAU following the recognition and admission of the Saharawi Arab Democratic Republic (SADR) into the organization (Zoubir 1996, 189–90; Munya 1999, 563–4).

governance as well as promoting and protecting human and peoples' rights in Africa, under the elaborate provisions of Article 3 of the Constitutive Act of the African Union, 2001.[2] The ACHPR was specifically conceived as the bedrock of this agenda (Olowu 2003; Murray 2004).

Apart from the Assembly, other principal organs of the AU that have critical roles to play in the promotion and protection of human rights in Africa include: the Executive Council, the Commission that serves as the Secretariat, the Pan-African Parliament, the African Court of Justice, the Economic, Social and Cultural Council, the Peace and Security Council, diverse specialized and technical committees, and three regional financial institutions. The nucleus of the day-to-day activities and programmes of the AU in all fields is the Commission, otherwise known as the Commission of the AU.

The Commission consists of the Chairperson, the Deputy Chairperson, eight commissioners and other personnel, and each commissioner is assigned a specific responsibility relating to the mandate and objectives of the AU. Human rights, democracy and good governance come under the 'Political Affairs' portfolio.

The African Charter on Human and Peoples' Rights

In terms of its conceptualization, the ACHPR bears greater resemblance to the contents of the Universal Declaration of Human Rights (UDHR) of 1948 than to the European and Inter-American regional human rights systems. The philosophical foundation for the equal emphasis of *all* human rights in the ACHPR is expressed in its seventh preambular paragraph as follows: 'Civil and political rights cannot be dissociated from economic, social and cultural rights in their conception as well as universality …'. This foundation represents one of the most distinctive features of the normative renditions of the ACHPR.

The ACHPR succeeded in uniting a diverse cultural body to agree upon common human rights values. The ACHPR established a supranational institutional system, which gives individuals, as well as states, the right to petition for redress of human rights violations. Until the coming into force of the Protocol of the African Court in 2004, the African Commission was the only organ that had the responsibility for monitoring implementation of the ACHPR.

Normative Content

Apart from its Preamble, underscoring the importance traditionally ascribed to human rights notions in Africa, the ACHPR is divided into three focal parts of 68 articles. Part I contains a set of 'Rights and Duties' (articles 1–29); Part II covers 'Measures and Safeguards' (articles 30–63) sub-divided into 'Establishment and Organization of the African Commission on Human and Peoples' Rights' (articles 30–44), 'Mandate of the Commission' (article 45), 'Procedure of the Commission' (articles 46–59) and 'Applicable Principles' (articles 60–63). Part III deals with 'General Provisions' (articles 64–8).

---

2   Constitutive Act of the African Union, AU Doc. CAB/LEG/23.15 (26 May 2001).

The ACHPR contains certain distinctive characteristics that are not found in any of the other existing regional human rights systems. Prominent among these is the inclusion of the concept of *duties* of the individual person. These duties include those towards family and society as well as other recognized communities and the duty to exercise one's rights within the context of collective social and moral interests (article 27); the duty towards fellow human beings in promoting and maintaining non-discrimination and social harmony (article 28); and the duty of an individual to promote and safeguard family life, parental care, national service, payment of taxes and the defence of social solidarity (article 29). Their inclusion reflects important African socio-cultural values that promote social harmony and cohesion.

Another striking feature of the ACHPR is the endorsement of the *interdependence* and *indivisibility* of the principles in the ACHPR. Accordingly it makes provision for *all* human rights, economic, civil, political, social and cultural rights, within the same context, and with equal force.

The treaty enumerates a long list of human rights couched as the entitlements of 'every individual' (articles 2–18) and of 'all peoples' (articles 19–24). The individual rights emphasize the prohibition against discrimination (article 2); the principle of equality before the law and equal protection of the law (article 3); the inviolability and integrity of the human person (article 4); the protection of 'human dignity' through the prohibition of all forms of exploitation and 'degradation' (article 5); the prohibition of arbitrary arrest and detention (article 6); the right to a fair trial and enabling rights (article 7); freedom of conscience and religion (article 8); and so forth.

The ACHPR thereafter proceeds to list a number of what are variously regarded as 'peoples' rights', 'solidarity rights' or 'collective rights' (Kiwanuka 1980; Benedek 1985; Mutua 1995; Heyns 2004). These are the inalienable right to self-determination and socio-economic development (articles 19–20); the right to exercise autonomy over their wealth and natural resources (article 21); the right to economic, social and cultural development as well as the right to development (article 22); the right to national and international peace and security (article 23); and the right to a satisfactory environment (article 24).

It is also significant to note that throughout the ACHPR, there is a marked absence of any explicit derogation clause as is customary in human rights treaties generally. The plain meaning of this is that no African government is permitted to abridge these rights even during emergencies (Umozurike 1983, 910). The African Commission reinforced this opinion in *Media Rights Agenda and Constitutional Rights Project v Nigeria*,[3] where it held that '[i]n contrast to other international human rights instruments, the ACHPR does not contain a derogation clause.'

Furthermore, it is important to mention that while much has been written about the 'claw-back' clauses (that is, those provisions which allow a state to limit the guaranteed rights to the extent permitted by municipal law) found in the body of the ACHPR (see Ankumah 1996, 8; Buergenthal 1995, 52–3; Flinterman and Henderson 1999, 390–91), it seems to have escaped the scrutiny of scholars that there are no

---

3   *Media Rights Agenda and Constitutional Rights Project* v *Nigeria*, Communication No. 105/93 (31 October 1998).

such claw-back clauses in respect of the economic, social, cultural and collective rights provisions in articles 15 to 24. These guarantees are all in plain, unrestricted, and unconditional language.

Nature and Scope of Obligations Created

The basic obligation of state parties to the ACHPR is to protect human rights and freedoms. Article 1 establishes the fundamental obligation of states to 'recognize the rights, duties and freedoms enshrined in this Charter and ... undertake to adopt legislative or other measures to give effect to them'. A corollary to this obligation is found in article 62, which makes it mandatory for state parties to submit biennial reports 'on the legislative or other measures' they have put in place to give effect to the ACHPR. Further, under article 25, it is the duty of state parties 'to promote and ensure through teaching, education and publication, the respect of the rights and freedoms' in the ACHPR. Complementing this is article 26, obliging state parties 'to guarantee the independence of courts and ... allow the establishment and improvement of appropriate national institutions entrusted with the promotion and protection of the rights and freedoms' in the ACHPR.

Some critical points emerge from these provisions. The language employed in articles 1 and 62 reveals the overall intention of creating an *active* human rights stance in African states, rather than mere idealistic goals. A state will thus be in violation of its obligation if it fails to '*adopt* legislative or other measures' to give effect to the provisions (article 1 [my emphasis]).

Also, the human rights profile created by the ACHPR encompasses *all* its provisions, meaning that civil and political rights are to be given as much priority as economic, social and cultural rights, as well as 'peoples' rights'.

Implementation Mechanisms

The principal mechanism that ACHPR provides to ensure and monitor the compliance of state parties with their treaty obligations is the African Commission (the Commission), established by article 30, with the tripartite mandate to promote, to ensure and to interpret the human and peoples' rights in the ACHPR (article 45(1)–(3)).

The Commission, established in 1987, is made up of 11 members acting in their individual and personal capacities (article 31). The election of Commission members is conducted by the Assembly of Heads of State and Government through secret ballot based on a list of candidates put forward by state parties (article 33). Members are elected for a period of six years and may stand for re-election, if put forward (article 36). The Commission meets for two weeks for its ordinary sessions, twice in a year, and can also meet in extraordinary sessions in urgent situations such as occurred in the aftermath of the execution of environmental rights activist, Ken Saro-Wiwa, by the Abacha-led military regime in Nigeria, in November 1995.[4] The

---

4 See generally Consolidated Communication Nos 137/94, 139/94, 161/97 – *International PEN, Constitutional Rights Project, Interights and Civil Liberties Organization (on behalf of Ken Saro-Wiwa Jnr) v Nigeria.*

Commission's headquarters are in Banjul, the Gambia, although it is at liberty to rotate its sittings among African states. Commission meetings are held in public and its Annual Activity Report is transmitted to the Assembly of Heads of State and Government. The Commission fulfils its mandate through the state reporting procedure, the complaints procedure and its promotional activities.

The state reporting procedure enables the Commission to examine measures a state party has put in place to secure the provisions of the ACHPR. The complaints procedure permits the consideration of both inter-state complaints (articles (47–54) as well as individual complaints (articles 55–6). There is an accessible database facility through which one may accurately monitor the status of treaty reporting; the Commission's web pages were updated in April 2007.[5] The Commission's promotional mandate enables it to 'undertake studies and researches on Africa's problems in the field of human and peoples' rights' and to pursue educative programmes; to formulate normative human rights standards and to embark on co-operative programmes that would enhance human rights protection in Africa (article 45).

States' periodic reports Over the years, the reporting procedure has become the mainstay of the Commission (Viljoen 2000; Gaer 1992), enabling the Commission to monitor the implementation of the ACHPR. However, the procedure remains fraught with many impediments to efficacy. A major problem is the sheer failure of states to submit their reports as and when due.[6] Even when states do submit reports, they frequently fail to send competent representatives to present them (Viljoen 1998, 189). This leads to long delays, and some reports have become very dated by the time they are examined. Commendably, the Commission later adopted a radical approach to this question, deciding at its 23rd Session in 1998 that it would henceforth consider states' reports without the presence of representatives once the affected state had been given adequate opportunity to attend and had failed to respond. In 2001, the Commission started issuing 'Concluding Observations', conforming to the practice of UN human rights treaty bodies.

Other problems have been identified relating to the administration of the reporting procedure. States frequently submit their reports in only one language, English or French, while the Arab states submit in two languages, including Arabic. The consequence is that not all commissioners are able to read the reports, and this hampers their ability to ask meaningful questions (Ankumah 1996, 97–108; Odinkalu 2001, 355–8).

Beyond procedural impediments, the Commission lacks any effective follow-up mechanism. Once it closes its consideration of a state party's report, no clear device exists to monitor what the affected state does with the recommendations. In fact, the Commission's manner of handling states' reports has been criticized as lacking 'seriousness [and] incisiveness' and as constituting 'a reduction of

---

5   See 'Status of Submission of State Periodic Reports to the African Commission on Human and Peoples' Rights as of May 2003', <http://www.achpr.org/state_periodic_reports. doc> (accessed 22 November 2007).

6   Ibid., showing that a total of 17 African states had never submitted any report as of November 2007.

the whole exercise into a rigmarole ...' (Quashigah 2002, 278). Nevertheless, it is auspicious that a platform exists where African states are obliged to make themselves available for scrutiny, with an opportunity for civil society to submit alternative or 'shadow' reports.

Individual complaints procedure   In contrast to criticisms around the state reporting procedures, the individual complaints procedure of the Commission has been kept remarkably active. However, there is an imbalance in the causes of action in the communications brought before it. A survey of the communications dealt with since inception reveals a huge gap between the number of communications dealing with civil and political rights, on the one hand, and economic, social and cultural rights, on the other (Olowu 2005). Even where there were communications that involved cross-cutting rights within the ACHPR, the Commission had traditionally been inclined not to consider economic, social and cultural rights in depth, or award remedies for established violations. In *Malawi African Association, Amnesty International* v *Mauritania*,[7] the Commission elaborated on the civil and political rights content of the ACHPR and pronounced concrete and specific remedies in unequivocal language. It held that the Government of Mauritania must establish an independent enquiry into the fate of disappeared persons; take diligent measures to replace the national identity documents seized from the expelled Mauritanian citizens; ensure appropriate compensation for the violations; reinstate persons dismissed from their jobs without due process; carry out an assessment of the deep-rooted causes of the degrading practices in the Mauritanian society; and enforce its legislative measures on the abolition of slavery.

Conversely, in *Free Legal Assistance Group, Lawyers' Committee for Human Rights, Union Interafricaine des Droits de l'Homme, and Les Témoins de Jehovah* v *Zaire*,[8] although the Commission held the Government of Zaire (now Democratic Republic of the Congo) to have violated the right to health and the right to education by failing to provide basic services such as 'safe drinking water and electricity and ... medicine' to the complainants during their detention as well as 'the [unjustifiable] closures of universities and secondary schools' (paragraphs 47–8), the Commission ended an otherwise lucid decision with '[f]or these reasons, the Commission holds that the facts constitute serious and massive violations of the African Charter, namely of articles ... 16 and 17' (paragraph 49), losing one of numerous opportunities it had to elaborate on the content of economic, social and cultural rights as well as to chart the path of granting appropriate remedies and relief for established violations.

In *Social and Economic Rights Action Center and the Center for Economic and Social Rights* v *Nigeria* (the *SERAC Case*),[9] however, the African Commission relied extensively on General Comments Nos 3, 4, 7 and 14 of the Committee on

---

    7   Communication Nos 54/91; 61/91; 98/93; 164/97; and 210/98, 13th Annual Activity Report: 1999–2000.
    8   Communication Nos 25/89; 47/90; 56/91; and 100/93, Ninth Annual Activity Report: 1995–1996.
    9   Communication No. 155/96, Decision of the African Commission on Human and Peoples' Rights, Thirtieth Ordinary Session, Banjul, The Gambia, 13–27 October 2001, OAU

Economic, Social and Cultural Rights (CESCR), the treaty monitoring body for the International Covenant on Economic, Social and Cultural Rights (ICESCR), to hold that the Federal Government of Nigeria had violated the rights to housing, food and health. Although hailed by notable scholars as a ground-breaking decision (see, for instance, Shelton 2002, 942; Coomans 2003, 749; Bekker 2003, 132), it can be criticized for uncritically adopting the 'progressive realization' paradigm adopted by the CESCR, which this author has argued has no legal or factual basis in the ACHPR (Olowu 2004, 197–8). The decision is bereft of any substantial remedy for the established violations, which may explain why there has been no tangible outcome from the decision in the troubled Niger-Delta region, long after its delivery (Olowu 2005).

Another complaints procedure recognized in the ACHPR is the inter-state communications mechanism. Although designed to enable African states to play a watchdog role, for all practical purposes, the inter-state mechanism has remained dormant. African states have thus generally shied away from accusing one another of violations, being reluctant to attract reprisal complaints. Perhaps the only ever recorded inter-state communications were those filed by the Democratic Republic of the Congo against Burundi, Rwanda and Uganda[10] alleging violations of ACHPR provisions by the bellicose activities of those states within its territory, as well as that filed by Ethiopia against Eritrea for similar reasons.[11]

The individual complaint system has also had inherent bottlenecks. After considering a communication, rather than making public its findings and making swift contact with the state party, article 59 of the ACHPR prohibits the Commission from publishing its findings until it has been considered by the Assembly of Heads of State and Government. This invariably translates into delay. However, since 1994, the Commission has steadily departed from that culture of 'rigid secrecy' as it now attaches its review of individual communications as an annexure to its report (Viljoen 1998, 154).

The above does not in any way diminish the significance of the critical jurisprudence emanating from the Commission. While it is not a court, it has been able to make remarkable pronouncements that have guided the interpretation of human rights norms in Africa. In *Legal Resources Foundation* v *Zambia*,[12] for instance, the Commission declared that 'international treaties which are not part of domestic law and which may not be directly enforceable in the national courts, nonetheless impose obligations on state parties …'. Equally significant was *The Law Offices of Ghazi* v *Sudan*,[13] where the complainant was stopped by state security officials from travelling to Blue Nile State to deliver a human rights lecture. They threatened to arrest the complainant should he choose to make the trip. The complainant contended

---

Doc. ACHPR/COMM/A044/1. See, further, for details of this case in Chirwa, Chapter 6 of this volume.

10 *Democratic Republic of the Congo* v *Burundi, Rwanda and Uganda*, Communication No. 227/99.

11 *Ethiopia* v *Eritrea*, Communication No. 233/99.

12 Communication No. 211/98, Fourteenth Annual Activity Report.

13 Communication No. 228/99, Sixteenth Annual Activity Report: 2002–2003.

that his rights, including those under article 9, had been violated.[14] The Commission upheld the complaint, stating,

> Mr. Ghazi Suleiman's speech is a unique and important part of political debate in his country. When an individual's freedom of expression is unlawfully restricted, it is not only the right of that individual that is being violated, but also the right of all others to 'receive' information and ideas. It is particularly grave when information that others are being denied concerns the human rights protected in the African Charter as did each instance in which Mr. Ghazi Suleiman was arrested. (Paragraphs 46 and 50)

In response, the government of Sudan had argued that his speech 'threatened national security and public order'.[15] Nevertheless, the Commission demonstrated its reluctance to permit restrictions on freedom of expression on the pretext of 'national security and public order'.

In yet another notable case, *Institute for Human Rights and Development in Africa (on behalf of Sierra Leonean Refugees in Guinea)* v *Republic of Guinea*,[16] the Commission held that it was:

> Aware that African countries generally and the Republic of Guinea in particular, face a lot of challenges when it comes to hosting refugees from neighboring war torn countries. In such circumstances some of these countries often resort to extreme measures to protect their citizens. However, such measures should not be taken to the detriment of the enjoyment of human rights. When countries ratify or sign international instruments, they do so willingly and in total cognizance of their obligation to apply the provisions of these instruments. Consequently, the Republic of Guinea has assumed the obligation of protecting human rights, notably the rights of all those refugees who seek protection in Guinea. (Paragraphs 67–8)

Promotional mandate   The Commission is to be commended for the numerous interactive programmes it has conducted with national human rights institutions in various states as well as with African and non-African civil society groups. These activities have been well documented over the years.[17] It is regrettable, however, that the Commission has not yet designed or implemented any concrete promotional agenda for economic, social and cultural rights in Africa beyond the rhetoric of plans and programmes of action (Olowu 2004). The Commission has extended its promotional mandate to the appointment of Special Rapporteurs to investigate, monitor and report on specific human rights issues under the ACHPR, based on the components of its promotional functions under article 45(1), namely, 'to collect documents, undertake studies and research …' (Essien 2000, 99–102). The first appointment was that of the Special Rapporteur on Arbitrary, Summary and Extra-

---

14 Article 9 of the African Charter provides: '1. Every individual shall have the right to receive information. 2. Every individual shall have the right to express and disseminate his opinions within the law.'

15 Communication No. 228/99, above note 13, paragraph 51.

16 Communication No. 249/2002.

17 See Seminars of the African Court on Human and Peoples' Rights, <http://www.achpr.org/html/seminarsconferences.html> (accessed 22 November 2007).

Judicial Killings, in 1994 (Danielsen 1995). Thereafter, there have been others, as enumerated in the introduction to this chapter.

Other African Regional Human Rights Protection Mechanisms

Although the ACHPR is the *grundnorm* of human rights within the African regional milieu, there are a number of other regional instruments that are of significance to human rights in Africa, including the ACRWC;[18] the Additional Protocol to the African Charter on Human and Peoples' Rights on the Establishment of the African Court on Human and Peoples' Rights, 1998 (the African Court Protocol);[19] and the AWP.[20]

The African Children's Charter (ACRWC)

Because the focus of this book is on the rights of children in Africa, it is desirable to highlight briefly this particular treaty, although other chapters will discuss it in greater detail.

The ACRWC emerged out of the sentiment that the Convention on the Rights of the Child (CRC) ignored vital socio-cultural and economic realities of the African milieu (Viljoen 2000; Olowu 2002). It stresses the need to consider African cultural peculiarities in matters relating to the rights of children (Olowu 2002, 128). Lloyd has suggested that the ACRWC 'offers a higher level of protection than that offered by the CRC' (2002a, 14). An in-depth analysis of the ACRWC and its monitoring mechanism is dealt with by her in detail in Chapter 3.

The African Women's Protocol (AWP)

Like the ACRWC, the AWP was born out of the feeling among African states parties to the Convention on the Elimination of All Forms of Discrimination Against Women (CEDAW) that it failed to take cognizance of specific African socio-cultural peculiarities (Olowu 2006).

One of the distinguishing features of the AWP lies in its overt concern with women's rights in the private domain. While CEDAW only sought to secure the equality of husband and wife in marriage (article 16 (1)(a)–(h)), the AWP aims at affecting traditional marital practices in a radical way. For example, whereas CEDAW is completely silent about polygamy, the AWP obliges state parties to take legislative and other measures to encourage monogamy (article 6(c)).

In addition, it recognizes and obliges state parties to take legislative and other measures to protect certain economic, social and cultural rights for women in Africa. These are: the right to education and training (article 12); the right to economic and social welfare (article 13); health and reproductive rights (article 14); the right

---

18 OAU Doc. CAB/LEG/153/Rev.2 (entered into force 29 November 1999).

19 OAU/LEGAL/MIN/AFCHPR/PROT. (I) Rev.2. AHG/Res. 230 (XXX) (1998) (entered into force 25 January 2004).

20 OAU Doc CAB/LEG/66.6 (entered into force 25 November 2005).

to food security (article 15); the right to adequate housing (article 16); the right to a healthy and sustainable environment (article 18); and the right to sustainable development (article 19).

In an innovative way, the AWP creates an obligation for state parties to provide 'appropriate remedies to any woman whose rights or freedoms ... have been violated' (article 25(a)). This puts the justiciability of the enumerated rights beyond controversy (Heyns 2004; Nmehielle 2004; Olowu 2006).

While the substantive provisions of AWP fall under the supervisory jurisdiction of the African Commission and the new African Court, Wing and Smith have argued that they nonetheless hold significant implications for virtually every other organ of the AU (2003, 72–9).

The African Human Rights Court

Numerous African scholars are enthusiastic about the prospects of a more efficient regional human rights system for Africa with the recent birth of the African Court on Human and Peoples' Rights (the African Court) (Naldi and Magliveras 1998; Udombana 1999; Udombana 2002a; Nmehielle 2000; Eno 2002; Hopkins 2002; Pityana 2004; Viljoen 2004). The African Court Protocol entered into force on 25 January 2004.[21] Apart from rendering advisory opinions on any legal matter relating to the ACHPR or any other relevant human rights instruments, the African Court has jurisdiction on the interpretation of its own jurisdiction (article 3). Its judgments are final and are not subject to appeal (article 28). Judgments of the Court are also binding (article 30). To reinforce this, the Council of Ministers, which serves as the Executive Council of the AU, monitors the implementation of judgments (article 29).

In relation to complaints about violations, the Commission, a state party that has lodged a complaint, and a state party against which a complaint is lodged, are eligible to appear before the Court (articles 5–6).

While further details about the composition and structures of the Court need not be discussed further here, it must be stressed that the Court might be able to perform judicial functions *stricto sensu* beyond the traditional purview of the Commission's mandate of merely interpreting and promoting the contents of the ACHPR (Viljoen 2004). Under article 3(1) of the African Court Protocol, the African Court has jurisdiction in respect of 'all cases and disputes submitted to it concerning the interpretation and application of the Charter, this Protocol and any other relevant Human Rights instrument ratified by the states concerned'. Under article 5(3), '[t]he court may recognize relevant NGOs with observer status before the Commission, and individuals to institute cases directly before it, in accordance with article 34(6) of this Protocol.' Article 34(6), in turn, provides: 'At the time of the ratification of this Protocol or any time thereafter, the State shall make a declaration accepting the competence of the court to receive cases under article 5(3) of this Protocol. The court shall not receive any petition under article 5(3) involving a state party which has not made such a declaration.'

---

21 For a list of countries that have signed, ratified or acceded to the African Court Protocol, see <http://www.african-union.org> (home page) (accessed 22 November 2007).

A particularly innovative element that is expected to invigorate human rights protection in Africa is the implicit competence of the emergent African Court to entertain cases from individuals and civil society groups in respect of the breach of the ACHPR and other relevant instruments. Even though some scholars have criticized the African Court Protocol for failing to make unequivocal provision granting *locus standi* to individuals and civil society groups to institute proceedings before the court (Naldi and Magliveras 1998; Udombana 1999; Udombana 2002a; Nmehielle 2000; Eno 2002; Hopkins 2002; Pityana 2004; Viljoen 2004), the declaration mentioned in articles 5(3) and 34(6) may make it possible for such persons and groups to bring actions. In the absence of states' declarations to grant such access, persons and groups can submit their complaints to the Commission, as has always been the case, and the Commission may then present these to the Court.

It is notable that since the fifth ordinary session of the Assembly of the AU in Sirte, Libya, in July 2005, despite fiscal and logistic constraints, there has been perceptible movement towards the election of judges, the determination of the budget, and the organization of the Court's registry. In sum, the entry into force of the African Court Protocol certainly promises a viable platform for Africans. How the emergent African Court will handle its historic responsibility once it comes into full operation remains to be seen in the course of time.

The New Partnership for Africa's Development (NEPAD) and the African Peer Review Mechanism (APRM)

Another innovative framework that is becoming significant in the regional promotion and protection of human rights in Africa is NEPAD.[22] NEPAD can be regarded as the vehicle for the attainment of regional integration and co-operation. Central to the NEPAD agenda, however, is its APRM component (Udombana 2002b; Olowu 2003, 226–7).[23] The APRM is the instrument through which African leaders are expected to hold one another accountable to the demands of, among others, genuine democracy, human rights, good governance, poverty alleviation, corruption eradication, the development of an integrated regional market and trade, as well as 'a new global partnership', all of which form the crux of the NEPAD vision for Africa (Obi 2002; Olowu 2003).

Equipped with an array of top-flight African bureaucrats, technocrats and policy makers, NEPAD's implementation structure revolves around the Heads of State and Government Implementation Committee (HSIC), supported by a steering committee and a secretariat, the APRM Forum of Heads of State and Government, the APRM Panel of Eminent Persons, and an APRM Country Team. Even though the APRM is a voluntary instrument, it is already growing into a viable vehicle for strengthening the protection of human rights in Africa. Today, there are 27 African states who have

---

22 Discussed also in Chirwa, Chapter 6 of this volume.

23 See the NEPAD APRM <http://www.schoolnetafrica.net/fileadmin/resources/APRM NEPAD.pdf> (accessed 22 November 2007). See also APRM Organization and Process, NEPAD/HGSIC-3/2003/APRM/Guideline/OandP (2003), setting out the working modalities of the APRM and its incorporation into the AU framework.

enlisted among state parties to the APRM.[24] Since inception, the APRM Panel of Eminent Persons has been on mission to Benin, Ghana, Kenya, Mauritius, Nigeria, Rwanda, South Africa, Sudan and Tanzania.[25]

Although the APRM is mainly discussed in terms of its economic dimensions (see, for example, Ngamau 2004; Mosoti 2004), and while it may be too early to assess its impact on human rights protection, there can be no gainsaying the fact that as the processes for the scrutiny of states under the APRM gather momentum, the mechanism will avail Africans of a valuable platform for addressing human rights concerns arising from the practices of their states.

'Soft Law' Regional Human Rights Instruments

Besides treaty-based mechanisms, there is a broad range of 'soft law' instruments in which African leaders have reaffirmed their faith in human rights. While these instruments are not legally binding, scholars have highlighted their importance in the elaboration of binding norms within the African regional human rights arrangement (Evans and Murray 2002; Udombana 2003; Viljoen 2004). Some of the most topical are the Grand Bay Declaration and Plan of Action, 1999, and the Kigali Declaration, 2003.

At Grand Bay in 1999, the first OAU Ministerial Conference on Human Rights in Africa unanimously affirmed 'the principle that human rights are universal, indivisible, interdependent and inter-related' and demanded of all African 'governments, in their policies, to give parity to economic, social and cultural rights as well as civil and political rights' (Grand Bay (Mauritius) Declaration and Plan of Action, paragraph 1). Furthermore, the AU's first Ministerial Conference on Human Rights in Africa, held in Kigali in 2003 reinforced the universality, indivisibility, interdependence and interrelatedness of *all* human rights (Kigali Declaration, paragraph 1), and proceeded to direct 'member states and regional institutions to accord the same importance to economic, social and cultural rights, and apply, at all levels, a rights-based approach to policy, programmes, planning, implementation and evaluation' (Kigali Declaration, paragraph 4). Viljoen has also identified the Kigali Declaration as a motivating factor for the timely entry into force of the African Court Protocol (2004, 11–12).

Conclusion

Notwithstanding persistent criticisms against the African regional framework for human rights protection, this chapter has highlighted some of the positive normative and institutional developments critical to the promotion of human rights in Africa. For a regional arrangement that only came into effective existence in 1987, many of these developments suggest both the resilience and the potential of the African

---

24 See List of Countries acceded to the APRM <http://www.nepad.org/2005/files/aprmcountries.php> (accessed 22 November 2007).

25 See NEPAD APRM <http://www.nepad.org/2005/files/aprm.php> (accessed 22 November 2006).

regional human rights protection system. The conclusion can be drawn that there is an adequate legal and ethical framework for strategic activism towards integrating all human rights into a concrete agenda for their promotion and protection on the African continent. Taken together, the various instruments, including the existing regional human rights instruments and monitoring mechanisms as well as the organs and structures created under the auspices of the OAU, the AU and NEPAD, hold the promise of dramatically increasing the capacity of African countries and peoples to work together in addressing the critical issues of democratization, human rights, sustainable regional peace and stability, and socio-economic development. The challenge remains how to galvanize them.

References

Articles, Books and Chapters in Books

Alston, P. and Steiner, H. (2000), *International Human Rights in Context* (Oxford: Oxford University Press).

Ankumah, E. (1996), *The African Commission on Human and Peoples' Rights: Practice and Procedures* (The Hague: Martinus Nijhoff Publishers).

Baah, R.A. (2000), *Human Rights in Africa: The Conflict of Implementation* (Lanham, MD: University Press of America).

Bekker, G. (2003), 'The Social and Economic Rights Action Center and the Center for Economic and Social Rights v. Nigeria', *Journal of African Law* 47, 107.

Benedek, W. (1985), 'Peoples' Rights and Individual Duties as Special Features of the African Charter on Human and Peoples' Rights', in Kunig, P. et al. (eds) 59–94.

Bondzie-Simpson, E. (1988), 'A Critique of the African Charter on Human and Peoples' Rights', *Howard Law Journal* 31, 643–65.

Buergenthal, T. (1995), *International Human Rights in a Nutshell*, 2nd edn (St Paul, MN: West Group).

Busia Jr, N.K.A. (1994), 'The Status of Human Rights in Pre-Colonial Africa: Implications for Contemporary Practices', in McCarthy-Arnolds, E. et al. (eds) 225–50.

Cobbah, J.A.M. (1987), 'African Values and the Human Rights Debate: An African Perspective', *Human Rights Quarterly* 9:3, 309–31.

Coomans, F. (2003), 'The Ogoni Case before the African Commission on Human and Peoples' Rights', *International and Comparative Law Quarterly* 52:3, 749–60.

Danielsen, A. et al. (1995), '16th Session of the African Commission on Human and Peoples' Rights', *Netherlands Quarterly of Human Rights* 13:1, 80–84.

Doebbler, C.F. (2003), 'A Complex Ambiguity: The Relationship Between the African Commission on Human and Peoples' Rights and Other African Union Initiatives Affecting Respect for Human Rights', *Transnational Law and Contemporary Problems* 13:1, 7–31.

Donnelly, J. (1984), 'The Right to Development', in Welch Jr, C.E. et al. (eds) 261–73.

El-Obaid, E.A. et al. (1996), 'Human Rights in Africa: A New Perspective on Linking the Past to the Present', *McGill Law Journal* 41, 819–54.

El-Sheikh, I.B. (1989), 'The African Commission on Human and People's Rights: Prospects and Problems', *Netherlands Quarterly of Human Rights* 7:3, 272–83.

Eno, R.W. (2002), 'The Jurisdiction of the African Court on Human and Peoples' Rights', *African Human Rights Law Journal* 2:2, 223–33.

Essien, U. (2000), 'The African Commission on Human and Peoples' Rights: Eleven Years After', *Buffalo Human Rights Law Review* 6, 93–103.

Evans, M.D. and Murray, R.H. (eds) (2002), *The African Charter on Human and People's Rights: The System at Work* (Cambridge: Cambridge University Press).

Eze, O. (1984), *Human Rights in Africa: Some Selected Problems* (New York: St. Martin's Press).

Eze, O. (1990), 'Human Rights Issues and Violations: The African Experience', in Shepherd Jr, G.W. and Anikpo, M.O.C. (eds) 95–103.

Flinterman, C. and Henderson, C. (1999), 'The African Charter on Human and Peoples' Rights', in Hanski et al. (eds) 387–96.

Flinterman, C. et al. (1992), 'The African Charter on Human and Peoples' Rights', in Hannum (ed.) 159–69.

Gaer, F.D. (1992), 'First Fruits: Reporting by States under the African Charter on Human and Peoples' Rights', *Netherlands Quarterly of Human Rights* 10:1, 29–42.

Gutto, S.B.O. (1993), *Human Rights for the Oppressed: Critical Essays on Theory and Practice from Sociology* (Lund: Lund University Press).

Gutto, S.B.O. (1999), *Human and Peoples' Rights for the Oppressed: Critical Essays on Theory and Practice from Sociology of Law Perspectives* (Lund: Lund University Press).

Gutto, S.B.O. (2001), 'The Reform and Renewal of the African Regional Human Rights and Peoples' Rights System', *African Human Rights Law Journal* 1:2, 175–84.

Hannum, H. (ed.) (1992), *Guide to International Human Rights Practice*, 2nd edn (Philadelphia, PA: University of Pennsylvania).

Hanski et al. (eds) (1999), *An Introduction to the International Protection of Human Rights: A Textbook*, 2nd edn (Turku: Institute for Human Rights, Åbo Akademi University).

Harrington, J. (2001), 'Special Rapporteurs of the African Commission on Human and Peoples' Rights', *African Human Rights Law Journal* 1:2, 247.

Heyns, C. (ed.) (1998), *Human Rights in Africa* (The Hague: Kluwer Law International).

Heyns, C. (2004), 'The African Regional Human Rights System: The African Charter', *Penn State Law Review* 108, 679–702.

Hopkins, K. (2002), 'The Effect of an African Court on the Domestic Legal Orders of African States', *African Human Rights Law Journal* 2:2, 234–51.

Howard, R. (1986), *Human Rights in Commonwealth Africa* (Ottawa: Rowman and Littlefield).

Institute for Human Rights and Development in Africa (2001), *Compilation of Decisions on Communications of the African Commission on Human and Peoples' Rights 1994–2001* (Banjul: Institute for Human Rights and Development in Africa).

Kiwanuka, R.N. (1980), 'The Meaning of "People" in the African Charter on Human and Peoples' Rights', *American Journal of International Law* 82, 80–101.

Kunig, P. et al. (eds) (1985), *Regional Protection of Human Rights by International Law: The Emerging African System* (Baden-Baden: Nomos Verlagsgesellschaft).

Lloyd, A. (2002a), 'A Theoretical Analysis of the Reality of Children's Rights in Africa: An Introduction to the African Charter on the Rights and Welfare of the Child', *African Human Rights Law Journal* 2:1, 11–32.

Lloyd, A. (2002b), 'Evolution of the African Charter on the Rights and Welfare of the Child and the African Committee of Experts: Raising the Gauntlet', *International Journal of Children's Rights* 10:2, 179–98.

McCarthy-Arnolds, E. et al. (eds) (1994), *Africa, Human Rights and the Global System* (Westport, CT: Greenwood Press).

Mosoti, V. (2004), 'The New Partnership for Africa's Development: Institutional and Legal Challenges of Investment Promotion', *San Diego International Law Journal* 5, 145–78.

Munya, P.M. (1999), 'The Organization of African Unity and Its Role in Regional Conflict Resolution and Dispute Settlement: A Critical Evaluation', *Boston College Third World Law Journal* 19, 537–91.

Murray, R. (1998), 'The African Commission on Human and People's Rights (Report of the 23rd Session)', *Netherlands Quarterly of Human Rights* 16:3, 394–401.

Murray, R. (2001), 'The African Charter on Human and Peoples' Rights 1987–2000: An Overview of Its Progress and Problems', *African Human Rights Law Journal* 1:1, 1–17.

Murray, R. (2004), *Human Rights in Africa: From the OAU to the African Union* (Cambridge: Cambridge University Press).

Mutua, M. (1995), 'The Banjul Charter and the African Cultural Fingerprints: An Evaluation of the Language of Duties', *Virginia Journal of International Law* 35, 339–80.

Naldi, G.J. and Magliveras, K. (1996), 'The Proposed African Court of Human Rights: Evaluation and Comparison', *African Journal of International and Comparative Law* 8, 944–69.

Naldi, G. and Magliveras, K. (1998), 'Reinforcing the African System of Human Rights: The Protocol on the Establishment of a Regional Court of Human Rights', *Netherlands Quarterly of Human Rights* 16:4, 431–56.

Ngamau, R. (2004), 'The Role of NEPAD in African Economic Regulation and Integration', *Law and Business Review of the Americas* 10, 515–42.

Nmehielle, V.O.O. (2000), 'Towards an African Court on Human Rights: Structuring of the Court', *Annual Survey of International and Comparative Law* 6, 27–50.

Nmehielle, V.O.O. (2004), 'A Decade in Human Rights Law: Development of the African Human Rights System in the Last Decade', 11 *Human Rights Brief* 6–11.

Odinkalu, C.A. (2001), 'Analysis of Paralysis or Paralysis by Analysis? Implementing Economic, Social and Cultural Rights under the African Charter on Human and Peoples' Rights', *Human Rights Quarterly* 23:2, 327–69.

Olowu, D. (2002), 'Protecting Children's Rights in Africa: A Critique of the African Charter on the Rights and Welfare of the Child', *International Journal of Children's Rights* 10:2, 127–36.

Olowu, D. (2003), 'Regional Integration, Development and the African Union Agenda: Challenges, Gaps and Opportunities', *Transnational Law and Contemporary Problems* 13:1, 211–53.

Olowu, D. (2004), 'Human Development Challenges in Africa: A Rights-Based Approach', *San Diego International Law Journal* 5, 179–223.

Olowu, D. (2005), 'Emerging Jurisprudence on Economic, Social and Cultural Rights in Africa: A Critique of the Decision in SERAC and Another v. Nigeria', *Turf Law Review* 2:1, 29–44.

Olowu, D. (2006), 'A Critique of the Rhetoric, Ambivalence and Promise in the Draft Protocol to the African Charter on Human and People's Rights on the Rights of Women in Africa', *Human Rights Review* 8:1, 78–101.

Quashigah, K. (2002), 'The African Charter on Human and People's Rights: Towards a More Effective Reporting Mechanism', *African Human Rights Law Journal* 2:2, 261–300.

Shelton, D. (1999), 'The Promise of Regional Human Rights Systems', in Weston, B.H. et al. (eds) 351–98.

Shelton, D. (2002), 'Decision Regarding Communication 155/96 SERAC v. Nigeria. Case No. ACHPR/COMM/A044/1', *American Journal of International Law* 96, 937–42.

Shepherd Jr, G.W. and Anikpo, M.O.C. (eds) (1990), *Emerging Human Rights: The African Political Economy Context* (Westport, CT: Greenwood Press).

Shivji, I.G. (1989), *The Concept of Human Rights in Africa* (London: CODESRIA Book Series).

Social and Economic Rights Action Center's Interview with E.V.O. Dankwa, a Member of the African Commission on Human and People's Rights (1999), *Access Quarterly* 1, 16–17.

Udombana, N.J. (1999), 'Towards the African Court on Human and Peoples' Rights: Better Late than Never', *Review of African Commission on Human and Peoples' Rights* 8:2, 338–58.

Udombana, N.J. (2002a), 'A Harmony or a Cacophony? The Music of Integration in the African Union Treaty and the New Partnership for Africa's Development', *Indiana International and Comparative Law Review* 13, 185–236.

Udombana, N.J. (2002b), 'How Should We Then Live? Globalization and the New Partnership for Africa's Development', *Boston University International Law* 20, 293–354.

Udombana, N.J. (2003), 'Articulating the Right to Democratic Governance in Africa', *Michigan Journal of International Law* 24, 1209–70.

Umozurike, O.U. (1983), 'The African Charter on Human and Peoples' Rights', *American Journal of International Law* 77:4, 902–12.

Viljoen, F. (1998), 'Overview of the African Regional Human Rights System', in Heyns (ed.) 128–205.

Viljoen, F. (2000), 'State Reporting under the African Charter on Human and Peoples' Rights: A Boost from the South', *Journal of African Law* 44:1, 110–18.

Viljoen, F. (2004), 'A Human Rights Court for Africa, and Africans', *Brooklyn Journal of International Law* 30, 1–66.

Welch, Jr, C.E. et al. (eds) (1984), *Human Rights and Development in Africa* (Albany, NY: State University of New York Press).

Weston, B.H. and Marks, S.P. (eds) (1999), *The Future of International Human Rights* (Ardsley, NY: Transnational Publishers).

Weston, B.H. et al. (1987), 'Regional Human Rights Regimes: A Comparison and Appraisal', *Vanderbilt Journal of Transnational Law* 20:4, 585–637.

Wing, A.K. and Smith, T.M. (2003), 'The New African Union and Women's Rights', *Transnational Law and Contemporary Problems* 13:1, 33–81.

Zoubir, Y.H. (1996), 'The Western Sahara Conflict: A Case Study in Failure of Prenegotiation and Prolongation of Conflict', *California Western International Law Journal* 26, 173–213.

General Comments, Unpublished Papers, Treaties, Declarations and Reports

Additional Protocol to the African Charter on Human and Peoples' Rights on the Establishment of the African Court on Human and Peoples' Rights, (1998), OAU/LEGAL/MIN/AFCHPR/PROT. (I) Rev.2. AHG/Resolution 230 (XXX) (1998) (entered into force 25 January 2004).

African Charter on the Rights and Welfare of the Child, (1990), OAU Doc CAB/LEG/153/Rev.2 (entered into force 29 November 1999).

African Peer Review Mechanism Organization and Process, NEPAD/HGSIC-3/2003/APRM/Guideline/OandP (2003).

Constitutive Act of the African Union, AU Doc. CAB/LEG/23.15 (26 May 2001).

Final Communiqué of the 28th Ordinary Session of the African Commission on Human and Peoples' Rights 23 October to 6 November 2000, Cotonou, Benin. <http://www.africaninstitute.org/html/28th_session.html> (accessed 1 November 2006).

Grand Bay (Mauritius) Declaration and Plan of Action, OAU First Ministerial Conference on Human Rights in Africa, 12–16 April 1999, OAU Doc. CONF/HRA/DECL. (I) (16 April 1999).

Kigali Declaration, AU First Ministerial Conference on Human Rights in Africa, AU Doc MIN/CONF/HRA/Decl.1 (I) (8 May 2003) <http://www.african-union.org> (home page) (accessed 22 November 2006).

Obi, C.I. (2002), 'Reconstructing Africa's Development in the New Millennium Through NEPAD: Can African Leaders Deliver the Goods?', Paper presented at the 10th CODESRIA General Assembly, Nile International Conference Centre, Kampala, Uganda, 8–12 December, 2002.

Protocol to the African Charter on Human and Peoples' Rights concerning the Rights of Women, 2003, OAU Doc CAB/LEG/66.6 (entered into force 25 November 2005).

Internet Based Sources

List of Countries Which Have Acceded to the African Peer Review Mechanism <http://www.nepad.org/2005/files/aprmcountries.php> (accessed 22 November 2007).

List of Countries Which Have Signed, Ratified/Acceded to the African Court Protocol <http://www.african-union.org> (home page) (accessed 22 November 2007).

New Partnership for Africa's Development (NEPAD) African Peer Review Mechanism (APRM) <http://www.nepad.org/2005/files/aprm.php> (accessed 22 November 2007).

Pityana, N.B. (2004), 'Reflections on the African Court on Human and Peoples' Rights'<http://www.unisa.ac.za/contents/about/principle/docs/HumanandPeople. doc> (accessed 22 November 2007).

Seminars of the African Court on Human and Peoples' Rights <http://www.achpr. org/html/seminarsconferences.html> (accessed 22 November 2007).

Cases

African Institute for Human Rights and Development (on behalf of Sierra Leonean Refugees in Guinea) v *Republic of Guinea*, Communication No. 249/2002.

Democratic Republic of the Congo v *Burundi, Rwanda and Uganda*, Communication No. 227/99.

Ethiopia v *Eritrea*, Communication No. 233/99.

Free Legal Assistance Group, Lawyers' Committee for Human Rights, Union Interafricaine des Droits de l'Homme, and Les Témoins de Jehovah v *Zaire*, Communication Nos 25/89; 47/90; 56/91; and 100/93, Ninth Annual Activity Report: 1995–1996.

International PEN, Constitutional Rights Project, Interights and Civil Liberties Organization (on behalf of Ken Saro-Wiwa Jnr) v *Nigeria*, Consolidated Communication Nos 137/94, 139/94, 161/97.

Legal Resources Foundation v *Zambia*, Communication No. 211/98, Fourteenth Annual Activity Report.

Malawi African Association, Amnesty International v *Mauritania*, Communication Nos 54/91; 61/91; 98/93; 164/97; and 210/98, Thirteenth Annual Activity Report: 1999–2000.

Media Rights Agenda and Constitutional Rights Project v *Nigeria*, Communication No. 105/93 (31 October 1998).

Social and Economic Rights Action Center and the Center for Economic and Social Rights v *Nigeria*, Communication No. 155/96, Decision of the African Commission on Human and Peoples' Rights, Thirtieth Ordinary Session, Banjul, The Gambia, 13–27 October 2001, OAU Doc. ACHPR/COMM/A044/1.

The Law Offices of Ghazi v *Sudan*, Communication No. 228/99, Sixteenth Annual Activity Report: 2002–2003.

Chapter 3

The African Regional System
for the Protection of Children's Rights

Amanda Lloyd

Introduction

The African regional system for the protection of children's rights is the most progressive achievement of all the regional systems, as it is the only system to provide a comprehensive mechanism for the protection and promotion of children's rights at a regional level. This serves as an innovation in the arena of children's rights.

Adopted in 1990, the African Charter on the Rights and Welfare of the Child (ACRWC) couches children's rights and welfare issues in familiar African language, allowing for the virtues of children's cultural heritage, historical background and the values of African civilization to be given priority. The ACRWC recognizes children in Africa as direct bearers of rights and, in turn, children bear responsibilities to others. This may be considered a controversial addition by Western thinkers, but it reflects the underpinning of African society, and positive conclusions can be drawn from this addition, once one understands the African concept of human rights.

The ACRWC has the potential to reverse the discriminatory practices that prevail in many parts of the continent and to educate social, administrative and judicial institutions about the way in which the child should be viewed and treated within society. It obliges states to ensure all domestic legislation and customary practices comply with the enshrined provisions.

The ACRWC clearly defines a 'child' – setting an age of 18 years – and explicitly provides for the prohibition of child betrothals, children participating in armed conflicts, child labour practices and child trafficking, to name but a few dangerous situations facing children in Africa. It promotes the child's right to become a fully-fledged and active member of society.

In 2002, the treaty's monitoring and enforcement mechanism was established in accordance with Part II of the ACRWC. The African Committee of Experts on the Rights and Welfare of the Child (ACERWC) has an extensive mandate to ensure state parties comply with their treaty obligations. The mandate of the committee extends further than the limited mandate of the UN Committee on the Rights of the Child (CRC committee), which only has the jurisdiction to receive and comment on state reports submitted periodically. The ACERWC has the remit to receive state reports, individual communications, as well as conduct ad hoc missions and onsite visits to states considered to be violating their treaty obligations. It also has standing before the newly established African Court on Human and Peoples' Rights.

The Development of the Protection System for Children's Rights in Africa

The paramountcy of children's rights in an African context has been formally recognized by the region since 1979 when the (non-binding) Declaration on the Rights and Welfare of the African Child (Declaration) was adopted by the Assembly of Heads of State and Government of the Organization of African Unity (OAU) at its 16th Ordinary Session in Monrovia.

The secretariat of the OAU had also displayed an interest in developing protection mechanisms for children's rights before the adoption of the ACRWC. It had been active regarding children's matters, such as child labour, child trafficking and children in situations of armed conflict. With regard to child labour, the OAU worked closely with the International Labour Organization's International Programme on the Elimination of Child Labour (ILO-IPEC), as well as the OAU Labour and Social Affairs Commission, which continuously discussed this issue.

African Heads of State and Government further committed to children's rights by ratifying the CRC, which entered into force in 1990. In order for the CRC to satisfy the culturally diverse international community that participated during the drafting and adoption process, some substantive provisions are rather vague. This is one of the reasons for the drafting and subsequent adoption of the ACRWC. Civil society organizations (CSOs)[1] followed the international development of children's rights eagerly and collectively drafted the document, taking the values of the CRC and adding African historical and cultural values. The draft was then presented to the OAU for consideration and potential adoption. The OAU African Heads of State and Government adopted it without amendment at the 26th Ordinary Session in Addis Ababa, Ethiopia in 1990.

While awaiting its entry into force, a Special Committee on Children in Situations of Armed Conflict (Special Committee) was established in 1997. The task of this committee was to follow up on the recommendations of the Conference on Children in Situations of Armed Conflict, held in June 1997 in Addis Ababa, Ethiopia. The Special Committee was composed of five OAU member states: Burkina Faso, South Africa, Togo, Uganda, and Zimbabwe. Working in co-operation with various CSOs, such as Save the Children and the African Network for the Prevention and Protection against Child Abuse and Neglect (ANPPCAN), the Special Committee was created on the understanding that when the ACRWC entered into force and the ACERWC was established, it would cease to exist.

During its five years of operation, the Special Committee actively lobbied OAU member states to ratify the ACRWC, as well as lobbying the OAU to ensure there was no discrimination on the basis of age within the OAU. The Special Committee also produced English and French versions of the ACRWC, as well as child-friendly versions for general distribution, produced a handbook and databank and identified good practice in culture. The Special Committee also importantly identified challenges hindering the effective provision of services to children in Africa.

---

1   The driver behind this development was the African Network for the Prevention and Protection against Child Abuse and Neglect (ANPPCAN) in 1989.

The African Charter on the Rights and Welfare of the Child (ACRWC)

The ACRWC was adopted on 11 July 1990 and entered into force on 29 November 1999. To date, it has received 41[2] out of 53 ratifications, and a number of states have signed the treaty. It has been criticized for the slow uptake by OAU member states (Lloyd 2002a, 181) as it took two years after adoption for any state to ratify or accede to it. Even after being adopted 16 years ago and in force for seven years, there still remain 12 states to agree to be bound by its principles and provisions.[3]

The ACRWC is divided into four principal sections: The Preamble and Part 1 'Rights and Duties'; Part 2 'The Establishment and Organisation of the African Committee of Experts'; Part 3 'The Mandate and Procedure'; Part 4 'Miscellaneous Provisions'.

Substantive Elements

The ACRWC reaffirms the proclamations of the Declaration, and explicitly recognizes that the child in Africa occupies a unique and privileged position in African society and that for the full harmonious development of the child's personality, the child should grow up in a family environment in an atmosphere of happiness, love and understanding (Preamble of the ACRWC). Furthermore, the ACRWC acknowledges the critical situation facing most children in Africa due to unique factors of their socio-economic, cultural, traditional and developmental circumstances, natural disasters, armed conflicts, exploitation and hunger, and that on account of children's physical and mental immaturity, they need special safeguards and care.

Who is a child? The ACRWC states that a child is 'every human being under 18 years' (article 2), providing a clear and concise definition. Unlike the CRC,[4] there are no limitations or attached considerations. However, the definition may yet come under scrutiny for its reference to the chronological age of children in Africa, as it is linked to effective birth registrations, physical capacity, initiation ceremonies and other cultural and traditional concepts of childhood in Africa.

Nature of state obligations The ACRWC contains a comprehensive, inclusive and progressive provision for the general obligations and responsibilities of state parties. This detailed provision provides evidence of a modern human rights-centric

---

2   Status at 25 October 2007. In 2006 there were no ratifications, in 2005 there were five.

3   Mezmur (2007b) records that subsequent to the 9th meeting, Gabon ratified the ACRWC on 12 June 2007, and Cote D'Ivoire on 18 June 2007. There is an unconfirmed report that the Charter was ratified by Sudan in a Presidential Decree in 2006 although the AU record does not confirm this.

4   Article 1 of the CRC states that a child is any human being under 18, unless majority is attained earlier under the law applicable to the child. This provision is ambiguous and weak, lacking specific protection within the African context, such as in relation to child betrothals, child participation in armed conflict and child labour.

approach,[5] bestowing many rights directly on the child by entitlement. Furthermore, the comprehensive provision could also be described as highlighting the importance of states adhering to the principles and putting them into the African context.[6]

The ACRWC obliges states to take necessary measures to implement its provisions and principles. 'Measures' include the adoption of legislation, the review and introduction of policies and other administrative measures, as well as budgetary allocation, in accordance with their constitutional processes (article 1, rule 8, Guidelines for Initial State Reports), to realize the rights and welfare of the child in the law of the state party, or in any other international convention or agreement in force in that state. It should also involve measures which promote positive cultural values and traditions as well as measures which discourage those traditions and values which are inconsistent with the rights, duties and obligations contained in the ACRWC. Furthermore, 'necessary steps' would also include the introduction and implementation of existing or planned mechanisms at the national or local level for co-ordinating policies relating to children.

Treaties come to life once the rights, freedoms and duties are 'incorporated' in accordance with a state's constitutional process, generally through an act of parliament, publication in the official gazette, or by other legislative measures. This is incredibly important as the executive arm of a state is not able to make law, and yet it is the executive which signs and ratifies international treaties.

The ACRWC contains 'general principles' for the protection of children's rights. These general principles also form the heart of the treaty, through which all other provisions should be interpreted and implemented. According to the ACERWC,[7] these 'core principles' underpin, inform and guide all the other provisions.[8] These 'underpinning principles' are: non-discrimination (articles 3 and 26), the best interests of the child (article 4), life, survival and development (article 5), and respect for the views of the child (article 7). Implementation priorities and specific future goals also need to be provided by state parties (Part IV, Guidelines for Initial State Reports). The ACRWC takes a more comprehensive approach than the CRC to the protection of children's rights, particularly with regard to the best interests principle.

Best interests   Within the framework of the ACRWC, the best interests of the child principle is paramount over the other three underpinning principles and is *the* primary consideration in all actions concerning the child.[9] This is in stark contrast to article

---

5   Refer to the Constitutive Act of the AU for further information on the human rights-based approach of the AU, in comparison to the former OAU. See, too, Olowu, Chapter 2 in this volume.

6   This is particularly pertinent in article 1(3) ACRWC.

7   The Guidelines for Initial Reports of States Parties, adopted at the second session of the ACERWC, Nairobi, Kenya, 17–21 February 2003. Cmttee/ACRWC/2 II.Rev 2.

8   States parties are requested to provide relevant information on the application of these principles in the implementation of the articles listed elsewhere in the ACRWC. Cmttee/ACRWC/2 II.Rev 2. Part IV, section 12.

9   Article 4(1) ACRWC states '*In all actions* concerning the child undertaken by any person or authority *the best interests of the child shall be the primary consideration*' (emphasis added).

3(1) of the CRC, which states that in all actions concerning children the best interests of the child shall be *a* primary consideration. The ACRWC goes further than the CRC by ensuring that all its provisions must be interpreted first and foremost in the child's best interests; moreover, this is contained in a binding document, rather than being predicated on non-binding, yet persuasive recommendations, made by a committee, as is the situation under the CRC. It has been observed (Gose 2002, 26–7) that the supremacy of the best interests principle in the ACRWC, though maximizing the influence of this overriding principle over other considerations, tends to reflect Western culture rather than embracing genuine African spirit. However, it must be noted that the best interests of the child have been the paramount consideration in determining a variety of children's issues, such as custody, in both customary law and formal civil law in Africa, dating back to the late eighteenth century, and has been applied consistently since.[10]

Life, survival and development   Life, survival and development principles ensure that children have the capacity to ascertain their rights and ensure the protection of their welfare. Furthermore, without the other provisions of the ACRWC being read in compliance with the child's right to life, survival and development, a child will always remain vulnerable and incapacitated. This underpinning principle refers to other overarching concepts and situations, such as poverty, disease, war and conflict, capital punishment and the disintegration of the traditional family unit.

The underlying principle of survival incorporates the inherent right to life, which by necessity, requires the eradication of the death penalty (article 5(3)), which is all the more significant considering at least 32 of 53 African states retain the death penalty (though not necessarily for children). Thus its eradication is imperative for the protection of children's rights in Africa. State parties' compliance with this obligation reflects the general policy to substitute life imprisonment for the death penalty. It is regrettable that the ACRWC does not explicitly provide for the implications of life imprisonment for children, akin to the CRC. However, article 5 of the ACRWC obligates states parties to ensure, to the maximum extent possible, the survival and development of the child. Life imprisonment would clearly impinge on the development of a child, mentally and physically, and thus would contravene article 17(3) of the ACRWC.

Non-discrimination   The principle of non-discrimination highlights the requirement to always ensure actions, decisions, policies and legislative enactments take heed of a child's rights to 'belong' and to be considered equal, not only among their own group, but as members of the whole community. The non-discrimination principle attaches to both the child and to the child's parents or legal guardians.

The CRC, in article 2(1), confines state parties to ensure children only 'within their jurisdiction' receive the rights in the CRC without discrimination. The ACRWC does not include any such restrictions or limitations, implying that states parties and individuals should ensure respect for, and realization of, children's rights without

---

10 *Tabb* v *Tabb* 1909 TPD 1033; *Mohapi* v *Masha* 1939 NAC (N&T) 154; *Hlope* v *Mahlalela* 1998 1 SA 449 (T).

discrimination across the continent. This has far reaching consequences for the sharing and mobilization of joint efforts and ventures with African states in need of additional assistance to ensure compliance with the ACRWC's provisions and principles.

The ACRWC has included explicit provisions on various forms of potential discrimination, to ensure special protection to children in certain circumstances, such as discriminatory regimes, war and conflict, as well as military destabilization, which are particularly acute problems in Africa. These explicit provisions are a positive contribution by the ACRWC, as they do not dilute the importance of non-discriminatory practices and directly confront some of the most relevant issues affecting children in Africa.

Participation　Participation is required for the effective realization of the other core principles and, indeed, the other substantive provisions contained in the ACRWC. Participation ensures that children are engaged actors rather than passive beneficiaries in the fulfilment of their rights. It also ensures children are capable of accessing their rights and have a voice, as well as a stake, in the protection of their rights and welfare.

The ACRWC contains many similar provisions to the CRC, albeit prescribed in an African context. However, there are certain provisions which provide for a higher threshold of protection for children, and some which are not provided for at all within the CRC. These provisions will be considered.

Nationality　Article 7(2) of the CRC can be regarded as an empty provision, requiring states to turn to other international agreements and national law for the provision of nationality for an otherwise stateless child. Thus, the right to acquire nationality is worthless if there is no recognizable state to which to make an application. Fortunately, article 6(4) of the ACRWC is much more comprehensive, explicitly providing for citizenship from the territory or residence in which the child is born.

Education　The ACRWC affords a much more detailed and protective measure on education, with no corresponding provision at the international level. Article 11(3)(e) of the ACRWC obliges states to take affirmative action and measures with regard to female, disadvantaged and gifted children. This provision attempts to address social imbalances, which can be corrected by state action.

Article 11(6) of the ACRWC provides protection for, and the promotion of, the rights of girls who fall pregnant while in education. It provides the opportunity for such girls to complete their education, on the grounds of their individual ability, without interruption, and pregnancy is not a legitimate ground for any kind of discrimination.

Disabled children　Article 13(1) of the ACRWC ensures that a mentally or physically disabled child should enjoy a full and decent life and shall be provided with special measures, obliging the state to take the financial burden.[11] States are also obliged to provide mobility and access to public institutions and facilities (article 13(3)). Unfortunately, the ACRWC did not provide for 'free of charge' assistance to the extent possible in the state, and is silent on access to rehabilitation services, health care services and education for disabled children.[12]

Health and health services   Article 14(2)(g) of the ACRWC prescribes the integration of basic health service programmes into national development plans. Parents, children, community leaders and community workers have the right to be supported and informed about the basic knowledge of child health and nutrition (article 14(2)(h)).[13] The ACRWC emphasizes a collegial approach by providing for the meaningful participation of the whole of society and NGOs in the planning and management of a basic health service programme for children (article 14(2)(i)). Moreover, it provides for technical and financial support for the mobilization of local community resources in the development of primary health care for children (article 14(2)(j)).

Child labour   As well as reinforcing the provisions at the international level, the ACRWC provides for the widespread dissemination of information on the dangers of child labour, and obliges states to facilitate and organize educational campaigns (article 15(2)(d)). It also requires states to legislate for minimum ages for admission into every form of employment (article 15(2)(a)).

Parental responsibilities   If parents or guardians are facing difficulties in providing material assistance to their children, states parties are obliged to provide such assistance and support programmes, especially in regard to health, education, clothing and housing. This could be an invaluable addition to tackle the problem of HIV/Aids: the primary responsibility is on parents and *de facto* carers, when they are no longer able to provide, or are no longer present, the responsibility falls back onto the state (article 20(2)(a)).

Harmful social and cultural practices   Africa is a continent rich in cultural practices which are embedded in the fabric of everyday life. Article 21 of the ACRWC, which protects children against harmful social and cultural practices, is one of the most important of all the enshrined provisions; a concurring clause has not been included in any other treaty at any level and this is a crucial step forward for the protection of children in Africa, especially in light of the recognition of African cultural heritage and African civilization. Many discriminatory and dangerous practices in Africa emanate from custom and from heritage. It has been very difficult to eradicate harmful practices, owing to the perceived threat to cultural 'values' and a 'western imposition'. This is, therefore, a welcome inclusion. States must take *all appropriate measures* to ensure the effective implementation of this provision.

---

11 Article 23(1) CRC does not oblige states to take special protection measures.
12 Article 23(3) CRC provides for this measure.
13 Article 24(2)(e) CRC only states that parents and children have this right.

Article 21(1) of the ACRWC is very broad: no practices or customs are expressly mentioned, leaving it open to interpretation, and it includes such practices as female genital mutilation (FGM);[14] the ACERWC has commented on FGM and article 21(1) in a number of its sessions,[15] but has not yet provided any further analysis or interpretation of this article.

Article 21(2) of the ACRWC specifically relates to the African customary practice of child betrothal and marriage, and interrelates with other clauses in the treaty, such as article 27 on sexual exploitation, article 11 on education, article 3 on discrimination, article 5 on the right to survival and development, and article 14 on health. Child marriage and betrothal is expressly prohibited, and effective action, including legislation, is to be taken to specify the minimum age of marriage as 18 years; it is compulsory to register all marriages in an official register. This has not been expressly recognized and regulated in any other treaty and is a welcome addition. It is not clear how African states will be able to ensure compulsory marriage registration, as resources are scarce in some jurisdictions. Nonetheless, states must make every effort to allocate enough budgetary resources to ensure this provision is fully implemented. Compulsory marriage registration has also a potentially immense impact on the law governing customary marriages in Africa.

Children in armed conflict   The ACRWC increases the protection of children between the ages of 15 and 18, which the CRC under article 38 fails to do. States must take all necessary measures to ensure no child takes a direct part in hostilities, although there is no further elaboration of the rights of those children caught up in conflict situations as non-direct participants, such as girls who cook, clean and are at the disposal of armies. State parties must refrain from recruiting any child (article 22(2)).[16]

Children's duties   Reflecting the African cultural and traditional concepts of family and society, the ACRWC bestows responsibilities on children to, *inter alia*, work for the cohesion of the family, to respect parents, superiors and elders at all times and assist in times of need, to serve the national community through physical and intellectual abilities, and to preserve and strengthen traditional values (article 31).

Child victims   One of the shortcomings of the ACRWC lies in the recognition of child victims, and the assistance states should provide. Such protection must be imported and interpreted by way of article 39 of the CRC, which establishes that states must take appropriate measures to promote physical and psychological recovery and social reintegration of a child victim. It is regrettable the ACRWC does not incorporate a better safeguard to support child victims.

---

14 This practice violates article 21(1)(a). See also, Arts 1992, 139.

15 The issues were discussed in technical discussions, and agenda time was allocated to the specific discussion of FGM at the 5th ordinary session, 8–12 November 2004.

16 See Chapter 12 on child soldiers for further discussion of the legal regulatory framework in this sphere.

The Establishment and Organization of the ACERWC

The Steps to the Creation of the ACERWC

The ACERWC was established according to Part II of the ACRWC (article 32) on 10 July 2001 following the entry into force of the treaty in November 1999. It is a body of 11 independent members of high moral standing, integrity, impartiality and competence in matters of the rights and welfare of the child (article 33(1)), serving in their personal capacity. Each state party could nominate up to two candidates, one of whom had to be a national (article 35). As far as possible, the election process takes into account gender and geographical balance. Despite the OAU requesting nominations, by November 2000 only five names had been proposed. The slow initial nomination process of candidates resulted in the delayed establishment of the ACERWC. However, as more states ratified the ACRWC, a larger pool from which candidates could be proposed materialized. Fortunately, by the 37th Assembly of Heads of State and Government, 12 candidates had been proposed, from which 11 were elected by secret ballot on 10 July 2001 in Lusaka, Zambia. The term of office is decided by drawing lots and is generally for five years; members cannot be re-elected. However, the term of office of four members elected at the first election expired after two years, and the term of six others after four years (article 37). This provided for rotation, while at the same time retaining members with a working knowledge of the ACERWC's methods.[17]

Composition and Bureau

To date, there have been four different compositions of members. This is partly due to the shorter term of office of some of the first elected members, and partly due to vacancies arising. All compositions have been gender and geographically balanced. The first composition comprised members from Guinea, Kenya, Lesotho, Rwanda, Senegal, South Africa, Chad, Togo, Uganda, Mauritius and Cameroon. The first ordinary session took place in 2002. At the second ordinary session in February 2003, three members had resigned due to taking up alternative positions which were deemed incompatible with committee membership. The member from Togo took up a ministerial position, the member from Chad joined UNICEF, and the member from Senegal was appointed to the UNICT for Rwanda. It is positive to note that the members take their role seriously and comply with such provisions.[18] Not all human rights protection and monitoring bodies have adhered so rigorously to the requirements of impartiality and independence of committee membership.[19]

---

17 For a more in depth look at the ACERWC and its work, see Lloyd 2002a, 179; Lloyd 2002b, 320; Lloyd 2003, 329; Lloyd 2004a, 139; Lloyd 2004b, 1; Mezmur 2006; Mezmur 2007a; Mezmur 2007b.

18 At the 9th ordinary meeting, the new posts of two members were ruled not to be incompatible with their role as members of the ACERWC: Mezmur 2007b.

19 For example, the history of the African Commission on Human and Peoples' Rights highlights that Ambassadors and Ministers have formed part of the Commission membership, even though such positions impair impartiality and independence.

At the third ordinary session, the term of office of the members from Guinea, Lesotho and Uganda expired after the mentioned two years, and they were replaced by members from Burkina Faso, Nigeria and Togo. At the seventh ordinary session, the term of office of the members from Kenya, Rwanda, South Africa, Chad (vacancy), Mauritius and Cameroon expired after the initial four years. These members were replaced by experts from Senegal, Côte d'Ivoire, Kenya, Lesotho, Botswana and Mali.[20] From 2005, the ACERWC comprised ten members (11 members since late 2006) improving its capacity to undertake its mandate effectively and foster credibility regionally and internationally.

Article 38 of the ACRWC establishes the Bureau of the African Committee: the Rules of Procedure (hereinafter also referred to as 'Rules'), the Officers, the Quorum and the Working Languages. The ACERWC established its own Rules of Procedure, which provide further information on its functions and its meetings. The consideration and adoption of the Rules of Procedure, adopted on 2 May 2002, formed the principal activity of the ACERWC during the first and second ordinary sessions.

The Relationship between the AU and the ACERWC

The ACERWC was established by the OAU, but during a period when the OAU was in transition. The original focus of the OAU was on political stability, peace and security. The focus was changing to be more human rights centred, and the OAU was to be replaced by the African Union (AU). This transition from OAU to AU has posed many challenges to the establishment and organization of the ACERWC, ranging from budgetary issues to the support of the OAU/AU from an institutional viewpoint. The infrastructure at the OAU/AU did not cope well with the establishment of new bodies. The Labour and Social Affairs Directorate (LSAD) took the responsibility of organizing the ACERWC's schedules; after the interim period this did not significantly change. The Labour and Social Affairs Commission (LSAC) is indirectly responsible for organizing the work of the ACERWC; the LSAC reports to the executive council of AU, as does the ACERWC. However, the AU by 2006 had still not established a secretariat for the ACERWC, which the chairperson of the commission of the AU was obliged to do by virtue of article 40 of the ACRWC. The secretariat would assist the ACERWC in the exercise of its functions, serve as intermediary for all communications, and be the custodian of the ACERWC's archives (rule 23).

Initially discussions about the secretariat, its establishment and staff were very positive and encouraging. Unfortunately, as the sessions progressed, and despite continual promises to the ACERWC that the secretariat would be established and a permanent secretary and other staff would be provided, this remained a dream. At best, temporary personnel fulfilled the administrative functions with the support of the LSAD. The main reason given for this was financial. At the second ordinary session, the representatives of the AU stated that provisional budget for the ACERWC

---

20 These experts were elected as members at the Assembly of the AU, 5th ordinary session, July 2005 in Sirte, Libya.

had not been completed, and due to the interim status of the AU, there would only be a temporary budget, as the AU was awaiting a complete structural reform, due to end in July 2003. The ACERWC became disenchanted with the broken promises and at its fourth ordinary session called the AU to account over the severe problems encountered by the lack of structures in place. The AU responded by highlighting that the ACERWC must mobilize themselves to ensure their mandate was performed and stated further the AU had been doing all it could with the means available. The ACERWC then considered the possibility of working with partners to create their own secretariat, but there were mixed feelings – while some members considered they needed to be proactive and mobilize their own resources, instruments and institutions, others thought this would relieve the AU of responsibilities, which was not acceptable. When the situation had not improved by the fifth ordinary session, the ACERWC submitted a request to the extraordinary session of the AU Executive Council in December 2004. The AU reaffirmed its commitment to the ACERWC and started the recruitment process for a permanent secretary; however, the recruitment process remained slow due to AU requirements for regional distribution and gender balance. Good news prevailed at the seventh ordinary session, when the ACERWC was informed that the AU Commission was finalizing the recruitment of a secretary and that UNICEF had approved funds for assisting the secretariat with a senior policy officer (legal) and an administrative secretary. However, at the eighth ordinary session in December 2006, information was shared that the recruitment process had failed to attract a suitable candidate to serve as permanent secretary; thereafter, an initial employee remained for only six months, and only in mid-2007 was the post eventually filled.

The regular budget for the ACERWC is provided by the AU, and donations to support its work programme can also be accepted (Rule 26). Due to the problems arising during the transitional period of the AU, the ACERWC has been resourced mainly through donations, inter-agency participation and collaboration. This has affected the work it has undertaken: there was a lengthy work plan from the outset, but when finance was not available, the ACERWC had to reduce its plans and rework priorities according to the donations received and conditions attached to some of the funding. The work has also suffered because members did not appreciate that any proposal they want to undertake in the name of the ACERWC, such as country visits, should be circulated to the chairperson of the Commission of the AU to prepare an estimated costing. This procedure has not been followed, and the ACERWC has simply relied on the AU to provide funding or on the generosity of partners. If proposals had been circulated through the Commission of the AU, more funding might have been allocated.

Collaboration and Co-operation between the ACERWC and its Partners

An important aspect for the effective facilitation of the ACERWC's work has been the participation of, and consultation with, non-members of the ACERWC, such as specialized institutions, inter-governmental organizations, and CSO's (article 42, rules 78–81). This has been a primary focus of work and without such consultation and collaboration, the ACERWC would have achieved far less during its six years of operation. In 2007, the African Children's Committee finalized 'Criteria for Granting Observer Status', in conformity with article 42 of the African Children's Charter and articles 34, 37, 81 and 82 of the Rules of Procedure, on representation and co-operation with civil society organizations. Granting observer status facilitates formally involving NGOs in the work of the African Children's Committee, be it in the preparation of complementary reports, submission of communications or undertaking of lobbying and/or investigation missions (Mezmur 2007b).

Steps were taken at the first ordinary session to establish links between the ACERWC and partners. The ACERWC had discussed adopting modalities for co-operation, but no formal document was ever concluded. Consideration was given to facilitating work through establishing a website, and Save the Children (Sweden) pledged to finance the design and creation of this, followed by a proposal from UNICEF. It took a while before this was taken up by the ACERWC. Throughout the various sessions, partners offered various types of support, such as assisting the ACERWC to distribute, disseminate and promote the ACRWC; to sensitize partners; to provide technical assistance and human resources support; to provide training workshops; and to undertake research.

The ACERWC took time to forge links with its sister organization, the African Commission on Human and Peoples' Rights (African Commission). There are many lessons to be learnt from the African Commission, as well as ensuring clear working procedures between the bodies, as the African Commission dealt with all human rights issues, including children, until the establishment of the ACERWC. Questions have been raised about how to consolidate work to prevent conflict and repetition. The relationship should be complementary, which can only be achieved through close collaboration and modalities of co-operation. The chairperson of the African Commission attended the seventh ordinary session of the ACERWC in December 2005 to begin the process of forging closer collaboration.

The Mandate of the ACERWC

General mandate   The ACERWC is the guardian of children's rights in Africa, and its role is manifold: it can collect and document information; commission inter-disciplinary assessments of situations on African problems in the field of children's rights; organize meetings; encourage relevant national and local institutions; and where necessary give its views and make recommendations to governments. Furthermore, the ACERWC can formulate and lay down principles and rules, derived from the substantive elements of the ACRWC and drawn up in line with the core principles, aimed at protecting the rights and welfare of children in Africa (article 42 supplemented by Rules 65, 70, 72 and 73, 75, 76 and 77). The ACERWC can also be creative and ensure that children's rights and welfare are guaranteed by interpreting the provisions of the ACRWC at the request of a state party, an institution of the AU, or any other person or institution recognized by the AU. These 'protect and promote' functions provide a policy-initiator role which allows the ACERWC to be innovative and an '*animateur*' in the area of child rights. Generally, this is undertaken through devoting ordinary sessions to general discussions on one specific provision of the ACRWC, to enhance a deeper understanding of the content and implications of the

ACRWC (rule 76).[21] Furthermore, the ACERWC may recommend to the Assembly of Heads of State and Government to request the chairperson of the commission of the AU to undertake, on its behalf, studies on specific issues relating to the rights and welfare of the child. Partners and other bodies can also be invited to undertake studies or submit studies on topics of relevance to the ACERWC.

The general mandate of the ACERWC to 'promote and protect' children's rights and welfare issues can be divided into procedural activities and substantive issues to be addressed. As far as the procedural activities are concerned, the lion's share of work has been to popularize the ACRWC among member states, partners and other stakeholders to bring about increased ratification and understanding of the ACRWC's principles and provisions. Other procedural priorities have included resource mobilization and the formulation of National Plans of Action for Children, where they do not already exist. Such activities fall within the ACERWC's responsibility to encourage relevant national and local institutions.

The substantive priorities addressed by the ACERWC under the general remit of article 42 of the ACRWC include a variety of thematic issues such as children in situations of armed conflict, child labour, child trafficking, sexual abuse and exploitation of children, including traditional practices, HIV/Aids, youth in conflict with the law, and birth registration. The highest priority has been accorded to HIV/Aids and child soldiers. These areas have been discussed at every meeting and formed the basis of country visits to Sudan and Northern Uganda. The International Committee of the Red Cross (ICRC) and the AU Labour and Social Affairs Commission have been driving the work of the ACERWC, through support, existing programmes and funding. As these priority areas form part of the mandate of these organizations, it could be suggested that the work of the ACERWC has been shaped and to an extent dictated by partners, as opposed to deciding for themselves in their expert capacity on issues to tackle, and then requesting support from relevant partners. Further, it would seem, from a substantive viewpoint, that the ACERWC has been guided by partners who provide funding, but not by those with collaborative project proposals, or those requiring this specialized AU monitoring body to pronounce recommendations and observations on issues that states parties need to implement, in order to satisfy their obligations under the ACRWC. Unfortunately, the ACERWC has not seemed to seize the opportunity to use the time devoted to technical discussions at the ordinary sessions to guide thinking about the conceptualization of children's rights through making recommendations and interpreting the ACRWC provisions accordingly. Thus far, the ACERWC has not been innovative with the information provided to it.

Within the arena of legislative amendments, there has been a drive for member states to strengthen, harmonize and consolidate their laws pertaining to children.[22] Members have discussed certain issues regarding legislative harmonization processes

---

21 Hence at the 10th ordinary meeting of the ACERWC, held in Cairo, Egypt, in October 2007, a presentation on the jurisprudential implications of the duties of the African child as spelt out in article 31 of the Charter was made and formed the basis of further discussion. See Sloth-Nielsen, J. and Mezmur, B.D. (2008), 'A Dutiful Child: The Implications of Article 31 of the African Children's Charter', *Journal of African Law* (forthcoming), 1.

22 See, in general, African Child Policy Forum 2007.

in Mauritius, Rwanda, Cameroon, and the drafting of a sub-regional convention on child trafficking in Francophone countries in West and Central Africa. However, the ACERWC has not yet used these recent country developments to formulate principles aimed at the legislative protection of children's rights and welfare in Africa.

The ACERWC has organized a variety of meetings over the past six years of operation aimed at promoting and protecting children's rights. Many have been with representatives of the UN and UNICEF, as well as with various organs of the AU. Country visits have also been undertaken to advise governments on ratifying the ACRWC, as well as to make other recommendations concerning the protection of children in Africa. Missions to Northern Uganda, Madagascar, Sudan and Namibia have been undertaken, during which meetings were organized with government officials, staff of UN agencies, academics, the media and NGOs. These visits were part of the ACERWC's popularization and sensitization campaigns, as well as being undertaken to assess the child protection systems of these countries. The country visits were financed by partners, thus the areas were limited to the donor requirements.

The Day of the African Child[23] (DAC), celebrated every year on 16 June, has been used as the main advocacy tool by the ACERWC, to not only popularize the ACRWC, but to also make member states aware of the work of the ACERWC and to draw attention to priority issues affecting children in Africa. Since the establishment of the ACERWC, the themes for DAC have covered: the African child and the family, birth registration, violence against children, orphans and child trafficking. The theme selected for 2008, as recommended by the 8th meeting of the Committee, is 'Right to participation: Let children be seen and heard'. Member states are obliged to submit reports on how the DAC was celebrated at the national and local level. These reports should be scrutinized by the ACERWC. However, to date, there have been very few reports submitted, and the ACERWC has stated that these were insufficient to constitute a basis for comprehensive assessment.

The ACERWC is also a guardian of children's interests through more bureaucratic and formal processes. The ACERWC can still have an important impact through these functions, but they are dependent on the action and input of states parties. The processes can be divided into three categories: the reporting procedure, communications and investigations.

Reporting procedure   Like most treaty-based bodies, states parties have an obligation to submit initial reports (within two years of ratification of the ACRWC (article 43(a)) and then periodic reports (every three years according to article 43 (b)); the content of reports must be based on the Guidelines drafted and adopted by the ACERWC. The procedure for the submission, formalities concerning non-submission, and attendance by states parties at the examination of the reports is covered in the Rules of Procedure.[24]

In theory, reports should contain sufficient information on the implementation of the ACRWC to provide the ACERWC with a comprehensive understanding

---

23 CM/Res. 1659 (LXIV) Rev. 1 1996.

24 Rules 66 (Submission), 67 (Non-Submission), 68 (Attendance of States Parties at Exam of Report), 69 (Request for Additional Reports or Information) of the Rules of Procedure.

of its implementation in the respective countries, and should include factors and difficulties encountered in fulfilling the ACRWC obligations.[25] However in practice, state reporting mechanisms have demonstrated that, as a general proposition, the quality of reports varies in detail and in content. States do not always provide sufficient information on the implementation of the treaty at a domestic level.

It must be borne in mind that the CRC committee also receives state reports on the implementation of the principles and provisions of the CRC. There is a significant duplication in the work of the two committees, and additional burdens on states parties to both treaties to provide adequate reports for both forums. This overlap has been considered by both committees,[26] and it was decided by the ACERWC that, in order to avoid repetition, and in order to encourage governments to fulfil their obligations towards both committees, whilst recognizing the specific nature of the several provisions of the ACRWC, if a state party has already submitted an initial report to the CRC committee, whether that report has been reviewed or not, that state party would be invited to update the information already submitted and add information on the different provisions contained in the ACRWC. Where a state party's initial report has been reviewed by the CRC committee, the recommendations may be considered by the ACERWC when preparing the list of issues for the government's response, and when adopting its own concluding observations and recommendations. If a state party has not yet submitted an initial report to the CRC Committee, it shall be invited to prepare a complete report on all of the provisions of the ACRWC. If either of the two committees intends to change its guidelines, a consultative process should be developed between them, but there remains a need to further develop modalities for co-operation between the CRC committee and the ACERWC.

In practice, the ACERWC has devoted time at every ordinary session to the state reporting procedure, affirming it would devise a timeframe for the receipt of state reports. However, this was not the reality. Instead much administrative work was dedicated to discussing state reports, but little progress was actually made. At the fourth ordinary session in 2004, the AU could not even confirm if the Guidelines had been sent to member states. However, by 2005, the Guidelines and Schedules for Submission had been dispatched. In spite of much discussion, the ACERWC still remains ill-equipped to deal with submissions of state reports. The state reports for Mauritius and Egypt were received by the seventh ordinary session in 2005. By the eighth ordinary session (in December 2006), Nigeria and Rwanda also submitted their reports. However, these reports could not be considered as procedures had still not been finalized. This is a good illustration of how the reporting procedure can be time consuming and ineffective.

It is suggested that the state reporting procedure is not a far-reaching tool for the protection of children's rights generally. Thus, the ACERWC should have devoted

---

25 Generally see article 43(2) ACRWC and Part I Guidelines 1–7; Part II Guidelines 8–9; specific information on substantive elements is provided in the remaining Parts of the Guidelines.

26 At the 1st ordinary session, May 2002, where particular attention was given to Paragraph 24 of the Guidelines for State Parties, defining the procedure to be followed to avoid duplication of reports to both the CRC committee and the ACERWC.

more time, attention and consideration to the other two (more innovative) procedural areas of potential work: communications and investigations. This, however, is not what the ACERWC has done so far in practice.

Communications   A noteworthy and innovative addition to the ACRWC is that of individual complaints (article 44). Since the CRC does not contain this enforcement mechanism, the ACERWC has the chance to make a valuable contribution to the development of children's rights through the receipt of communications and holding individual states accountable for violating the provisions and principles contained in the ACRWC. Communications can be made by any person, group or NGO recognized by the AU, by a member state, or the UN, and relating to any matter covered by the ACRWC.

It could be argued that the inclusion of a complaints mechanism runs counter to African culture and tradition, which emphasizes community-based resolution systems, as opposed to individualistic complaints procedures. On the other hand, it reflects a move towards recognizing the inherent vulnerability of children and provides an avenue for the whole of society to take responsibility for the protection of children's rights, reflecting a very traditional African approach: society and the community protecting each other.

There is ambiguity surrounding who can actually submit a communication and this has not been interpreted by the ACERWC, despite it being asked on many occasions.[27] The provision could be interpreted as allowing everyone a right to submit a complaint, though this is only theoretical, given that individuals would first have to know of the mechanism in order to use it. It is debatable if those in rural areas in Africa would have been informed of this mechanism, let alone know how to access it.

The ACERWC has devoted very few meeting hours to the elaboration of communication guidelines, criteria, and the need for a filter mechanism, to ensure the complaints procedure does not become overburdened and the work of the ACERWC backlogged and inefficient. The first formal discussion of the communications procedure was during the seventh session in late 2005. This discussion was forced on the ACERWC, as the AU had received various individual communications from NGOs. One example is that from Uganda. The memo and document were distributed to all members for consideration and action. However, the ACERWC would only acknowledge receipt of the communications, as it felt it could not react without adopting and developing its own procedures.

The ACERWC compared documents submitted by the Institute for Human Rights and Development in Africa (IHRDA) and those of the African Commission. However, the communication procedure contained within the African Charter on Human and Peoples' Rights (ACHPR) for the African Commission is more extensive, or at least more detailed in content than the ACRWC, which simply provides that the 'Committee may receive communications from any person,

---

27 For example, observers at the 6th and 7th ordinary sessions raised such points. The AU representatives referred to the criteria adopted at the Sirte Summit in July 2005, stating the ACERWC is also able to adopt its own criteria. This was not further elaborated.

group or non-governmental organization recognized by the Organisation of African Unity, by a Member State, or the United Nations relating to any matter covered by this Charter' (article 44). The procedure contained in the ACHPR spans seven different articles elaborating different conditions for submission and receipt of communications. Although the ACERWC's mandate is basic, this does not mean it is a weaker mechanism. It simply allows room for interpretation and for Guidelines and Procedures to be established which set out submission and receipt conditions.

In a positive turn of events, during the eighth ordinary session in December 2006, a detailed 'Guideline for the consideration of individual complaints' was prepared and submitted for discussion by one of the ACERWC members (Mezmur 2007a). The draft was considered provision by provision and the necessary amendments were made. At the closing session of the meeting it was agreed that the draft document be adopted as amended, pending the finalization of some technical issues by the Legal Counsel of the AU. The Guideline contains detailed procedures on the submission and examination of individual complaints, including the requirement that local remedies be exhausted.

The individual complaints mandate provides an area where the ACERWC has the potential to make positive contributions to the protection of children's rights and welfare. This is a tool for ensuring that individual violations by states can be directly addressed, and states held to account by the ACERWC. Though no prescriptive sanctions are provided by the ACRWC, the AU could take action to ensure the enforcement of breaches of any sanctions imposed. Moreover, responses to individual complaints will help to shape the development of an indigenous children's rights jurisprudence.

Investigations   The investigation procedure provided by the ACHPR for the African Commission forms a part of the communications procedure; it is not a separate procedure. The ACRWC dedicates a specific provision to the investigation of any matter falling within the ambit of the treaty, a power provided for by article 45 of the ACRWC. Rather than states parties instigating this procedure, the ACERWC by its own motion may seek any relevant information regarding the implementation of the ACRWC provisions, and the nature and scope of implementing the measures adopted. The power of investigation is also rather vague and requires elaboration by drawing inspiration from other sources, such as the ACHPR. Accordingly, during the eighth ordinary session, a draft 'Guideline on investigations' was submitted and discussed, and after deliberation, adopted by the ACERWC members (Mezmur 2007a). It is suggested that both articles 44 and 45 should be read together to understand the situations that would require investigation by the African Committee, by its own motion. If a communication is submitted against a state party, then it is suggested that, as part of the consideration of this communication, the ACERWC could launch an investigation to assess the validity of the complaint. The preliminary investigation may lead to an in-depth study of the cases brought to the attention of the ACERWC.

It is difficult to assess how effective the enforcement mechanisms of the ACERWC will be, considering the undertaking of investigations must be with the agreement of the state party. The provisions are also wholly dependent on the extent to which states parties are prepared and willing to give full effect at a national level to any recommendations and proposals. Article 45 of the ACRWC will further require state party commitment to provide the necessary financial and logistical support to enable investigations by the ACERWC to occur.

As the ACERWC is mandated to take note of other sources of inspiration in the delivery of and fulfilment of its mandate (see, for instance, article 46), the effectiveness of the enforcement procedures may depend on the extent to which the ACERWC is prepared, willing and able to utilize, using their knowledge as experts, the available data, information, resources and experiences of institutions with comparable objectives.

Conclusion

At present, the ACERWC can still be considered a fledging organization, and it is perhaps too early to examine the efficacy of the ACRWC's provisions, along with its monitoring and enforcement procedures. Time will tell if the ACERWC can be creative in untangling the complexities and intricacies of what needs to be protected and promoted, as well as what needs to be abandoned in African culture and tradition, to provide a new dimension to the status of children in Africa: a status of value and worth, where a child has recognized rights and a child's welfare is guaranteed.

References

Articles, Books and Chapters in Books

Arts, K. (1992), 'The International Protection of Children's Rights in Africa: The 1990 OAU Charter on the Rights and Welfare of the Child', *RADIC* 5, 139.
Gose, M. (2002), *The African Charter on the Rights and Welfare of the Child: An Assessment of the Legal Value of its Substantive Provisions by Means of a Direct Comparison to the Convention on the Rights of the Child* (Bellville: Community Law Centre, University of the Western Cape).
Lloyd, A. (2002a), 'Evolution of the African Charter on the Rights and Welfare of the Child and the African Committee of Experts: Raising the Gauntlet', *International Journal of Children's Rights* 10, 179–98.
Lloyd, A. (2002b), 'The First Meeting of the African Committee of Experts on the Rights and Welfare of the Child', *African Human Rights Law Journal* 2:2, 320–27.
Lloyd, A. (2003), 'A Report of the Second Ordinary Session of the African Committee of Experts on the Rights and Welfare of the Child', *African Human Rights Law Journal* 3:2, 329–47.
Lloyd, A. (2004a), 'The Third Ordinary Session of the African Committee of Experts on the Rights and Welfare of the Child', *African Human Rights Law Journal* 4:1, 139–58.
Lloyd, A. (2004b), 'How to Guarantee Credence: Recommendations and Proposals for the African Committee of Experts on the Rights and Welfare of the Child', *International Journal of Children's Rights* 12:1, 1–21.

Mezmur, B.D. (2006), 'The African Committee of Experts on the Rights and Welfare of the Child: An Update', *African Human Rights Law Journal* 6, 2.

Mezmur, B.D. (2007a), 'Still an Infant or a Toddler? The Work of the African Committee of Experts on the Rights and Welfare of the Child and its 8th Ordinary Session', *African Human Rights Law Journal* 7:1.

Mezmur, B.D. (2007b), 'Looking Back to Looking Ahead: The 9th Meeting of the African Committee of Experts on the Rights and Welfare of the Child', *African Human Rights Law Journal* 7:2.

Sloth-Nielsen, J. and Mezmur, B.D. (2008), 'A Dutiful Child: The Implications of Article 31 of the African Children's Charter', *Journal of African Law* (forthcoming).

Reports

African Child Policy Forum (2007), *Realising their Rights: Harmonization of Law for Children in Eastern and Southern Africa* (Addis Ababa: African Child Policy Forum).

Cases

Hlope v *Mahlalela* 1998 1 SA 449 (T).
Mohapi v *Masha* 1939 NAC (N&T) 154.
Tabb v *Tabb* 1909 TPD 1033.

Chapter 4

Domestication of Children's Rights in National Legal Systems in African Context: Progress and Prospects

Julia Sloth-Nielsen

Introduction

Children's rights have made a measurable impact on the legal and policy environment in Africa. The journey of assimilation, formulation, adaptation, specialization and implementation is an unfinished one, but the contours of domestication on the continent bear some hallmarks of distinction, which are worthy of exploration in this chapter. Further, it will be argued that the ongoing project of legal and, in some instances, constitutional reform or judicial development of children's rights lays a sound framework for children's survival and development on the continent in a much broader sense: that far from being merely an exercise in recording legal words on paper, the developments traced here link directly to economic imperatives, to programming and service delivery, to achievement (at least partially) of the Millennium Development Goals (MDGs), and to the recognition of African children as actors in the human rights family.

This chapter commences with a brief analysis of both international law imperatives driving law reform on the continent, as well as other factors which have propelled legal and policy developments. Thereafter, attention turns to the extent to which children's rights feature in national constitutions. The argument is made that as significant parts of Africa entered the era of constitutional democracy from the mid-1990s, the value and significance of enshrining children's rights has become increasingly apparent. The next section provides an overview of domestication processes within national legal systems in selected African countries, drawing out signal features of both law reform processes and of innovative approaches that have characterized law reform to enhance children's rights in Africa. Lessons and challenges derived from the domestication initiatives are also highlighted. In conclusion, some comments on the role of law in developing countries are proffered.

International Law Factors and Other Imperatives Impelling Legal Reform in Children's Rights Related Spheres

International Law Framework for Legal Reform

Article 4 of the Convention on the Rights of the Child (CRC) lays an obvious basis for assuring that legal reform is a core obligation that ratifying states parties agree to undertake. It provides that '[s]tate parties shall undertake all appropriate legislative, administrative and other measures for the implementation of the rights recognized in the Convention ...' which, according to Doek (2007, 3), entails 'the activities of government to ensure that national laws and related administrative regulations are in full compliance with the CRC ...'. It is further noted that harmonization should be an ongoing process, commencing with a review – audit – of existing laws and continuing with the systematic checking of compliance of proposed legislation with the CRC, the African Children's Charter and the Optional Protocols, where ratified. These statements are underscored by General Comment no. 5 (General Measures of Implementation of the Convention on the Rights of the Child) of the CRC Committee, issued in 2003. Paragraph 1 contains the foundational principle, 'ensuring that all domestic legislation is fully compatible with the Convention and that the Convention's principles and provisions can be directly applied and enforced is fundamental'. And although other measures (such as institutions for monitoring children's rights implementation) are accorded equal significance in the implementation of general rights as spelt out in the General Comment, legislative reform is mentioned as inescapable in para. 9, para. 11 ('States must see their role as fulfilling clear legal obligations to each and every child') and para. 12 (requiring active measures by governments, parliaments and judiciaries to embed the best interests of the child principle, which clearly point to the need for legal measures to ensure its application), and the nature of the state obligation described in considerable detail in part IV, paras 18–23.

Noting (in 2003, more than a decade after the entry into force of the CRC) that review processes at national level had started in many cases, but that they needed to be more rigorous, the General Comment points to the advantage of participation by a wider array of bodies and organs of civil society in the review of legislation (para. 18). Stating that clarification of the extent of applicability – or justiciability – of the CRC provisions under domestic law remains murky in many jurisdictions, the Comment appears to suggest that the preferred position, even where the CRC is allegedly 'self executing', or 'has constitutional status' (para. 19), is to ensure (by legal means) that the provisions of the Convention can be invoked before courts and national authorities (see also Hodgkin and Newell 2002, 66), and that its provisions prevail where there is conflict between the children's right provisions of the CRC and those of domestic law. That the obligation to legislate within the framework of the CRC rests at all levels of government is clear from para. 20. The extent to which consolidated statutes or comprehensive child laws are mandated is still moot: whilst the endeavour to develop such unified statutes has been epitomized in some of the early African child law reform processes, such as those in Uganda and Nigeria, the increasing complexity of legal responses to issues such as trafficking of children and sexual offences, as well as debates about the desirability of the separation of welfare and protection-oriented child statutes from ones dealing with the procedures and institutions for children in conflict with the law, has led to divided legislative processes in many other countries of late – South Africa, Ghana and Namibia, to name three examples (discussed further in Chapter 9). All three have enacted, or are aiming to enact, separate juvenile justice statutes, alongside legislation dealing with welfare, status or affiliation.

In the process of legal reform, the General Comment emphasizes the need for attention to be paid to domestic incorporation of the four general principles which go to the heart of the children's right framework, namely non-discrimination (article 2), the primacy of the child's best interests (article 3), the child's right to survival and development (article 6) and the child's right to participate and to have his or her views considered (article 12).[1] Hodgkin and Newell also emphasize this point. Furthermore, since rights are inextricably interwoven with enforcement and the availability of remedies, appropriate procedures, sanctions and other measures in the event of breaches should be provided in sufficient detail, according to the General Comment (para. 25).

That other general measures of implementation of children's rights required by General Comment no. 5 can be furthered through law reform efforts is also worth mentioning. For instance, the need for co-ordination of children's rights across different spheres and levels of government can – should? – find expression in legally mandated structures and bodies. Equally, although the monitoring of implementation of child rights programmes and their impact is a practical, rather than a legal, activity, there can be no doubt that providing for data collection, evidence-based policy formulation and ongoing review of progress or impact at regular intervals via some or other legal or quasi-legal form can buttress the fulfilment of these essential developmental tools. This will be explored further below (see 'Children's Rights in African Constitutions').

Of course, in African context, the issue of compatibility of children's legal rights with customary and religious laws poses particularly sharp problems when law reform, harmonization and domestication are considered. That the obligation to harmonize all legal systems to which children are subject with the rights framework established by the CRC and the African Charter extends to customary and religious laws has been articulated frequently in the CRC Committee's concluding observations (see Hodgkin and Newell 2002, 65). Further, in the light of the African Children's Charter's prohibition on harmful cultural practices prejudicial to the health of children (article 24(3)), it must be argued that clear legal measures to proscribe such practices, and to provide sanctions for their violation, is an essential tool in the effort to eradicate them, again bringing culture and the role of law in responding to it into possible opposition. But although the law is but one tool in the elimination of harmful practices rooted in culture, along with civic education, it remains an indispensable part of entrenching a children's rights approach in the legal system of countries in Africa.

---

1   See further Chapter 7 in this volume concerning child participation.

Other Factors Impelling Legal Reform in Africa

In 1997, in a review of child law reform in African context, it was noted that pre-child law reform Africa was often characterized by a plethora of different legislative enactments affecting children (66 in Kenya identified during the drafting of the Children's Act, 2001), and that these were often of colonial origin (Sloth-Nielsen and Van Heerden 1997) and very dated, seldom being still relevant even in their place of origin. Modernizing such legislation, catering to the new globalized world of migration and technological advances, and consolidating applicable provisions in one central and more accessible source were therefore powerful additional motivating factors.

To the above can be added the need to formalize in legal terms the changing nature of family forms that has been a consequence of the transformation from a rural, communitarian, agrarian and subsistence society to a vastly more urbanized, diverse population moving steadfastly towards a cash-based economy. At the same time, law reforms were predicated upon the need to strengthen and reinforce the family as the primary social unit in which children are raised (Sloth-Nielsen and Van Heerden 1997, 269), albeit that it is not necessarily a narrow nuclear concept of the family that had to prevail. The impetus towards the legal reformulation of the 'family' in African countries, including the place of children in it and the identification of the bearers of parental responsibilities towards them has, in addition, been bolstered by growing support for democratization of women's roles in the family, for equal rights for women, and a diminishing concern for the status of illegitimacy. Towards the end of the millennium, the realization of the impact of HIV/Aids on the structure and shape of the family, especially in sub-Saharan Africa, further motivated changing legal norms.[2]

In this regard, the role of law in Africa's economic resurgence should also be noted, although its relevance to children's rights is not necessarily obviously apparent. With regard to gender equality, however, the need to foster women's economic development through access to property, land and other economic resources has underpinned a number of family law reform processes which have occurred, and which have affected the status of children as well: examples in point are family law reforms in Lesotho, Namibia, South Africa and Mozambique. In some instances, child law reform and economic development initiatives have run in tandem, the one supporting the other, particularly given the need for socio-economic support to vulnerable and orphaned children that has become particularly prominent since the late 1990s. From that period, the international community has begun to support programmes giving effect to children's right of access to social security as a preventive strategy to provide a minimum floor of protection against poverty, often also as a frontline response to HIV/Aids. There have been positive evaluations of the spin-off effects of cash transfers or small grants in relieving the worst effects of poverty, and, especially where economic growth has been positive, African governments have been encouraged to support schemes that were initially

---

2   See Chapter 15 in this volume for an account of some of the legal changes in the children's rights sphere brought about in the era of HIV/Aids.

donor funded.[3] Some of these schemes have found expression in legal provisions, notably in South Africa, where children's entitlement to a basic social grant, the child support grant payable to the primary care-giver of a child aged below 15 years, is founded in the Social Assistance Act of 2004.[4]

In sum, it is argued that law, development and transformative agendas are inextricably linked, and are of special relevance in the African context, given the historic under-development characterizing the continent and the particular challenges faced by her children. Of course, implementation on the requisite scale remains an ongoing project in many countries; but even in this regard, some good practices relating to child participation (see Chapter 7) and to costing and implementation planning have emerged in which African experiences can serve as a benchmark for other regions of the world (Innocenti Centre 2008).

Children's Rights in African Constitutions

Children's rights are commonly referred to in African constitutions. It has previously been pointed out that modern bills of rights on the continent frequently single out children for special mention, over and above according children the rights that they may otherwise enjoy as citizens, and that at least 34 constitutions[5] can be identified in which children's rights feature (Sloth-Nielsen 2007a). Furthermore, several are of recent origin, such as the 2005 constitution of Burundi, the 2006 constitution of the Democratic Republic of Congo, and the Constitution of Sudan. It has been noted, though, that constitutional provisions tend to refer to children in a variety of different ways, using 'minors', 'young persons', 'youth' and 'infants', some even employing more than one term in the same text (for example, the constitution of Benin, referring to the education of children and the education of youths in articles 12 and 13). These are clearly rather indefinite concepts, and preference must be shown for constitutional provisions that clearly delineate 18 as the cut-off age for childhood (as the South African constitution in section 28(1) does), and which specify their applicability to children (as opposed to some other imprecise term). In addition, some constitutional protections are expressly limited to categories of children aged younger than 18 years, for instance those pertaining to child labour (Namibian constitution, section 15(2), which limits protection to children aged below 16 years; see too, the limitation of the children's rights protection to those under 16 in the constitution of Malawi, discussed in Sloth-Nielsen 2007a, 87). This distinction also arises in the context of

---

3   See Nyamweya et al. 2006; Kakwani et al. 2005; Kakwani et al. 2006; Schubert and Slater 2006; Sridhar and Duffield 2006.

4   The age at which the grant is payable has been gradually extended over the decade since its introduction from seven years to this age.

5   Algeria, Republic of Angola, Republic of Benin, Burkina Faso, Republic of Burundi, Republic of Cameroon, Republic of Cape Verde, Central African Republic, Republic of Chad, Comoros, Republic of Cote D'Ivoire, Democratic Republic of the Congo, The Arab Republic of Egypt, Equatorial Guinea, Federal Democratic Republic of Ethiopia, Gabon, The Gambia, Ghana, Guinea, Lesotho, Republic of Madagascar, Malawi, Mozambique, Namibia, Niger, Sao Tome et Principe, Senegal, South Africa, Sudan, Togo, Uganda and Zambia.

juvenile detention: the age at which children should be kept separately from adults is set at 16 years (rather than 18) in the 2005 transitional constitution of Burundi, for instance. With these caveats in mind, some constitutional elements pertinent to children's rights derived from African constitutions are discussed next.

Civil and Political Rights

Echoing the central pillar of the CRC and the African Children's Charter, non-discrimination clauses specifically protecting children are found in several constitutions, notably that of Burkina Faso, and that of Lesotho (Heyns 2004). The former provides, for instance, that 'children are equal in rights and duties within their familial relations' (article 23), whilst the latter provides for the 'protection and assistance [of] all children and young persons without any discrimination for reasons of their parentage or other conditions. Article 56(4) of the constitution of Mozambique similarly enshrines the principle that 'children may not be discriminated against on the ground of their birth ...'. It has been pointed out that African constitutions have adopted gender neutral language (Sloth-Nielsen 2007a, 91) and that girl children benefit from constitutional clauses which proscribe discrimination on the basis of gender.

Nor can equality be singled out amongst children's civil and political rights in African constitutional context. South Africa's constitution expressly recognizes the child's right to a name and a nationality from birth (section 28(1)(a)), and the constitution of the Federal Republic of Ethiopia contains an equivalent provision (article 36(1)(b)), as does the recent constitution of the Democratic Republic of Congo. The child's right to know and be cared for by parents or legal guardians regularly appears (constitution of South Africa, Ethiopia, Namibia, Uganda). The Seychellois constitution enacts the principle of article 9 of the CRC and article XIX of the African Charter on the Rights and Welfare of the Child (ACRWC) that, save in exceptional and judicially recognized circumstances, children (of young age) should not be separated from their parents. The right to life also finds expression from time to time. An unusual provision is found in the constitution of Cameroon relating to the child's right to adoption only in accordance with the law, and there are a number of constitutional provisions enshrining the principle that children may not be detained except as a matter of last resort and when this occurs, such detention must be for the shortest appropriate period of time (article 37(b) of the CRC): viz. the constitutions of The Gambia, South Africa, Uganda and Ethiopia. In South Africa, this constitutional provision has significantly shaped judicial sentencing policy, for instance in a landmark case concerning the application of legislation containing prescribed sentences to persons aged below 18 at the time of the commission of the offence (*Brandt* v *S*, 2006 (1) SACR 311 (SCA)), which legislation was held to contravene the principle that the determination of sentence length should be only for the shortest appropriate period of time.

Socio-economic and Cultural Rights[6]

Education rights of children are mentioned very frequently in African constitutions, which often afford an elaborate guarantee in this regard. Provisions which constitutionally entrench free or basic education, as is required by article 28 of the CRC and article 11(3)(a) of the ACRWC, can be found in a number of constitutions, illustrating the highest domestic level of protection of this right. According to a report by Action Aid (2007), '[f]irst, education is an entitlement that is sanctioned by states, through legislation and national constitutions – twenty-seven sub-Saharan African countries have a constitutional guarantee of free basic education for all children, ... and therefore education is a justiciable right.' For instance, article 20 of Namibia's constitution provides that all people should have access to education and basic education shall be free and compulsory. The constitution of 2005 of Southern Sudan provides that 'education is a right for every citizen' (article 44(1)) and that '[p]rimary education is compulsory and the State shall provide it free' (article 44(2)). In Uganda, the wording is to the effect that 'a child is entitled to basic education which shall be the responsibility of the state'.

The constitution of Nigeria, which places economic and social rights in directives of state policy in Chapter 11, places the duty on government to 'strive to eradicate illiteracy and to this end, government shall as and when practicable provide ... free, compulsory and universal primary education' (article 18(3)).[7] The constitution of Mali states that 'public education shall be obligatory, free and secular' (article 18). And the constitution of Ghana provides that 'all persons shall have the right to equal education opportunities and facilities and with a view to achieving the full realization of that right ... basic education shall be free, compulsory and available to all.' It is worth pointing out that the constitutional provisions concerning education frequently apply to all citizens and not only to children, and are therefore provided for separately from children's rights provisions. The mentioned example from Ghana is a case in point, as is South Africa's constitutional provision in section 29, applicable to 'everyone'.

As a general proposition, socio-economic rights for children are not commonly provided for in African constitutions outside of directive principles of state policy (Sloth-Nielsen 2007a, 92), although there are exceptions.[8] The socio-economic rights accorded children in the South African constitution stand out, not only in respect of their reach – section 28(1)(c) gives every child the right to basic nutrition, shelter, basic health care services and social services – but because these and other socio-economic rights provided for in this constitution are justiciable in courts of law.

---

6   See Chapter 6 in this volume for a more detailed discussion of the role of socio-economic rights in combating child poverty.

7   The placement of socio-economic rights as a principle of state policies does diminish their status as directly enforceable constitutional rights, a point also made by Chirwa.

8   Such as the constitution of Angola, which, in article 31, requires the state in collaboration with the family and society, 'to promote the harmonious development of the personality of young people and create conditions for the fulfilment of the economic social and cultural rights of youth ...'.

They may be used to resist government interference, to strike down programmes not fully compatible with the requisite constitutional standard, or as development tools to compel action where appropriate programmes have not been put in place. A vast domestic and international literature concerning the jurisprudence of South Africa's Constitutional Court (in particular) surrounding socio-economic rights and their enforcement has been authored (see, for instance, Liebenberg 2005; Mbazira 2007; Davis 2006; Brand and Russell 2002; Bilchitz 2003), and children's social economic rights have additionally earned sustained attention in academia and in advocacy quarters (for example, Mbazira and Sloth-Nielsen 2007; Creamer 2004). The promise of a minimum, if basic, floor of entitlements for children which appeared to arise from the evident absence of any qualification (such as that the rights be implemented progressively or within available resources) was initially regarded as a constitutionally sanctioned 'first call' for children in the allocation of resources in South Africa.

But the jurisprudence of the Constitutional Court in elaborating the nature of the state obligation *vis-à-vis* the rights contained in section 28(1)(c) has tempered these expectations to an extent, notably in *Government of the Republic of South Africa and others* v *Grootboom and others* (2000 (11) BCLR 1169 (CC)). In this landmark case involving housing rights and children's rights to shelter, the Constitutional Court (CC) declined to interpret the child's constitutional socio-economic rights to encompass a directly enforceable claim for destitute children, unless such children were orphaned, abandoned or otherwise lacked a family environment. This seemingly stark position was somewhat ameliorated in *Minister of Health and Others* v *Treatment Action Campaign and Others* (2002 (10) BCLR 1033 (CC) (*TAC*)).[9]

Here an attempt was made to force the government to expand and roll out the provision of anti-retrovirals to HIV-positive pregnant mothers giving birth in state clinics to prevent mother-to-child transmission of the disease. The rights concerned were everyone's right to have access to health care (section 27 of the Constitution), and children's rights to basic health care (section 28 (1)(c)). The existing programme was challenged as unreasonable because of its restriction to selected hospitals serving as pilot sites, thereby excluding an HIV/Aids positive mother (and her child) who did not have access to these designated hospitals. The CC, expanding the ruling in the *Grootboom* case, held that the primary obligation to provide children with basic health care no doubt rests on those parents who can afford to pay for the services (para. 77). However, the State bears the primary responsibility as regards basic health care for children when '[…] the implementation of parental or family care is lacking' (para. 79). The Court also reasoned that: '[…] in evaluating government's policy, regard must be had to the fact that this case is concerned with new born babies whose lives might be saved by the administration of Nevirapine' (para. 72). Children's '[…] needs are "most urgent" and their inability to have access to Nevirapine profoundly affects their ability to enjoy all rights to which they are entitled' (para. 78). Limiting the provisions of anti-retrovirals to certain test sites would imperil mothers giving birth to vulnerable children in the public health system, and infringe their children's rights to survival and development. The *TAC* case appears to have, to a limited

---

9   See for a similar discussion, Chapter 6 of this volume.

extent, restored the confidence of children's rights advocates that the constitution is capable of protecting children as a vulnerable group, even though the court did not conclude that children had a core right to claim basic services on demand.

The constitutional promise and transformative potential of children's socio-economic rights can further be gleaned from the recent case of *Centre for Child Law and Others* v *MEC for Education and Others*.[10] The case revolved around the nature of the state obligation towards children placed by a court in alternative care. The hostels in which the children were housed were in a state of deterioration, most dormitories had no windows, the floors were in poor condition and there were neither cubicles to provide privacy in the showers, nor doors to the toilets. The lack of ceiling boards and window glass meant that the children were exposed to freezing weather conditions in their sleeping quarters. There was no heating and the children's beds consisted of old dirty foam mattresses, with one (sometimes two) thin grey blankets similar to those used in prisons. The children were cold and miserable, and sought fulfilment of their (socio-economic) rights to an adequate standard of care. The court recorded:

> [W]hat is notable about the children's rights in comparison to other socio-economic rights is that section 28 contains no internal limitation subjecting them to the availability of resources and legislative measures for their progressive realisation. Like all rights, they remain subject to reasonable and proportional limitation, but the absence of any internal limitation entrenches the rights as unqualified and immediate.[11]

The court consequently gave an order compelling the authorities to provide each child with a sleeping bag, and to put in place proper access control and psychological support. The court further noted that 'the minimal costs or budgetary allocation problems in this instance are far outweighed by the urgent need to advance the children's interests in accordance with our constitutional values' (at pp. 7–8).

Providing for justiciable socio-economic rights at a constitutional level, as in South Africa, has been hailed internationally, and singling out children as beneficiaries can be highlighted for the potential it has to ensure that resource allocation for the fulfilment of children's rights is prioritized (see, further, Sloth-Nielsen et al. 2007), as well as for the fashioning of creative remedies, such as that evident in the *Centre for Child Law* case discussed above.

---

10 Case No. 19559/06 (30 June 2006).

11 Page 7, lines 13–20 of the judgment. Acknowledging the budgetary implications of the decision, the Court noted that 'our Constitution recognizes, particularly in relation to children's rights and the right to a fair trial, that budgetary implications ought not to compromise the justiciability of the rights. Each case must be looked at on its own merits, with proper consideration of the circumstances and the potential for negative or irreconcilable resource allocations. The minimal costs or budgetary allocation problems in this instance are far outweighed by the urgent need to advance the children's interests in accordance with our constitutional values' (pp. 7–8).

Protection

The language of protection is commonplace in constitutional clauses dedicated to children in African context. In the Ugandan constitution, at least three clauses to this effect can be highlighted: the entitlement of children to protection from social and economic exploitation (clause 34(4)), protection via the requirement that children in detention be kept separately from adults (clauses 34(6)), and the unique requirement mandating the law to accord 'special protection to orphans and other vulnerable children' (clause 34(7)). Extensive further examples of protective constitutional provisions can be cited, including both general provisions (for example, according protection against abuse, maltreatment and neglect) and specific provisions targeting areas in respect of which children are especially vulnerable, notably in the arena of child labour and armed conflict. A sample includes:

- 'Every child has the right to individual measures to ensure or improve the care that is necessary to his or her well being, health and physical safety and to be protected against abuse, acts of violence or exploitation' (transitional constitution of Burundi).
- 'All children shall have the right to special protection in the case of illness, becoming orphans, abandoned and deprived of family environment' (constitution of Cape Verde, as amended).
- 'No young person shall be the subject of traffic in any form' (constitution of Zambia).
- 'Children shall be given absolute priority and shall therefore enjoy special protection from the family, the state and society with a view to their all round development' (constitution of Algeria).

The constitution of the Democratic Republic of Congo requires public authorities to ensure the protection of children in difficult circumstances and to bring to justice the authors and accomplices of acts of violence against children. It specifically identifies the need for the special protection of the state for girl children, orphans, children either of whose parents are in prison, children with disabilities, and refugee and homeless children (clause 41). Particularly noteworthy in the recent constitution of Southern Sudan (2005) is a provision assuring to children protection from all acts of violence both inside and outside their home, thereby constituting the first prohibition on corporal punishment in Africa.

The Best Interest Standard

The constitutions of South Africa and Ethiopia enshrine this cardinal principle, which as a result of the justiciability of constitutional rights in South African context, has led to an elaborate array of instances in which the principle has influenced or advanced judicial decision-making. The child's best interests have, moreover, been held to apply to matters beyond the rights enumerated in the children's rights clause itself, and a recent example of this is to be found in the Constitutional Court's judgment in *S* v *M* (CCT 53/06), an appeal against a custodial sentence by a single parent (mother) of three young children. At stake was the relevance of their best interests in the sentencing process, and future care, were their mother to be imprisoned. Writing for the majority and expounding on the significance of the best interests standard, Judge Sachs said,

> The four great principles of the CRC which have become international currency, and as such guide all policy in South Africa in relation to children, are said to be survival, development, protection and participation. What unites these principles, and lies at the heart of section 28, I believe, is the right of a child to be a child and enjoy special care ... Every child has his or her own dignity. If a child is to be constitutionally imagined as an individual with a distinctive personality, and not merely as a miniature adult waiting to reach full size, he or she cannot be treated as a mere extension of his or her parents, umbilically destined to sink or swim with them. The unusually comprehensive and emancipatory character of section 28 presupposes that in our new dispensation the sins and traumas of fathers and mothers should not be visited on their children (paras 18 and 19) ... It follows that section 28 requires the law to make best efforts to avoid, where possible, any breakdown of family life or parental care that may threaten to put children at increased risk. Similarly, in situations where rupture of the family becomes inevitable, the State is obliged to minimise the consequent negative effect on children as far as it can. (Para. 20)

Conceding that there was no formula to indicate how the difficult act of balancing the interests of the children with the requirements of sentencing policy be determined, the court was nevertheless of the view that the constitutional principle of the child's best interests required that a sentencing officer must establish whether there will be an impact on a child in the decision to be made; must consider independently the child's best interests; must attach appropriate weight to those interests; and ensure that the child will be taken care of if the primary caregiver is sent to prison.

Given the potential of the best interests principle to meaningfully advance children's rights, its wider incorporation in Africa constitutions is worth motivating for.

The Duties of Children and Parents

As may be expected, given the African human rights conception of duties for her citizens (discussed more fully in Sloth-Nielsen and Mezmur 2008; see too, Gose 2002, Mutua 1995; Udombana 2004), African constitutions do not eschew mention of duties on the part of both parents and children. As an example of the former, the constitution of Togo provides that 'parents shall have the duty to train and to educate their children ...' (article 31), which continues to note that 'the State shall support them in this task'. A prime instance of constitutional duties placed upon children (and parents) is to be found in the constitution of Eritrea, specified as follows:

> Parents have the right and duty to bring up their children with due care and affection; and, in turn, children shall have the right and the duty to respect their parents and to sustain them in their old age. (Article 22)

The constitution of Guinea provides that 'children owe care and assistance to their parents' (article 16), whilst that of Cape Verde refers to children's duty to obey their parents and to respect their authority. These provisions reflect the spirit and purport of the related provision of the African Children's Charter, which provides extensively for duties of children towards their families, communities and societies in article 31. And, as has been suggested, far from duties creating an environment for a gratuitous invasion of rights, duties should be understood as reinforcing rights (Sloth-Nielsen and Mezmur 2008; Pityana 1999). Furthermore, the preambular paragraph, before the specifics of the duties provided for further in article 31 are enumerated, contains within it two internal limitations. Firstly, the duties of the child are subject to his or her age and ability; and secondly, the child's duties are subject to 'such limitations as may be contained in the present Charter', recalling all other rights and protections afforded children in the ACRWC. It cannot justifiably be argued, therefore, that the language of duties paves the way to rights violations.

Intudi (2007) points out that in pre-colonial African societies children were prized as an asset to the family, and that the positive consequence inherent in providing for children's duties towards their families is that the child is not merely an object upon whom protection and welfare is bestowed, but an actor, a subject, upon whom the responsibility to promote the overall well-being of the family unit is placed. These sentiments are reinforced by constitutional recognition of children's and parents' duties.

Promoting Constitutionalism in Children's Rights Context

Modern constitutions not only spell out commitments of democratic governments, embody ideals and values underpinning a society, and chart the limits of the exercise of state power *vis-à-vis* citizens, they also lay the foundation, in a number of ways, for further implementation of children's rights at the national level. First, the South African experience of justiciability of the rights provided for in the Bill of Rights – which includes an elaborate clause providing for children's rights – has had measurable impact in child rights constitutional litigation, commencing with the judicial abolition of the sanction of juvenile whipping as early as 1995 by the Constitutional Court in *S* v *Williams* (1995). Second, constitutional provisions can form the backdrop to the activities and focus of national Human Rights institutions, insofar as the constitution is the supreme law to which all organs of state must be held accountable. Third, the really innovative developments – which to a great extent lie in the future – revolve around designing suitable and progressive remedies for violations of children's constitutional rights, a development hinted at in relation to socio-economic rights jurisprudence earlier in this chapter. Creative mechanisms must be sought to ensure that children can gain as a class of beneficiaries, and it is contended that this can best be furthered by the inclusion of justiciable children's rights in national constitutions.

Domestication of International Children's Rights Principles in National Legal Systems

There has recently been a sustained examination of the role of child law reform in domesticating the principles of the CRC and the ACRWC: two notable international publications in this regard are the 2008 (forthcoming) Innocenti report, *Law Reform and Implementation of the Convention on the Rights of the Child* and the report *In the Best Interests of the Child: Harmonising Laws in Eastern and Southern Africa* (African Child Policy Forum 2007a). Whilst Africa is not the exclusive focus of the former, which examines experiences from some 60 countries of which six are in sub-Saharan Africa and a further few reside under the category devoted to Islamic legal systems (Egypt, Morocco, Tunisia, Libya and Sudan), the latter profiles efforts in 17 countries of southern and eastern Africa. Indicative of the impact of the CRC at the national level, the raft of legislative changes that has occurred, or is in the process of occurring, has been previously described as a 'continent wide revolution' (Sloth-Nielsen 2007a, 98). Alluding to the Ugandan Children Act of 1996, followed by legislative reform in Ghana, Kenya, Rwanda, Nigeria, South Africa, Namibia, and with pending bills in Mozambique, Malawi and Lesotho, to cite a few examples, it is clear that children's interests have moved to the mainstream in Africa's renaissance. The Innocenti Report notes, for instance, that providing for children's rights to be heard, as a new concept, is now featuring in African children's legislation (referring to the Child Rights Act of Nigeria, 2003, the Child Rights and Protection Legislation of Rwanda, 2001, to which can be added a host of provisions of South Africa's Children's Act 38 of 2005 providing for the child's right to participate in proceedings, to express views and have these taken into account and given due weight, and to approach courts independently).

A further area of considerable change relates to reforms concerning the parent/child relationship, with new standards for parental responsibilities of mothers and fathers in conformity with the gradual move towards recognizing equal rights for women in society, and also in accordance with the child's right not to be discriminated against (for example, on the grounds of birth or his or her parents' marital status). The Child Rights Act of Nigeria proceeds from a premise of joint custody, whilst the 2006 Namibian Children's Status Act (not yet in operation) provides that 'both parents of a child born outside of marriage have equal rights to become the custodian of the child' (section 11(1)).

This section focuses on three key themes which appear to characterize the law reform processes that are underway: process and the development of institutional mechanisms for implementation, targeting, and the role of civil society.

Process and the Development of Institutional Mechanisms for Implementation

It is a matter of record that apparently lengthy periods have elapsed between the commencement of domestication initiatives and their conclusion (African Child Policy Forum 2007a). In the case of South Africa, for example, the establishment of a project committee to investigate proposals for a new juvenile justice system took place in 1996, and while the initial draft of the Child Justice Bill was tabled in 2002, the legislation was not yet passed by parliament at the time of writing. The Children's

Act 38 of 2005 was born of a similar review process commenced in 1997, and the composite legislation envisaged by the South African Law Reform Commission had not reached its final stages by end of 2007 either (the split process necessitated by the constitutional procedures attendant upon bills affecting national competencies and those of concerning provincial competencies is described more fully in Chapter 16 of this volume and partly explains the drawn out nature of the law-making required). The Nigerian Child's Rights Act was first passed at Federal level in 2003, but thereafter had to be introduced and passed by all state legislatures as well. The Lesotho draft Child Care and Protection Bill (2004), which was first mooted around the turn of the millennium, has also taken longer than expected to be considered by the Attorney General's office and to enter the parliamentary process (Kimane 2006). Malawi's Law Reform Commission completed a similar bill in 2005, which has also not yet formally been considered. The drawn out process which lead to the Kenyan Children's Act of 2001 has been described elsewhere (Odongo 2005), and in some instances, whilst the principal legislative framework has been completed, the absence of regulations impede implementation (for example, Ghana's juvenile justice legislation of 2003: personal communication with the Attorney General's office).

However, lest it be thought that this is an entirely adverse scenario, developments at the practical level may suggest the contrary, as the intervening period between inception and culmination of the law reform process has been used to lay solid foundations for eventual implementation. Two main arenas of activity can be recorded in this regard: first, the establishment of national fora to oversee the process of embedding reforms at a practical level; and second, human and infrastructural development to support the planned new laws.

In the sphere of juvenile justice in Malawi, for instance, a national juvenile justice forum (chaired by a judge) is now well established, with specialized services – child friendly courts and access to diversion – unfolding in a phased manner throughout the country (Twea 2007, 2008). Similar developments have come to fruition in Zambia, commencing with a child friendly court project in the capital city, Lusaka, in 2003 (Sloth-Nielsen and Gallinetti 2004), and now culminating in the development of legislation under the auspices of the Zambian Law Development Commission. The Swazi experience has lead to the formation of a children's co-ordinating unit at national level, to take ownership of the law reform process and involving a number of Ministries and other relevant arms of government (such as the Attorney General's office) (Rodgers 2008). It can be concluded that the mere existence of law reform processes themselves may have the added spin-off of furthering intersectoral capacity via the parallel emergence of focused co-ordinating teams at the national level, with great potential to deliver a range of children's rights-oriented improvements (including data collection and monitoring).

As regards the second issue, namely human resource and infrastructural development whilst the law is in the making, the obvious example pertains to South Africa's juvenile justice reforms; this unfolding story of the progress made over the decade since law reform was first conceptualized has been extensively documented (Skelton 2005; Odongo 2005; Innocenti Centre 2008; Sloth-Nielsen 2007b; Gallinetti, Kassan and Ehlers 2006). The decade since the establishment of a separate juvenile justice system was first mooted has seen the expansion of probation services and the development nationally of diversion services, offered by an increasing variety of service providers and in an ever-growing range of programmes, as well as the building of specialized one stop child justice centres at which all services related to children in conflict with the law are located. Secure care facilities as alternatives to incarceration in prisons have been commissioned to the extent that more children are now detained in these facilities than are accommodated in prisons while awaiting trial, and still more such facilities are in planning. Training and awareness-raising has been extensive, especially as far as the judiciary is concerned, easing the path of embedding new ideas about alternative methods of dealing with child offenders. The law-making process has thus offered an opportunity to try out and test new ideas, to adapt foreign models to local contexts and to begin the time consuming task of getting the right people for the (eventual) job in place.

Targeting

It is evident that many African law reform processes have endeavoured to deal with the specifics of child rights violations within their respective societies. The law reform process in Mozambique, for example, commenced with the identification of five categories of children regarded as being especially vulnerable (children involved in commercial sexual exploitation, children in prison, orphaned and vulnerable children in the context of HIV/Aids, children involved in child labour and child victims of trafficking), in respect of whom legal reform efforts were to be targeted. In the case of Lesotho, children with disabilities and children in institutions were additional thematic areas regarded as being worthy of particular concern (African Child Policy Forum 2007b). Concern for the rights of disabled children is especially evident in South Africa's Children's Act 38 of 2005 and the Children's Act Amendment Bill 19F of 2006, and it is in no small measure due to the influence of disabled parliamentarians themselves that the final version of the legislation reflects a welcome bias towards inclusive provisions. The ongoing ratification of the African Women's Protocol is going to require dedicated legislation in all countries to outlaw female genital mutilation (FGM) and similar practices, as some countries – for instance Togo – have already done. Anti-trafficking legislation is under development or has been passed in a number of jurisdictions (at a sub-regional level, involving the Southern Africa Network against Trafficking and Abuse of Children, a consortium which includes Malawi, Zimbabwe, Zambia, Mozambique and South Africa; see too, Benin, Burkina Faso and Cameroon, and Chapter 14 of this volume). Sexual offences against children are receiving legislative attention in any number of jurisdictions, again indicative of an approach that hones in on protection of categories of child victims identified as warranting enhanced legal protection.

The Kenya Children's Act, adopted in 2001, is already being reviewed for enhancement: diversion provisions are to be added, along with more comprehensive provisions relating to children in alternative care (ANPPCAN 2007, 26). Elsewhere in this volume, the dedicated legal attention being paid to child victims of the worst forms of child labour is detailed,[12] as are South African legal provisions enumerating the role

---

12 See Chapter 18 of this volume.

of child headed households in society (see Chapter 16). Dedicated juvenile justice legislation has been enacted in a number of countries (Tunisia, Gambia, Ghana), and its formulation underway in a number of others. It can be discerned, thus, that African law makers are to an ever increasing extent focusing their efforts on the specificities of vulnerable groups of children in African societies, and tailoring their legislative endeavours to flesh out the required state responses, actions and measures.

The Role of Civil Society

Child participation in law reform processes in Africa is described elsewhere in this volume.[13] However, less attention has been paid in the extant literature to the various roles that civil society groups and movements have played in children's law reform, and here a few examples may be worthy of mention. In Nigeria, the civil society organization ANPPCAN (African Network for the Prevention and Protection against Child Abuse and Neglect) was at the forefront of efforts to develop a comprehensive Child's Right's Act (personal Communication, Prof. P. Ebigbo, ANPPCAN Nigeria). Lesotho's development of legislation was accompanied by an extensive civic education process (African Child Policy Forum 2007b), which included radio programmes, law publications and consultations with tribal chieftains who will ultimately be custodians of some of the conflict resolution processes provided for in the envisaged law. Indeed the inclusive process in Lesotho has been identified as a best practice model, and it may need repeating that the chairperson of the law reform process was herself drawn from civil society (and was not a lawyer!). In South Africa, the 'Children's Bill Working Group' is a network of civil society organizations (in fact, a network of networks)[14] who supported the legislative passage of the Children's Act in critical ways, including through information sharing, advocacy, briefings and research (Children's Institute 2007). In Namibia, the Legal Assistance Centre has played an important role in guiding law reform processes. In Swaziland, the fact that the impetus for the ongoing child law reform process came from a civil society organization has been regarded as significant (Gallinetti 2006).

In Kenya, civil society participation has been accorded formal recognition through the involvement of civil society membership of the National Council for Children's Services, an umbrella body falling in the Office of the Vice President and co-ordinating the implementation (amongst other things) of the 2001 Children's Act (ANPPCAN 2007, 26). In Egypt, too, national strategies concerning implementation of children's rights are driven by a committee with membership drawn from government and civil society (IBCR 2007, 66). Civil society involvement in domestication of children's rights may not be unique to the African continent; but it can be concluded that these partnerships with governments that have come to the fore significantly strengthen the (relatively lower) capacity of these governments to steer implementation and drive ongoing development in the children's rights domain.

---

13 See Chapter 7 of this volume.

14 Further details of the activities of the working group can be accessed at http://www.ci.org.za.

Conclusions

This chapter has attempted to provide, in overview, a sense of the achievements that have taken place since efforts started in earnest to incorporate children's rights in African legal systems. Undoubtedly, this journey is an uneven one, and challenges to law making and implementation remain acute. For instance, conservative and culturally hogtied parliaments can derail progressive rights based proposals (South Africa's enactment of legal provisions sanctioning the potentially harmful cultural practice of virginity testing providing one such example [section 12 of the Children's Act 38 of 2005]). Lack of fiscal resources often see progressive reforms being implemented only in large urban areas, and examples of advances being made on any scale are not yet easy to find. Yet, as has been asserted before (Sloth-Nielsen 2007a), law reform remains a key policy planning instrument which can set in motion a host of associated developmental processes to the benefit of children. And examples of the joint efforts of governments and civil society partners reflects the democratization of child rights mainstreaming, which will serve to embed the law reform processes much more effectively over time. At the very least, it can be concluded that the development of dedicated children's law in the modern era serves to focus the public mind on children's role in African society, rendering children all the more visible as rights bearers and citizens.

References

Articles, Books and Chapters in Books

Alen, A. et al. (eds) (2007), *The UN Children's Rights Convention: Theory Meets Practice* (Antwerp and Oxford: Intersentia).

Bilchitz, D. (2003), 'Towards a Reasonable Approach to the Minimum Core: Laying the Foundations for Future Socio-economic Rights Jurisprudence', *South African Journal on Human Rights* 19:1.

Brand, D. and Russell, S. (eds) (2002), *Exploring the Core Content of Socio-economic Rights: South African and International Perspectives* (Pretoria: Protea Book House).

Children's Institute (2007), *Children's Rights in Focus* 6 (March).

Creamer, K. (2004), 'The Implication of Socio-economic Rights Jurisprudence for Government Planning and Budgeting: The Case of Children's Socio-economic Rights', *Law Democracy and Development* 8, 221.

Davis, D. (2006), 'Adjudicating the Socio-Economic Rights in the South African Constitution: Towards "Deference Lite"', *South African Journal on Human Rights* 22, 301.

Evans, M. and Murray, R. (eds) (2002), *The African Charter on Human and Peoples' Rights: The System in Practice 1986–2000* (Cambridge: Cambridge University Press).

Gallinetti, J., Kassan, D. and Ehlers, L. (2006), *Child Justice in South Africa: Children's Rights under Construction* (Cape Town: Open Society Foundation for South Africa and Child Justice Alliance).

Gose, M. (2002), *The African Charter on the Rights and Welfare of the Child* (Bellville: Community Law Centre, University of the Western Cape).

Heyns, C. (2004), *Human Rights Law in Africa* (Leiden: Brill Academic Publishers).

Hodgkin, R. and Newell, P. (2002), *Implementation Handbook for the Convention on the Rights of the Child* (Geneva: UNICEF).

International Bureau for Children's Rights (IBCR) (2007), *Making Children's Rights Work in North Africa: Country Profiles on Algeria, Egypt, Libya, Morocco and Tunisia* (Montreal: International Bureau for Children's Rights).

Intudi, R. (2007), 'The Application of the International Convention on the Rights of the Child in Africa: When the Law is Tested by Reality', in Alen, A. et al. (eds).

Kakwani, N., Soares, F. and Son, H. (2005), *Conditional Cash Transfers in African Countries* (Brasilia: International Poverty Centre).

Kakwani, N., Soares, F. and Son, H. (2006), 'Cash Transfers for School-Age Children in African Countries: Simulation of Impacts on Poverty and School Attendance', *Development Policy Review* 24:5.

Liebenberg, S. (2005), 'Socio-Economic Rights', in Woolman, S. et al. (eds) *Constitutional Law of South Africa*, 2nd edn (Cape Town: Juta and Co.).

Mbazira, C. and Sloth-Nielsen, J. (2007), 'Incy Wincy Spider Went Climbing up Again: Prospects for Constitutional (Re) Interpretation of Section 28(1)(c) of the South African Constitution in the Next Decade of Democracy', *Speculum Juris* 2, 147–67.

Mutua, M. (1995), 'The Banjul Charter and the African Cultural Fingerprint: An Evaluation of the Language of Duties', *Virginia Journal of International Law* 35, 339.

Pityana, B. (1999), 'The Renewal of African Moral Values', in Makgoba, M.W. (ed.) *The African Renaissance: The New Struggle* (Sandton: Mafuba/Cape Town: Tafelberg).

Pityana, B. (2002), 'The Challenge of Culture for Human Rights in Africa', in Evans, M. and Murray, R. (eds).

Schubert, B. and Slater, R. (2006), 'Social Cash Transfers in Low-Income African Countries: Conditional or Unconditional?', *Development Policy Review* 24:5, 571–8.

Sloth-Nielsen, J. (2007a), 'Strengthening the Promotion, Protection and Fulfillment of Children's Rights in the African Context', in Alen, A. et al. (eds).

Sloth-Nielsen, J. (2007b), 'A Short History of Time: Charting the Contribution of Social Development Service Delivery to Enhance Child Justice 1996–2006', *Social Work/Maatskaplike Werk* 43:4, 317.

Sloth-Nielsen, J. and Gallinetti, J. (eds) (2004), *Child Justice in Africa: A Guide to Good Practice* (Cape Town: University of the Western Cape).

Sloth-Nielsen, J. and Mezmur, B.D. (2008), '2 + 2 =5? Exploring the Domestication of the CRC in South African Jurisprudence 2002–2006', *International Journal on Children's Rights* 1, 1–28.

Sloth-Nielsen, J. and Mezmur, B.D. (2008), 'A Dutiful Child: The Implications of Article 31 of the African Children's Charter', *Journal of African Law* (forthcoming).

Sloth-Nielsen, J. and Van Heerden, B. (1997), 'New Child Care and Protection Legislation for South Africa: Lessons from Africa', *Stellenbosch Law Review* 8:3, 260.

Udombana, N.J. (2004), 'Between Promise and Performance: Revisiting States' Obligations under the African Human Rights Charter', *Stanford Journal of International Law* 40, 111.

Woolman, S. et al. (eds) (2005), *Constitutional Law of South Africa*, 2nd edn (Lansdowne: Juta and Co.).

Unpublished Documents, Reports and Internet Sources

Action Aid, 'Education in Africa: Responding to a Human Rights Violation' <http://www.actionaid.org.uk/doc_lib/135_1_education_in_africa.pdf> (accessed 23 October 2007).

African Child Policy Forum (2007a), *In the Best Interests of the Child: Harmonising Laws in Eastern and Southern Africa* (Addis Ababa: African Child Policy Forum).

African Child Policy Forum (2007b), *Realising Rights for Children: Good Practice in Eastern and Southern Africa* (Addis Ababa: African Child Policy Forum).

ANPPCAN (2007), *Report of the 1st African Conference on Child Sexual Abuse, Nairobi, 24–26th September 2007.*

CRC Committee (2003), 'General Comment no. 5: General Measure of Implementation of the Convention on the Right of the Child' (CRC/GC/2003/5).

Doek, J. (2007), 'Harmonisation of Laws on Children: Some Practical Guidance' (Addis Ababa: African Child Policy Forum).

Gallinetti, J. (2006), 'Country Report: Swaziland', unpublished paper prepared for the African Child Policy Form, 2006.

Innocenti Centre (2008 forthcoming), *Law Reform and Implementation of the Convention on the Rights of the Child*, <www.unicef-irc.org/publications> (accessed 12 January 2008).

Kimane, I. (2006), 'The Lesotho Child Protection and Welfare Bill 2005: Why the Delays in Enacting the Children's Law' (unpublished paper presented at the Miller du Toit/University of the Western Cape Child and Family Law Conference, Cape Town, January 2006).

Mbazira, C. (2007), 'Enforcing the Economic, Social and Cultural Rights in the South African Constitution' (unpublished LLD thesis, University of the Western Cape).

Nyamweya, P. et al. (2006), 'Evaluation of Sida Support to Unicef Country Programme, Kenya', <www.oecd.org/dataoecd/5/8/39125999.pdf>.

Odongo, G. (2005), 'The Domestication of International Standards on the Rights of the Child with Specific Reference to Juvenile Justice in the African Context' (unpublished LLD thesis, University of the Western Cape).

Rodgers, J. (2008), unpublished presentations on the work of the Malawi National Juvenile Justice Forum at the Miller Du Toit/University of the Western Cape Child and Family Law conference, Cape Town.

Skelton, A. (2005), 'The Influence of the Theory and Practice of Restorative Justice in South Africa with Special Reference to the Child Justice Bill' (unpublished LLD thesis, University of Pretoria).

Sloth-Nielsen, J. and Mezmur, B.D. (2007), 'A Dutiful Child: The Implications of Article 31 of the African Children's Charter', paper presented at the 10th ordinary meeting of the African Committee of Experts on the Rights and Welfare of the Child, Cairo, Egypt.

Sloth-Nielsen, J. et al. (2007), 'Available Resources: The African Context; An African Perspective' (unpublished paper prepared for the CRC Committee Day of General Discussion, September 2007, available at <www.crin.org>).

Sridhar, D. and Duffield, A. (2006), 'A Review of the Impact of Cash Transfer Programmes on Child Nutritional Status' (Save the Children UK, available at <www. savethechildren.org.uk> (accessed 21 November 2007)).

Twea, E., Judge (2007, 2008), unpublished presentations on the work of the Malawi National Juvenile Justice Forum at the Miller Du Toit/University of the Western Cape Child and Family Law conference, Cape Town.

Cases

Brandt v *S*, (2006) (1) SACR 311 (SCA).

Centre for Child Law and Others v *MEC for Education and Others* (Case No. 19559/06 (30 June 2006).

Government of the Republic of South Africa and Others v *Grootboom and Others* (2000) (11) BCLR 1169 (CC).

Minister of Health and Others v *Treatment Action Campaign and Others* (2002) (10) BCLR 1033 (CC).

Chapter 5

African Customary Law and Children's Rights: Intersections and Domains in a New Era

Chuma Himonga

Introduction

Along with received Western law, African customary law has been applied to large sections of Africa's population ever since the colonization of Africa, especially in the fields of family law, succession and land law. It has therefore occupied a central place in the regulation of children's lives for hundreds of years. It intersects mainly with norms of Western law, which were received in the territories by colonial states. The last few decades have, however, witnessed a change, precipitated largely by international and regional human rights norms, as well as the constitutional norms of some countries. Since the idea of children's rights took root in the Convention on the Rights of the Child (CRC), Africa, like most of the rest of the world, has embarked on a search for new ways of protecting the rights of children within its continental borders, including inaugurating its own child rights charter, the African Charter on the Rights and Welfare of the Child (ACRWC); increasingly enacting constitutions bearing rights of children in their Bills of Rights; and enacting consolidated national legislation aimed at the promotion and protection of children's rights, as discussed in Chapter 4 of this volume. With these developments, a new era, characterized by new intersections between customary law and human rights, has dawned on the African continent.

The new intersections may be mapped at three levels: the recognition of customary law by international and constitutional law; children's rights legislation; and internal conflicts of law. These levels of intersection also broadly represent the new domains or enclaves occupied by customary law in the children's rights framework in African legal systems. Within these broad intersections may be found yet smaller enclaves in which customary law continues to influence the rights of children.

This chapter examines the intersections and domains as they appear from the legal systems of countries that have enacted special legislation to protect the rights of children. It shows, firstly, that human rights norms are the axis for customary law's role in the protection of children's rights in the new era. In short, the recognition of customary law by human rights legal frameworks constitutes the broad level at which customary law intersects with children's rights. This intersection anticipates the incorporation of 'harmless' customary law norms into domestic laws for the promotion and protection of the rights of children. Secondly, the chapter shows the role allocated to customary law in the promotion and protection of children's rights through an analysis of its intersections with children's rights in domestic legislation specifically designed to promote and protect children's rights (hereafter called children's rights legislation). Finally, the chapter shows how customary law intersects with children's rights in the context of its application by the courts, against the backdrop of internal conflicts of law.

The Recognition of Customary Law Intersection

If any justification is required for the role allocated to customary law in the implementation of children's rights in Africa, it is the recognition of cultural rights (by which is meant rights associated with customary law) by international law, on the one hand, and by the constitutional law of an increasing number of African countries on the other.

A considerable body of literature on cultural rights and customary law as they relate to the human rights of children already exists (Lloyd 2002; Ncube 1998a; Grant 2006; Himonga 2002). It is therefore not necessary to rehearse its themes. It is only important, for our purposes, to underscore the point that the recognition of the role of customary law in the protection of children's rights is embedded in the human rights framework itself.

Thus the Universal Declaration of Human Rights (UDHR), which is recognized as customary international law, devotes two articles specifically to cultural rights. Article 22 states: 'Everyone, as a member of society … is entitled to the realization of the economic, social and cultural rights indispensable for his dignity and the free development of his personality.' Article 27 takes the right to culture a step further by awarding everyone the right to participate in 'the cultural life of the community …'.[1] The protection of the cultural rights of minorities is specifically ensured by article 27 of the International Covenant on Civil and Political Rights (ICCPR), which provides:

> In those states in which ethnic, religious or linguistic minorities exist, persons belonging to such minorities shall not be denied the right, in community with the other members of their group, to enjoy their own culture, to profess and practice their own religion, or to use their own language.

The CRC also countenances one of the core values of African culture, a person's ties to the extended family and community, when it places the rights of the child in the context of the community and the extended family.[2]

---

1   See also Article 15 of the International Covenant on Economic, Social and Cultural Rights (ICESCR).

2   Article 5 of the CRC. See also articles 14(2) and 18(1). See, furthermore, on the recognition of African customs and traditions that may impinge on the rights of the child, article 18 of the African Charter on Human and Peoples' Rights ACHPR.

The ACRWC, which not only reflects 'the spirit of traditional cultural values' (Lloyd 2002), but also stresses the African *cultural context*[3] for the implementation of children's rights on the continent, deserves special mention. The ACRWC shows remarkable tolerance for African cultural values and customary law. For example, it states in its preamble that 'the African approach to children's rights takes cognizance of the virtues of the African cultural heritage and the values of African civilization' which should inspire and characterize the content of the rights of the African child. Furthermore, the ACRWC is unique among children's human rights instruments in placing culture and tradition-loaded duties on the child, such as the duty of the child to 'preserve and strengthen African cultural values in his relationship with other members of the society ...' (ACRWC, article 31(d); Thompson 1992, 432). Thus it sends a very strong message that customary practices are not to be lightly dismissed with regard to the protection and interpretation of children's rights in the African context.

It has also been noted that the incorporation of cultural rights into African constitutions was largely influenced by international law (Grant 2006, 5). In the case of South Africa, for example,[4] the inclusion of cultural rights in the constitution was intended to implement the cultural rights under international law (Grant 2006, 5). Other African constitutions, enacted after the South African constitution, apparently followed the precedent of the latter in guaranteeing the right to culture in their respective Bills of Rights.[5] In addition, these constitutions recognize customary law, in varying degrees, in their provisions other than within the Bills of Rights.[6] Some constitutions furthermore explicitly recognize the co-existence of customary law rights with the Bill of Rights, provided that the former are consistent with the Bill of Rights,[7] or provide for the development of customary law by the courts,[8] thereby ensuring that customary law develops in accordance with the spirit of the constitution and its values.

With regard to the hierarchy of rights, Lloyd (2002, 17) argues that cultural rights (presumably including those guaranteed by constitutional law) are relatively weaker and subordinate to other human rights, so that 'whenever the right to preserve a culture conflicts with [the rights of the child – in this case the 'best interests of the child' principle] the latter prevails.'

---

3   See Preamble to the ACRWC.

4   See sections 30 and 31 of the Constitution of the Republic of South Africa of 1996, which state: 'Everyone has the right to use the language and to participate in the cultural life of their choice, but no one exercising these rights may do so in a manner inconsistent with any provision of the Bill of Rights' and 'Persons belonging to a cultural, religious or linguistic community may not be denied the right, with other members of that community – (a) to enjoy their culture, practise their religion and use their language; and (b) to form, join and maintain cultural, religious and linguistic associations and other organs of civil society.'

5   See Constitution of Uganda of 1995, s. 37, and the Constitution of Malawi, s. 26.

6   See, for example, the preamble to the Ugandan Constitution; s. 211(3) of the Constitution of South Africa.

7   See, for example, South African Constitution, s. 39(3).

8   See, for example, s. 39(2) of the South African Constitution.

Ncube (1998a, 14–15) provides, arguably, a more nuanced and balanced view of the relationship between cultural and children's rights when he observes that the various cultural rights provisions in international and regional human rights instruments 'merely recognize that the rights granted to children should in their localization and implementation bear the local cultural fingerprints without, however, extinguishing the essential core of the right itself'. In other words, 'the substantive rights granted are primary over cultural considerations which could negate the essence of the right. However, the substantive rights will often get their complexion from the local cultural environment within which they have to be given concrete, practical meaning.'

Thus, while it is conceded that customary practices that are inconsistent with the rights of the child have to give way, the human rights instruments and the ACRWC, in particular, give more than sufficient recognition to those customary practices that promote and protect the rights of the child. As Lloyd (2002, 23) points out, the ACRWC 'has regard to and respect for cultural practices … but prevents cultural practices which may be harmful or prejudicial to a child's health and bans other practices such as child marriages'.

To sum up, the inclusion and role of customary law in the legal framework for the protection of children's rights are founded on international and constitutional law human rights norms. Furthermore, these norms anticipate the incorporation of 'harmless' customary law norms into domestic laws for the promotion and protection of the rights of children. The African states that have so far enacted children's rights legislation seem to take this view, insofar as they have included certain aspects of customary law in the legislation concerned. Whether or not the level of inclusion of customary law in these statutes adequately reflects the stature accorded to customary law in international law and constitutional law, as the case may be, is beyond the scope of this chapter, but it certainly merits consideration in other contexts. Of interest at present are the various domains in which customary law intersects with children's rights in countries that have enacted children's rights statutes in the last decade. The following section identifies and evaluates this in respect of four countries.

Children's Rights Legislation Intersections

Amongst the countries that have enacted children's rights legislation are Uganda (Children's Act cap. 59 of the Laws of Uganda), Kenya (Children's Act 8 of 2001), Ghana (Children's Act 560 of 1998) and South Africa (Children's Act 38 of 2005).[9] A sample of the preambles to the acts reveals the human rights motivation (Odongo 2006) for the enactment of the acts: 'to give effect to certain rights of children as

---

9   There are also countries that have not yet consolidated their child laws but have nevertheless reformed their marriage and succession customary laws by legislation in ways that promote certain rights of children. Examples are Tanzania (the Law of Marriage Act 5 of 1971) and Zambia (the Intestate Succession Act cap 59 of the Laws of Zambia and the Affiliation and Maintenance of Children Act cap 64 of the Laws of Zambia). A draft children's statute is currently under discussion in Zambia, Malawi and Lesotho. See further Chapter 4 of this volume.

contained in the Constitution' (South Africa); 'to give effect to the principles of the Convention on the Rights of the Child and the African Charter on the Rights and Welfare of the Child' (Kenya); 'to provide for the rights of the child' (Ghana). For some countries, the rights contained in the statute represent to an extent a children's 'Bill of Rights' since their constitutions do not have a provision on children's rights. For instance, Kenya does not have a provision for children's rights in its constitution, but Part II of the Kenya Children's Act is entitled 'safeguards for the rights and welfare of the child'.

It should be noted, however, that these statutes have not completely abandoned the African cultural values. This approach not only echoes the cultural orientation of the ACRWC, already alluded to, but it apparently represents the UN General Assembly's outlook on the protection of human rights in different regions of the world. In this respect, Lloyd (2002, 14) notes that the 'UN General Assembly has affirmed the value of regional agreements to promote and protect human rights situations, whilst upholding cultures, traditions and histories unique to the region.' A glance at the children's rights legislation reveals that customary law plays a role, albeit restricted, in the promotion and protection of children's rights frameworks in areas involving the African extended family, damages for extra-marital pregnancy, the communal ethic, decision-making, 'harmful cultural practices' and dispute resolution. In the process, customary law intersects with various rights of the child. These domains will now be discussed, in turn, in relation to the rights of the child with which they intersect.

Extended Family Domain

The concept of the extended family intersects with a number of rights of the child protected by children's rights legislation, particularly the right to parental care,[10] the right to grow up with parents,[11] and the 'best interest or welfare' principle.[12] The South African Children's Act allocates a role to the extended family in the protection of these rights by including extended family members – grandparents, brothers, sisters, uncles, aunts and cousins – in its definition of a child's 'family member' for the purposes of the Act (section 1(1)). It is also noteworthy that the need for a child to remain in the care of his or her family or to maintain a connection with his or her family, including the extended family, are among the criteria to be considered whenever a provision of the Act requires the 'best interests of the child' standard to be applied.[13] Thus the customary concept and values of the extended family intersects with another important area of the right of the child – the 'best interests of the child' standard – that underpins all the other rights of the child.

---

10 See section 6 of the Kenyan Children's Act; section 8 of the South African Children's Act, which adopts the rights of the child enshrined in the Constitution, including the right to parental care and alternative parental care.

11 See section 5 of the Ghanaian Children's Act.

12 See section 2 of the Ghanaian Children's Act; section 8 of the South African Children's Act, which incorporates and elaborates the right in section 28(2) of the Constitution.

13 See section 7(1)(f) of the Act.

The Ghana Children's Act (section 111) also allocates a role to the extended family by providing that a relative (other than a parent or guardian) of a child who has been placed in a home may be ordered by a family tribunal to contribute towards the maintenance of the child in the home.

The extended family has not been precisely delineated for legal purposes. The definition by Rwezaura (1988, 169) probably conveys the idea of the extended family contemplated by children's rights legislation. It is 'a traditional African social unit consisting of people who are genealogically related, as well as those who are related to them through marriage … [and] whose social and economic welfare is closely associated'. In the traditional setting, the members of this social unit often live in close proximity to each other or in a homestead 'headed by a senior male relative who directed important economic, religious and political activities of the unit'. Status relations (for example, through marriage) and kinship relations were created, maintained and reinforced through the transfer of property and various forms of economic exchanges and services (Rwezaura 1988, 170). Furthermore, individual members of the family looked to the group to safeguard their welfare and interests when these were threatened by other members within the group or by outsiders.

Changing social and economic conditions have, unquestionably, transformed and weakened the extended family's role in safeguarding the social and economic welfare of its members. However, it would be wrong to argue that this social unit is completely of no relevance to the welfare of many an African person. Members of the extended family continue to support each other as much as their changed circumstances allow.[14] Rwezaura (1988, 183) correctly concludes, after a careful and critical analysis of the transformation of the extended family, that 'it is not possible to argue that the extended family has completely ceased to function as a source of economic support for some of its members.' The following statement speaks to the way the extended family functions in modern changed conditions. Because of its relevance today, it is quoted in the present tense (the specific context is different, but the general idea is typical of what still happens today):

---

14 In the recent South African case, *Fosi v Road Accident Fund and Fosi* (N.O.) (case no. 1934/2005 Cape of Good Hope Eastern Circuit Local Division), the customary law duty of members of the family to support each other was considered to be an African inborn consciousness of one's roots, of where one has come from in relation to the role played by other members of his or her family in his or her own life, as well as an actionable wrong. 'It is for this reason that the Plaintiff was puzzled on being asked in cross-examination, why did the deceased send her money. Her answer was rather telling, "because the deceased knew where he was coming from". The duty of a child to support a needy and deserving parent is well-known in indigenous/customary law. It is observed by such children. There is always an expectation on the part of a parent that his child will honour this duty. In African law it is most certainly an actionable wrong on the part of the child who is financially able, not to provide support to his needy and deserving parents. … The parent can successfully civilly proceed against such a child in traditional courts. It is also a morally reprehensible act to fail to maintain one's own parents who are in need of such maintenance. If the parents were to decide not to lodge a complaint before the tribal Court, but opt somehow to alert members of the immediate family about this predicament, such a child would be ostracised and be looked down upon as a person who has no *ubuntu*. The latter scenario is rather rare because as stated above every African child is born with this duty of consciousness never to forget his/her roots' (paras 16 and 17).

The response of most African societies to economic change is not characterized by inaction or passiveness. Individuals faced with these challenges try to combine the traditional system with the new system in order to minimize losses as well as to maximize gains. Fathers, for example, gain an income from their son's wages by invoking tradition, and from their sons-in-law by maintaining control over marriageable women. While women are escaping into the urban centers, elders try to utilize the state's authority to restrain them. Thus they do not abandon whatever advantages they can gain by invoking their status relation. Where the external system enables them to gain some economic advantages or to enforce certain rights under tradition, these are also used. For example, kinsmen claim the self-acquired properties of their deceased male relatives against their female children by relying on tradition. (Rwezaura 1988, 183)

The picture that emerges from this statement seems to leave women and children completely passive and helpless. But this is apparently not the case, for Rwezaura pictures them using similar kinds of strategies to manage their lives within the changed context of the extended family:

As far as women and children are concerned, they too never abandon certain traditional arrangements which are still capable of providing them with some economic support. Hence they escape into urban centers to look for jobs, some seek temporary accommodation with relatives who are already there ... After securing work, they send some money back to their parents to purchase land and livestock for them. These properties are then looked after by their relatives.

Although these statements seem to suggest a power-based form of reciprocity (that is, seniors against juniors and males against females), which may not have been the basis of reciprocity in pre-colonial contexts, it does not detract from the argument that the extended family still plays a role in the support of its members. In this context, the customary law concept of an extended family intersects with the rights of the child to parental care. Children may look to relatives, other than their nuclear family, for the promotion and protection of their right to parental care and support. The importance of this intersection in Africa must be viewed against the backgrounds, firstly, of the lack of effective state social security systems, secondly, of the prevalence of poor rural communities in which many people still live in close proximity to each other and, thirdly, of the effects of HIV/Aids on young families whose children must be left in the care of their adult (or even young) members of the extended family.

Armstrong (1998, 141) has also noted the benefits of the extended family to the rights of children in the context of rape and sexual abuse in Zimbabwe. She observes that the interests the family (group) has in its members sometimes 'benefits children by protecting them from rape and helps rape victims to recover more easily through relying on the support provided by the family.' However, she also alludes to occasions when the family or group interests work to the disadvantage of the child. This is the case when the child's individual needs are ignored in favour of family or group interests (Armstrong 1998, 147; Himonga 1998, 115). Letuka (1998, 212) has furthermore shown that some members of the extended family who take care of their relatives' children in Lesotho abuse and exploit them, including using them as cheap labour. Similarly, Nhlapo (1991, 137) maintains that the African family and its emphasis on group rights masks inequalities between men and women in customary law under the guise of group interests in which women, including girl children, are disadvantaged, because they do not, among other things, have a say in the articulation of the group interests. Clearly, there is an inherent conflict between the child's individual rights and his or her family's interests.

According to Armstrong (1998, 147) some people have argued that the solution to this conflict is an approach that emphasizes 'the individual and individual rights at the expense of the community and family rights and duties'. She submits, however, that the child would in the end lose out, 'because the community and family also protect her [or him] from child abuse and help to heal her [or him] when she [or he] is abused.' Consequently, she concludes, correctly, that the community 'and state solutions are not necessarily mutually exclusive. There is a role for involving the family and community in the state system.' She furthermore makes the point that there is a need for solutions that 'work with both the individual and the community, which support individual rights and autonomy but at the same time support the family and belonging' (Armstrong 1998, 148). It is submitted that the children's rights statutes that include the extended family as part of their child-rights protection frameworks constitute an attempt towards a solution that strikes a reasonable balance between group rights, on the one hand, and the individual rights and autonomy of the child, on the other hand, as envisaged by Armstrong.

With regard to Nhlapo's argument, it is submitted that the dichotomy between living customary law and official customary law should not be lost sight of when considering the inequalities between men and women in customary law. Rigidified norms of official customary law, framed in colonial contexts and through the medium of Western-style courts, are more likely to infringe the rights of women and children than living customary law. The latter's dynamic and flexible nature gives it greater potential to respond positively to women's and children's rights than official customary law. Cornell (2004, 666) seems to share this view when she opines that 'social custom, including the day-to-day on the ground status of women, is dynamic' and that there are, therefore, 'sources within the practice of social custom itself that can be imagined and re-imagined so as to reconfigure the norms of customary law'. This reconfiguration of the living norms of customary law may include their synchronization with the rights of women (and children), as they are engaged in by women (and children) themselves (Cornell 2004, 671).

To sum up, while the extended family has elements that undermine the rights of children, and which need to be guarded against, it still provides its members, including children, with a certain degree of broad-based support and care networks, beyond their immediate group of relatives. Given the potential the extended family has to contribute to the protection of children's rights, Odongo (2006, 22) rightly bemoans the absence of explicit provisions in the Kenyan Children's Act creating a role for the family – nuclear or extended – in providing care and protection for children in need of either or both, including children who have no parents or guardians, abandoned children, children who beg for a livelihood, abused children and children who are terminally ill.

Communal Ethic Domain

Closely connected to the concept of the extended family is the African communal value, which intersects with the duties and responsibilities aspect of children's rights, on the one hand, and the rights concerning the abuse and exploitation of children on the other. Both these intersections will be considered after a brief consideration of the meaning of communal ethic.

The communal ethic is perhaps better explained by reference to another African core value, *ubuntu*, which is said to express itself, metaphorically, in *umuntu ngumuntu ngabantu*, describing the significance of group solidarity on survival issues. An attempt to define this value was made by the South African Constitutional Court in the well-known case of *S v Makwanyane*, which abolished the death sentence in South Africa. The Court (para. 224) defined *ubuntu* as:

> [A] culture which places some emphasis on communality and on the interdependence of the members of a community. It recognizes a person's status as a human being, entitled to unconditional respect, dignity, value and acceptance from the members of the community such person happens to be part of. It also entails the converse, however. The person has a corresponding duty to give the same respect, dignity, value and acceptance to each member of that community. More importantly, it regulates the exercise of rights by the emphasis it lays on sharing and co-responsibility and the mutual enjoyment of rights by all.

In the *DPP* v *Pete*, the Court of Appeal of the Republic of Tanzania considered the African communal ethic to be:

> [the] co-existence of the individual and society, and also the reality of co-existence of rights and duties of the individual on the one hand, and the collective of communitarian rights and duties of society on the other [which in effect] means that the rights and duties of the individual are limited by the rights and duties of society, and vice versa.[15]

Mokgoro (1998, 15) also identifies 'group solidarity, conformity, compassion, respect, human dignity, humanistic orientation and collective unity' to be the key social values of *ubuntu*. And in her consideration of the practical effects of *ubuntu*, she suggests a strong connection between the concept of the extended family and *ubuntu* in the following terms: 'a society based on *ubuntu* places strong emphasis on family obligations. Family members are obliged to help one another.'

The African communal value or *ubuntu* intersects with an aspect of children's rights that is unique to the African continent, contained in article 31 of the ACRWC, and adopted by both the Kenyan and South African Children's Acts. Section 21 of the Kenyan Act reproduces, almost verbatim, article 31 of the ACRWC on the duties and responsibilities of the child. These include the duties of the child to work for the cohesion of the family and to 'preserve and strengthen the positive cultural values of his community in his relations with other members of that community'. The South African Children's Act has a similar provision on the duties and responsibilities of the child, whose inclusion was intended to promote the incorporation of article 31 of the ACRWC.

---

15 As quoted by the Constitutional Court in *S* v *Makwanyane* (see para. 224).

Thus the incorporation of the communal ethic into the children's rights legislation ensures that the child sees the family and community of which he or she is a member as significant parts of his or her life. On the other hand, the child's discharge of duties and responsibilities to the group leads to an expectation that the group will reciprocate by respecting his or her rights as a child.

The communal ethic also intersects with the right of the child to be free from abuse and exploitation. One way the communal ethic expresses itself in relation to the upbringing and protection of children is in the idiom 'a child belongs to everyone', which is probably more prevalent in rural areas, where traditional child-rearing practices and concepts still have considerable influence (see, for example, Himonga 1998, 116–17). The idiom bears the idea that the upbringing of a child is as much the responsibility and concern of his or her parents as it is of the whole community in which the child lives. This is coupled with the idea that there are 'mutually accepted community controls of adult behaviour towards children' (Himonga 1998, 117). For example, a parent (or care-giver) may be restrained by any member of the community from abusing his or her child, or from using excessive forms of discipline to correct the child. In other words, any member of the community who witnesses the abuse of a child may intervene on the child's behalf. Such intervention may include initiating a process, involving local networks and authorities, for the removal of the child from the abusive parent or care-giver and his or her placement with another relative. Thus the concept of 'a child belongs to everyone' intersects with those rights of the child that protect him or her from abuse and exploitation (sections 10 and 13 of the Kenyan Children's Act; sections 12 and 13 of the Ghanaian Children's Act).

However, legitimate concerns may be raised concerning both the communal ethic and its intersection with children's rights. In the first place, the inherent conflict between the interests of the group and those of the child, noted above in relation to the extended family, also applies to the communal ethic. The benefit of the latter to the promotion of children's rights should therefore be assessed and guarded in the same manner as the benefit of the extended family discussed above.

Second, it has been argued (Odongo 2006, 12) that calling upon children to be responsible for adults and their communities in the context of children's rights is amenable to abuse, to the detriment of children. In any case, the ACRWC and the children's rights legislation do not place duties and responsibilities on adults similar to those they place on children. The answer to this concern seems to be that the over-arching 'best interests of the child' principle within which the child is to discharge his or her responsibilities should be used to guard against the possible abuse of children by adults. In this context, it is worthy of note that the 'best interest of the child' principle has already been used in other contexts to disallow the application of customary law where it was considered not to serve the rights of the child,[16] as shown later below. Furthermore the value of reciprocity, embedded in the communal ethic and *ubuntu*, seems to make up for the fact that no duties and responsibilities are placed on adults by children's rights legislation.

16　See, for example *Hlophe* v *Mahlalela* 1998 (1) SA 449 (T).

Damages for Extra-marital Pregnancy Domain

The customary law concerning the payment of damages by a man for extra-marital pregnancy intersects with a number of rights of children, particularly the right to parental care and the right to grow up with one's parents. In customary law, a man who makes a woman pregnant out of wedlock is liable to pay damages to the woman's family. Although these damages are considered to be 'delictual', they are also part of the rules for the affiliation of children born outside wedlock. For example, in terms of section 98(1) of the KwaZulu-Natal codes, a beast is payable in respect of each pregnancy 'provided that should such child or children be born during the subsistence of an engagement no claim for damages shall be recognized unless the marriage does not take place: provided further that should the seducer marry the woman, payments other than the ngquthu beast made in respect of her seduction shall be regarded as forming part of the lobolo.'

The South African Children's Act incorporates the customary practice of the payment of damages for extra-marital pregnancy in its allocation of parental rights and responsibilities in respect of the child. Section 21(1)(b) of the Act provides that the unmarried 'biological father of a child who does not have parental responsibilities and rights in respect of the child ... acquires full parental responsibilities and rights in respect of the child ... if ... he pays damages in terms of customary law'.

The incorporation of this customary practice ensures that the child's right to the father's care is achieved by giving the father full parental responsibilities and rights, along with the child's mother.[17] At face value, section 21(1)(b) seems to run counter to the decision in *Hlophe* v *Mahlalela*, in which the High Court of South Africa applied the 'best interests of the child' principle as a basis for allocating parental authority. The court held that the principle of the best interests of the child contained in section 28(2) of the Constitution of 1996 prevailed over the application of customary rules that allocated parental powers or responsibilities and rights in accordance with the payment of bride wealth upon the marriage of the child's parents. In its reasoning the court stated (at paras 458–9) that: 'arrangements that smack of sale or trafficking of children cannot be enforced; thus issues relating to the custody of children cannot be determined by the mere delivery or non-delivery of cattle.' It accordingly gave the custody of the child in respect of whom the matter had arisen to its father, as opposed to the maternal grandparents who claimed that *lobolo* had not been paid and therefore the father was not entitled to have custody of the child. The court considered this approach to be a development of customary law in terms of the country's Bill of Rights.

However, on a close analysis, it appears that the approach taken by section 21 of the new South African Children's Act is correct. The case to which it applies is one in which the payment of damages is in the best interests of the child, because it promotes the rights of the child to parental care and to grow up with both of its parents. The criticism against *Hlophe* is simply that it did not consider whether there may be instances in which the payment of 'goods' with regard to the acquisition of parental responsibilities and rights may be in the interests of the child.

17　According to section 19(1), the unmarried mother has full parental responsibilities and rights in respect of her child.

Decision-making Domain

The child's culture, and customs and practices of the community to which the child belongs, generally intersect with the basic principles on which decision-making concerning children are made in terms of the children's rights legislation. In this respect, the Kenya Children's Act provides that in considering whether the court is to make an order with regard to a child, the court is to have particular regard to the 'child's cultural background' and to 'the customs and practices of the community to which the child belongs'(sections 76(3)(d) and (g)). Similarly the 'best interest of the child' standard in South Africa is to be considered by reference, among other things, to the child's connection to culture or tradition, as already stated.

A consideration of these cultural and customary practices may, of course, not always lead to a decision that is necessarily in favour of the preservation of customary law, but their inclusion for purposes of decision-making not only underlines the role customary law plays in the interpretation of children's rights, but also ensures that this system of law is not passed by or simply ignored in decision-making processes concerning children.

'Harmful Cultural Practices' Domain

'Harmful cultural practices' have not been defined precisely, but they seem to include practices that 'are likely to negatively affect the child's life, health, social welfare, dignity or physical or psychological development', such as circumcision and other genital mutilations, virginity testing, child betrothals and child marriages. Some countries have banned these practices outright. For example, section 14 of the Kenyan Children's Act provides that '[n]o person shall subject a child to female circumcision, early marriage or other cultural rites, customs or traditional practices that are likely to negatively affect the child's life, health, social welfare, dignity or physical or psychological development.' Others seem to countenance all or some of these practices provided that they are not forced on the child (section 14 of the Ghana Children's Act; sections 12 (3), (4), and (8) of the South African Children's Act), or not performed on a child who is below a prescribed age (such as section 12(2)(5) of the South African Children's Act). Thus, in the latter group of countries, the customary law practices concerned are not banned, but merely regulated.

To the extent that 'harmful practices' have been allowed by the children's rights legislation, they intersect with various rights of the child, such as the right to life, dignity and health, as the case may be, and the 'right not to be subjected to social, cultural and religious practices which are detrimental to his or her well-being' (section 12(1) of the South African Children's Act). Without entering into a discussion about the advantages or disadvantages of legal banning or regulation of the practices in question,[18] there can be no doubt that practices that are harmful to the child can never be in the child's best interests. This underlines the concern about merely regulating as opposed to banning harmful practices by some children's rights statutes. In other

---

18 For a discussion of this and other aspects of harmful cultural practices in the context of human rights, see Banda 2005, 207–46.

words, the acts or events that fall under the description of 'harmful cultural practices' would not be in the best interests of the child, notwithstanding their traditional cultural importance or value. The inescapable conclusion seems to be that unless the practice concerned is deemed to serve the best interests of the child, its intersection with children's rights would be problematic and unacceptable. But there is no real prospect for the practice in question ever being in the best interests of the child.

Dispute Resolution Domain

African dispute resolution mechanisms intersect with the rights of children to have their rights enforced in courts of law.[19] The enforcement of children's rights or any other rights, for that matter, is critical. Unless they are enforced, rights are without value and not worth the paper they are written on. Thus the structures for the enforcement and promotion of rights are as important as the substantive rights themselves. Courts are the primary agents for the enforcement of rights in modern legal systems, including African ones. Yet access to these courts is notoriously difficult, if not impossible, especially for African rural communities, where most children living under customary law reside. It is probably in this context that the children's rights legislation in some countries marks out a role for traditional authorities to play in protecting and promoting the welfare of children living within their jurisdiction. The South African Law Reform Commission conceived of these traditional authorities playing this role by participating at government levels provided for by the Constitution and local government legislation (South African Law Reform Commission 2002, para. 8.5).

Furthermore, the South African Children's Act provides for the role of traditional leaders in court processes aimed at protecting and promoting the rights of children. It provides that the children's court may refer a matter brought before it to a 'lay forum, including a traditional authority, in an attempt to settle the matter by way of mediation out of court' (section 71). A traditional authority would, obviously, include a traditional leader, who in terms of customary law administers the affairs of any group of indigenous people resident within the area under his or her control.[20] The Uganda children's statute and the draft Lesotho Child Care and Protection Bill (2004) similarly provide for dispute resolution structures at village level (Mbazira 2006; Sloth-Nielsen 2006; African Child Policy Forum 2007).

Besides alleviating problems of access to formal, state mechanisms of justice, the traditional leaders fora bring to the scene of enforcement of children's rights the benefit of African 'adjudication' as a method of resolving disputes. Among the underlying values of this method is the reconciliation of the parties to disputes. The advantages of this value to the enforcement of children's rights is to be seen against the background

---

19 See, for example, section 15 of the Ghanaian Children's Act, which creates criminal sanctions for any contravention of provision relating to children's rights; section 22 of the Kenyan Children's Act, which provides for the enforcement of children's rights by applications to the High Court.

20 See, for example, the definition of traditional authority in the South African Children's Act, s. 1(1).

of difficulties associated with the enforcement of Western court judgments and the alienation of community members from each other that the win-or-lose elements of these judgments entail (Scharf and Nina 2001, 47; Himonga 1997, 88).

However, the involvement of traditional leaders in resolving disputes concerning children poses the risk that traditional values and practices that are inimical to the rights of children are invoked. This would be unacceptable, but the answer seems to lie in civic education for communities and their leaders and particularly sensitizing traditional leaders to the rights of children, in addition, perhaps, to restricting their role regarding serious problems affecting children.[21]

The Internal Conflicts of Law Intersection

The received laws and judicial institutions, passed on by colonial states after the attainment of political independence along with state-recognized customary and religious systems of law, make up the legal systems of post-colonial Africa. The colonial states introduced their own laws, especially those governing private relations and land tenure, while retaining the indigenous systems of law for the governance of Africans in these areas. To date, customary law operates largely in the same fields, and applies to the same people, as it did in colonial times.

The prevalence of more than one culture and legal system in Africa and the fact that most of the courts in African countries have jurisdiction to apply customary law raises the question: when does customary law apply to a given situation or case? The circumstances under which customary law applies are determined by internal conflicts of law regimes, the details of which differ from one country to another. A number of broad post-colonial approaches in Africa are, however, evident (Bennett 1996, 49). The first approach presumes that customary law applies only to certain matters, such as succession, marriage and land tenure, or classes of parties to disputes (litigants).[22] This approach is based on the premise that the cause or matter or class of disputants 'provides an indication of overall cultural orientation' (Bennett 1996, 51) of the parties concerned either as tied to African or to Western culture. The second approach deems customary law as applicable to particular groups, such as members of a traditional or cultural community or tribe. The third approach determines the application of customary law according to the status of the disputing parties as complainants or defendants, so that if the complainant is subject to customary law, then the matter is decided by customary law or vice versa (Bennett 1996, 51). The last approach gives discretion to courts to determine when customary law should be applied but using judicially defined guidelines, including those that focus on the cultural orientation indicators.

In sum, the effect of these technical rules, particularly their cultural orientation elements, is that customary law applies primarily in private matters to African children and not to other racial groups.

---

21 In South Africa, for example, traditional authorities are not allowed to deal with matters of child abuse or sexual abuse (see s. 71(2) of the Children's Act).

22 See, for example, section 16 of the Subordinate Courts Act Cap 28 of the Laws of Zambia (discussed in Himonga, 1997, 52; Bennett 1996, 50).

However, it is worthy of note that in its intersection with children's rights, the application of customary law seems to be controlled by the 'best interests of the child' principle, which is one of the fundamental rights of the child in international law, as well as in the constitutional law of some countries, in that solutions to conflicts of law are directed by this principle. This approach entails that, in matters affecting the child, the courts choose to apply the system of law, whether it be customary law or received law, that serves the best interests of the child.

Thus, in *Hlophe* v *Mahlalela* the High Court of South Africa applied the best interests of the child principle, guaranteed as a right of the child by the South African Bill of Rights, to a case where customary law should most probably have applied if the matter had been decided purely on the basis of conflicts of law rules. There are also examples from Zambia and Kenya of the application of the best interests or welfare of the child principle over customary law (Himonga 1995, 67; Odongo 2006, 10) even though these countries do not have a provision in their Bills of Rights that makes the 'best interests of the child' principle a child's right. Moreover, it may be argued that, since this principle is part of international law, contained in the CRC and the ACRWC, it should direct the choice of law rules in all countries that have ratified these treaties, so that in all matters concerning children, only the system of law – whether this be received law or customary law – that serves the best interest of the child should be applied to a given case.

There is, however, a qualification to the argument that the 'best interests of the child' principle should direct the internal conflicts of law decisions. The qualification is that, as a value, the 'best interests of the child' is not reserved to the received law only. To the contrary, it is arguable that embedded in some of the rules for the affiliation of children under customary law is the value of the welfare of the child, which may well be compatible with the child's human rights, even though it is not expressed or understood in the same way or terms as 'the best interests of the child' are understood in other systems of law, including received law. For example, it has been argued elsewhere that the importance attached to kinship (that is, the mother's or father's kinship group) in determining custody under customary law constitutes an aspect of the welfare of the child principle (Himonga 1990, 207). 'Granting custody to a parent to whom the child "belongs" by descent may be seen as taking the child's welfare into account by providing for its security within the kinship group.' Placing this argument in a traditional context, Wanitzek (1995, 19) states:

> In traditional society, it was considered basic and 'best' for anybody to be clearly affiliated to a certain kinship group, because an individual could survive physically and psychologically only with the group's support. Basic material and immaterial needs could be met only through the community. The system of labour, of communal work, of reciprocal help and responsibility among group members ... made it necessary to belong clearly to a certain kinship group.

Similarly, in commenting on the value of social group membership to the individual and vice versa in traditional contexts in Sierra Leone, Harrell-Bond and Rijnsdorp (1975, 20) say 'each individual's security was bound up in the welfare of the whole group.'

The transformation of the extended family and its relevance to the well-being of its individual members, including children, has already been considered in relation to the extended family above. It is only necessary to emphasize that the transformation of the extended family or kinship group may have affected, but not completely eroded, its value as an aspect of the welfare of the child principle under customary law. Therefore, in determining the internal conflicts of law, and in using the best interests of the child principle to direct the choice of the applicable system of law, the courts should not assume that all aspects of the customary rules concerning the affiliation of children have no attributes of the welfare of the child principle. As already stated, this is the criticism levelled against the decision of the High Court in *Hlophe* v *Mahlalela*, in which the court gave no consideration as to whether the payment of *lobolo* could ever be in the interests of the child.

Conclusion

In the changing environment, characterized by children's rights and growing efforts by states to protect these rights in domestic law, African customary child law is increasingly acquiring a new face. This face represents new intersections between this system of law and children's rights created by children's rights legislation. This chapter has attempted to give an overview of the major intersections between customary law and children's rights, as well as the domains in which customary law constitutes a part of the new child-rights frameworks in the African context. At the same time, the chapter has alluded to some concerns that should not be lost sight of in the assessment of these frameworks.

References

Articles, Books and Chapters in Books

Armstrong, A. (1998), 'Consent and Compensation: The Sexual Abuse of Girls in Zimbabwe', in Ncube, W. (ed.) 129–49.
Banda, F. (2005), *Women, Law and Human Rights: An African Perspective* (Oxford: Hart Publishers) 207–46.
Bennett, T.W. (1996), *Customary Law in South Africa* (Cape Town: Juta and Co.).
Blanpain, R. (ed.) (1997), *International Encyclopaedia of Laws World Law Conference: Law in Motion* (The Hague: Kluwer) 75–98.
Cornell, A. (2004), 'A Call for a Nuanced Constitutional Jurisprudence: Ubuntu, Dignity, and Reconciliation', *SAPR/PL* 19, 666–75.
Grant, E. (2006), 'Human Rights, Cultural Diversity and Customary Law in South Africa', *Journal of African Law* 50:1, 2–23.
Harrell-Bond, B. and Rijnsdorp, U. (1975), *Family Law in Sierra Leone, A Research Report* (Leiden: Afrika-Studiecentrum).
Himonga, C. (1997), 'The Legal Culture of a Society in Transition: The Case of South Africa', in Blanpain, R. (ed.).

Himonga, C. (1998), 'The Right of the Child to Participate in Decision Making: A Perspective from Zambia', in Ncube, W. (ed.) 115–16.

Himonga, C. (2002), 'Implementing the Rights of the Child in African Legal Systems: The Mthembu Journey in Search of Justice', *International Journal of Children's Rights* 9, 89–122.

Letuka, P. (1998), 'The Best Interests of the Child and Child Labour in Lesotho', in Ncube, W. (ed.) 203–24.

Lloyd, A. (2002), 'Evolution of the African Charter on the Rights and Welfare of the Child and the African Committee of Experts: Raising the Gauntlet', *International Journal of Children's Rights* 10, 179–98.

Meulders-Klein, M.T. and Eekelaar, J. (1998), *Family, State and Individual Economic Security* (London: Kluwer Tax and Law).

Mokgoro, Y., Justice (1998), 'Ubuntu and the Law in South Africa', *Buffalo Human Rights Law Review* 4, 15.

Ncube, W. (1998a), 'The African Cultural Fingerprint? The Changing Concept of Childhood' in Ncube, W. (ed.).

Ncube, W. (ed.) (1998b), *Law, Culture, Tradition and Children's Rights in Eastern and Southern Africa* (Aldershot and Brookfield: Ashgate).

Nhlapo, T. (1991), 'The African Family and Women's Rights: Friends or Foes?', *Acta Juridica*, 135–46.

Rwezaura, B.A. (1988), 'The Changing Role of the Extended Family in Providing Economic Support for an Individual', in Meulders-Klein, M.T. and Eekelaar, J. 167–85.

Scharf, W. and Nina, D, (2001), *The Other Law: Non State Ordering in South Africa* (Cape Town: Juta and Co.).

Thompson, B. (1992), 'Africa's Charter on Children's Rights: A Normative Break with Cultural Traditionalism', *International and Comparative Law Quarterly* 41, 432–41.

Conference Papers, Reports, Internet Sources and Other Documents

African Child Policy Forum (2007), *Realising Rights for Children: Good Practice in Eastern and Southern Africa* (Addis Ababa: African Child Policy Forum).

Himonga, C. (1990), 'International "Kidnapping" of Children and Determination of Custody: An African Perspective with Special Reference to Zambia', in *9th Common Law Conference: Conference Papers*, 291–300.

Himonga, C. (1995), *Family and Succession Laws in Zambia: Developments since Independence* (Bayreuth: University of Bayreuth Press).

Mbazira, C. (2006), 'Harmonization of National and International Laws to Protect Children's Rights: The Uganda Case Study', paper presented at the African Child Policy Forum Conference on harmonization of laws in eastern and southern Africa, Nairobi, Kenya, 25–27 October 2006.

Odongo, G.O. (2006), 'Harmonization of National and International Laws to Protect Children's Rights: The Kenya Case Study', paper presented at the African Child Policy Forum Conference on harmonization of laws in eastern and southern Africa, Nairobi, Kenya, 25–27 October 2006.

Sloth-Nielsen, J. (2006), 'Harmonization of National and International Laws to Protect Children's Rights: The Lesotho Case Study', paper presented at the African Child Policy Forum Conference on harmonization of laws in eastern and southern Africa, Nairobi, Kenya, 25–27 October 2006.

South African Law Reform Commission (2002), *Report on the Review of the Child Care Act* (Pretoria: South Africa Law Reform Commission).

Wanitzek, U. (1995), 'The Legal Status of Children in Tanzania: Patrilineal or Welfare Principle', paper presented at the 31st Annual Meeting of the African Studies Association, Chicago, Illinois, 19.

Codes, Laws, Reports

Ghana (Children's Act 560 of 1998).

Kenya (Children's Act 8 of 2001).

The Kwa Zulu Law on the Code of Zulu Law 16 of 1985 and the Natal Code of Zulu Law Proc R151 of 1987.

Lesotho (Child Care and Protection Bill), 2004.

South Africa (Children's Act 38 of 2005).

Uganda Children's Act cap. 59 of the Laws of Uganda.

Cases

DPP v *Pete (Tanzania)*.

Hlophe v *Mahlalela* 1998 (1) SA 449 (T).

S v *Makwanyane* 1995 (3) SA 391 (CC).

Chapter 6

Combating Child Poverty: The Role of Economic, Social and Cultural Rights

Danwood M. Chirwa

Introduction

Although statistics on the prevalence of poverty in Africa belong to familiar terrain, they have not become any less shocking. It has been estimated that about 310 million people in sub-Saharan Africa eke out a living on less than a dollar per day.[1] This figure represents half of Africa's population and is expected to rise to 365 million by 2015 (Thomas 2005, 3). Africa is host to 32 of the 48 poorest countries in the world. These statistics are not child specific and do not provide a full picture of the extent to which children are affected by poverty. Nevertheless, evidence abounds that a larger proportion of the poor in Africa are children. According to UNICEF, 'children are disproportionately represented among the poor' (UNICEF 2000, 41). About 50–60 per cent of the population of sub-Saharan Africa consists of children below the age of 18 years (Thomas 2005, 4). According to the World Bank, 29.4 per cent of children under the age of five were malnourished in 2004[2] and most of these children die before the age of five.

Poverty presents wide-ranging challenges to children. In poor families, children feel the full weight of the yoke of poverty as they have to work from very tender ages to provide for their families. Girl children in particular face enormous difficulties. Not only do they walk long distances to fetch food and water for their families, they also are primarily responsible for taking care of sick members of their families. Sometimes, they are married off prematurely with the hope of improving the economic position of their families.[3]

Children are, on account of their age alone, a vulnerable group of people. Poverty just worsens their vulnerability. This chapter contends that the fight against child poverty requires holistic approaches that place economic, social and cultural rights[4] at

---

1   UNDP 'Facts on Poverty in Africa' at <http://www.africa2015.org/factspoverty.pdf> (accessed 14 February 2007).

2   See World Bank 'Sub-Saharan Africa Data Profile' at < http://www.worldbank.org/> (accessed 14 February 2007).

3   For example, during the food shortage of 2002–2003 in Malawi, it was reported that child marriages had increased as a means of accessing food in the country. See Centre for Human Rights and Rehabilitation, *Human Rights Report 2005* (2006).

4   Hereafter, the term 'socio-economic rights' is used merely as shorthand, and not to exclude cultural rights.

their centre. Human rights offer a useful framework within which poverty alleviation efforts must be moulded. It is a framework that emphasizes the need for preferential treatment for children. Efforts at poverty alleviation (international, regional and municipal) should therefore include specific and targeted measures for children.

Defining Child Poverty and the Significance of Socio-economic Rights

Defining child poverty is a complex task, firstly, because the term poverty does not lend itself to easy definition and, secondly, because methodologies for measuring poverty have thus far lacked a child focus. What renders the notion of poverty particularly difficult to define is the fact that poverty is a relative condition and, as a result, the determination of the poor across disparate societies living under different circumstances is extremely difficult (UNICEF 2005, 6).

The World Summit for Social Development held in 1995 in Copenhagen helped to clarify the meaning of poverty. There, it was agreed:

> Poverty has various manifestations, including lack of income and productive resources sufficient to ensure sustainable livelihoods; hunger and malnutrition; ill health; limited or lack of access to education and other basic services; increased morbidity and mortality from illness; homelessness and inadequate housing; unsafe environments; and social discrimination and exclusion. It is also characterized by a lack of participation in decision-making and in civil, social and cultural life. (Programme of Action of the World Summit for Social Development, 1995, para. 19)

Understood in this broad sense, poverty means something more than income or material deprivation. It denotes a state in which a person is unable to live a long, healthy and creative life, or to enjoy a decent life worthy of self-respect and the respect of others (UNDP 2000, 73). A poor child may therefore be defined as a person below the age of 18 years who lacks access to what is required to fulfil basic human needs.

Human rights are entitlements claimable primarily against states. Although the temptation to conflate human rights with poverty should be avoided, there are strong synergies between the two concepts (International Council on Human Rights Policy 2003, 17–18; Alston 2005, 785–9). Conditions of poverty are closely linked to socio-economic rights, whose primary aim is to ensure access by all to the resources, opportunities and services necessary for an adequate standard of living (Liebenberg and Pillay 2000, 16). Socio-economic rights are violated where a significant number of individuals are deprived of minimum essential levels of basic services such as health care, primary education, food, water, social security and housing (CESCR 1990, para. 9). People living in poverty cannot exercise or enjoy their socio-economic rights, and it follows that these rights are a key to breaking the downward spiral of entrapment in poverty. Poverty alleviation efforts must therefore be moulded within a human rights framework that places the realization of socio-economic rights at its fore.

The Socio-economic Rights of the Child in International Law

The International Covenant on Economic, Social and Cultural Rights (ICESCR) is a general treaty that protects a wide spectrum of socio-economic rights that can be claimed by everyone. However, this treaty also recognizes a set of specific rights of children. Among other things, article 10(3) of the ICESCR provides that '[S]pecial measures of protection and assistance should be taken on behalf of all children and young persons without any discrimination for reasons of parentage or other conditions.' Van Bueren has rightly argued that this provision is capable of being interpreted quite broadly and in a manner that advances the rights of the child (Van Bueren 1999, 56). Crucially, it 'lays down the basic principle that all children, because of their vulnerability, are entitled to special protection and assistance additional to that provided for adults' (Van Bueren 1999, 56). According to the Committee on Economic, Social and Cultural Rights (CESCR), which oversees the implementation of ICESCR, article 10(3) is self-executing and therefore 'capable of immediate application by judicial and other organs in many legal systems' (CESCR 1990, para. 5). However, the fact that the ICESCR was adopted without a complaints procedure has limited its significance.

The adoption of the Convention on the Rights of the Child (CRC) in 1989 bolstered the protection of children's socio-economic rights in two critical ways. It protected both civil and political rights and socio-economic rights in one treaty, and adopted new nomenclature for categorizing child rights. In defiance of the traditional divide, the CRC is predicated on four key principles: participation, prevention, provision and protection (Van Bueren 1995, 294–5). These principles are inseparable, mutually supporting and interdependent. For example, aspects of prevention, protection and provision are all embedded in the right to survival and development, which is regarded as the umbrella right from which a range of key children's socio-economic rights can be derived. This right protects the right to life in its traditional sense – as an injunction against the state, restraining it from interfering with the enjoyment of one's life – as well as the right to protective and other positive measures that are necessary for the survival and development of the child (Hammerberg 2001, 357). In so doing, the CRC underscores the fact that socio-economic rights are rights deserving of recognition on a par with civil and political rights and, therefore, that child poverty is an issue that courts cannot skirt.[5]

The CRC does not support the notion that children's socio-economic rights are realizable primarily through the agency of adults.[6] This notion is a misinterpretation of the principle enshrined in the CRC, which posits that parents or legal guardians have the primary responsibility for the upbringing and development of the child (for example, articles 18 and 27). The significance of parents in the upbringing of children cannot be gainsaid. However, it must not be interpreted as a claw-back clause on the responsibilities of states towards children. The CRC, for one thing, clearly grants children a range of socio-economic rights claimable directly against

---

5   However, the failure to include a complaints mechanism in the CRC has to some extent weakened that theoretical exposition.

6   See below.

the state. These include the right to education, the right to health and the rights of disabled children to a full and decent life. Even the right to social security is couched in terms that suggest that children have a direct claim against states even when they are under parental care.[7] Cumulatively, these provisions summon the state to adopt child-specific polices and to include children as direct beneficiaries in general measures.

It must be conceded that the CRC falls short of expressly placing a general obligation on states to accord priority to implementing children's socio-economic rights. However, one can still interpret some of its provisions as suggesting that states have the obligation to display preference to children when implementing human rights. This is evident in article 37, for example, which lists a number of procedural and substantive rights in favour of children in conflict with the law. Among other things, this article prohibits the imposition of capital punishment or life imprisonment on children without the possibility of release and requires that children are detained under more humane conditions than those applicable to adults. Similarly, preferential treatment of children can be found in article 38 of the CRC, which proscribes the conscription of children below the age of 15 years in direct hostilities and imposes limitations on the recruitment of any child between 15 and 18 years into armed forces.

These provisions are premised on common sense. Children are the future of humanity and deserve to live in circumstances that would ensure that they develop optimally and realize their full potential. The absence of express provisions requiring preferential positive measures to realize children's socio-economic rights can be attributed to the lack of proper recognition of socio-economic rights in international and comparative constitutional law at the time that the drafting of the CRC was taking place. However, international human rights law appears to be moving in the direction of imposing an obligation of a 'first call for children' in the arena of socio-economic rights as well. It is duty that posits that 'the essential needs of children should be given high priority in the allocation of resources, in bad times as well as in good times, at national and international as well as at family levels.'[8] This idea was coined a year after the CRC was adopted, at the World Summit in 1990, where world leaders agreed that 'the fulfilment of the basic needs of children must receive a high priority' and that '[e]very possible opportunity should be explored to ensure that programmes benefiting children, women and other vulnerable groups are protected in times of structural adjustments and other economic restructuring.'[9] The CRC Committee, which monitors the implementation of the CRC, is increasingly leaning towards an interpretation of the CRC which manifests this view. For example, while

---

7   Article 26 provides that 'States Parties shall recognize for every child the right to benefit from social security, including social assistance' and that the benefits should be granted considering, among other things, the resources and circumstances of the child, and legal guardians.

8   Para. 33, Plan of Action for Implementing the World Declaration on the Survival, Protection and Development of Children in the 1990s, adopted on 30 September 1990 at the World Summit for Children held in New York.

9   Ibid., para. 31.

pointing out the practical impact of the CRC on domestic policies and legislation, it has observed that the CRC has changed the perception of the child's place in society to one that displays 'a willingness [by states] to give higher political priority to children and an increasing sensitivity to the impact of governance on children and their human rights' (CRC 2003, para. 10).[10] Furthermore, the CRC Committee has called for 'particular attention' to be paid to the most vulnerable groups of young children regarding the obligation of states to ensure that all young children are guaranteed access to appropriate and effective services such as health, care and education (CRC 2005, para. 24). Such children include,

> ... girls, children living in poverty, children with disabilities, children belonging to indigenous or minority groups, children from migrant families, children who are orphaned or lack parental care for other reasons, children living in institutions, children with mothers in prison, refugee and asylum-seeking children, children infected with or affected by HIV/ Aids, and children of alcohol- or drug-addicted parents. (CRC 2005, para. 24)

In its concluding observations consequent upon the 2007 General Day of Discussion on Resources for the Rights of the Child: Responsibilities of States, the CRC Committee has elaborated in considerable detail the ambit and scope of the obligation of states towards harnessing and tracking resources for the fulfilment of socio-economic rights, and underscored the importance of ensuring the justiciability of these rights in domestic courts, especially with regard to the allocation of resources for the rights of the child.[11]

It can be concluded, therefore, that international law recognizes the importance of socio-economic rights in combating poverty. It requires, at a minimum, that child-specific measures are adopted and, at most, that states accord priority to the realization of children's rights, including socio-economic rights. For international law to make a real impact on the plight of children on the ground, greater efforts are needed to make socio-economic rights fully and directly justiciable at the international level.[12] Furthermore, the concept of the 'first call for children' ought to be given more prominence by the CRC Committee and other relevant monitoring bodies than has been the case thus far.[13]

---

10 See Sloth-Nielsen, J. et al., Submission by ad hoc working group on 'Available Resources: the Africa Context; An African Perspective', prepared for the CROC Day of General Discussion on Resources for the Rights of the Child (21 September 2007) available at <www.crin.org>.

11 CRC Committee Day of General Discussion on 'Resources for the Rights of the Child – Responsibility of States' (5 October 2007) available at <www.unhchr.org>.

12 The CRC still does not have a complaints procedure and efforts to adopt an Optional Protocol to the ICESCR are proceeding at a very slow pace.

13 In its concluding observations following the Day of General Discussion (note 11 above), the CRC Committee recommended that 'states parties make children a priority in budgetary allocations as a means to ensure the highest return of the limited available resources' (para. 30).

The Socio-economic Rights of the Child within the African Regional System

The African Charter on Human and Peoples' Rights (ACHPR) has received wide acclaim for recognizing socio-economic rights on the same footing as civil and political rights (Odinkalu 2002, 178). It remains the only international treaty that subjects the whole range of socio-economic rights protected under it to the communications procedure. The ACHPR includes the right to health, education, family protection and work. In addition, it protects the so-called 'third generation' rights to existence and self-determination, to sovereignty over natural resources, development, peace and a generally satisfactory environment. All these rights are critical to the fight against deprivation, and their realization holds the key to unlocking the full potential of children in Africa.

However, the ACHPR has been rightly been criticized for paying lip-service only to children's and women's rights. It deals with the rights of these special groups in one provision only, which obliges states to 'ensure the protection of the rights of the woman and the child as stipulated in international declarations and conventions' (article 18(3)). The trouble with this provision is that it is located within an article dealing with family protection. It has been argued that the family in Africa represents an oppressive context within which serious human rights abuses against children and women are committed (Mutua 1992, 27).

Curiously, the African Charter on the Rights and Welfare of the Child (ACRWC) was not adopted as a direct response to these concerns. Rather, it arose as part of rearguard action to the CRC adopted a year earlier, which was considered by African leaders to have failed to incorporate sufficiently the socio-cultural and economic realities of the African child (Olowu 2002, 128; Viljoen 2000, 218–19). Like the CRC, the ACRWC employs the principles of participation, prevention, provision and protection as the organizing matrix for defining child rights. It has been lauded for placing children's rights within the African context (Viljoen 2000, 218–19; Chirwa 2002a, 157), and has done so by blending universal principles with those of an African flavour such as the notion of individual duties, group rights, peoples' rights, solidarity rights and family-related rights.

However, insofar as socio-economic rights are concerned, the contribution of the ACRWC is limited. It does not add any new rights, but simply defines the rights already entrenched in the ACHPR with children as the beneficiaries and in greater detail. For example, the right to education in the ACHPR is defined so briefly that one may not easily discern its meaning. The ACRWC defines the right to education as encompassing free and compulsory primary education and requires states to, amongst other things, encourage the development of secondary schools and make higher education accessible to all (article 11). Likewise, it also outlines the measures that states should implement in order to realize the right to health including the allocation of adequate resources to the health portfolio, allowing for the participation of civil society and local communities in the planning and management of basic services programmes for children, and mobilizing local community resources in the development of primary health care for children (article 14).

Like the ACHPR, the ACRWC does not explicitly recognize the rights to social security, adequate housing, an adequate standard of living and adequate food. The failure of the ACRWC to recognize these rights has been described as a significant let-down (Oloka-Onyango 1995, 51). The African Committee of Experts on the Rights and Welfare of the Child (ACERWC), which monitors the implementation of the ACRWC, will have to draw inspiration from the African Commission on Human and Peoples' Rights (African Commission), which monitors the implementation of the ACHPR, regarding innovative tools for interpreting Charter provisions in a way that lends indirect protection to these rights. In *The Social and Economic Rights Action Centre & the Centre for Economic and Social Rights v Nigeria*,[14] the African Commission found Nigeria to be in violation of the rights to housing and food even though these rights are not expressly recognized in the Charter. It did so after finding that the right to housing was implicitly entrenched in the rights to property, family protection, and in the right to the enjoyment of the best attainable state of mental and physical health;[15] the right to food was implicitly recognized by a combined reading of the provisions guaranteeing the rights to life, to enjoy the best attainable state of physical and mental health, and to economic, social and cultural development.[16]

The ACERWC may also use the Protocol to the African Charter on Human and Peoples' Rights on the Rights of Women in Africa (AWP) to boost the protection of children's socio-economic rights (Chirwa 2006, 63). This instrument recognizes the rights of women to social security and insurance, housing, and food security and food,[17] which are not expressly recognized in either the ACHPR or in the ACRWC. The Protocol also gives express recognition to reproductive rights,[18] which are important for ensuring the autonomy of the girl child. Significantly, the AWP recognizes the right of women, including girl children, to inherit from their parents. These rights are critical to the empowerment of women in the African context where many women and children are thrown into desperation upon the death of their spouses or parents due to oppressive and gender-skewed inheritance customs (Fenrich and Higgins 2001, 259).

The right to sustainable development, recognized in article 19 of the AWP, is arguably one of the most important rights it protects. This article requires states to introduce gender perspectives in national development planning procedures and ensure the participation of women at all levels in the conceptualization, decision-making, implementation and evaluation of development policies and programmes. It also obliges states to promote women's access to land and control over productive resources. Article 19 of the AWP also imposes an obligation on states parties to ensure that the negative effects of globalization and any adverse effects of the implementation of trade and economic policies and programmes are reduced to the minimum for women. These provisions are very important to women and, by extension, to children in the African context, where women and children are rarely

---

14 Communication 155/96 (2001) AHRLR 60 ('*SERAC* Case'). For reviews of the case, see Chirwa 2002b, 14; Coomans 2003, 749. See, too, for a discussion of this case, Olowu, Chapter 2 in this volume.

15 Para. 60.

16 Para. 64.

17 Arts 13–16.

18 Art. 14.

or poorly represented at all levels of decision-making. They emphasize the need for development policies to be scrutinized from a gender perspective and for assessments of their impact on vulnerable groups such as women. Moreover, for development policies to have the desired positive impact on the lives of the people, they ought to be formulated and implemented with the participation of the intended beneficiaries. These principles could be incorporated into the provisions of the ACRWC through progressive interpretation to ensure that children's socio-economic rights are given effective protection.

For socio-economic rights to be enforced meaningfully, courts must develop appropriate benchmarks for measuring state compliance with its obligations. This is a task that has presented problems to the African Commission. In the *SERAC Case*, the African Commission appeared to use the language of the 'minimum core obligations' concept when defining the duties of the state implicit in the rights to food and shelter.[19] Yet in the same case, it construed the right to a healthy environment under article 24 of the ACHPR as obligating states to 'take reasonable' measures to 'prevent pollution and ecological degradation, to promote conservation, and to secure an ecologically sustainable development and use of natural resources',[20] thereby suggesting that it was applying the 'reasonableness' test developed by the South African Constitutional Court, which has thus far refused to follow the concept of a minimum core of socio-economic rights adopted by the CESCR in its General Comments.

In *Purohit and Moore* v *The Gambia*,[21] the African Commission missed an opportunity to clarify its jurisprudence especially with regard to the nature of positive obligations of states. This case concerned a challenge that the Lunatic Detention Act of the Gambia, the principal legislation governing mental health, was outdated and inadequate to provide protection for the rights of mental patients, in that the Act did not provide safeguards to protect the rights of persons undergoing diagnosis for mental illness, and during their subsequent certification and detention. It was also alleged that the psychiatric unit, where mental patients were detained, was overcrowded, the living conditions in the unit were poor, and that patients were treated without giving consent. In finding the Gambia to be in violation of the right to enjoy the best attainable physical and mental health, the African Commission stated that this right requires states to '*take concrete and targeted steps, while taking full advantage of its available resources*, to ensure that [it] is fully realized in all its aspects without discrimination of any kind'.[22] This pronouncement was made after the Commission had pointed out that it was aware that millions of people in Africa were unable to enjoy this right maximally because African countries were generally

---

19 It stated that 'the minimum core of the right to food requires that the Nigerian government should not destroy or contaminate food sources.' It stated similarly that the minimum obligation embodied in the right to shelter obliged the Nigerian government 'not to destroy the houses of its citizens and not to obstruct efforts by individuals or communities to rebuild lost homes'. See above, note 14, paras 47 and 65 respectively.

20 *SERAC* Case (note 14 above) para. 52.

21 Communication 241/2001 (2003) AHRLR 96 ('*Purohit* Case').

22 Note 21 above (emphasis added).

faced with the problem of poverty.[23] This case resolved the long standing question as to whether resource constraints could constitute a defence by the state for the failure to meet its socio-economic rights obligations, given that the ACHPR does not define these rights with the traditional internal limitations such as 'to the maximum of available resources' and 'subject to progressive realization'.

However, no reference was made in this case to the *SERAC Case* and the statements made in it cannot be easily reconciled with that earlier decision. For example, it is difficult to tell whether 'concrete and targeted steps' means the same thing as 'reasonable measures' as stated in the *SERAC Case* or as defined by the CESCR in its General Comment No. 3. Furthermore, it is not clear whether the socio-economic rights obligations forming part of the minimum core should be discharged as a matter of priority in the context where resources are lacking. By contrast, the CESCR has stated that while the lack of availability of resources could constitute an acceptable ground for exonerating states from liability for failing to realize socio-economic rights, states shoulder the burden of proving that they have used the available resources optimally to meet the basic needs of their people as a matter of priority (CESCR 1990, para. 10).

It is clear therefore that the three human rights monitoring bodies – African Commission, ACERWC, and the newly established African Court on Human and Peoples' Rights[24] – have the obligation to provide clarity on the question of the nature of the states' positive obligations in respect of social and economic rights. The laxity or stringency of the standard for measuring state compliance with its positive obligations will determine the extent to which socio-economic rights and the courts can contribute to efforts aimed at poverty alleviation. In the African context, where democratic norms have not yet taken effective hold, where parliamentary mechanisms are not yet fully functional and effective, where corruption is frequently unchecked, and states often lack the capacity to devise and implement development programmes, models for enforcing rights which prevent courts from adjudicating upon positive obligations of states may not be appropriate. The African situation requires stringent benchmarks directing states to give priority to implementing the rights of such vulnerable groups as children.

The Place of the Child in Regional Development and Policy Frameworks: NEPAD

The human rights commitments that African states have made at both international and regional levels are rarely reflected in the regional policy frameworks. Nowhere is this more apparent than in the infamous New Partnership for Africa's Development (NEPAD) framework.[25] NEPAD is the major regional agenda adopted in 2001 through which African leaders seek to disentangle the continent and its people from

---

23 Note 21 above para. 84.

24 This Court has powers to hear communications against states alleging violations of the ACHPR. See article 2 of the African Court's Protocol establishing the African Court on Human and Peoples' Rights adopted in 1998, entered into force 25 January 2004.

25 Discussed also in Chapter 2 in this volume.

underdevelopment, and marginalization from the globalization process. It constitutes a pledge by African leaders to eradicate poverty, to 'place their countries, both collectively and individually, on a path of sustainable growth and development', and to participate actively in the world economy (NEPAD 2001, para. 1.1).

Rooted in the belief that globalization presents opportunities for future economic prosperity and poverty reduction on the continent, the stated long-term objectives of NEPAD are two-fold: to eradicate poverty in Africa and to place African countries, both individually and collectively, on a path of sustainable growth and development and, thus, halt the marginalization of Africa in the globalizing process; as well as to promote the role of women in all activities (NEPAD 2001, para. 67). Its expected outcomes are economic growth and development and increased employment, reduction in poverty and inequality, diversification of productive activities, enhanced international competitiveness and increased exports, and increased African integration (NEPAD 2001, para. 69).

In order to achieve these objectives and goals, NEPAD has a Programme of Action which calls for particular attention and immediate action regarding the creation of the conditions for sustainable development, the undertaking of policy reforms and increasing investment in certain identified priority sectors, and the mobilization of resources through increasing domestic savings, improving public revenue collection systems and sourcing external funding to support development programmes. The sectoral areas of priority identified in NEPAD for increased investment are agriculture, human resource development, bridging infrastructural gaps, protection of culture, promotion of development and the assimilation of technology, and the environment.

NEPAD has generated considerable interest and support from foreign governments and international organizations, which can be seen as an indication of its potential. Compared with its predecessors, it is relatively well-designed conceptually, with clear objectives and goals and the means for realizing them. The adoption of the African Peer Review Mechanism (APRM),[26] a voluntary review procedure for assessing the quality and feasibility of a participating country's draft Programme of Action and following up on the country's progress regarding the implementation of the Programme of Action, has been welcomed as an especially positive feature of the initiative.

However, NEPAD is dangerously insensitive to children. While poverty alleviation is a primary goal of NEPAD, the amelioration of child poverty or the improvement of the quality of the life of the child is listed neither as a specific objective nor as a specific outcome of NEPAD. Only two child-specific goals are included, namely to enrol all children in school by 2015 and to reduce child and infant mortality by two-thirds by the same year. Although some of the priority areas that require states' urgent action concern health, education, water and other basic goods and services, these are neither couched within a human rights framework, nor do they display a special concern for children. Instead, they are defined within the context of creating conditions that are conducive to international

---

26 Declaration on the Implementation of the New Partnership for Africa's Development (NEPAD), 2003.

trade. NEPAD, through its Democracy and Political Governance Initiative, seeks to promote adherence to global standards of democracy whose core components include political pluralism and respect for human rights and the promotion of the rule of law.[27] However, NEPAD itself lacks a clear legal basis. As it is not a treaty but an economic and development regional programme, NEPAD has dubious status in international law. Its monitoring mechanism is voluntary with no powers to name and shame non-compliant states. It also does not have a concrete mandate regarding human rights. Furthermore, NEPAD's institutional links to the African Union (AU) and other institutions under it, including the African Commission and the African Court, are altogether unclear. What is perhaps more concerning is that NEPAD considers poverty alleviation as an offshoot of economic growth and development. Some of the principles promoted by it are intrinsically incompatible with human rights. For example, it places much premium on the need to increase domestic savings and tighten fiscal discipline, restructure the public service and, above all, attract foreign direct investment. Thus, the primacy given to micro-economic objectives is not adequately counterbalanced by people's claims to socio-economic rights within NEPAD. This is problematic, as the achievement of economic objectives does not automatically result in poverty reduction.

There is no doubt that, conceptually, NEPAD offers prospects for addressing poverty and underdevelopment. However, child rights and human rights generally have been given peripheral attention within NEPAD. Opportunities still exist for agitating for greater attention to be given to children's socio-economic rights. One of them is through domestic Programmes of Action. Civil society can use the APRM process to highlight the plight of children in the relevant countries and advocate for targeted measures to address children's socio-economic rights issues, including child poverty. Above all, this section has demonstrated that key instruments for fighting poverty need to be structured by human rights standards and should, more importantly, be sensitive to the needs of the most vulnerable groups affected by poverty, such as children.

The Constitutionalization of Children's Socio-economic Rights[28]

The internationalization of human rights dealt a heavy blow to the previously impregnable doctrine of state sovereignty by elevating the concern for individual and group rights to the international level. However, it has not resulted in the reduced significance of domestic mechanisms for realizing human rights. Thus, socio-economic rights provisions in international and regional treaties will have no real impact on the ground without the hand of individual states.

Contrary to the rhetoric propagated by African leaders in the post-colonial era about the need for accelerated development and the centrality of socio-economic rights to the African conception of rights, most African countries did not include these rights in their constitutions and, instead, entrenched catalogues of civil and

---

27 In its Declaration on Democracy, Political, Economic and Corporate Governance, human rights are defined quite widely to include the rights in the ACHPR and the ACRWC.

28 See also Chapter 4 of this volume.

political rights only. Human rights generally were viewed with unease due in part to the perception that they were intended to benefit the white settlers in these countries and the fear that they would derail accelerated development (Oloka-Onyango 1995, 2–3). It is not surprising, therefore, that independent Africa was marked by dictatorial and corrupt regimes, which failed both to achieve the desired accelerated development and to uphold human rights.

A wave of democratization that swept across the continent after the fall of the Berlin Wall has dramatically changed the political landscape on the continent. Since then, democratically elected regimes have been installed in many countries under new constitutional arrangements. According to Heyns and Kaguongo, almost all the 53 countries of Africa now make provision for human rights in their constitutions, although the bias is still in favour of civil and political rights (Heyns and Kaguongo 2006). Socio-economic rights are recognized in three principal ways (Chirwa 2005, 207). Some countries, such as Egypt, Lesotho, Nigeria, Sierra Leone and Sudan, protect these rights as directory principles of state policy. Others, such as Eritrea, Ethiopia, the Gambia, Liberia, Malawi, Namibia, Swaziland, Tanzania, Uganda and Zambia, use a mixed model with a few of these rights in the bill of rights, the rest being protected as directory principles of state policy. There are also an increasing number of African constitutions that protect socio-economic rights directly in their bills of rights as full rights with the power of enforcement. They include the constitutions of Benin, Cape Verde, São Tomé and Príncipe, Burkina Faso, Gabon, Madagascar, Mali, Niger, Togo, Seychelles and South Africa.

Constitutionalizing social and economic rights has the effect of placing poverty alleviation among the state's topmost priorities. Courts are thereby given constitutional legitimacy to play a part in finding solutions to deprivation and systemic causes of inequalities in society. Constitutionalizing these rights provides a solid basis for civil society, individuals and other interested persons to challenge legislation and policies that do not adequately give effect to these rights, or to demand that new legislation and policies should be put in place.

A closer look at African constitutions reveals that socio-economic rights continue to be a neglected set of rights. More disturbing is the fact that children's socio-economic rights are rarely given adequate constitutional protection. The most widely recognized socio-economic rights in African constitutions generally are the rights to and in work, to education, to family protection, to social security, and environmental rights (Heyns and Kaguongo 2006, 22–31). Certain key socio-economic rights of importance to children are not widely recognized. For example, very few constitutions recognize the right to social security in respect of orphans, widowhood and indigence (Heyns and Kaguongo 2006, 32–3). The right to an adequate standard of living is protected in 14 African constitutions while the right to housing and shelter is recognized in 12 constitutions only (Heyns and Kaguongo 2006, 34). The right to food and water, by contrast, is recognized only in eight and six constitutions respectively (Heyns and Kaguongo 2006, 34–5).

While a total of 34 countries expressly provide for the specific rights of children in their constitutions, as discussed in more detail in Chapter 4 of this volume, most of these do not address children's socio-economic rights. The most commonly recognized socio-economic rights of children are the right to protection from exploitation and the right to education. Unfortunately, the right to education is defined predominantly as the responsibility of parents, while the duty of the state in relation to this right is defined in weak language, suggesting that its duty is simply one of assistance to parents.[29]

The constitutions of Rwanda and São Tomé and Principé are somewhat unique in that they require the respective states to undertake special measures to protect children and do not place undue emphasis on the role of parents *vis-à-vis* the state regarding the upbringing and development of children. Article 28 of the Rwandese Constitution provides that '[e]very child is entitled to special measures of protection by his or her family, society and the state that are necessary, depending on the status of the child, under national and international law.' Article 52 of the Constitution of São Tomé and Principé states that '[t]he youth, especially the young workers, enjoy special protection in order to render effective their economic, social and cultural rights.' Both these provisions could be interpreted broadly to impose the duty on the respective states not only to protect a wide range of socio-economic rights of children but also in a manner that displays preferential treatment to children in order to accord wider protection to children's socio-economic rights. Article 34 of the Ugandan Constitution has potential to afford greater protection to children's social rights if interpreted as more than just a prohibition against discrimination and as entailing more than the duty to respect this right. It provides that '[n]o child shall be deprived by any person of medical treatment, education or any other social or economic benefit by reason of religious or other beliefs.'

It is, however, the Constitution of South Africa which, on paper, appears to be quite progressive regarding the protection of children's socio-economic rights. Section 28(1)(c) of the South African Constitution provides that '[e]very child has the right to basic nutrition, shelter, basic health care services and social services.' This provision is couched without reference to the concepts of 'progressive realization' and 'within the limits of available resources', as is the case with sections 26 and 27 of the same Constitution, which enshrine the rights of everyone to have access to housing, and health, food, water and social security respectively. It was initially thought that the omission of these terms from section 28 meant that children were entitled to enjoy priority allocation over everyone's socio-economic rights. This view was rejected in *Government of the Republic of South Africa* v *Grootboom,*[30] which dealt with the issue as to whether the state could be ordered to provide shelter to a group of people who were living in intolerable conditions without basic shelter (by virtue either of section 26 (protecting the general right of everyone to housing) or section 28(1)(c) (protecting the child's right to basic shelter)). Regarding the latter, the Constitutional Court took the view that section 28(1)(c) imposed a primary duty on parents to take care of their children, including providing them with shelter. The state incurred a primary obligation only where children were removed from,

---

29 See, for example, article 17 of the Constitution of Gabon; article 17 of the Constitution of Guinea; section 31(3) of the Constitution of Malawi; article 15(2) of the Constitution of Namibia; article 19 of the Constitution of Niger; article 36 of the Constitution of Togo; and article 24 of the Constitution of Zambia.

30 2001 (1) SA 46 (CC) (*Grootboom*).

or lacked, parental care. This decision raised eyebrows among children's rights activists and scholars, not least because it brought confusion as to the proper role of section 28(1)(c) in South African constitutional jurisprudence, given the existence of sections 26 and 27 (Sloth-Nielsen 2001, 210). The Court held that this section had to be read together with section 26 of the Constitution, so that the internal limitations of 'available resources' and 'progressive realization' are brought to bear on the meaning of the children's entitlement to the fulfilment of their socio-economic rights. The net effect of this ruling is that children's rights are of subordinate significance, since the state's obligations in relation to children are to a large extent conceptualized as being indirect and exercisable through the agency of parents.

The sweeping effect of this decision was mitigated to some limited extent in *Minister of Health and Others* v *Treatment Action Campaign (TAC)*,[31] where it was held that that the state incurs 'the primary obligation to provide basic shelter [which] rests on those *parents who can afford to pay*'.[32] Acknowledging that the provision of a single dose of Nevirapine to a mother and her child to prevent transmission of HIV was essential to a child, the Constitutional Court of South Africa held that the government violated the right to health by adopting and implementing a policy that prevented poor mothers and their children from accessing the drug. This decision means that the state has a primary obligation with regard to children's socio-economic rights in section 28(1)(c) at least where their parents are indigent.

However, both *Grootboom* and *TAC* fell short of requiring the state to implement socio-economic rights in a manner that accorded priority to vulnerable groups such as children and women (Chirwa and Khoza 2005, 148). Worse still, these decisions did not require the state to develop measures that at least made specific and adequate provision for children and women, despite that fact that more than half of the plaintiffs in *Grootboom* were children and that the intended beneficiaries of the comprehensive programme on HIV/Aids treatment in *TAC* were children.

The nub of this discussion, therefore, is that children's socio-economic rights remain underprotected at the domestic level, despite the commitments made by African states at the international and regional levels. In order for the fight against child poverty to bear fruit, it is critical that domestic constitutions (supported by appropriate policies and legislation) entrench socio-economic rights generally and specifically for children. These rights should be interpreted to require states to adopt measures that are general as well as child-specific, or that sufficiently incorporate the needs of children.

Conclusion

Poverty alleviation constitutes one of the enduring and greatest challenges facing Africa. A majority of the poor in Africa are children. Yet, efforts to address poverty often neglect the composition of the poor. General measures to combat poverty may not bring about the desired effect for certain sections of poor people. Socio-economic

---

31 2002 (10) BCLR 1033 (CC) (*TAC*), discussed further in Chapter 14 of this volume.
32 Para. 77 (emphasis added).

rights are important in Africa because they hold the key to liberating many people from entrapment in poverty. The African regional system of human rights complements the international system very well by recognizing the justiciability of social and economic rights. Indeed, Africa is the only region that has specialized instruments addressing the rights of the child and those of women. Between them, these treaties bolster the ACHPR by recognizing a wide range of socio-economic rights that are essential to uplifting the plight of an African child. One of the key outstanding issues to be addressed is the question of the development of the benchmarks for measuring state compliance with its positive obligations in relation to socio-economic rights. Thus far, the African Commission has been uncertain about the appropriate standard. It is critical for such benchmarks to require states at least to make specific provision for children in all development measures, or to set the advancement of children's rights as a standard for measuring the success of any such measures. Ideally, states should be obliged to accord priority or special protection to children in poverty alleviation efforts. Another challenge is to ensure that human rights are reflected more prominently in regional development initiatives. As this chapter has shown, using NEPAD as an example, this goal remains elusive in Africa.

Unlike at the regional level, the status of socio-economic rights at the constitutional level is markedly less promising. While African constitutions are increasingly making dedicated provision for children's rights, they do not generally include specific socio-economic rights for children. The focus has mostly been on measures to protect children from exploitation and the right to education. The protection of these rights is to be commended, but they are by no means the only – or even the most important – rights. African states ought to move beyond the common law conception of placing primacy on parental duties to children, in order to ensure that children's socio-economic rights are given full effect. The undue weight given to the notion of parental duties in the first instance has meant that most constitutions do not recognize the direct obligations of states in relation to children's socio-economic rights and, as a result, children are often not the direct beneficiaries of state policies. Holistic approaches to poverty alleviation are needed, but they need to be accompanied by child-specific measures in order for the challenge of child poverty to be overcome.

References

Articles, Books and Chapters in Books

Alston, P. (2005), 'Ships Passing in the Night: The Current State of the Human Rights and Development Debate Seen through the Lens of the Millennium Development Goals', *Human Rights Quarterly* 17, 785–9.
Benedek, W. et al. (eds) (2002), *Human Rights of Women: International Instruments and African Experiences* (London: Zed Books).
Chirwa, D.M. (2002a), 'The Merits and Demerits of the African Charter on the Rights and Welfare of the Child', *International Journal of Children's Rights* 10:2, 157.

Chirwa, D.M. (2002b), 'Toward Revitalising Economic, Social and Cultural Rights in Africa: Social and Economic Rights Action Centre and the Centre for Economic and Social Rights v Nigeria', *Human Rights Brief* 10:1, 14.

Chirwa, D.M. (2005), 'A Full Loaf is Better than Half: The Constitutional Protection of Economic, Social and Cultural Rights in Malawi', *Journal of African Law* 49:2, 207.

Chirwa, D.M. (2006), 'Reclaiming (W)omanity: The Merits and Demerits of the African Protocol on Women's Rights', *Netherlands International Law Review* LIII, 63.

Chirwa, D.M. and Khoza, S. (2005), 'Towards Enhanced Citizenship and Poverty Eradication: A Critique of *Grootboom* from a Gender Perspective', in Gouws, A. (ed.).

Coomans, F. (2003), 'The Ogoni Case before the African Commission on Human and Peoples' Rights', *International and Comparative Law Review* 53, 749.

Davel, C.J. (ed.) (2000), *Introduction to Child Law in South Africa* (Cape Town: Juta and Co.).

Eide, A. et al. (eds) (2001), *Economic, Social and Cultural Rights: A Text Book* (The Hague: Kluwer Law International).

Evans, M. and Murray, R. (eds) (2002), *The African Charter on Human and Peoples' Rights: The System in Practice, 1986–2000* (Cambridge: Cambridge University Press).

Fenrich, J. and Higgins, T. (2001), 'Promise Unfulfilled: Law, Culture, and Women's Inheritance Rights in Ghana', *Fordham International Law Journal* 25, 259.

Gouws, A. (ed.) (2005), *Unthinking Citizenship: Feminist Debates in Contemporary South Africa* (Aldershot: Ashgate).

Hammerberg, T. (2001), 'Children', in Eide, A. et al. (eds).

Liebenberg, S. and Pillay, K. (eds) (2000), *Socio-Economic Rights in South Africa* (Cape Town: Community Law Centre).

Mutua, M. (1992), 'The African Human Rights System in a Comparative Perspective: The Need for Urgent Reformulation', in Benedek, W. et al. (eds).

Odinkalu, C.A. (2002), 'Implementing Economic, Social and Cultural Rights under the African Charter on Human and Peoples' Rights', in Evans, M. and Murray, R. (eds).

Oloka-Onyango, J. (1995), 'Beyond the Rhetoric: Reinvigorating the Struggle for Economic, Social, and Cultural Rights in Africa', *California Western International Law Journal* 26:1.

Olowu, D. (2002), 'Protecting Children's Rights in Africa: A Critique of the African Charter on the Rights and Welfare of the Child', *International Journal of Children's Rights* 10:2, 127.

Sloth-Nielsen, J. (2001), 'The Child's Right to Social Services, the Right to Social Security, and Primary Prevention of Child Abuse: Some Conclusions in the Aftermath of *Grootboom*', *South African Journal on Human Rights* 17, 210.

Van Bueren, G. (1995), *The International Law on Rights of the Child* (Dordrecht: Marthinus Nijhoff).

Van Bueren, G. (1999), 'Alleviating Poverty through the Constitutional Court', *South African Journal on Human Rights* 15:1, 56.

Viljoen, F. (2000), 'The African Charter on the Rights and Welfare of the Child', in Davel, C. (ed.).

General Comments, Unpublished Papers, Declarations and Reports and Internet-based Sources

Centre for Human Rights and Rehabilitation (2006), *Human Rights Report 2005*.
CESCR (1990), 'General Comment No. 3: The Nature of States Parties Obligations (Art. 2, para.1 of the Covenant)', E/C.12/1991/23.
CRC (2003), 'General Comment No. 5: General Measures of Implementation of the Convention on the Rights of the Child (arts 4, 42 and 44, para. 6)', CRC/GC/2003/5.
CRC (2005), 'General Comment No. 7: Implementing Child Rights in Early Childhood', CRC/C/GC/7/Rev.1.
CROC Concluding Observations on the Day of General Discussion on 'Resources for the Rights of the Child – Responsibility of States' (unedited version, 5 October 2007, available at <www.ohrhr.org>).
Heyns, C. and Kaguongo, W. (2006), 'Constitutional Human Rights Law in Africa' (unpublished).
International Council on Human Rights Policy (2003), *Duties sans Frontières: Human Rights and Global Social Justice* (Versoix: ICHRP).
New Partnership for African Development (NEPAD) (2001), <http://www.nepad.org> (home page), accessed 11 February 2007.
Plan of Action for Implementing the World Declaration on the Survival, Protection and Development of Children in the 1990s, adopted on 30 September 1990 at the World Summit for Children held in New York <http://www.unicef.org/wsc/plan.htm> (home page), accessed 12 February 2007.
Resolution 1 of the World Summit for Social Development, Copenhagen 1995, A/CONF. 166/9.
Sloth-Nielsen, J. et al., Submission by ad hoc working group on 'Available Resources: The African Context; An African Perspective' for the CROC Day of General Discussion on Resources for the Rights of the Child, 21 September 2007 (available at <www.crin.org>).
Thomas, P. (2005), 'Ending Child Poverty and Securing Child Rights: The Role of Social Protection' (Plan: United Kingdom) (unpublished).
UNDP (2000), *Human Development Report* 73 <http://hdr.undp.org/reports/global/2000/en/> (accessed 14 February 2007).
UNDP, 'Facts on Poverty in Africa' at <http://www.africa2015.org/factspoverty.pdf> (accessed 14 February 2007).
UNICEF (2000), *Poverty Reduction Begins with Children* 41 <http://www.unicef.org/publications/pub_poverty_reduction_en.pdf> (accessed 14 February 2007).
UNICEF (2005), *Child Poverty in Rich Countries 2005*, Report Card No. 5, 2005, UNICEF Innocenti Research Centre, Florence <http://www.unicef.org/brazil/repcard6e.pdf>, accessed 14 February 2007.
World Bank, 'Sub-Saharan Africa Data Profile' at <http://www.worldbank.org/> (home page) (accessed 14 February 2007).

National Constitutions

Constitution of Gabon, 1991.
Constitution of Guinea, 1984.
Constitution of Malawi, 1994.
Constitution of Namibia, 1990.
Constitution of Niger, 1999.
Constitution of Togo, 1992.
Constitution of Zambia, 1991.

Cases

Government of the Republic of South Africa v *Grootboom*, 2001 (1) SA 46 (CC).
Minister of Health and Others v *Treatment Action Campaign* 2002 (10) BCLR 1033 (CC) (*TAC*).
Purohit and Moore v *The Gambia*, Communication 241/2001, (2003) AHRLR 96.
The Social and Economic Rights Action Centre & the Centre for Economic and Social Rights v *Nigeria*, Communication 155/96, (2001) AHRLR 60.

PART II

Chapter 7

Child Participation in Africa

Louise Ehlers and Cheryl Frank

Introduction

Engaging children in participation or consultation is a relatively recent advent within the children's rights arena and, at least at first glance, is an idea alive with promise and potential. In Africa, this promise has special significance, given the range of conditions on the continent that render its children particularly vulnerable. The need to consult children is especially pressing in the light of the move in Africa towards the reform of laws and policies relating to children, and particularly because of the potential for giving effect to unique provisions in the Convention on the Rights of the Child (CRC) and the African Charter on the Rights and Welfare of the Child (ACRWC) relating to children's participation. The vast diversity of conditions that prevail on the African continent offer both opportunities and challenges for this massive children's rights project that must be undertaken. There is no doubt, however, that children in Africa live under incredibly challenging circumstances, and it is these conditions that may in fact present some of the greatest barriers to the full recognition of children as the rights-holders that they are.

There have been a wide range of efforts at engaging children in participation in the African context. This chapter grapples with the question of how well such efforts have served children on the continent, and it seeks to present key considerations for future participation endeavours. The primary question that arises is how these efforts should be evaluated in terms of their value for children in Africa? This chapter takes the view that this must necessarily be assessed from two broad perspectives. The first is the ethics of child participation. This chapter charts some of the central ethical concerns relating to child participation and assesses how some exercises of this nature in Africa have addressed themselves to these concerns. The second lens through which child participation efforts in Africa should be viewed, we argue, revolves around whether and how such efforts have enabled African children to engage with the many unique problems that carve out their daily existence. The lives of children in Africa are shaped by a range of social, economic, political and environmental conditions including poverty, development efforts, conflict, HIV/ Aids, weak governance and corruption. In fact, it has been said that African children are more likely to be victims of human rights violations than adults, and they are also more likely to be victims than children on other continents (Viljoen 2000). We argue that these conditions render the recognition of children as rights holders, and the realization of children's rights, even more difficult. In the discussion that follows, we seek to review some child participation efforts on the continent against the backdrop of the ways in which they engage with the difficulties and complications created by these conditions.

In reviewing child participation processes undertaken in the African context, the discussion that follows has been centred around the following three considerations:

- Do child participation efforts seek to identify and address the specific challenges faced by African children?
- Have child participation exercises been undertaken with due consideration for ethical issues in relation to child participation?
- How have participation efforts been harnessed towards improving the lives of children in Africa?

Two notes of clarity need to be made at the outset. First, there are very few examples on the continent of child participation processes that have been fully evaluated, and this review has been limited by this fact. Second, throughout this chapter, the terms 'participation' and 'consultation' are used interchangeably.

Child Participation and Children's Rights Instruments

It has been argued that an explicit right to participation is non-existent in international human rights law. However, elements of participation can be found throughout the rights contained in the CRC (Ang et al. 2006). Ang et al. (2006) consider children's participation rights as a 'cluster of rights' comprised primarily of the respect for the views of the child (article 12), the right to freedom of expression (article 13), the right to freedom of thought, conscience and religion (article 14), the right to freedom of association and peaceful assembly (article 15) and the evolving capacities of children as a legitimate ground for parental guidance (article 5).

Articles 12 and 13 in particular have the intention of ensuring that children are afforded a direct stake in all the processes that relate to them, and articles 12 (1) and (2) of the CRC make the following provision:

> (1) State parties shall assure to the child who is capable of forming his or her own views the right to express those views freely in all matters affecting the child, the views of the child being given due weight in accordance with the age and maturity of the child.

> (2) For this purpose, the child shall in particular be provided the opportunity to be heard in any judicial and administrative proceedings affecting the child, either directly, or through a representative or an appropriate body, in a manner consistent with the procedural rules of national law.

Article 13 of the CRC provides that '[t]he child shall have the right of freedom of expression; this right shall include freedom to seek, receive and impart information and ideas of all kinds, regardless of frontiers, either orally, in writing or in print, in the form of art, or through any other media of the child's choice.'

It is noteworthy that article 12 is unique in that it has no precedent in any other international law document and in that it focuses on the role of the child (the beneficiary of the instrument) as an active participant in the implementation of the instrument. When contemplating article 12, it is important for the analyst to distinguish between sub-clauses 1 and 2. Article 12(2) relates specifically to the right of an individual child to participate in judicial and administrative proceedings such as divorce and custody hearings. It can thus be viewed as the more limiting of the two clauses. Article 12(1) refers to 'the right to express those views freely in *all matters* affecting the child' and can be interpreted as including the participation of the child in all levels of decision-making. It can be argued that it thereby creates a vehicle for children's participation in broader law and policy reform processes. Article 12(1) is a useful starting point for institutionalizing children's participation, because it stipulates a three-pronged test according to which the opinions of children are given relative weight – their capacity to form views, their age and their psychological maturity (Van Bueren 2000).

The ACRWC, the regional children's rights treaty, does not differ greatly from the spirit of the CRC, but its intention is to afford African children *additional* protection in the light of their particular vulnerability. This has been attributed to their socio-economic, cultural, traditional and developmental circumstances, natural disasters, armed conflicts, exploitation and hunger (Preamble to the ACRWC). The ACRWC also recognizes the position that the child occupies in African society, and his or her cultural heritage, historical background and values. A number of clauses in the ACRWC provide for children's participation (see articles 4 and 12). The most specific provision is article 7 on freedom of expression, which states:

> Every child who is capable of communicating his or her own views shall be assured the rights to express his opinions freely in all matters and to disseminate these opinions subject to such restrictions as are prescribed by laws.

Olowu (2002) notes that the ACRWC was not developed in opposition to the CRC, but rather in tandem. The two treaties are complementary: both contribute to a framework in which the rights of children in Africa may be discussed.

Substantial interest and debate has been generated by the inclusion of participation clauses in the CRC and, to a lesser extent, the ACRWC. The concept of participation is still, however, open to interpretation. Consequently, the degree to which children's voices have to be incorporated into policy and law reform processes by the state parties to these conventions is far from clear. The discussion that follows explores the current thinking underpinning participation.

Child Participation: Definitions and Debates

Kjorholt and Qvortrup (2000, 9) suggest three arguments supporting children's participation. First, it is in the best interests of children in that it contributes to their development of individual identity, competence and a sense of responsibility. Second, children's involvement in debate constitutes an important area for social democratization because it represents the extension of some democratic rights to a disenfranchised group. Finally, the contribution of children gives us access to essential information that we could get from no other source. It has further been said that the observations of children not only breathe life into the tenets of international instruments such as the CRC, but also expose the real discrepancies between the good intentions articulated in these instruments and the realities of children's lives. The human rights abuses and procedural failures in judicial systems that are identified by children emphasize the need for urgent and far-reaching law reform if their rights are to be realized in a concrete way (Community Law Centre 1999; Clacherty 2001, 9).

Participation may be defined in a range of different ways. Roger Hart (1992, 5) characterizes public participation as a critical element in any democratic process, describing it as:

> [t]he process of sharing decisions which affect one's life and the life of the community in which one lives. It is the means by which democracy is built and it is the standard against which democracies can be measured. Participation is the fundamental right of citizenship.

He suggests, further, that a process in which children are consulted needs to meet four important requirements before it can be viewed as participatory. These are that children involved understand the intentions of the project; that they know who made the decisions concerning their involvement, and why; that they have a meaningful role; and that they volunteer for the project *after* its nature has been made clear to them (Hart 1992). Similarly, Boyden and Ennew (1997, 11) suggest that: 'to participate meaningfully, children need information about the reasons and the consequences of what they are doing…'.

While an array of theorists have written on the subject, initial thinking about children's participation was strongly influenced by the writings of Roger Hart and Gill Westhorpe. Hart (1992) conceptualizes participation as a ladder with eight rungs,[1] each symbolizing an increasing level of participation. He describes (1992, 8–14) a range of scenarios for adult-child interaction from manipulation as the least participative interaction or first rung; followed by decoration and tokenism (both viewed as non-participatory); assigned but informed participation; consulted and informed participation; adult initiated-shared decisions with children and child initiated and directed participation. Child initiated-shared decisions with adults is the top rung, and therefore the most participatory.

More recently, Cattrijsse and Delens-Ravier (2006, 33) have argued that while Hart and others believe that it is possible to evaluate the 'quality' of participation initiatives by classifying them according to a defined scale, in practice there is far less of a distinction between a methodical–technical approach to participation and a critical–political approach. They believe that the way in which participation is put into practice will always have to be considered in the light of the specific context and the prevailing circumstances.

Hart himself describes the ladder of participation as 'the beginning of a typology for thinking about children's participation in projects' (1992, 8). He cautions that the ladder should not be considered a simple measuring stick of the quality of any programme, as there are many factors affecting the extent to which children

---

1   Hart acknowledges borrowing the metaphor of the ladder from Arnstein (see Arnstein, S., 'A Ladder of Citizen Participation', *Journal of American Planning Association* 35:4 [1969]) but has created his own categories.

participate, one of them being the design of the programme. Others are the age and maturity of the child and cultural issues.

It is the view of the authors that the levels of participation described by Hart should be viewed as a flexible continuum rather than a rigid, upwardly ascending ladder. It should serve as a guide rather than an unyielding empirical tool for assessing the value of participatory efforts. The regimented gradation of the 'rungs' of participation militates against flexibility with regard to the intention of the participative process, which could affect proposed outcomes. Notwithstanding some criticism, Hart's model provides a useful framework within which to assess the level and authenticity of children's participation processes, given the relatively recent introduction of the concept in Africa and the largely unregulated environment in which participation is taking place.

Westhorpe offers an alternative to Hart's model in the form of a six-stage continuum of youth involvement. The stages are ad hoc input, structured consultation, influence, delegation, negotiation and control. A series of questions are posed to ascertain the level and authenticity of participation. These questions explore the levels of participation, the mechanics of the process, selection criteria, and evaluation strategies. Howard, Newman, Harris and Harcourt (2002, 6) point out that this continuum does not imply that more or less control is better, just that certain stages will be more appropriate in some situations than others.

Another useful tool for assessing the manner in which a particular process was carried out is suggested by Stuart Hart (1996, 15–16), quoting one of the founders of the International School Psychology Colloquium: '[We] have four choices in relating to children: to do things *to* them; to do things *for* them; to do things *around* them or to do things *with* them.' His message is essentially that the knowledge of children's capabilities gained in recent years should encourage the creation of more opportunities for participation and self-determination, with a greater emphasis on doing things with and around children than was allowed or thought possible in earlier generations.

One issue that has been written about extensively with regard to the participation of children concerns the ethical implications of involving children in these processes. There is a need to ensure that when children are consulted one is not merely paying lip service to international conventions. One should strive to avoid tokenism in favour of allowing the contribution of children to make a real impact on the issues that affect their lives. While conscious manipulation of children to serve a particular agenda is indisputably unethical, tokenism and decoration (the second and third rungs on Hart's ladder) are common traps into which organizations involved in the promotion of children's participation can fall. Tokenism is a particularly difficult issue to deal with, because such efforts are often carried out by adults who are strongly concerned with giving children a voice, but have not begun to think carefully and self-critically about doing so. The result is that they design projects in which children seem to have a voice, but in fact have little or no choice about the subject or the style of communicating it, or no time to formulate their own opinions (Hart, R.A. 1996).

Another issue that is frequently raised is how one ensures that the authentic voices of children are heard, that is, that the views reflected by adults following a participation process are indeed those articulated by the children.

... [Not] all child participation is active, social, purposeful, meaningful or constructive. Too often, the participation of children, even when designed by well-meaning adults, amounts to non-participation if children are manipulated ... (Hart 1992, 5)

Bearing the above in mind, it is critical that practitioners engaging in the promotion of children's participation move beyond a superficial understanding of the concept and develop a more nuanced understanding of how children can contribute in a truly meaningful way to discussions of issues affecting them. The question of how one ensures ethical and meaningful engagement with children remains. It would seem from the literature on the subject that theorists agree that in designing projects, adults need to be mindful of three considerations. The first is how the information gathered in a participation process can benefit the child; the second, what mechanisms have been provided to ensure that the information is channelled in order to create material improvements in the child's circumstances. The last is to ensure that the intervention will in no way harm the child, or infringe on his or her rights.

According to the Children's Rights Centre (Children's Rights Resource Handbook, undated), when assessing whether or not a children's participation process has been conducted ethically, a number of essential criteria need to be met. These include treating the children involved with respect; recognizing their capabilities regardless of their age; and listening to what they have to say. The process should support and protect the child, and allow him or her to participate meaningfully. A child should be able to argue his or her case and interact with adult role-players. The participants also need to be properly briefed, because they cannot be said to be representing children if they have not had the opportunity to discuss the issue with their peers. Finally, children need to be given the opportunity to express views that are rooted in their own experience.

Experiences from Africa

Bearing the above in mind, this section of the chapter looks at four case studies from Africa, and assesses these in terms of the three central considerations set out earlier, which are:

- Does the child participation effort seek to identify and address the specific challenges faced by African children?
- Has the child participation exercise been undertaken with due consideration for ethical issues in relation to child participation?
- How have the findings from the participation effort been harnessed towards improving the lives of children in Africa?

Consultation with Ugandan Children on Violence against Children – Save the Children Uganda

Save the Children Uganda (SAVE)[2] undertook a study in 2005 which examined the views of children and adults on violence against children. SAVE took as its point of

---

2   See too, Chapter 10 in this volume for a discussion of this process.

departure article 19 in the CRC that articulates the responsibility to protect children from all forms of violence. According to the authors, it is widely acknowledged that globally, obligations by state parties in respect of article 19 have not been translated into practice, and it was assumed that Uganda was no different to other countries in this regard. However, in Uganda, very little was known from a children's perspective about the nature and extent of violence against them, the perpetrators of this violence and their views about what ought to be done about it. The purpose of the study was therefore to generate credible information to inform the development of policy and programmes and to develop a meaningful response to the problem (Naker 2005).

The study examined the views and opinions of 1,406 children (719 girls and 687 boys) aged between eight and 18 years, drawn from five districts in Uganda. The areas were selected based primarily on geographical diversity, existing infrastructure to support the project, accessibility to participants and safety of the researchers. The sites were selected to reflect cultural diversity, and the urban, semi-urban and rural mix that they offered. In addition to the children, the researchers interviewed 1,093 adults (520 women and 573 men), primarily parents, teachers and community leaders in order to reflect on how their views corroborated or differed from those of the children.

Using five complementary research methods, children were asked about their experiences of the violence used against them, how the violence manifests itself, how often it occurs, who commits it, how it makes them feel, how they react, and what they believe should be done to prevent it. Adults were also asked about their perspectives on violence against children including: how they understand the term 'violence against children', how they and other adults in their communities punish children, how they rationalize the types of punishment they use, and what they believe should be done to prevent violence against children.

The process undertaken by SAVE provides a useful example of the direct application of ethical principles in undertaking a child participation initiative as described by Hart. The researchers developed the project plan based on an ethical policy that guided all their interactions with children. In line with these guiding principles, they ensured that children were informed of the purpose of the project and how the information would be used. Participation in the project was voluntary and confidentiality was ensured. Given the sometimes traumatic nature of the subject matter, plans were also put in place for children who required further support to be referred to the appropriate local services.

In considering whether this participation effort sought to identify and address the specific challenges faced by African children, one may easily argue that the object of interest in this case (that is, violence against children) specifically responded to the vulnerability of children in Africa as noted by the ACRWC, and was particularly relevant given the findings of more recent studies such as the UN Study on Violence against Children. The means of addressing this issue also warrants mention. The researchers made deliberate efforts to utilize multiple research methods within the design of the project to enable them to allow children to speak in different ways. The design of the study also took into account some of the issues that need always to be considered in the African context, that is, diversity, infrastructure, accessibility to participants and the safety of the researchers.

The extent to which the findings of this study have been harnessed towards improving the lives of children is difficult to assess, particularly in the absence of longitudinal information in this regard. However, it may be noted that prior to the implementation of the study there had been a dearth of information relating to violence against children in Uganda. The cumulative results of this process confirmed empirically the urgent need for what the authors term a 'multi-layered response' to the rampant use of violence against children in that country. By eliciting the voices and opinions of children and those of adults in the same communities, the researchers were able to make concrete suggestions with regard to proposed interventions, including the need to develop a comprehensive framework to address the issue of violence against children; the need to develop outreach programmes to promote alternative models for the adult-child relationship; and the need to establish community-based mechanisms that respond proactively to children experiencing violence (Naker 2005, iv). By documenting the voices of children on this issue, SAVE in Uganda has also brought their views to a wide audience and has attempted to draw attention to what they see as the disconnection between actions and intentions, experiences and perceptions.

Consultation with Mozambican Children as Part of the Legal Reform Process
Towards the Development of a Comprehensive Children's Act

In 2003, Mozambique began a process of reviewing all its legislation pertaining to children. The Community Law Centre (CLC) at the University of the Western Cape in South Africa was contracted by UNICEF and UTREL (Unidade Técnica da Reforma Legal, the office in the Ministry of Justice responsible for law reform in Mozambique) to undertake this process in preparation for the development of a new children's code for Mozambique. The government's brief to CLC was that the opinions of children should be sought before developing their recommendations, and this child participation process sought to explore the views of Mozambican children on children's rights, and establish where they felt the realization of these rights was lacking (Ehlers and Mathiti 2003). The process involved 58 children ranging in age from six to 19 that had had direct experience of child labour, orphanhood, human trafficking, incarceration (in prison and police cells) or sexual exploitation. The study also included consultation with one group of children that had not had personal experience of any of these issues. They were selected from institutions and schools in two provinces, Maputo and Gaza. These provinces were selected because they provided an even balance between urban and rural children. Focus group discussions were used as the primary research methodology. All facilitators were affiliated to registered children's rights organizations in Mozambique and had extensive experience of working with children and families. The facilitators were responsible for recruiting children, ensuring that their participation was voluntary, and that they understood the purpose of the study. Seven focus group workshops were held during which children were encouraged to discuss their experiences, feelings and attitudes freely. While facilitators used a schedule of questions to guide the process, they also utilized techniques such as role-playing, discussion and debate to gather the necessary information.

As regards its scope and attempts to address contextual issues, the Mozambican consultation process addresses very specific concerns that relate to the African child. Child labour, the plight of orphans and vulnerable children as a result of the HIV/ Aids pandemic, human trafficking, the rights of children in trouble with the law and sexual exploitation have all been identified by the Mozambican government, and indeed by aid agencies in many other countries on the continent, as requiring urgent attention in order to protect children and promote their rights. It is arguable that a targeted approach such as this is critical in Africa, due to the diversity of circumstances and the particular vulnerabilities that may be faced by children on the continent.

As far as ethical issues were concerned, this study appears to have been undertaken with due care for the preparation of the children involved, with careful attention being given to the issues of voluntary involvement and consent. Efforts were also made to ensure that the facilitators had the appropriate qualifications and were adequately trained prior to the commencement of the project. It may be argued that the central weakness of this process from an ethical point of view was the lack of feedback to the children on the report ultimately provided to the government, as well as communication to them regarding to the ultimate outcomes of the process (that is, the development of new legislation).

In respect of the extent to which the findings from this participation effort have been harnessed towards improving the lives of children, the following key issues may be noted. Firstly, one needs to recognize the limitations of this particular process as a result of the sample size. While it is not always possible to be totally inclusive, this sample group was especially small, with only 58 children participating. Thus, while the views and opinions expressed by the children in the study are legitimate and based on real experience, they cannot necessarily be attributed to Mozambican children more broadly. This being said, the researchers developed a comprehensive report to the Mozambican government which included recommendations with regard to reform of the law, making explicit reference to the views of children and to the challenges expressed by them. The Mozambican government has now drafted two proposed bills dealing with child rights and child protection and justice issues.

It is often argued that there is insufficient political will with regard to the institutionalization of child participation. This case study is interesting in that UNICEF was instrumental in ensuring that children's voices would be included in the drafting process and orchestrated this through the creation of a partnership with the Mozambican government to ensure that children's participation was recognized and that the results would be integrated into the final recommendations. In implementing the process, the facilitators were therefore able to give the children involved the assurance that their participation had been formally mandated by the government and that the views they expressed would be heard and considered in the drafting of new laws.

Consultation with South African Children on the Legislative Proposals Preceding the Drafting of the Child Justice Bill

A project committee was established in 1996 by the South African Law Reform Commission (SALRC) to draft legislative proposals for the development of a new system to respond to children that come into conflict in the law (Community Law Centre 1999). The committee announced that submissions received from civil society organizations and the views of children would both be used in the development of a report which would form the basis of the new legislation. A range of workshops and meetings were held with specific interest groups, and their views were recorded for inclusion in the final report.

The National Institute for Crime Prevention and the Reintegration of Offenders (NICRO) was commissioned by the SALRC to co-ordinate children's participation in this process.[3] The study was undertaken at institutions in the Gauteng and the Western Cape provinces and included children who were: in diversion programmes; over the age of 14 years and awaiting trial in a place of safety; under the age of 12 and awaiting trial in a place of safety; awaiting trial in prison; serving sentences in a reformatory and in a prison; attending school. The groups were asked to provide their views on ten key themes: the minimum age of criminal capacity; police powers; alternatives to arrest; assessment; diversion; the proposed preliminary inquiry; child justice courts; sentencing; legal representation; and the expunging of criminal records of young persons. Methods used to elicit responses included role-plays, small group discussions and written feedback using structured worksheets. Children were also asked to share their personal experiences of the criminal justice system, and to make recommendations or propose changes to the legislation. A total of 70 worksheets were processed. Following the consultation phase, the SALRC prepared a report documenting all the submissions (SALRC Project 106, Juvenile Justice Report, July 2000), accompanied by a draft Child Justice Bill. In drafting the report, the SALRC made extensive use of the contributions of the children and made direct reference to their views.

In considering whether this child participation effort addresses the specific challenges faced by African children, the following should be noted: the recognition of the need to abolish all forms of cruel, inhumane or degrading treatment of children in the criminal justice system has in recent years found a solid footing in many countries on the African continent. It is further recognized that through the deprivation of their liberty, children are rendered particularly vulnerable to a range of institutional and systemic abuses.

As regards the ethics of this process, considerable efforts were made to ensure that children understood the purpose of the process and participated voluntarily. However, feedback to the children is again an area of weakness. To the knowledge of the authors, neither the SALRC nor NICRO had further engagement with these children to provide feedback to them on the value of their participation or in relation to the extent to which their views were adopted in the Child Justice Bill. This is a

---

3   NICRO is a South African non-government organization working in the field of child justice and crime prevention. This process was sub-contracted to Louise Ehlers, one of the authors of this chapter.

critical flaw in this and many other participation processes, as it undermines the value gained from engaging children in the first place, and weakens any meaningful attempt to empower them or promote further civic participation.

The extent to which this participation effort has been harnessed towards improving the experiences of children in the criminal justice system in South Africa is not easy to gauge. However, this case study is an interesting example of how the voices of children were used directly in the drafting of an official, government-mandated report. The SALRC makes clear and explicit reference to the views of the children involved in the participation discussions throughout its report, and explains in detail if and when these views influenced the drafting of the legislation. Where the process fell short was ensuring a meaningful role for the children in the longer-term process of law reform. While attempts were made to involve children in later parts of the drafting process, these were not officially mandated and no explicit reference is made to the views of children after the SALRC report.

The Law Reform Process in Lesotho[4]

The process of reforming children's legislation in Lesotho began in 2000. The Lesotho government recognized that the existing Children's Protection Act of 1980 had a range of shortcomings.[5] The fact that Lesotho is a party to a number of conventions meant that domestic legislation needed to be aligned to these obligations. The revised law (the Child Welfare and Protection Bill, 2004) aims to promote the rights of children and provide a comprehensive legal framework for the promotion and protection of the best interests of the child.

Save the Children Sweden, UNICEF and Save the Children UK funded the law reform process. The main partner in the project was the Lesotho Law Reform Commission (LLRC). The LLRC sought to involve different stakeholders in the development of the new legislation, and to this end, established the multi-sectoral Child Legislative Reform Project Committee whose membership included government representatives and NGOs. This Committee established five thematic areas in order to create the framework for the new legislation. These included children in conflict with the law, children in parental care, children with disabilities, child victims of violence and other forms of exploitation, and children infected or affected by HIV and Aids. The Committee sought to make the process as consultative as possible and to this end conducted a range of consultations amongst professionals, children, youth and traditional leadership structures to source input on the intended legislation. These inputs were then collated and fed into the drafting process.

---

4   At the time of writing, the Lesotho children's participation process had not as yet been documented and this information was obtained via personal correspondence with the children's participation consultant, Selloane Mokuku, who was responsible for implementing the children's participation aspect of the Lesotho law reform process and finalizing the reports to UNICEF and the LLRC in this regard.

5   Lesotho, Juvenile Justice Situation 1980–2004, presentation made by UNICEF representative at the Southern African Juvenile Justice Network meeting held on 11 and 12 November 2004 at the University of the Western Cape, South Africa.

It was fortuitous that the law reform process coincided with preparations for the UN Special Session on Children (UNGASSoC) in 2002. At the time, Save the Children UK in Lesotho promoted the Save the Children Alliance mandate of ensuring child participation in the UN process and the issue of children's participation was placed high on government's agenda. In order to prepare for UNGASSoC, a national consultative meeting was held with children drawn from all ten districts in Lesotho. They represented a diverse range including school children, out of school youths, teenage mothers, herders, initiates and children with disabilities, among others. The main aim of the meeting was to make inputs on the document 'A World Fit for Children' which was due to be finalized in September 2002.

Through the UNGASSoC process, the children who participated in the meeting were made aware of the law reform process in Lesotho. As a result, a Junior Committee was established consisting of children nominated by the UNGASSoC participants with a specific mandate to ensure that the experiences of children were recognized and considered when the new laws were developed. This process was facilitated by a children's participation consultant contracted to Save the Children UK.

The Junior Committee was briefed by the LLRC about progress on law reform and the children were then engaged with on the particular issue being discussed. In order to ensure that the Junior Committee members were in fact representing the authentic voices of children more broadly, they in turn consulted extensively with children in their regions through mechanisms such as drama, poetry and storytelling. They also convened community events that would appeal to young people (with music, food and so on) and used these events as a vehicle for eliciting children's experiences and informing children about the proposed legislative reform.

As regards the extent to which the findings from the participation effort have been harnessed towards improving the plight of Lesotho's children, it may be too early to make any concrete assessment, although the Lesotho experience has been identified as a regional best practice (African Child Policy Forum 2007). The final revisions to the Children's Protection Bill were completed in 2004 and it has been presented to the Minister of Law, Constitutional and Parliamentary Affairs for tabling in parliament.

Concerning the issue of ethical considerations, it is important to note that children cannot be viewed as a homogeneous group and the views of one child or group of children may not necessarily reflect those of another. One of the major challenges in ensuring the ethical and authentic participation of children in largely adult-driven initiatives (such as law reform) is to clarify whose views the children are representing – are they speaking on behalf of a particular constituency or are they expressing individual views? When the opinions of children are presented to law makers, policy makers or people in positions of influence in any sphere, there should be a genuine effort to ensure clarity with regard to this issue. The Lesotho process is a useful example of how this may be achieved. Instead of simply eliciting the views of the Junior Committee members, the child participation co-ordinator was able to access a far wider spectrum of views and opinions through the consultation efforts in the regions of the members themselves. The members were also able to draw on the views of their peers through age and culturally appropriate activities and events, an exercise which would arguably have been less successful if implemented solely by adults for the benefit of children.

Child Participation in Africa: Future Considerations

Child participation exercises in Africa have addressed themselves to a wide range of issues faced on the continent. These have included the consultation of children on the reform of legislation (Lesotho, South Africa, Mozambique), programme and policy development, for instance in South Africa (Frank and Muntingh 2005), Uganda (Naker 2005), Swaziland and Zambia,[6] and the inclusion of children in post-conflict reconciliation efforts such as the Truth and Reconciliation Commission in Sierra Leone (UNICEF 2004). In addition to these, there have been other innovative exercises undertaken to engage children on issues that concern them. For example, in Egypt, UNICEF engaged children in the development of a short animated film relating to corporal punishment.[7] In recent years there has also been a move towards the development of schools' and children's parliaments[8] and African children have formed part of a number of United Nations delegations invited to discuss matters of interest on the continent.

While it is apparent that these exercises have engaged African children on a range of issues, it is also clear that there are many aspects that are central to children's experiences in Africa that have not been addressed in any depth. Some of the most obvious issues are poverty, development, HIV/Aids,[9] good governance, democracy, conflict and corruption. If future participation efforts are to be ethical (and therefore meaningful to children), it seems obvious that they need to engage in a far more realistic way with the day-to-day issues that shape the lives of children. It is also important to note that the problems faced by African children are not unique to this continent and much can be learned from the efforts of other developing nations.[10]

A related question is whether and how participation efforts actively seek to address some of the very real barriers that conditions in Africa may place in the way of children's participation. It has been suggested that despite the acceptance of children's rights by governments around the world as demonstrated by the widespread ratification of the CRC, there is a lack of national policies that allow

---

6　The Save the Children Alliance commissioned child participation processes in Zambia, South Africa and Swaziland on the issue of corporal punishment, also referred to in Chapter 10 of this volume.

7　*The Revenge of the Canes*, DVD, UNICEF Egypt, 2005.

8　The setting up of children's parliaments and school parliaments is a common way in which countries are responding to the need to increase the level of children's participation and to create a forum in which children's voices can be heard. These structures take different forms in different countries and the level at which they engage with the formal state structures varies greatly, with some having direct access to the decision makers and others having very little impact on issues that affect them (Hodgkin and Newell 2002).

9　Although some pioneering work on child participation in the HIV/Aids sphere has recently been undertaken by a range of organizations, including the Children's Institute at the University of Cape Town (www.ci.org.za).

10　See, for example, a 'child study' aimed at gathering data on the situation, experiences and ideas of 2,000 children in two conflict-ridden areas in East Sri Lanka. The primary aim of the study was to inform the training of personnel in government and NGOs working with children in the war-torn areas of Sri Lanka (Hart 2002).

for the formal, ongoing participation of children (Ackermann et al. 2003). We argue also, that even amongst children's rights organizations, there have been few attempts to integrate the participation of children into the way in which these organizations do their business, and that both national policy and general practice needs to be addressed to accommodate this.

It has also been noted that, at the project level, there are cultural and familial practices that may inhibit or act against the participation of children (Ackerman et al. 2003). According to UNICEF (2003), the principle that children should be consulted on issues that affect them often meets with resistance from people who see it as undermining adult authority within the family and society. Although scholars argue that decision-making in accordance with the CRC ought to be influenced by the child's wishes, a number of cultures hold to the traditional belief that children are less rational, less secure about their identity and less autonomous than adults (Van Bueren 2000, 206).

Twum-Danso notes that another barrier to children's participation experienced in the African context is the emphasis placed on children's performance of duties. She argues that children participate extensively in the daily work of their communities as, like adults, they are seen as having a responsibility to contribute to the subsistence of their families and the wider community. Despite this, children's participation in matters affecting them has met with formidable opposition from adults in social and political structures.[11]

These brief examples provide a stark reminder of some of the more specific and practical realities that relate to the lives of children on the continent. Seeking to engage children in participation under these conditions requires not only careful planning, but a nuanced understanding of the social and cultural systems that govern children's lives. Throughout this chapter, the need has been emphasized for formalized, institutionalized channels for children's ongoing participation on issues that affect them. When assessing the extent to which this has been achieved on the continent, it is significant to note that most of the child participation exercises reviewed, as well as others noted whilst undertaking research for this study, have been actively driven by international agencies such as the members of the Save the Children Alliance, UNICEF and the International Labour Organization. The Mozambican example discussed above illustrates that, while it is commendable that children's participation was included in the original project brief for the legislative review, it would seem that the initiative came largely from UNICEF, and that it is unclear whether the Mozambican government would have included children's participation without the intervention of this agency. In the future, it will be critical to examine the extent to which international players continue to dominate such processes or whether local organizations are able to capitalize on the momentum that has been created. More important, it will be critical to assess the extent to which these players continue to 'set the agenda' in relation to the specific issues on which children's participation is engaged.

---

11 Twum-Danso, A. (n.d.), *Africa: A Hostile Environment for Child Participation*, Thematic reports, p. 66. <http://www.ecpat.net/eng/A4A02-03_online/ENG_A4A/Thematic_ Africa.pdf > (accessed 7 July 2005).

There is no question that the rights and welfare of children in Africa are inextricably linked to the development fortunes of the continent. Participation is deeply embedded in a human rights approach to development, as are other critical concerns such as equality, empowerment and accountability. As with child participation, the principles that are contained in this approach may be seen as both an end in themselves and a means to the broader ends of development on the continent. It is an open question to what extent this approach will gain ascendancy among efforts to bring better lives and prospects to those on the continent. This paradigm does, however, offer increased opportunities to engage children in processes that affect them and it seems clear that ensuring that children's voices are heard in such processes will only enrich and legitimize these efforts. Into the future, assessing to what extent a clear role for children has been carved into development efforts may be a critical factor in ensuring investment in the eventual development outcomes.

One of the questions arising from the discourse on development relates to the scale of participation. From the child participation exercises discussed earlier, it seems that there have been limited efforts to engage children on a large scale, with the Lesotho example reflecting the strongest initiative in this regard. Both from a children's rights perspective and a development perspective, it may be argued that it is not the representivity of the outcome that is of importance but rather the act of participation. This obviously cannot be understood in isolation, but should be juxtaposed against the length and depth of children's participation that is achieved within such exercises. From the examples noted, most were of a one-off nature, offering little by way of ongoing engagement with children, illustrating the tension between the scale of such exercises and the length and depth of children's involvement. Another factor that should be added to these considerations is that of cost, which may be a feature that above all else shapes and defines the nature of children's participation, especially in Africa where there may be far more immediate needs that compete for attention. We argue that while there are no easy ways of navigating these challenges, they remain issues that must receive active and specific consideration in the planning of child participation processes.

Concluding Comments

Child participation in Africa is a notion that, both theoretically and practically, is caught up in the bewildering array of features that define the African condition. It is subject to all the diversities of the African continent; it is dependent on those processes that define and interpret broad notions such as rights, democracy and development; it is subject to the actions and reactions of international agencies and local interests; it competes for both attention and funding and its reality is ultimately shaped by the political will of those who choose to believe in its importance.

For all those engaged in the children's rights project, in Africa and across the globe, notwithstanding the many questions that beset it, the challenge that ultimately remains in relation to child participation is how we integrate the authentic voices of children into all aspects of our engagement with them and on their behalf. Most fundamentally, this calls for an ongoing and deeper engagement with children, it asks for the establishment of respectful and accountable relationships with children, and demands the conscious and cautious negotiation of the many barriers that stand in the way.

References

Articles, Books and Chapters in Books

Ackerman, L., Feeny, T., Hart, J. and Newman, J. (2003), *Understanding and Evaluating Children's Participation: A Review of Contemporary Literature* (Children in Development).

Ang, F., Berghmans, L., Cattrijsse, L., Delens-Ravier, I., Delplace, M., Staelens, V., Vandewiele, T., Vandresse, C. and Verheyde, M. (2006), *Participation Rights of Children* (Antwerp and Oxford: Intersentia).

Arnstein, S. (1969), 'A Ladder of Citizen Participation', *Journal of American Planning Association* 35:4.

Boyden, J. and Ennew, J. (eds) (1997), *Children in Focus: A Manual for Participatory Research with Children* (Stockholm: Radda Barnen) quoted in Clacherty, G. (2001).

Cattrijsse, L. and Delens-Ravier, I. (2006), 'Reflections on the Concept of Participation', in Ang, F. et al. (eds).

Davel, C.J. (ed.) (2001), *Introduction to Child Law in South Africa* (Lansdowne: Juta and Co.).

Hart, R.A. (1992), *Children's Participation: From Tokenism to Citizenship* (Innocenti essays, No. 4, Florence: UNICEF).

Hart, R.A. (1996), *Children's Participation: The Theory and Practice of Involving Young Citizens in Community Development and Environmental Care* (London: Earthscan Publishers).

Hart, S. (1996), 'Children's Perspectives on the Culture: Cross-national Research', in John, M. *Children in Charge: The Child's Right to a Fair Hearing* (London: Jessica Kingsley Publishers).

Hodgkin, R. and Newell, P. (2002), *Implementation Handbook for the Convention on the Rights of the Child* (Geneva: UNICEF).

Olowu, D. (2002), 'Protecting Children's Rights in Africa: A Critique of the African Charter on the Rights and Welfare of the Child', *International Journal of Children's Rights* 10:2, 127–36.

Van Bueren, G. (2000), 'The UN Convention on the Rights of the Child: An Evolutionary Revolution', in Davel, C.J. (ed.).

Viljoen, F. (2000), 'The African Charter on the Rights and Welfare of the Child', in Davel, C.J. (ed.).

Reports and Unpublished Papers

African Child Policy Forum (2007), *Realising Rights for Children: Good Practice in Eastern and Southern Africa* (Addis Ababa: African Child Policy Forum).

Children's Rights Centre (no date provided), *Children's Rights Resource Handbook* (Durban).

Clacherty, G. (2001), 'Evaluation of the South African Law Reform Commission Child Participation Process' (unpublished, Johannesburg: Clacherty and Associates).

Community Law Centre (1999), *What the Children Said ...* (Cape Town: University of the Western Cape).

Ehlers, L. and Mathiti, V. (2003), *Children's Perspectives on Children's Rights in Mozambique* (Cape Town: Community Law Centre, University of the Western Cape).

Frank, C. and Muntingh, L. (2005), *Children's Perceptions of their Use by Adults to Commit Crime* (Pretoria: International Labour Organization).

Hart, J. (2002), 'Participation of Conflict-affected Children in Humanitarian Action: Learning from East Sri Lanka', draft report prepared for the Canadian International Development Agency (CIDA).

Howard, S., Newman, L., Harris, V. and Harcourt, J. (2002), 'Talking about Youth Participation: Where, When and Why?' paper presented at the annual conference of the Australian Association for Research in Education, Brisbane, 2–5 December 2002.

Kjorholt, A.T. and Qvortrup, J. (2000), 'Children's Participation in Social and Political Change: Western Europe', quoted in Clacherty, G. (2001).

Naker, D. (2005), *Violence Against Children: The Voices of Ugandan Children and Adults, Raising Voices* (Uganda: Save the Children Uganda).

South African Law Reform Commission (SALRC) (2006), *Report on Juvenile Justice*.

UNICEF (2003), *The State of the World's Children* (New York: UNICEF).

UNICEF (2004), *Truth and Reconciliation Commission Report for the Children of Sierra Leone, Child Friendly Version* (Graphic Packaging Limited Publishers).

Chapter 8

Restorative Justice in Child Justice Systems in Africa

Ann Skelton

Introduction to Restorative Justice

Restorative justice has become a buzzword in progressive criminal justice reform throughout the world. It is a theory of justice which focuses on the harm caused to the victim and the community by crime, and endeavours to find ways to repair the harm. This is done by bringing stakeholders together in co-operative processes. Reconciliation, restitution and the restoration of peace are all very important features of restorative justice. Examples of modern restorative justice practice are victim–offender mediation, family group conferences and sentencing circles.

Internationally, much of the early work in restorative justice has been done with children in the criminal justice system, a sector which is referred to in this chapter as 'child justice'. Some African countries also boast existing projects and emerging law reform measures which reflect the modern revival of restorative justice. This chapter will explain this 'modern' restorative justice approach within the context of African traditional justice processes, and will provide exciting, cutting-edge examples of restorative justice in action for children on the African continent today.

Restorative justice is both a new and an ancient paradigm of justice that has recently been given increasing attention by lawmakers and justice practitioners in a number of countries around the world. Although it is new as a modern theory in criminal justice thinking (it emerged in the second half of the twentieth century), it is also an old paradigm because restorative justice theorists and practitioners have drawn on indigenous justice systems around the world to develop the theory and practice of restorative justice (see Skelton 2005, 164–203).

Restorative Justice History in Context

Prisons were brought to Africa by the colonizers. It is interesting to note, however, that if one examines the early penal history of colonizing countries such as Great Britain, France and Portugal, they too did not initially use imprisonment as a sentence (Gallinetti, Muntingh and Skelton 2004, 36). Originally, when crimes were committed in these countries, Western law emphasized the need for offenders and their families to settle disputes with victims and their families (Van Ness and Heetderks Strong 2006, 7–9). Compensation was considered to be more important than punishment in Saxon law (Hamilton 1979, 2). Prior to the eleventh century, an offence was not considered a crime against the state, as it is seen in Western legal systems today, but as a crime against the victim and the victim's family. In the eleventh century, however, this began to change, with the monarch and later the state taking over as the main protagonist in criminal matters. This effectively removed victims as major role players in the criminal justice system, and the old processes of settlement or restitution were replaced with meting out pain or punishment to the offender. The punishments were quite barbaric – public humiliation, torture and death. Strangely enough, therefore, the introduction of imprisonment as a sentence was originally intended as a measure of reform, which was enthusiastically supported by the American Quakers (Zehr 1990, 120). Before the eighteenth century, prisons or dungeons were mainly used for those awaiting trial. The idea of using imprisonment as a sentence was linked to the concept of 'penitence' – the offender should spend time in seclusion thinking about his or her sins, thus some prisons in America were called 'penitentiaries'. This approach really heralded the beginning of what later came to be called 'rehabilitation'. It is today generally agreed, however, that prison is not a useful environment for rehabilitation – indeed the whole idea of rehabilitation itself has given way to the paradigm of reintegration (Allen 1981). Meanwhile, the actual purpose of prison has become more about punishment and keeping communities safe from criminals who are perceived as dangerous. It is common knowledge, however, that an offender who has been in prison is unlikely to emerge from there a less dangerous person than when he or she was admitted. The real reason for sentencing more and more people to prison is that criminal justice systems in most countries in the world today are, by and large, retributive in nature. The aim is to mete out punishment, and to deter others in society from committing crimes by making an example of those convicted (Gallinetti, Muntingh and Skelton 2004, 36).

The Western system of justice was inherited by the colonies and was superimposed over, or operated in a dual system with, indigenous African justice systems. In this way, African justice practices were kept alive, though they were not given adequate recognition during the colonial era. During the 1960s and 1970s, there was an era of disillusionment in the field of criminal justice in the Western world. During this period, there was a rediscovery of African traditional justice methods by Western mediation practitioners, with linkages being made between the modern development of mediation and African models of conflict resolution (Wright 1991, 50).

The contemporary theory of restorative justice began to grow from its roots in the mediation movement in the late 1970s, and was developed into a theory of justice during the last two decades of the twentieth century. The original writers were American, British and European. Soon however, an interesting trend began to emerge: in countries with a colonial history where there was still a living indigenous justice movement, this began to come to the fore. Increasingly, traditional justice systems were looked to in order to inspire present day criminal justice practitioners and writers trying to find a better way of doing justice.

In New Zealand, for example, Maori traditions were used as the basis for a new way of dealing with child offenders – known as the family group conference. In Canada, the first nations' people's traditions were drawn on in the use of sentencing circles. Johnstone (2004, 10) argues that in order to obtain a comprehensive understanding of restorative justice it is necessary to 'engage with accounts of its use in historical societies and in contemporary indigenous communities'. Such engagement may help people to overcome the impediment that a Western education and socialization creates to grasping an alternative vision of justice. In Western society, state punishment is the norm, and people educated in this system struggle to understand that it is not the only way of doing justice. As explained above, however, the Western system of prosecution by the state was preceded by systems which rested on compensation and restitution. In many indigenous societies, these principles remain prominent.

The Links between Restorative Justice and African Traditional Approaches to Conflict Resolution

Informal Justice Systems

A search for harmony and healing is common to many indigenous justice systems, including those systems which existed in Africa prior to colonization. Customary law processes are still used in Africa today, especially in chief's courts in rural areas. With the emphasis on 'problems' rather than offences, traditional structures hear the stories of the parties involved and then make decisions regarding outcomes. These outcomes aim to heal relationships, and they ensure restitution or compensation to victims. Symbolic gestures such as sacrifice of animals and the sharing of a meal indicate that the crime has been expiated and the offender can now be reintegrated (Kgosimore 2001).

In many African countries, traditional courts are still part of informal systems to which people take their disputes directly, rather than going to the police. In some countries, such as Uganda, Mozambique and South Africa, there are popular forums which have been based on or modelled on traditional systems, but have grown out of a lack of faith in the colonial or imposed systems (Sachs and Honwana Welch 1990, 5; Scharf and Nina 2001). In some countries, NGOs or even governments have developed other dispute resolution structures that are used as alternatives to the formal system (Shearing 2001, 14–34; Roche 2002, 514–33).

Resonance of Restorative Justice with African Justice Processes

Tshehla (2004, 1) has observed that there is a 'resounding resonance between restorative justice and justice as practiced by Africans through community courts and chief's courts'. In fact, some African authors go further and say that African traditional justice *is* restorative justice. Elechi (2004) comments:

> The African indigenous justice system is community based, human centred and employs restorative and transformative principles in conflict resolution. Restorative justice is negotiative and democratic; hence it empowers the community to mediate in conflicts. Ideally, African indigenous justice systems provide opportunities for dialogue amongst the victim, the offender, their families and friends, and the community. Conflict provides opportunities for primary stake-holders to examine and bring about changes to the society's social, institutional and economic structure.

Bishop Desmond Tutu, Nobel Peace Prize winner, has made it quite clear that he sees African justice as restorative justice. He says that retributive justice is largely Western, and that the African understanding is far more restorative – not so much to punish as to redress or restore a balance that has been knocked askew. 'The justice we hope for is restorative of the dignity of the people' (cited in Minow 1998, 81). Penal Reform International, in a publication entitled *Access to Justice in Sub-Saharan Africa* (Stevens 2001), identifies the following features of African non-state traditional justice systems: the problem is viewed as that of the whole community or group; there is an emphasis on reconciliation and restoring social harmony; traditional arbitrators are appointed from within the community; there is a high degree of public participation; customary law is merely one factor to be considered in reaching a compromise; the rules of evidence and procedure are flexible; there is no professional legal representation; the process is voluntary and the decisions made are based on agreement; there is an emphasis on restorative penalties; enforcement of decisions is secured through social pressure; and the decision is confirmed through rituals aimed at reintegration. Stevens (2001, 22) adds the characteristic that like cases need not be treated alike. All of these features accord with the prevailing understanding of restorative justice, although the developing debates about minimum standards do raise some questions about the need to protect the rights of people going through restorative justice systems, and these will be dealt with later in this chapter.

Law Reform and Practice Examples of the Application of Restorative Justice in African Child Justice Systems

Uganda

Uganda was one of the first countries to embark on law reform to bring its laws in line with the Convention on the Rights of the Child (CRC). The Children's Statute was passed in 1996, and includes both child protection and child justice issues. The general approach is to ensure that families and communities are fully involved and that the formal system only comes into play as a last resort.

In 1987 the 'resistance committees', which had developed as informal dispute resolution structures, were given formal recognition as part of the legal system. The committees were renamed 'local council courts'. The Children's Statute gave jurisdiction to the local council courts at village level regarding civil matters, as well as criminal matters where children are accused of the following crimes: affray, common assault, actual bodily harm, theft, trespass and malicious damage to property. The local council courts can use the following remedies: reconciliation, compensation, restitution, apology, caution or a guidance order of up to six months.

Children charged with most other offences are to be tried in Family and Children's Courts, with only capital cases being tried in the mainstream criminal courts. The Family and Children's Courts are intended to be separate from the mainstream courts and are required to protect children from adversarial proceedings. However, it seems that these courts are not operating throughout the country as yet, and are still being established (Odongo 2003; Sloth-Nielsen et al. 2007, 61). Trials before these courts are not supposed to be prolonged; matters are supposed to be handled expeditiously and without unnecessary delay. Cases, if not completed in three months after the plea was taken, have to be dismissed and the child is then not liable to be the subject of any further proceedings for the same offence. Furthermore, to avoid stigmatization during and after the trial, the Statute proscribes the use of such terms as 'conviction' or 'sentence'. Instead, such terms as 'proof of an offence against a child' and 'order' are to be used.

Furthermore, the legal recognition of the district council courts is a great starting point for making the child justice system in Uganda more restorative, because it brings the victim and offender together in a forum that is managed by the community. The possible outcomes of the forum (such as an apology, restitution and compensation) are very typical of restorative justice outcomes. They focus on healing and restoring rather than on punishment.

A limitation of the system is that it has given very narrow jurisdiction to the district council courts, as it is only relatively petty offences that can be dealt with by these courts. However, the protection is provided at sentencing stage for children who do go through the formal court system. Imprisonment is regarded as a last resort and section 95(1)(g) of the Statute provides that children who are below the age of 14 years can be detained for a maximum of three months, whilst those who are between the ages of 16 and 18 years are to be detained for no longer than 12 months. In capital cases, for which the maximum penalty for adult offenders is the death penalty, it is for children a maximum of three years imprisonment.

Ghana

Ghana's Children's Act (Act 560 of 1998) made provision for the establishment of child panels at district or community level. The panel is intended to assist with victim–offender mediation in minor criminal matters involving the child, the outcomes of which may include an apology, restitution or service to the community. The panels were established by the district assemblies (legislatures) in collaboration with the ministry in charge of children's affairs. Their composition includes a district social worker, a representative from a women's organization, a representative of the traditional council and people from the community in which the panel is constituted. The role of these child panels is to bring about reconciliation between the child and the victims of crime within a community context. The children's panels can encourage apology, restitution from the child and his or her family, or service by the child to the victims in the course of, or subsequent to, the mediation process. The panel also has the power to place a child under the guidance and supervision of a person of good standing in the local community for a period not exceeding six months.

The measures described above have been maintained and enhanced by the new Ghanaian Juvenile Justice Act 653 of 2003. The new Act also allows for the use by the police of (pre-trial) formal or informal cautions where 'it is in the best interests of the juvenile to do so'. Although formal cautions are to be recorded and may be with or without conditions, they must be expunged after a definite period of time. In a similar way to the Ugandan Statute, the new Act allows for the use of a range of alternative sentences, which also allow for restorative justice approaches.

Odongo (2005, 231) points out the similarities between the Ghanaian system and the Ugandan system. Both use community-based structures as a first level intervention, which encourages restorative justice approaches. Another feature common to both is that the community structures can only deal with relatively minor offences. In criminal matters involving children, the panel is tasked with the facilitation of victim–offender mediation in minor criminal matters such as 'petty theft and threatening offences'. A distinction can be observed, however, in the fact that the Ghanaian Children's Act is not specific on the particular criminal offences that may go to local courts, referring broadly to 'petty theft and threatening offences'. The Ugandan Children's Act is more specific, providing details the criminal offences in respect of which local courts may adjudicate. In both systems, offences deemed serious are totally excluded from the community-based processes, and the adjudication of such cases is left to the formal juvenile justice system. At the sentencing stage, however, there are possibilities for restorative sentences, and both the Ugandan and Ghanaian system place limits on the length of imprisonment to which children can be sentenced. Both allow for other forms of custodial sentences in facilities such as approved schools, and, according to Odongo, there is still a heavy reliance on custodial options (2005, 379).

South Africa

Description of Child Justice Bill   South Africa's Child Justice Bill has been in development for a decade. The law-making process began when the Minister of Justice requested the South African Law Reform Commission (SALRC) to include an investigation into juvenile justice in its programme. A project committee was set up which commenced its work in 1997. A consultative method of law-making was followed. The Child Justice Bill was the culmination of this process. It was tabled before parliament in 2002 but had not yet been enacted at the time of writing. South African criminal justice practitioners and activists became aware of the modern restorative justice movement in the early 1990s, and this had a strong influence on the drafting of the Child Justice Bill.

The Bill includes the following as part of the objectives clause:

The objectives of the Act are to promote *ubuntu*[1] in the child justice system through –

(i) fostering of children's sense of dignity and worth;

(ii) reinforcing children's respect for human rights and the fundamental freedoms of others by holding children accountable for their actions and safe-guarding the interests of victims and the community;

(iii) supporting reconciliation by means of a restorative justice response; and

(iv) involving parents, families, victims and communities in child justice processes in order to encourage the reintegration of children who are subject to the provisions of the Act.

---

1   The concept of *ubuntu* is discussed in detail by Himonga in Chapter 5 of this volume.

Restorative justice is defined in the draft Bill as follows: 'Restorative justice means the promotion of reconciliation, restitution and responsibility through the involvement of a child, a child's parent, family members, victims and communities.'

The new system aims to divert as many children as possible, and all forms of diversion rest on children first acknowledging responsibility for the offence. If they do not, then cases will be referred for trial where the children can plead not guilty, and in instances where their liberty may be at risk, they will be guaranteed legal representation.

Most children coming into the system will have to be assessed by a probation officer within 48 hours of arrest. Those charged with petty offences can be diverted by a prosecutor. Those charged with more serious crimes must go to a preliminary inquiry, which will be chaired by a magistrate and will take the form of a case conference, the main purpose of which is to promote the use of diversion. The prosecutor, probation officer, and police official will attend this inquiry, as well as the child and his or her family. Certain very serious offences such as murder and armed robbery may be excluded from the possibility of diversion.

Diversion is a core component of the new system, and the draft Bill offers two 'levels' of diversion. Level one includes programmes, which are not particularly intensive and are of short duration. They rely to a great extent on the family and the community as a resource, with children being referred back to their family under an order directing them to do or not to do certain things. Level one includes an apology, restitution and compensation. The second level, however, contains programmes of increasing intensity, which can be set for longer periods of time. The clear intention of setting out a range of options in this way is to encourage those working in the system to use diversion in a range of different situations, even with regard to relatively serious offences.

Children can be referred to family group conferences, victim–offender mediation and 'other restorative processes', the outcomes of which are determined by the process itself. The Bill includes detailed procedures for the setting up and running of family group conferences. A probation officer has the responsibility of convening the conference as soon as possible, but not longer than 21 days after the decision has been made that such a conference must take place. The persons entitled to attend a family group conference are the child and his or her parent or an appropriate adult, any other person requested by the child, the probation officer, prosecutor, relevant police official, the victim and, where the victim is under the age of 18 years, his or her parent or guardian and other family members, a member of the community in which the child is normally resident, the legal representative of the child and any other person authorized by the probation officer to attend the conference.

The family group conference is empowered to regulate its own procedure and to make such plans as it deems fit, provided that they are appropriate to the child and family, and are consistent with the principles contained elsewhere in the law. The plan must specify the objectives for the child and the family, as well as the period over which they are to be achieved, must contain details of the services and assistance to be provided for the child and family, and must include such other matters relating to education, employment, recreation and welfare of the child as are relevant.

According to the Bill, family group conferences can happen as diversion options prior to trial, or the court can stop the proceedings in the middle of a trial and refer the matter to a family group conference. The court can also, after conviction, send the matter to a family group conference to determine a suitable plan, which the court can then make into a court order for the purposes of sentencing. The Bill includes provisions for the failure of family group conferences to reach agreed outcomes, as well as for non-compliance with the plans arising from the conference.

In addition to the possibility of referral to a family group conference, the Bill also allows for referral to a 'victim offender mediation or other restorative justice process'. The idea behind the wording 'other restorative justice process' is to allow for creative or indigenous models of restorative justice procedures to be developed or to re-emerge.

Family group conferencing   Despite the fact that there has until now been no legal framework to allow for family group conferencing, there have been various pilot projects in South Africa. An important pilot project was set up by a government-led initiative (that involved non-government stakeholders), the Inter-Ministerial Committee on Young People at Risk, in 1997. The project was evaluated and the findings were published in a document that is both a practice research study and an implementation manual (Branken and Batley 1998).

In this project, family group conferences were established as diversionary alternatives for child offenders, with the aim of testing the model in 80 cases in the Pretoria area. This project specifically sought to divert cases involving offending deemed to be relatively serious, such as assault, theft of, and out of, motor vehicles, housebreaking and robbery. These categories of offences were not ordinarily considered to be 'divertable' by the actors in the criminal justice system, who were accustomed only to the diversion of cases involving minor offences such as shoplifting and injury to property. The project attempted to insert family group conferences as a diversion option at the earliest stage of a child's interaction with the criminal justice system by obtaining referrals directly from the police. This too was unusual, as all diversions in the country up to this stage were done through referrals from prosecutors just prior to a child's first appearance in court. However, it was found that seeking referrals directly from the police did not yield cases as successfully as was hoped, and the project reverted to working directly with prosecutors to obtain referrals. Working directly with prosecutors proved to have its own problems. The project struggled to obtain 'the right kind' of cases, as prosecutors continued to consider only the very minor offences to be suitable for diversion. The implementation manual makes the following observations in this regard;

> People involved in setting up and running family group conferences should bear in mind that while restorative justice is the philosophy on which family group conferences are based, this is largely foreign to criminal justice staff, who have been trained and socialized firmly within a retributive philosophy.

The document goes on to say that prosecutors see diversion as 'doing nothing' or as a 'soft option' and concludes that, in order to ensure appropriate referrals, the prosecutor doing the referrals must be fully informed and convinced about the process and value of conferencing. Despite the difficulties described though, the project did manage to process some fairly serious offences, including housebreaking and theft, assault with intent to do grievous bodily harm, common assault, malicious injury to property, theft from a motor vehicle and possession of an unlicensed firearm.

The research study raises some other interesting issues, which are particularly relevant to the South African context, and perhaps to some other countries in Africa as well. Firstly, the project experienced difficulties with regard to interpretation when the victims and offenders spoke different languages from one another or from the facilitator. In South Africa, where there are 11 official languages, it is inevitable that language difficulties will emerge. In a court room, this is dealt with through the services of an interpreter. In the conferencing project, no official interpreters were appointed, and the conference organizers often undertook translations themselves, which, as the research study points out, created problems because the participants in the conference then related strongly to the conference organizer and the facilitator's role was seriously weakened. The research study noted that independent interpreters would be a better option, but then they would need to be carefully trained. However, the majority of family group conferences undertaken by this project involved victims and offenders from the same racial and socio-economic groups.

A more detailed study to explore the impact of race and class in conferencing processes in South Africa was undertaken and the findings published in 2004 (Gallinetti, Redpath and Sloth-Nielsen 2004). This survey found, again, that the pattern of family group conferencing in the youth justice system was that victims and offenders tended to come from similar backgrounds. When they were from different racial or socio-economic backgrounds, however, this was found not to be an insurmountable obstacle to successful resolution of the matter, although the study did suggest that practitioners in South Africa need to work hard to transcend the power imbalances that are likely to arise in family group conferences that bring together people from different races or socio-economic backgrounds.

The sample produced by the project for analysis by the 1997 research study was small, and it is therefore difficult to indicate fully levels of satisfaction by either victims or offenders. Nevertheless, the stories which emerged from the project richly illustrated the healing possibilities of family group conferences (Skelton and Frank 2001). Furthermore, the implementation manual arising from the project has been used as the basis of training for probation officers and non-government practitioners. Family group conferences are now happening in all of the nine provinces of South Africa, albeit on a limited scale in some areas (Skelton and Batley 2006, 115–19).

Victim Offender Conferencing project (VOC)   A group of NGOs under the banner of the 'Restorative Justice Initiative' established a Victim Offender Conferencing (VOC) project which focused on the resolution of disputes between parties that were criminal in nature. This operated in a partnership with three community based organizations in township[2] areas (Dissel 2002).

---

2   Townships are the colloquial term given to urban areas set aside for Black residents under apartheid, Soweto perhaps being the most famous internationally.

The aims and objectives of the project were to provide a safe space for people most affected by a criminal act to have the opportunity to enter into dialogue with each other. This enabled them to talk about how they were affected by the act, it provided an opportunity to answer any questions affected people may have had about the event, and it facilitated the development of a plan for dealing with the consequences of the act and the harm caused to any of the parties. The project was intended to allow the parties affected by crime to deal with the human issues of crime, the feelings involved, and also the events that had led up to the commission of the offence. The project also sought to develop a model that was more familiar to African customary values and that could draw on the experiences and principles of African customary traditions.

The first principle underpinning the VOC is the acknowledgment of the injustice: the offender needs to acknowledge responsibility for the offence before being referred to VOC. The offender is obliged to confront the consequences of his or her action, and see the victim as a person with real feelings, needs and concerns. A second key principle is that of restoring the inequity. This involves a delicate process of levelling the power imbalances that exist between offender and victim as a result of the offence, or the nature of the relationship between them. The third principle introduces a forward-looking perspective, developing an appropriate and concrete plan of action acceptable to all parties concerned. The plan should address the symbolic as well as material needs of the victims, and must sufficiently spell out the future intentions of the offending parties.

The project was set up by selecting and training mediators from each of the communities associated with the VOC partners. They received an initial week-long training course with a follow-up week-long course. Cases were referred to the VOC partners by the courts, the police and the community-based organizations. In all cases the mediators did a screening and completed an interview to establish the facts of the case and the parties' interest in proceeding with a VOC. There was some preparation of the individuals prior to the VOC, and the parties were invited to bring along people to support them. If an agreement was reached at the conclusion of the VOC, this was reduced to writing and signed by both parties. In cases that had been referred by the police or courts, a report was sent to the relevant bodies. In the second phase of the project (the last for which a report is available), 384 cases were dealt with and 91 per cent successfully resolved (Dissel 2002).

Namibia

The child justice system in Namibia is currently undergoing changes. There is a draft Bill, which is based on principles of restorative justice and is very similar to South Africa's Child Justice Bill (Schulz and Hamutenya 2004). The Namibian Child Justice Bill had not, at the time of writing, been passed by parliament.

Despite the absence of an enabling legal framework, there has been substantial work done in the area of diversion. One of the options for diversion is an option called 'consensus decision making'.

This is a therapeutic process which is used at the pre-trial stage, following a referral by a prosecutor. The victim, the offender and their families are brought together to discuss the offence, their feelings, and the restorative effort that each party can make. A Juvenile Justice Project staff member, who acts as a mediator, facilitates the meeting between the parties. It is designed to allow the victim and offender an opportunity to reconcile and mutually agree on reparation. (Schulz 2002, 363)

Consensus decision making is similar in its style and intended outcomes to family group conferencing, and is typical of a modern restorative justice process. The Juvenile Justice Project of the Legal Assistance Centre in Windhoek describes a core objective of its work as being to advocate and lobby for restorative justice instead of retributive justice in cases involving children (Mukondo 1999).

Lesotho

Qubu (2005) speaks of restorative justice being 'revived' in Lesotho 'because it is a common feeling in our country that only the name is new to Basotho [people] while the practice has always been there'. The probation services, located in the Ministry of Justice, began to pilot family group conferences and victim–offender mediation as diversion programmes for young offenders in 1999, with very positive results. The probation service began using restorative justice strategies with adult offenders as part of community-based sentencing. A draft Bill has been prepared (Lesotho Children's Protection and Welfare Bill, 2004) which appears to have drawn inspiration from the South African Child Justice Bill, as well as from the Ugandan and Ghanaian systems. It is based on restorative justice principles and aims to utilize traditional justice structures. The Bill provides for the establishment of village child justice committees, which shall comprise the village chief and six other members elected by the community. The Bill requires that the village child justice committee shall elect a chairperson from amongst its members – an indication of a modern and more democratic approach to community dispute resolution. A village child justice committee can convene an 'open village healing circle'. This is done in cases where there are two or more acts of 'anti-social behaviour', where two or more children are involved, and where the acts impact on members of the community (for example, vandalism or burning of grass). An open village healing circle shall be attended by the child and his or her family, representatives of the village, members of organizations such as youth organizations, and a probation officer (Sloth-Nielsen 2006).

A victim–offender mediation, which can also be convened by a village child justice committee chairperson, is a meeting between the victim and offender with the assistance of a trained mediator. The stated functions of the victim–offender mediation are:

a. to enable the victim and offender to talk about the crime, express their feelings and concerns;
b. to participate directly in developing an option for trying to make things right; and
c. to afford the offender an opportunity to make apologies, provide information and develop reparative plans and gain insight for personal growth (Section 129 of the Bill).

The Bill explains that there are many mechanisms via which a child may be referred to a restorative justice process – the child may self-refer, or may be referred by his parent, guardian or any other appropriate adult, or by the local chief. Such referrals then come directly from the community, and are not linked with the criminal justice system. Police, prosecutors, probation officers or courts may also refer children to the restorative justice processes.

Twenty-two principal chiefs have been trained in restorative justice, and pilot projects to prepare for the new system are already underway. The Lesotho model presents an innovative approach that makes a commendable effort to blend present-day restorative justice approaches with traditional structures. It is also submitted that the legislative proposals are both practical, given the local context, and cost effective (Sloth-Nielsen 2006).

Ensuring Good Restorative Justice Practice

It is clear that restorative justice has the potential to become an important feature of child justice systems in Africa. Although restorative justice has wider application than in cases where children have committed crimes, many writers have observed that when restorative justice is used to enable diversion of child offenders, this has usually worked well and is less controversial than when it is used in areas such as domestic violence. Of course, there were, and indeed still are, practices in traditional justice processes that do not accord with an ideal restorative justice practice in a modern constitutional society. Children's rights activists, for example, would be concerned about the lack of participation by children in customary courts, and they would also seek a commitment to move away from the practice of corporal punishment, which is still widely used by traditional courts.

One further area in which there may be some controversy is when restorative justice methods are used with young offenders who commit sexual offences. In these offences, it is likely that the victim is also a vulnerable person, and care must be taken to ensure that victims are not re-victimized by the process. Another danger is that the seriousness of sexual offences may be minimized, especially in cultures where it is or was common to deal with such matters through the payment of 'damages'. Some women's organizations have fought hard to eradicate such practices. Nevertheless, despite all these dangers, restorative justice processes may still be suitable for young sex offenders, provided there are sufficient safeguards (Gallinetti 2004, 70).

Safeguards may in fact be necessary for many types of restorative justice. Some authors have warned that communities are not always restorative in their approach.

> The idea that 'it takes a village to raise a child' seems to be mutating into 'it takes a village to punish a child' as community members, frustrated with high levels of crime, from time to time take the law into their own hands. A report by the Restorative Justice Centre (an NGO based in Pretoria) records the findings of a field study of four incidents during the year 2000 in which children accused of offences were assaulted, degraded and in one instance, killed by community members taking the law into their own hands. (Skelton 2002, 508)

Restorative justice means giving communities a bigger stake in justice, and their participation in the process and outcomes of justice can make them more aware of their important role in the raising of children. However, when opportunities are created for communities to have this increased involvement, it must at the same time be ensured that children in the system are safe, and that their rights are being protected.

There has been considerable discussion about the setting of standards or guidelines in restorative justice. Experts have warned, however, that care must be taken not to set standards that stifle creativity, or ones that lose indigenous knowledge in the process. Australian restorative justice writer, John Braithwaite, puts it like this:

> While it is good that we are now having debates on standards for restorative justice, it is a dangerous debate. Accreditation for mediators that raises the spectre of a Western accreditation agency telling an aboriginal elder that a centuries-old restorative practice does not comply with the accreditation standards is a profound worry. We must avert accreditation that crushes indigenous empowerment. We should also worry about standards that are so prescriptive that they inhibit restorative justice innovation. We are still learning how to do restorative justice well. (Braithwaite 2002, 565)

Nevertheless, not all processes that are described as 'restorative' are examples of good practice, and children could be at risk. Advocates for restorative justice therefore agree that there do have to be standards in order to provide protection for people going through these processes. At an international level, there has been a concerted effort to develop principles and standards relating to restorative justice. An expert group was mandated by the UN Commission on Crime Prevention and Criminal Justice to develop basic principles on restorative justice. According to Van Ness, it was acknowledged by the expert group that theories of restorative justice are still evolving and therefore the group avoided using prescriptive or narrow definitions that might impede further developments (2002).

The basic principles require that restorative justice programmes should be generally available, and should be voluntary. Such processes are typically used when the facts are not disputed, and participation by an offender is not going to be regarded as a sign of guilt if the matter ends up going to trial. The basic principles place emphasis on fairness for both victims and offenders, and stress that all parties are to be protected from intimidation.

The operation of restorative justice programmes should provide that fundamental due process rights are protected, and that the discussions during proceedings be kept confidential. According to the basic principles, facilitators of restorative justice processes should be selected from the community and should be familiar with local traditions and cultures.

A resolution was passed by the Commission taking note of the basic principles developed by the expert group and encouraging states to draw on them as they develop and implement restorative justice programmes. They should not be seen as hard and fast rules or minimum standards, but rather as a resource to draw on (Van Ness 2003, 165–76).

Ideally, standards should be set through discussing shared values and approaches, and seeing how they accord with international, regional and national norms on human rights. This is best done using a 'bottom up' approach, rather than a 'top-down' one (Boyack, Bowen and Marshall 2004, 265–71). Some have called for a broader discourse relating to rights, acknowledging that the individual rights model favoured by the Western legal tradition may be a less useful model for the setting of standards in restorative justice than rights rooted in a more communitarian tradition, such as that found in Africa (Skelton and Frank 2004, 209–10).

Conclusions

In conclusion, a useful African example is offered that was developed by the Community Peace Programme (Shearing 2001, 21). Although it is not a comprehensive set of standards it offers a simple and practical code of good practice that must be adhered to by members of the Committee that is concerned with implementing the programme:

- We help to create a safe and secure environment in our community.
- We respect the South African constitution.
- We work within the law.
- We do not use force or violence.
- We do not take sides in disputes.
- We work in the community as a co-operative team, not as individuals.
- We follow procedures which are open for the community to see.
- We do not gossip about our work or about other people.
- We are committed in what we do.
- Our aim is to heal not to hurt.

References

Articles, Books and Chapters in Books

Adayemi, A. (1994), 'Personal Reparations in Africa: Nigeria and Gambia', in Zvekic, U. (ed.).
Allen, F. (1981), *The Decline of the Rehabilitative Ideal: Penal Policy and Social Purpose* (New Haven, CT: Yale University Press).
Boyack, J., Bowen, H. and Marshall, C. (2004), 'How Does Restorative Justice Ensure Good Practice?', in Zehr, H. and Toews, B. (eds).
Braithwaite, J. (2002), 'Setting Standards in Restorative Justice', *British Journal of Criminology* 42:3, 563–77.
Cantwell, N. (1997), *Starting from Zero* (Florence: UNICEF).
Consedine, J. (1999), *Restorative Justice: Healing the Effects of Crime* (Lyttleton: Ploughshare Publications).
Gallinetti, J. (2004), 'Diversion', in Sloth-Nielsen, J. and Gallinetti, J. (eds).
Gallinetti, J., Muntingh, L. and Skelton, A. (2004), 'Child Justice Concepts', in Sloth-Nielsen, J. and Gallinetti, J. (eds).

Gallinetti, J., Redpath, J. and Sloth Nielsen, J. (2004), 'Race, Class and Restorative Justice in South Africa: Achilles Heel, Glass Slipper or Crowning Glory?', *South African Journal on Criminal Justice* 17.

Hamilton, D. (1979), *Foul Bills and Dagger Money: 800 Years of Lawyers and Lawbreakers* (London: Billing and Sons).

Johnstone, G. (2002), *Restorative Justice: Ideas, Values, Debates* (Cullompton: Willan Publishing).

Johnstone, G. (2004), 'How, and in What Terms Should Restorative Justice be Conceived?', in Zehr, H. and Toews, B. (eds).

Maepa, T. (2004), 'The Truth and Reconciliation Commission as a Model of Restorative Justice', in Maepa, T. (ed.) *Beyond Retribution: Prospects for Restorative Justice in South Africa* (Pretoria: Institute for Security Studies and Restorative Justice Centre).

Minow, M. (1998), *Between Vengeance and Forgiveness* (Boston, MA: Beacon Press).

Morris, A. and Maxwell, G. (eds) (2001), *Restorative Justice for Juveniles: Conferencing, Mediation and Circles* (Oxford: Hart Publishing).

Petty, C. and Brown, M. (1998), *Justice for Children: Challenges for Policy and Practice in Sub-Saharan Africa* (London: Save the Children).

Roche, D. (2002), 'Restorative Justice and the Regulatory State in South African Townships', *British Journal of Criminology* 42:3, 514–33.

Sachs, A. and Honwana Welch, G. (1990), *Liberating the Law: Creating Popular Justice in Mozambique* (London: Zed Books).

Scharf, W. and Nina, D. (2001), *The Other Law: Non-State Ordering in South Africa* (Lansdowne: Juta and Co.).

Schulz, S. (2002), 'Juvenile Justice in Namibia: A System in Transition', in Winterdyk, J. (ed.).

Shearing, C. (2001), 'Transforming Security: A South African Experiment', in Strang, H. and Braithwaite, J. (eds).

Skelton, A. (2002), 'Restorative Justice as a Framework for Juvenile Justice Reform: A South African Perspective', *British Journal of Criminology* 42:3, 496–513.

Skelton, A. and Batley, M. (2006), *Charting Progress, Mapping the Future: Restorative Justice in South Africa* (Pretoria: Institute for Security Studies and Restorative Justice Centre).

Skelton, A. and Frank, C. (2001), 'Conferencing in South Africa: Returning to our Future', in Morris, A. and Maxwell, G. (eds).

Skelton, A. and Frank, C. (2004), 'How does Restorative Justice Address Human Rights and Due Process Issues?', in Zehr, H. and Toews, B. (eds).

Sloth-Nielsen, J. and Gallinetti, J. (eds) (2004), *Child Justice in Africa: A Guide to Good Practice* (Cape Town: University of the Western Cape).

Stevens, J. (2001), *Access to Justice in Sub-Saharan Africa* (London: Penal Reform International).

Strang, H. and Braithwaite, J. (eds) (2001), *Restorative Justice and Civil Society* (Cambridge: Cambridge University Press).

Tshehla, B. (2004), 'The Restorative Justice Bug Bites the South African Criminal Justice System', *South African Journal on Criminal Justice* 16.

Van Ness, D. (2003), 'Proposed Basic Principles on the Use of Restorative Justice: Recognising the Aims and Limits of Restorative Justice', in von Hirsch, A. et al. (eds).

Van Ness, D. and Heetderks Strong, K. (2006), *Restoring Justice: An Introduction to Restorative Justice* (Cincinnati, OH: LexisNexis and Anderson Publishing).

von Hirsch, A. et al. (eds) (2003), *Restorative Justice and Criminal Justice: Competing or Reconcilable Paradigms?* (Oxford: Hart Publishing).

Winterdyk, J. (ed.) (2002), *Juvenile Justice Systems* (Toronto: Canadian Scholar's Press Inc).

Wright, M. (1991), *Justice for Victims and Offenders: A Restorative Justice Response to Crime* (Milton Keynes: Open University Press).

Zehr, H. (1990), *Changing Lenses: A New Focus for Crime and Justice* (Scottdale, PA: Herald Press).

Zehr, H. and Toews, B. (eds) (2004), *Critical Issues in Restorative Justice* (Monsey, NY: Criminal Justice Press and Willan Publishing).

Zvekic, U. (ed.) (1994), *Alternatives to Imprisonment in Comparative Perspective* (Chicago, IL: Nelson Hall).

Reports, Unpublished Documents and Theses

Branken, N. and Batley, M. (1998), *Family Group Conferences: Putting the Wrong Right* (Pretoria: Inter Ministerial Committee in Young People at Risk).

Odongo, G. (2003), 'Report on the Juvenile Justice System in Uganda in the Light of Best Practices and Challenges', unpublished paper.

Odongo, G. (2005), 'The Domestication of International Law Standards on the Rights of the Child with Specific Reference to Juvenile Justice in the African Context' (unpublished LLD thesis, University of the Western Cape).

Qubu, N. (2005), 'The Development of Restorative Justice in Lesotho', unpublished paper presented at the Association of Law Reform Agencies for Eastern and Southern Africa Conference, Cape Town.

Skelton, A. (2005), 'The Influence of the Theory and Practice of Restorative Justice in South Africa with Special Reference to the Child Justice Bill' (unpublished LLD thesis, University of Pretoria).

South African Law Commission (2000), *Report on Juvenile Justice*, Project 106, Pretoria.

Internet Sources

Dissel, A. (2002), 'Restorative Justice Initiative: Gauteng – Victim Offender Mediation Project', in *Restorative Justice: From Theory to Implementation*. Report of a National Conference held 18–20 November 2002 under the auspices of the National Crime Prevention Strategy. Available at <www.childjustice.gov.za>.

Elechi, O. (2004), 'Human Rights and the African Indigenous Justice System', an unpublished paper presented at the International Conference of the International Society for the Reform of Criminal Law, Montreal, Quebec, 8–12 August 2004, available at <www.isrd.org/papers> (accessed 13 June 2005).

Kakama, P. (1999), 'Juvenile Justice in Uganda', paper presented at a seminar on Juvenile Justice held in Lilongwe, Malawi 23–25 November 1999. Available at <http://www.pernalreform.org/english/vuln_jjuganda.htm>.

Kgosimore, D. (2001), 'Restorative Justice as an Alternative to Dealing with Crime', report of a National Conference held 18–20 November 2002 under the auspices of the National Crime Prevention Strategy. Available on <www.childjustice.gov. za>.

Mukondo, R. (1999), 'Juvenile Justice Project in Namibia', paper presented at a seminar on Juvenile Justice held in Lilongwe, Malawi, 23–25 November 1999. Available at <http://www.penalreform.org/english/frset_theme_en.htm>.

Schulz, S. and Hamutenya, M. (2004), 'Juvenile Justice in Namibia: Law Reform Towards Reconciliation and Restorative Justice', unpublished paper, available at <www.restorativejustice.org> (accessed 12 September 2005).

Sloth-Nielsen, J. (2006), 'Report on the Harmonisation of Laws with the Convention on the Rights of the Child and the African Charter on the Rights and Welfare of the Child: Lesotho' (Addis Ababa: African Child Policy Forum).

Sloth-Nielsen, J. et al. (2007), 'Report on Child Friendly Laws and Policies in Africa', unpublished paper prepared for the African Child Policy Forum, Addis Ababa.

Van Ness, D. (2002), 'UN Crime Commission Acts on Basic Principles', available at <http://www.restorativejustice.org/rj3/Feature>.

Chapter 9

The Impact of International Law on Children's Rights on Juvenile Justice Law Reform in the African Context

Godfrey O. Odongo

Introduction

The Convention on the Rights of the Child (CRC) and other international law standards on the rights of the child have revolutionized the area of child law in all its facets with a clear move from the doctrine of *parens patriae* which, by and large, entrusted parents with rights (rather than responsibilities) over their children, and with the State as the ultimate guardian of children. Juvenile justice[1] – referring to the set of laws, policies, procedures and institutions put in place to deal with children alleged or accused of committing crimes – is part of this revolution.

Predating the 'child rights-centred' approach to the issue of juvenile justice, the philosophical underpinning of the idea that children accused of committing offences should be treated differently from adults has been argued from a number of theoretical standpoints. This debate is mainly captured in views in criminology where juvenile justice theory is seen as being based on either the 'welfare model' or the 'justice model' (although neither prevails entirely).[2]

The point of departure in this chapter is that by acknowledging children as bearers of certain minimum universally agreed standards, the CRC and other international norms on the rights of the child stand at the forefront of the theoretical justification of any issue regarding the child. The subject of juvenile justice is no exception. The extent to which this is reflected in practice is assessed in light of selected juvenile justice law reforms in the African context. The analysis draws examples from African countries that have engaged in the process of comprehensive law reforms that seek to comply with their obligations under international law.

---

1 UNICEF (2004) adopts an expansive definition of juvenile justice pointing out that 'juvenile justice is an issue that affects not only children in criminal activities but also child victims of poverty, abuse and exploitation including street children and illegal child immigrants [often] treated as criminals …'.

2 For a recent discussion of these theories, see Zimring 2002.

Children's Rights as a Model for Juvenile Justice?

The CRC has increasingly come to supplant 'the paternalistic notion of "the best interests of the child" to be protected by the principle that children have a right to express their views and have their wishes taken into account in legal decisions which concern them' (Franklin 2002). This has far-reaching implications for the paternalist basis upon which juvenile justice theory prior to the CRC was based. Admittedly there may still not be practical realization of the CRC's ideals of child autonomy, but it is clear that the CRC attempts to straddle the divide between protectionist (paternalist) and participatory rights. Some of the juvenile justice provisions of the CRC and the trio of non-binding international juvenile justice instruments (Beijing Rules, United Nations Rules for the Protection of Juveniles Deprived of their Liberty [UN JDL Rules] and Riyadh Guidelines) represent a blend of both justice and welfare theories. It is, however, submitted that the CRC and other instruments offer a new model for considering juvenile justice in light of the overall vision of child autonomy and respect for the child's rights. Indeed, in his analysis of juvenile justice systems in modern day Europe, Doek (2002, 524) considers the aspect of autonomy of the child as most important in examining whether children's rights have had an impact on juvenile justice in these countries. Further, the CRC reveals an attempt to move away from paternalistic views of juvenile justice by the emphasis it places on *reintegration* as the primary objective of the juvenile justice system rather than *rehabilitation* (Van Bueren 1995). Sloth-Nielsen (2001, 67) argues that six entirely new features can be discerned from the provisions of articles 37 and 40 of the CRC which usher in a new normative standard for juvenile justice. A child rights orientation has recently been elaborated in the CRC Committee's General Comment no. 10: Children's rights in juvenile justice (CRC Committee 2007). This chapter will analyse the content of new juvenile justice laws in domestic systems of particular African countries in light of the provisions of the CRC, the African Charter on the Rights and Welfare of the Child (ACRWC) and those international law standards which call for children's rights-oriented juvenile justice systems.

A General Overview of some Child Law Reform Initiatives in Africa after 1990

For a number of African countries, ratification of the CRC and the ACRWC provided a climate within which to re-examine child laws (Sloth-Nielsen and Van Heerden 1997). Examples include reform processes in Ghana, Kenya, Namibia, Lesotho, South Africa and Uganda resulting in new or proposed laws which are considered further in this chapter.

The pioneering law reform project is that of Uganda. The product of the reform initiative is the Children's Statute of Uganda (no. 8 of 1996) under which both child social welfare and juvenile justice issues are covered. In Ghana, reform efforts saw the promulgation of the Children's Act 560 of 1998 dealing mainly with issues of child social welfare but excluding juvenile justice. A separate and dedicated Bill on juvenile justice was passed by parliament in 2003 (Act 650 of 2003).[3] Soon after Kenya's ratification of the CRC in July 1990 a child law reform process was started and the resultant product was the Children's Act of 2001 that was passed into law in March 2002.

In South Africa the process of juvenile justice law reform formally started with the establishment of the South African Law Reform Commission's (SALRC) Project Committee on Juvenile Justice in 1996, which led to the Child Justice Bill, 49 of 2002, referred to further here as the South African Bill. The Bill seeks to provide for a dedicated juvenile justice system in South Africa. The South African Bill was debated in parliament during 2002 and 2003, but thereafter lay dormant. A revised version will be debated in parliament in early 2008. Further to this, a new Children's Act 38 of 2005 dealing with matters of child social welfare has now been signed into law, although at the time of writing it is only partially in operation.

The Namibian child law reform process started in 1992 and culminated in the Child Care and Protection Bill of 1996 that provides for matters of child social welfare, care and protection. The search for juvenile justice legislation remains high on the Namibian reform agenda with the redrafting in 2002 of the Child Justice Bill (the Namibian Bill is at the time of writing still awaiting introduction into parliament).

Lesotho's reform process has so far led to the Children's Protection and Welfare Bill (2004)[4] which seeks to reform the whole area of child law in Lesotho, and it too awaits introduction to parliament. Like the Kenyan and Ugandan examples, this Bill includes both child social welfare and juvenile justice issues in one legislative enactment.

The Influence of International Child Rights Law on the Content of Legislation in the Six African Countries

Reforming Issues of Age and Criminal Capacity

Cardinal principles of international child rights law underpin the child law reform efforts in the six mentioned countries relating to the issue of age and criminal responsibility. This influence relates to both the issue of a maximum (upper) age and minimum (lower) age of criminal capacity.

It is significant that the new child and juvenile justice laws of Ghana, Kenya and Uganda and the proposed legislation in Lesotho, Namibia and South Africa all provide that the upper limit of the new juvenile justice systems will be 18 years, as provided for in the CRC and the ACRWC.

The question of a minimum age of criminal capacity is, however, a more vexing issue, partly on account of the fact that international law has until recently been silent on this issue.[5] Article 40(3)(a) of the CRC requires state parties to establish 'a

---

3   In this chapter also referred to as 'the Ghanaian Act'.

4   In this chapter also referred to as 'the Lesotho Bill'. The South African and Lesotho law reform processes are also discussed in Chapter 7 of this volume.

5   General Comment no. 10 (Children's Rights in Juvenile Justice) of the CRC Committee, released in February 2007, does now suggest a clear minimum age of 12 years.

minimum age below which children shall be presumed not to have the capacity to infringe the penal law'. This obligation is reiterated in the ACRWC which is worded in similar terms (article 17(4)). However, these provisions fall short of prescribing a specific age.

Since the adoption of the CRC there have been significant developments in relation to how the CRC Committee has interpreted this obligation on the part of states. First, the Committee has been unequivocal that failure to establish a minimum age of criminal capacity is a violation of the CRC (Abramson 2001, 3). The second prong of the CRC Committee's interpretation has considered certain minimum ages set by states as astonishingly low and hence a violation of the CRC. In an eight-year examination of state reports submitted between 1993 and 2000, the Committee was found to have expressed disapproval of the minimum age of criminal responsibility set by 35 states and found these states in violation of the treaty, while recommending that they review their criminal responsibility laws for CRC compliance (Abramson 2001). Cantwell (1998, 3) noted that the Committee was, at the time, consistent in its criticism of countries that have set the minimum age of criminal capacity at ten years and below. Later studies (Urbas 2000) record that while still not recommending a specific age, the Committee has tended to criticize the setting of a minimum age at 12 years or less.

The third prong of the CRC Committee's jurisprudence deals with the *doli incapax* rule under which children between certain ages are presumed to lack criminal capacity to commit crimes unless and until it is proved otherwise.[6] In its reaction to a proposal that sought to abolish this doctrine in the Isle of Man (under the United Kingdom's [UK] jurisdiction), the Committee was of the view that abolition would be in violation of the CRC.[7] More recently, in General Comment no. 10, the Committee has rejected a 'split' age of criminal capacity that is inherently brought about by keeping the *doli incapax* rule.

The approach to reforming issues of age in the countries under study   Both Namibia[8] and Kenya[9] have retained the age of seven and eight years respectively as the minimum age of criminal capacity with the *doli incapax* presumption applying for children between this age and the age of 14 (in Namibia's case) and 12 (in Kenya's case). In Kenya's case the retention of the doctrine in its original form (with eight as the minimum age) is all the more glaring due to the fact that the eventual enactment of the new child legislation by parliament took place well after the country's initial report under the CRC had been examined by the CRC Committee. In its concluding

---

6   Under Roman Dutch common law, which forms the basis of law in South Africa, Lesotho, Namibia and several other Southern African countries, children falling under this doctrine's rubric were those between the ages of seven and 14, the latter age being considered as signalling the end of puberty.

7   CRC Committee, *Concluding Observations*: Isle of Man (United Kingdom of Great Britain and Northern Ireland), CRC/C/15/Add.134, 16 October 2000 Paras 18–19.

8   Namibian Bill, section 6.

9   Penal Code (Chapter 63 Laws of Kenya), section 14(1). To date, this legislation is the general penal law in Kenya which was in place at the time of the child law reform. The new Act does not legislate on the doctrine, leaving the Penal Code's provision to apply.

observations the Committee had observed, 'the minimum age of eight years is too low.'[10] The Committee did not comment on the rebuttable presumption of *doli incapax*.

In Namibia's case, the reform body behind the new legislation in Namibia had proposed a minimum age of ten and retention of the presumption of incapacity for children aged between ten and 14 years (Schulz and Hamutenya 2004). Section 6 of the first Draft Bill reflected this position. But the result of the government's position is that the common law rule is to be left intact in the final draft Bill, hence a low minimum age of seven and the *doli* doctrine's application to determine the question of criminal capacity for children between this age and 14 years.

An important new introduction is the Namibian Bill's provision detailing an array of options for rebutting the *doli* presumption. Section 93 made provision for more emphasis on proof of age, the onus of such proof being on the prosecution, and upon the need for expert evidence on a child's mental capacity in all cases where this is in contestation. These measures can enhance the doctrine's protective value, especially in light of evidence that suggests that it is far too easily rebutted in practice (Schulz and Hamutenya 2004, 11). Of significance is the provision in the Bill which requires that at the 'instance of the prosecution or the child or his representative, an evaluation of the child's cognitive, emotional, psychological, and social development must be ordered by the court'. It has been argued that the drafter's intention here was to redress frequent court situations where assuming children's criminal capacity was the norm, even in the absence of proof (because of a disregard either of the doctrine's rebuttal procedure or disregard of the doctrine altogether).

A second approach is that taken by the new legislation of Uganda and Ghana. Both new laws provide for (increased) minimum ages of criminal responsibility while abolishing the *doli incapax* rule. In both countries the minimum age was previously set at seven, with the *doli* presumption applying until the age of 12 years. In Ghana, the abolition of the doctrine and concomitant increase of the minimum age were part of earlier reforms initiated well before the process of developing the recent comprehensive Juvenile Justice Act of 2003. A 1998 legislative amendment to the general penal code had increased the minimum age to 14 years in Ghana (1998 Ghana Criminal Code (Amendment) Act). This amendment also abolished the doctrine. In Uganda's case, abolition of the doctrine and an increase of the minimum age to 12 was part of the comprehensive law reforms that culminated in the Ugandan Children's Statute of 1996. Although the debates in both reform processes were largely based on the local contexts of these countries and a reference to comparative examples (see the Child Law Review Committee [CLRC] (Uganda) Report 1992), it is of note that the minimum ages set in the new laws are compliant with the CRC Committee's approach which has consistently called for increased minimum ages of criminal responsibility where such ages are set too low.

A third approach that can be identified is evident in the proposed South African and Lesotho bills (sections 5 and 83 respectively). In both cases, there has been a

---

10 See CRC Committee *Concluding Observations*: Kenya, CRC/C/15/Add.160 07 November 2001 Para. 22. At the time of writing, Kenya's next report (2006) had been considered by the CRC Committee but concluding observations were not yet available.

proposal to increase in the minimum age of criminal capacity from seven to ten years, coupled with the retention of the rebuttable presumption of incapacity for children aged between ten and 14. (It must be conceded that the juvenile justice law reform process in South Africa did inspire the process of development of the Lesotho Bill [Kimane 2004].) The motivations for adopting this position are canvassed in the SALRC's Report (SALRC 2000), and include the (then) jurisprudence of the CRC Committee and, in particular, studies that illustrated the Committee's criticisms of countries that had set their minimum age at ten years and below. It seems, though that this debate has now been overtaken by jurisprudence pointing to the threshold of 12 years as a minimum. In setting the minimum age, the SALRC's approach was very consultative and included the hosting of an international experts' seminar specifically dedicated to this issue, bringing legal, psychological and criminological perspectives into the debate.[11] Setting the age at ten was also linked to the SALRC's desire to retain the rebuttable presumption for children between this age and 14 years, calling it 'a protective mantle' (SALRC 2000, para. 3.10). This view was premised, firstly, on the point that the presumption comes into effect automatically by the simple fact of a child's age and thus once applicable, the onus is on the state to present evidence overturning the presumption. Second, the SALRC highlighted the flexible nature of the presumption. Thus the younger the child, the 'greater the cloak of the presumption' because it then requires more evidence to rebut. The SALRC noted that in this scheme of flexibility, the actual age of the child was an important factor to be considered, while not being in itself a conclusive one. However, there is a further dimension of the SALRC's view that is of significant relevance to other African countries. That is, that it provides for the rural–urban dichotomy and the possibility of children developing and hence maturing under very different conditions, even within the same country. Retaining the doctrine, it was argued, could accommodate the diverse nature of society and differing rates of child development in African context.

This section has suggested that the retention of low minimum ages in Kenya (eight years), Namibia (seven years), and the likely minimum age of ten years in South Africa and Lesotho, is in violation of the CRC. By exposing the non-compliance of these countries' positions with the emerging principles of the CRC, the value of using international children's rights law as a benchmark in examining the issue of age and criminal capacity is evident. Of significance is the common approach by Ghana and Uganda which adjusted the minimum age of criminal responsibility upwards, with children's rights as a main reference point for this development.

Enacting for Diversion of Child Offenders

Diversion refers to 'programmes and practices which are employed for young people who have initial contact with the police, but are diverted from traditional juvenile justice processes before children's court adjudication' (Polk 2003). Although pre-trial

---

11 For an analysis of this seminar's proceedings on the age issue, see 'Report of the South African Law Commission Seminar on Age and Criminal Capacity' (1999) 1(2) *Article 40* 5–6.

diversion represents the earliest stage at which child offenders may be channelled away from the formal criminal justice process, diversion may occur at any stage. In most juvenile justice systems in Africa, the use of diversion remains a relatively new concept, though different forms of diversion became an integral part of juvenile justice systems in most Western countries from the 1970s (Sarre 1999).

Article 40(3) of the CRC expressly provides for alternative diversionary measures over formal judicial proceedings, giving diversion binding status for the first time in international law (Sloth-Nielsen 1995). The CRC provisions borrow from rule 11 of the Beijing Rules, which provides clarity on some of the principles which are of guidance to states in this regard (rule 11.1–rule 11.4). Read together with the overarching principle that detention should be used as a last resort and, when resorted to, used for the shortest period of time (article 37(b) of the CRC), article 40(3) of the CRC therefore calls for alternative, non-custodial measures to traditional criminal trials.

In its examination of states parties' reports submitted under the CRC, the CRC Committee has consistently examined alternatives to the deprivation of liberty in formal juvenile justice systems. General Comment no. 10 elaborates the requirements for diversion in child rights juvenile justice systems, emphasizing that human rights and other safeguards must nevertheless be fully protected. Repeatedly calling for the strengthening of such measures, the CRC Committee responses to country reports include within their ambit the institutions and availability of diversion programmes. Diversion programmes must also comply with the overarching principles in the CRC pertaining to the best interests of the child principle (article 3), the right to non-discrimination (article 2), the right to be protected from cruel, inhuman and degrading treatment (article 37) and the right of children to participate in decisions affecting them (including judicial and administrative proceedings, in article 12).

Diversion in the African countries under study   The history of pre-trial diversion in the six African countries discussed in this chapter is fairly recent. Hence in Ghana, Kenya, Lesotho and Uganda, pre-trial referrals of children to diversion were not formally recognized by law up and until the mid- to end-1990s. Further, prior to the period after the enactment or development of the proposed new laws, pre-trial diversions were rarely used, if at all, by the formal juvenile justice systems of these four countries (Odongo 2003; Kassan 2003).

The possibility for the use of post-trial diversions did exist, by virtue of wide-ranging alternative sentences, which by their nature involved a child's removal from the formal criminal justice system (and from possible detention) into community-based programmes. The array of non-custodial or non-formal measures included orders for compensation, conditional discharge of a child with a warning, placement into parental care and the possibility of referring children to community service. However, past juvenile justice practice in these countries reveals an over-reliance on custodial sentences involving deprivation of liberty, rather than on these alternative sentences. Another consideration concerning the possibility of post-trial diversion in these countries is that it remains unclear whether the 'diverted' children were spared from acquiring a criminal label, one of the central tenets of diversion insofar as it aims at the elimination of stigma that attaches with a criminal label.

In contrast, both Namibia and South Africa have experimented widely with pre-trial diversion. However, even for these two countries, the use of diversion has been limited largely to the last decade (Mbambo 2005; Gallinetti 2004; Wood 2003). South African diversion has been premised on the practice that in the majority of cases where diversion is authorized, the prosecutor withdraws the criminal charges on condition that the child completes a specified activity such as participation in a diversion programme or performance of community service. In a similar vein, in 1997, the Namibian Prosecutor General delegated powers on the exercise of the decision whether to divert a child offender or not to prosecutors countrywide (Schulz and Hamutenya 2004), thereby providing a legal basis for pre-trial diversions, particularly for less serious offences. Further, in both Namibia and South Africa, the range of alternative sentences that sentencing courts may use at the post-trial stage has been a useful avenue for referrals to diversion programmes at the sentencing phase.

Comparison of Namibian diversion practice with that of the South African counterpart reveals many similarities in the nature and types of diversion programmes and methods used (Mukondo 1999). The only difference is that the Namibian diversion practice took off much later than it did in South Africa.

The absence of formal legal regulation or recognition of diversion under both South African and Namibian law has led to constraints in practice over the years. Wood (2003) points out that in South Africa 'children who committed offences have experienced very cautious and highly discretionary diversion'. This is also so in Namibia's case, where Schulz and Hamutenya (2004) note that despite the fact of the Prosecutor General's permission for diversion, there remains a lack of uniformity in the way children are assessed in preparation for decisions concerning diversion, meaning that not all children in Namibia receive the same treatment in this regard.

Although few written accounts in both countries reveal instances of violations of due process safeguards and other children's rights in the process of diversion, this danger lurks in an unregulated diversion system (Mbambo 2005; Mukondo 1999), especially in the absence of legal provisions to this effect. The potential for unequal access and discrimination in referral of child offenders to diversion calls for the need for diversion to be underpinned by legislation.

Three diverse approaches to diversion in the new and proposed laws   Three diverse approaches characterize the new laws and bills regarding diversion. Through 'indirect' provisions, the Kenyan Children's Act holds promise for the establishment of, access to and regulation of diversion. This is in relation to the provisions restricting the use of detention at all stages of juvenile justice procedure, the broad powers of the National Council for Children Services and provisions legislating for a wide range of alternative sentences which can be used to enable post-trial diversion measures.[12] However, the Act adopts an approach that still gives considerable leeway to prosecutorial authority on access to diversion. Therefore there remains an implicit danger for the abuse or non-exercise of such discretion, although it has

---

12 Kenyan Act, 'Child Offender Rules' in Schedule 5 of the Act and sections 30–46, 191(1).

been indicated that the Act may, in 2008, be augmented with the addition of more elaborate provisions on diversion. At present, though, the Kenyan approach fails to include direct provisions on when pre-trial diversions may be used.

The second approach is evident in the new juvenile justice laws in Ghana and Uganda. Both new laws are similar in making provision for community participation and affording a prominent role to village courts or community panels in the adjudication of some child offending cases.[13] The aim of this approach is to channel child offenders away from the formal criminal justice system. Besides, this will ensure that there is wide scope for community-based diversion programmes which allow the child to remain in his or her community. These premises are further explained by the fact that the local courts are legislatively made the courts of first instance in relation to minor offences. Hence, the decision to refer child offenders to these courts does not hinge on the exercise of prosecutorial discretion. In addition, the new Ghanaian and Ugandan laws make explicit provision for the possibility of post-trial diversions by virtue of an array of alternative sentences. This could also be a useful diversion mechanism for children whose cases are not dealt with by the local courts.

The third approach is that represented by the Lesotho, South African and Namibian bills. These bills propose diversion as central to the envisaged new juvenile justice systems. The three bills seek to comply with international law in a number of respects. The bills all envisage provisions which introduce a new pre-trial forum (the preliminary inquiry) to be held at the pre-trial stage with the aim of determining, *inter alia*, how to best deal with individual cases of children. Consideration of diversion is an express objective. The preliminary inquiry is expected to strengthen referral procedures for diversion by involving role-players (such as social workers, judicial officers and police) other than the prosecutor alone. It is submitted that this will ensure the development and growth of pre-trial diversion and assure more uniformity in the process of referral. Secondly, a wider access to diversion is envisaged through provision for a wide range of innovative diversion options by the introduction of different levels of diversion and an array of alternative sentences in the draft bills. In this regard, provisions have been included to encourage the development of innovative diversion practices which need not be cost intensive. This is highly relevant in light of scarcity of resources on the continent and the need for diversion practice in rural areas where formal diversion programmes may be rare, if not non-existent. Thirdly, the three bills propose a legislative framework for restorative justice diversion practices such as family group conferences which, while drawing from practices in Western juvenile justice systems, resonate with African concepts of restorative justice and reconciliation.[14] Finally, all the laws and bills of the six countries considered include minimum standards and human rights safeguards in relation to the different diversion approaches.

---

13 Ghanaian Act, 'Preamble to the Memorandum Accompanying the Act' and sections 25 and 26; Uganda Act section 93 and Schedule 3 (making provision for the adjudicative roles of community-based child panels and village level local court in Ghana and Uganda respectively).

14 On restorative justice more generally, see Chapter 8 in this volume.

One criticism that stands out in relation to the proposed diversion systems in the new or proposed laws of Ghana, Kenya, South Africa and Uganda[15] is the potential for a bifurcated system of diversion which would potentially totally exclude certain categories of child offenders from being considered for diversion. At the time of writing, all these four new laws and bills limit the use of diversion by prescribing that certain categories of offenders (related to the offence with which they have been charged) must be dealt with within the traditional formal juvenile justice system (that is, by way of prosecution and penal punishment).

The Need for Separate Procedures and Courts at the Pre-trial and Trial Stages of the Juvenile Justice System

A 'juvenile justice system' requires the institution of separate laws, procedures and institutions that apply specifically to children in conflict with the law in contrast to, or alongside but distinct from, the criminal justice system applicable to adult offenders.

As noted, an overarching principle of the juvenile justice scheme in the CRC is the rule that the arrest, detention or imprisonment of children must be considered as a last resort, and, if nevertheless ordered, be limited to the shortest period of time (article 37(b)). The import of the principle of arrest and detention as a last resort and, when resorted to, for the shortest period of time, is that alternative measures to arrest and detention must be used at all stages of the juvenile justice procedure including in relation to pre-trial detention. This principle aims to restrict institutionalization in two respects: in quantity ('last resort') and time ('minimum necessary period') (see Commentary to the Beijing Rules, rule 19(1)). The term 'detention' must be construed in the widest meaning possible. This is in light of the UN JDL Rules. These rules adopt an expansive definition of detention as 'any form of detention or imprisonment or the placement of a person in a public or private custodial setting from which this person is not permitted to leave at will' (rule 11(b)).

In terms of the provisions of article 40(3) of the CRC, there should be separate specialized courts that uphold the aims of the juvenile justice system. These courts must strive for informality of proceedings such as may be sensitive to the need for effective participation by children and to prevent the stigmatization of children. In striving for such informality, however, the procedures in these courts must incorporate children's due process and fundamental procedural rights (Van Bueren 1995, 179). States have 'a margin of discretion' whether to establish specialized courts or whether to adopt a different approach (Detrick 1999). Hence different approaches for the determination of whether children are criminally responsible, including the use of specialized (juvenile) courts on the one hand, or adult courts and or non-judicial bodies (such as lay tribunals) on the other, are in keeping with this 'margin of discretion'.

---

15 Lesotho and Namibia's bills still reflect the original South African position of the SALRC (prior to the parliamentary debates) that all cases may be considered for diversion. Despite indications that certain children charged with serious offences would be excluded from diversion, ultimately the version approved by one house of the South African Parliament in June 2008 did not completely exclude this as a possibility in serious cases.

The overall emphasis is to be placed on the competence of the forum and whether its procedure adheres to the aims of a juvenile justice system in international law.

The requirement of separate procedures and courts applicable to children has been described as being 'a means for the fulfilment of the aims of juvenile justice in international law' (Van Bueren 1995, 175). The rationale is that 'a separate juvenile justice system can be attuned to the specific needs of children and can better ensure their successful reintegration.' A juvenile justice system must however be underpinned by the due process safeguards guaranteed in article 40 of the CRC. The first of these provisions is article 40(2)(vii) of the CRC which stipulates the right of the child 'to have his or her privacy fully respected at all stages of the proceedings'. The Beijing Rules (rule 8.1) go as far as prohibiting the publication of information which may lead to the identification of a juvenile offender, and the CRC Committee's General Comment no. 10 elaborates the required standard in some detail. Further, in non-exhaustive lists of due process rights, both the Beijing Rules (rule 7(1)) and the CRC (article 40(2)) provide for the right not to be charged under the penal law for acts or omissions which were not prohibited by law at the time they were committed; the right to a presumption of innocence; the right to be promptly notified of the charges; the right to remain silent; the right to counsel (legal representation); the right to confront and cross examine witnesses; and the right to appeal to a higher authority at all stages of proceedings.

The ideal of a separate juvenile justice system in the new African laws   Provisions in the new acts and bills relating to police arrest and subsequent release procedures in all the new laws under study reveal that the principle of detention as a last resort (and for the shortest period of time) has had considerable influence in shaping their content. This is in relation to provisions on the police powers to use alternatives to arrest and detention, guidelines for the judicial determination and restriction of the use of pre-trial detention, enabling bail conditions and general provisions on the release of children.[16]

The ideal of having distinct procedures that are child rights-centred is clearly evident in the novel introduction of an inquisitorial pre-trial procedure – the preliminary inquiry referred to above – in the otherwise adversarial legal systems of Lesotho, Namibia and South Africa. This also provides an example of further incorporation of international child law standards in these three proposed juvenile justice systems since the preliminary inquiry is not only intended to widen access to diversion, but also to limit the need for detention in general[17] and pre-trial detention in particular.[18]

The new laws also reveal an attempt at establishing 'specialized courts' in all the countries under study to put in place systems that will be sensitive to a child's ability

---

16 Ghanaian Act, section 15(2); Kenyan Act, 'Child Offender Rules', Schedule 5; Lesotho Bill, sections 98 and 105; Namibian Bill, section 11; South African Bill, section 6(1); and Ugandan Act, section 90(7).

17 Through an expected increase in the use of diversion.

18 Through an obligation placed upon the inquiry magistrate to review any pre-trial detention of a child appearing before a preliminary inquiry.

to participate in proceedings by comparison to the formal adult courts. However, there is reluctance in all six countries to establish 'truly' (physically) separate systems of courts for children. Rather, all the new laws expand or redefine the powers of existing courts rather than recommending an overhaul of the system of courts and calling for new court structures or buildings. It is significant that the new laws all seek to give a national reach to the concept of specialized courts in contrast to past practice where specialized criminal courts for children were either non-existent (Namibia and South Africa) or limited to the capitals (Ghana, Kenya, Lesotho and Uganda).

The example of legislative provision to facilitate the creation of one-stop child justice centres in two of the case studies (Namibia and South Africa) points to an endeavour to comply not only with the requirement of separate institutions, personnel and courts, but also with the requirement of detention as a last resort and for the shortest period of time. This premise draws from the fact that these centres will be specifically dedicated to children and will aim for greater co-ordination between all the juvenile justice role players – the police, probation, residential care facilities, prosecutors and court officers, all hosted in one building. An existing one-stop child justice centre in Mangaung, in operation since 2002, has been regarded as a best practice example on the continent, and frequently visited by delegates from other African countries seeking to reform their juvenile justice systems.

The influence of international law is further evident through the incorporation of relevant standards in relation to the ambiance and procedures in the proposed specialized courts, with the need for informality in court proceedings involving children being expressed in the Ghanaian Act (section 16), Kenyan Act (section 188), Lesotho Bill (section 142(3)), Namibian Bill (sections 85(6), 91(4)), South African Bill (sections 50(1)(b), 53(4)) and the Ugandan Act (section 17(1)(c)).

All six laws include provisions enshrining the child's right to legal representation.[19] The proposed provisions in the new bills of Lesotho, Namibia and South Africa challenge conventional understandings of the lawyer–client relationship in order to give primacy to the notion of child autonomy.[20] The very recognition of the child's right to legal representation (in certain cases at the state's expense) in all the countries under study is a landmark achievement, having regard to an endemic lack of legal representation in current and past juvenile justice practice in these countries (Odongo 2004) and in large parts of the continent for that matter.

Sentencing and Alternative Sentencing Regimes

Decisions about sentencing and punishment of criminal offenders (children and adults alike) have traditionally been within the sovereignty of each nation state (Kurki 2001, 331). This is no longer true, as international standards for criminal

---

19 Ghanaian Act, section 22(c); Kenyan Act, section 186(b); Lesotho Bill, sections 139(1)(e), 151–3; Namibian Bill, sections 98–102; South African Bill, sections 73–6; and Ugandan Bill, section 17(1)(e).

20 Sections 151(2), 98(1)(a) and 73(1) of Lesotho, Namibian and South African Bills respectively stipulate that legal representatives should allow 'as far as is reasonably possible for the child to give independent instructions concerning the case'.

justice are now common and cover areas that have no international dimension, falling exclusively within the domestic domain. Relevant applicable standards are to be found in a number of UN and regional human rights instruments. In relation to sentencing of children in particular, the standards in international children's rights law are derived from the CRC and the Beijing Rules. The first set of standards involves the principles which should underpin and provide the aims of sentencing. Secondly, international law places restrictions and prohibitions on sentences that may be imposed on children.

The 'principle of proportionality' has been included in the CRC, which provides that the adjudication and dispositions in the administration of juvenile justice must aim 'to ensure that children are dealt with in a manner appropriate to their well-being and proportionate both to their circumstances and the offence' (article 40(4); see too, General Comment no. 10, 2007). Juvenile justice should aim at ensuring that children are treated in a manner consistent with their 'age and the desirability of promoting the child's reintegration and his or her assuming a constructive role in society'. In realizing this aim, the CRC emphasizes the 'promotion of the child's sense of dignity and worth' (article 40). Van Bueren has asserted that a state party to the CRC which adopts a sentencing policy for children which is punitive and primarily aimed at general deterrence cannot attain this aim (1995, 183). The principle that deprivation of liberty (including institutionalization in prisons, residential facilities of a public and private nature, and institutionalization in welfare settings), if used at all, should only be used as a measure of last resort and for the shortest period of time must also be reflected in the sentencing policy of any state party to the CRC. This principle is expressed in article 37(b) of the CRC and recommended by rule 17(1)(b) of the Beijing Rules.

Article 37(a) of the CRC prohibits the imposition of life imprisonment without the possibility of parole or release for offences committed by persons below 18 years of age. This prohibition accords with the principle limiting detention to the shortest period of time. The prohibition against corporal punishment as a sentence in juvenile justice system draws from the right of the child to be protected from torture or other cruel, inhuman or degrading treatment or punishment (article 37(a) of the CRC; article 17 of the ACRWC; article 5 of the African Charter on Human and Peoples' Rights (ACHPR); article 5(2) of the American Convention on Human Rights; and Article 3 of the European Convention on Human Rights). In addition, article 19 of the CRC provides for the right of the child to be protected against abuse and neglect while in the care of parent(s), legal guardian(s) or other persons who have the care of the child. The Beijing Rules are more direct, providing expressly that 'juveniles shall not be subject to corporal punishment' (rule 17(3); see, too, rule 67 of the UN JDL Rules). In addition, the imposition of the death penalty for children who commit offences whilst under the age of 18 years is prohibited under article 6(5) of the International Covenant on Civil and Political Rights (ICCPR) and article 37(a) of the CRC, and this rule is so universally practised and accepted, it has reached the level of a norm of *jus cogens*.

Provisions in relation to sentencing in the new laws of the countries under study   The new and proposed laws of the countries under study illustrate the influence of international law in a number of respects. In relation to the lack of a sentencing policy for custodial sentences in the past, it is significant that the new laws now provide for, or propose, fetters on judicial discretion. These restrictions are applicable to three main areas. First, there are provisions for new forms of alternative sentences (for instance in the case of Lesotho, Namibia and South Africa), new types of 'community-based sentences' and 'restorative justice sentences'. Second, there is a prohibition on the use of imprisonment (in the laws of Ghana, Kenya and Uganda) on the one hand, or, on the other, explicit limitations on its use (in the proposed laws of Lesotho, Namibia and South Africa). Third, all six new or proposed laws place restrictions on the use and duration of custodial sentences to be served in facilities other than prison. The above provisions in relation to alternative sentences further suggest that the provisions of article 40(4) of the CRC (stating that juvenile justice systems must provide for a variety of dispositions and alternatives to institutional care) were influential.

In addition, the provisions in all the new laws which require the consideration of pre-sentencing reports in the process of sentencing are aimed at making the use of alternative sentences and diversion more attainable, in the sense that the social background and personal disposition of every child would be more readily available to the sentencing officer.[21]

The imposition of juvenile death penalty was prohibited long before the recent juvenile justice law reforms in all of the six countries reviewed in this chapter. However, the Kenyan and Ghanaian positions which allow for the detention, at the pleasure of the president, of any child convicted of a capital offence (Ghanaian Act, section 32(3); Kenyan Penal Code (Chapter 63 Laws of Kenya), section 25(2)) may lead to long periods of imprisonment and even life imprisonment for such children. This is in violation of the principle in international law which recommends the use of detention as a last resort and for the shortest period of time.

All the legislation, or proposed laws, prohibit the imposition of life imprisonment, although the position in the instance of South Africa is confounded by the recent adoption of general sentencing legislation purporting to introduce life sentences as a prescribed minimum in certain instances, and evidently applicable to children aged 16 and 17 years of age.[22]

The prohibition on the use of judicial corporal punishment in all the countries under study also bears further testimony to the influence of international law in relation to juvenile sentencing laws on the new and proposed laws.[23]

---

21 In the Kenyan Act, section 78 provides that the sentencing court has the discretion to resort to an oral or written social background report while considering 'any question with respect to a child under the Act'.

22 The Criminal Law (Sentencing) Amendment Act 32 of 2007, in force from 31 December 2007. However, the latest version of the Child Justice Bill specifies the term of 25 years as a maximum sentence that can be imposed upon a child, presumably including a sentence to life imprisonment.

23 Abolished before the law reform processes in Ghana (by the 1992 Constitution) and by judicial case law in Namibia and South Africa.

Conclusion

Examination of the contents of the new and proposed African juvenile justice laws shows that children's rights norms provide an overarching framework within which these juvenile justice law reforms are situated. This is in contrast to predicating juvenile justice reforms on other competing themes, especially a more punitive and populist model of juvenile justice as witnessed in contemporary reforms in Western juvenile justice systems, which can easily lead to violations of international child rights law.

The discussion in this chapter shows that these African juvenile justice law reforms considered have to a great extent incorporated a children's rights approach to provisions raising the minimum age of criminal capacity (with the exception of Kenya and Namibia), to the legal recognition and expansion of access to diversion, to their recognition of the need for separate juvenile justice systems and to their approach to juvenile sentencing and alternative sentencing regimes.

It is submitted that implementation of the new laws will, however, involve further work in four key areas. These are: (a) sensitization of professionals and the general public on the value of a children's rights approach in the penal sphere;[24] (b) training of professionals such as court judges, probation officers, the police and diversion providers charged with implementation of the new laws; (c) budgeting at all levels of government (national, regional and local) for increased capacity and resources to breathe life into the new laws and ensure that minimum standards are maintained; and (d) procedural reform within state institutions, which requires innovation and the dedication of different officials in the implementation process (Wadri 1998).

References

Articles, Books and Chapters in Books

Abramson, B. (2001), 'An Analysis and Commentary on Issues of Juvenile Justice in the Concluding Observations of the Committee on the Rights of the Child', in *Juvenile Justice: The Unwanted Child of State Responsibilities* (Geneva: Defence for Children International).

Cantwell, N. (1998), 'Juvenile Justice', *Innocenti Digest No. 3 on Juvenile Justice* (Florence: UNICEF).

Detrick, S. (1999), *A Commentary on the Convention on the Rights of the Child* (The Hague: Marthinus Nijhoff).

Doek, J. (2002), 'Modern Juvenile Justice in Europe', in Rosenheim, M.K. et al. (eds).

Franklin, B. (2002), 'Children's Rights: An Introduction', in Franklin, B. (ed.) *The New Handbook of Children's Rights: Comparative Policy and Practice* (London and New York: Routledge).

Gallinetti, J. (2004), 'Diversion', in Sloth-Nielsen, J. and Gallinetti, J. (eds).

---

24 In the context of Lesotho and Namibia this extends to sustaining advocacy efforts to ensure the enactment by these countries' parliaments of the respective bills into law.

Kurki, L. (2001), 'International Standards for Sentencing and Punishment', in Tonry, M. and Frase, S. (eds).

Maepa, T. (ed.) (2005), *Beyond Retribution: Prospects for Restorative Justice in South Africa Monograph No. 111* (Pretoria: Institute for Security Studies).

Mbambo, B. (2005), 'Diversion: A Central Feature of the New Child Justice System', in Maepa, T. (ed.).

Petty, C. and Brown, M. (eds) (1998), *Justice for Children: Challenges for Policy and Practice in Sub-Saharan Africa* (London: Save the Children).

Rosenheim, M.K. et al. (eds) (2002), *A Century of Juvenile Justice* (Chicago, IL and London: University of Chicago Press).

Sarre, R. (1999), 'Destructuring and Criminal Justice Reforms: Rescuing Diversion Ideas from the Waste Paper Basket', *Current Issues in Criminal Justice* 10:3, 259.

Sloth-Nielsen, J. (1995), 'Ratification of the UN Convention on the Rights of the Child (1989): Some Implications for South Africa', *South African Journal on Human Rights* 11, 401.

Sloth-Nielsen, J. (2001), 'The Influence of International Law on South Africa's Juvenile Justice Reform Process', *Law, Democracy and Development* 67.

Sloth-Nielsen, J. and Gallinetti, J. (eds) (2004), *Child Justice in Africa: A Guide to Good Practice* (Cape Town: Community Law Centre, University of the Western Cape).

Sloth-Nielsen, J. and Van Heerden, B. (1997), 'New Child Care and Protection Legislation in Africa: Lessons for South Africa', *Stellenbosch Law Review* 261.

South African Law Reform Commission (SALRC) (2000), *Juvenile Justice Report (Project 106)*.

Tonry, M. and Frase, S. (eds) (2001), *Sentencing and Sanctions in Western Countries* (New York: Oxford University Press).

Urbas, G. (2000), 'The Age of Criminal Responsibility', *Trends and Issues in Crime and Criminal Justice Series No. 181* (Canberra: Australian Institute of Criminology).

Van Bueren, G. (1995), *The International Law on the Rights of the Child* (The Hague: Marthinus Nijhoff).

Wadri, K. (1998), 'Introducing Child Rights through Law Reform in Uganda', in Petty, C. and Brown, M. (eds).

Wood, C. (2003), *Diversion in South Africa*, ISS Occasional Paper no. 79 (Pretoria: Institute of Security Studies).

Zimring, F.E. (2002), 'The Common Thread: Diversion in the Jurisprudence of Juvenile Courts', in Rosenheim, M.K. et al. (eds).

Reports and Unpublished Documents

Child Law Review Committee (CLRC) (Uganda) (1992), *Report of the Child Law Review Committee of the Ministry of Labour and Social Welfare* (CLRC (Uganda) Report).

Kassan, D. (2003), 'Report on the Ghanaian Juvenile Justice System in Light of Best Practices and New Developments' (submitted to Community Law Centre, University of the Western Cape).

Kimane, I. (2004), 'The Children's Law Reform Process in Lesotho' (unpublished paper on file).

Mukondo, R. (1999), 'Juvenile Justice Project in Namibia', paper presented at a seminar on Juvenile Justice held in Lilongwe, Malawi, 23–25 November 1999, available at <http://www.penalreform.org/english/frset_theme_en.htm>.

Odongo, G.O. (2003), 'Report on the Juvenile Justice System in Kenya in Light of Best Practices and Challenges' (submitted to Community Law Centre, University of the Western Cape).

Odongo, G.O. (2004), 'The Birth of a Regional Juvenile Justice Network in East Africa', *Article 40* 6:1. Available at <http://www.communitylawcentre.org.za>.

Polk, K. (2003), 'Juvenile Diversion in Australia: A National Review', unpublished paper presented at the conference 'Juvenile Justice: From Lessons of the Past to a Road Map for the Future' convened by the Australian Institute of Criminology in conjunction with the New South Wales Department of Juvenile Justice, Sydney, 1–2 December 2003.

Schulz, S. and Hamutenya, M. (2004), 'Juvenile Justice in Namibia: Law Reform towards Reconciliation and Restorative Justice?', unpublished paper, available at <www.restorativejustice.org>.

UNICEF (2004), *Justice for Children: Detention as a Last Resort: Innovative Initiatives in the East Asia and Pacific Region* (New York: UNICEF).

Legislation and International Law Documents

Chapter 586 Laws of Kenya.

Child Care and Protection Bill of 1996 (Namibia).

Children's Statute of Uganda, Act No. 8 of 1996.

CRC Committee (2007), 'General Comment No 10: Children's Rights in Juvenile Justice'.

Criminal Law (Sentencing) Amendment Act 32 of 2007.

Ghana Act No. 560 of 1998.

Ghana Juvenile Justice Act No. 650 of 2003.

Lesotho Children's Protection and Welfare Bill, 2004.

Namibia Child Justice Bill.

South Africa Children's Act 38 of 2005.

South African Child Justice Bill No. 49 of 2002.

United Nations Rules for the Protection of Juveniles Deprived of their Liberty (Adopted by the UN General Assembly 14 December 1990, Resolution 45/113).

United Nations Standard Minimum Rules for the Administration of Juvenile Justice (adopted by the UN General Assembly 29 November 1985, Resolution 40/33, known as the 'Beijing Rules').

Chapter 10

The Protection of Children from All Forms of Violence – African Experiences

Daksha Kassan

Introduction

According to the World Health Organization (WHO), as many as 40 million children under the age of 15 are victims of violence each year (African Child Policy Forum 2006a, 2006b, 2006c). The recently completed UN Study on Violence Against Children, that was undertaken upon the recommendation of the Convention on the Rights of the Child (CRC) Committee and led by Professor Pinheiro, confirms that violence against children exists in every country of the world, cutting across culture, class, education, income and ethnic origin (Secretary General's report 2006, 5). It also confirms that in every region, in contradiction with human rights obligations and children's developmental needs, violence against children is socially approved and is frequently both legal and state-authorized.

Many children, despite their vulnerability, are frequently subjected to abuse, exploitation and various forms of violence. This often happens at the hands of those who are meant to protect them such as the state, their teachers, employers and even their families who have the responsibility to defend and guard their children against harm. What is even more alarming is the fact that violence against children occurs despite the entrenchment of various provisions in numerous international and regional instruments, as well as in domestic constitutions, ensuring the protection of children. These instruments and laws call upon governments and others to protect children from all forms of violence and oblige state parties to take all appropriate measures to ensure that violence against children is eradicated.

In assessing the efforts made in Africa, this chapter will examine what the concept of violence entails, discuss applicable provisions in international and regional instruments, briefly sketch the situation in Africa and finally provide selected examples of the ways in which specific African countries have sought to address certain issues relating to violence against children.

Understanding the Concept of Violence

Though there are many provisions contained in both international and regional instruments that relate to the protection of children against violence, there appears to be no universally accepted definition of violence against children. Nevertheless, violence is generally considered to be a violation of certain rights that every human being should have – namely the right to life, security, dignity and physical and psychological wellbeing (African Child Policy Forum 2006a). According to the 2002 World Health Organization's World Report on Violence and Health, 'violence' is defined as 'the intentional use of physical force or power, threatened or actual, against oneself, another person, or against a group or community that either results in or has a high likelihood of resulting in injury, death, psychological harm, maldevelopment or deprivation' (Krug et al. 2002, 5).[1] This definition covers a broad range of outcomes – including psychological harm, deprivation and maldevelopment – thus reflecting a growing recognition amongst researchers and practitioners of the need to include violence of types that do not necessarily result in injury or death, but that nonetheless pose a substantial burden on individuals, families, communities and health care systems (Krug et al. 2002, 5). Since violence can result in physical, psychological and social problems that do not necessarily lead to disability, injury or death, it is noted that to define 'violence' solely in terms of injury or death limits the understanding of the full impact of violence on individuals, communities and society at large.

In the context of violence against women and girls, some human rights activists prefer a broad-based definition that includes 'structural violence' such as poverty and unequal access to health care and education, while others argue for a more limited definition in order not to lose the rich descriptive power of the term (African Child Policy Forum 2006a, 11). Supporters of this broad-based definition argue that structural violence – which includes any situation where a woman is disadvantaged solely because of her gender, for example, being deprived of carrying out a profession or from having a bank account of her own – prevents women from exercising their fundamental rights (African Child Policy Forum 2006a, 13). They argue that these inequalities, which are often ingrained in societies, engender violence against women and encourage men and boys to perpetrate it. However, because it is less obvious and less direct than physical violence, its magnitude is often underestimated.

Violence against children thus manifests itself in every conceivable manner and comprises various forms, namely, physical, sexual and mental, emotional or psychological. It has existed since the beginning of recorded history (Ten Bensel et al. 1997, 3). Physical violence against a child generally involves any act or interaction in which an adult or another person aims to inflict physical pain on the child (Naker 2005, 18). It can include acts such as, but not limited to, punching, kicking, choking, stabbing and mutilation. Sexual violence involves any act or interaction – such as rape, unwanted touching or other unwanted acts of a sexual nature – where a child's sexuality is exploited by an adult or another person for such adult person's gratification or benefit (Naker 2005, 26). Emotional violence involves any act or interaction intentionally attacking the feelings of a child, undermining a child's opinion or withholding affection from a child resulting in an adverse effect upon a child's self-confidence. Such acts can include threats to harm the child, repeated

---

1   It must be noted that for the purposes of the UN Study, the definition of violence contained in article 19(1) of the CRC was used and the definition in the WHO's World Report on Violence and Health was drawn upon. See Secretary General's report (2006, 6).

insults, forced isolation from friends and relatives and the destruction of a child's belongings (African Child Policy Forum 2006a, 11). Similarly, mental violence includes humiliation, harassment, verbal abuse, the effects of isolation and other practices that cause or may result in psychological harm (Hodgkin and Newell 2002, 260). The subjection of children, especially girls, to financial or economic violence and also to structural violence (as mentioned above) has also been recognized (African Child Policy Forum 2006b). Financial violence involves the taking away of a women's wages or other income, limiting or forbidding access to family income, other forms of control, and abuse of power. Economic violence against girls involves unjustly denying them access to resources in the community and exposing them to excessive and exploitative forms of labour.

These forms of violence can occur in various settings, such as in the home or within the family, within the community, at school and in alternative care institutions and detention facilities, places where children work and also in situations where children are engaged in armed conflict. In order to guarantee that children are protected from violence, it is important to ensure that legislation, policy and programmes effectively recognize all of these forms of violence that children may be subjected to, and address them in the various settings that they may occur.

International and Regional Instruments

There are many international instruments that guarantee 'everyone', including children, a range of rights relevant to freedom from violence. These are the International Covenant on Civil and Political Rights (ICCPR) (1966), articles 3, 7 and 24 read with General Comments 28, 20 and 17; the International Covenant on Economic, Social and Cultural Rights (ICESCR) (1966) – where General Comment no. 13 on the right to education addresses discipline in schools and the issue of corporal punishment; the International Convention on the Elimination of all Forms of Racial Discrimination (ICERD) – where the Committee's General Recommendation XV on article 4 states that all racially motivated violence is unacceptable; the Convention Against Torture and other Cruel, Inhuman or Degrading Treatment or Punishment. Other instruments addressing the issue of violence, with particular reference to women, include the Declaration on the Elimination of Violence Against Women (DEVAW) (1993) and the Convention on the Elimination of All Forms of Discrimination Against Women (CEDAW) (1979).

The CRC and the ACRWC

With regard to children, the CRC and the African Charter on the Rights and Welfare of the Child (ACRWC) contain various provisions relating to the protection of children from violence. Of particular importance are articles 19 of the CRC and 16 of the ACRWC. Article 19(1) of the CRC provides that:

> States parties shall take all appropriate legislative, administrative, social and educational measures to protect the child from all forms of physical or mental violence, injury or abuse, neglect or negligent treatment, maltreatment or exploitation, including sexual

abuse, while in the care or parent(s), legal guardian(s) or any other person who has the care of the child.[2]

Similarly article 16(1) of the ACRWC provides that:

> States Parties to the present Charter shall take specific legislative, administrative, social and educational measures to protect the child from all forms torture, inhuman or degrading treatment and especially physical or mental injury or abuse, neglect or maltreatment including sexual abuse, while in the care of a parent, legal guardian or school authority or any other person who has the care of the child.[3]

According to Hodgkin and Newell (2002, 257), article 19 of the CRC goes beyond children's rights to protection from what is arbitrarily defined as 'abuse' in different societies as it requires children's protection from 'all forms of physical or mental violence' while in the care of parents or others. They further state that article 19 asserts children's equal human rights to respect for their dignity and physical and personal integrity, and it is linked to the right to life and to maximum survival and development guaranteed under article 6 of the CRC.

Both articles 19 and 16 place an obligation on states parties to take a variety of steps – namely, legislative, administrative, social and educational – to ensure that no level of violence is condoned and that children are protected from all forms of violence. Usually, a first step in this process involves an examination of the existing national framework, including legislation and policies, to see if they comply with the principles of the international law; and where they do not, to harmonize them with the international principles either through their repeal or revision (Zuberi 2005, 9). These provisions also require states parties to undertake protective measures which should include the establishment of social programmes (in the case of the CRC) or special monitoring units (in the case of the ACRWC) to provide necessary support for the child as well as for those who have the care of the child, and to provide other forms of prevention, as well as to engage in identification, reporting, referral, investigation, treatment and follow-up of instances of child maltreatment, abuse and neglect.

---

2   Other important and related articles in the CRC include article 24(3) – the protection of children against harmful traditional practices; article 28(2) – administration of school discipline in a manner consistent with a child's human dignity; article 34 – protection against sexual abuse and sexual exploitation; article 36 – protection against all forms of exploitation which is prejudicial to any aspect of a child's welfare; article 37(a) – protection against torture or other cruel, inhuman or degrading treatment or punishment; and article 39 – promotion of physical and psychological recovery and social reintegration of child victims of any form of neglect, exploitation, or abuse, torture or any form of cruel, inhuman or degrading treatment or punishment or armed conflict.

3   Other relevant articles in the ACRWC include article 11(5) – which ensures that a child who is subjected to parental or school discipline shall be treated with humanity and with respect for the child's inherent dignity; article 17 – dealing with child justice and the protection of children against torture and inhuman or degrading treatment or punishment; article 21 – protection against harmful and social cultural practices; article 27 – protection against all forms of sexual exploitation and abuse; and article 22 – armed conflict affecting children.

The concept of violence as referred to in article 19(1) includes physical and mental violence, injury or abuse, neglect or negligent treatment, maltreatment or exploitation including sexual abuse. However, article 16(1) of the ACRWC extends the concept further to include torture and inhuman or degrading treatment thereby encompassing all the different types of violence that children may be subjected to.[4]

General Comment No. 8 of the CRC Committee

In order to assist and guide states parties in understanding the provisions of the CRC and their obligations concerning the protection of children against all forms of violence, the CRC Committee recently released General Comment no. 8 specifically dealing with articles 19, 28(2)[5] and 37.[6] This is evidently the first of a series of comments that the Committee resolved to issue related to this theme, following its two General Discussion Days on Violence Against Children held in 2000 and 2001.

General Comment no. 8 particularly relates to the right of the child to protection from corporal punishment and other cruel or degrading forms of punishment, stating that these are currently very widely accepted and practised forms of violence against children (para. 1). It highlights the obligation of all states parties to move quickly to prohibit and eliminate all corporal punishment and all cruel or degrading forms of punishment of children and outlines the legislative and other awareness-raising and educational measures that states must take. Importantly, the General Comment notes that addressing the widespread acceptance and tolerance of corporal punishment of children and eliminating it in the family, school and other settings is not only an obligation of states parties under the Convention, but is also a key strategy for reducing and preventing all forms of violence in societies. This point is integral in the advocacy efforts to prohibit corporal punishment by parents, since many parents feel that it is their right to bring their children up as they choose. They do not realize that by imposing physical punishment on their children they are teaching their children that resorting to violence is the only way to resolve conflict, thereby perpetuating cycles of violence.

UN Study on Violence Against Children

In response to the growing awareness of violence against children internationally, the United Nations General Assembly, in 2001, requested the Secretary General to conduct an in-depth study on the question of violence against children (resolution

---

4   The CRC also, in article 37(a), protects a child against torture or other cruel, inhuman or degrading treatment or punishment. However, this section is focused more on the issue of depriving a child of his or her liberty than on the general protection of children against violence.

5   Article 28(2) provides that 'States parties shall take all appropriate measures to ensure that school discipline is administered in a manner consistent with the child's human dignity and in conformity with the present Convention.'

6   Article 37(a) provides that 'no child shall be subjected to torture or other cruel, inhuman or degrading treatment or punishment.'

56/138). Acting upon this recommendation, in 2003, the Secretary General appointed Professor Paulo Sergio Pinheiro to lead this study. The purpose of this study was to provide a global picture of violence against children and propose clear recommendations for the improvement of legislation, policy and programmes relating to the prevention of, and response to, violence against children for consideration by states for appropriate action. The study was prepared through a participatory process which included regional,[7] sub-regional and national consultations, expert thematic meetings and field visits. A detailed questionnaire to governments on their approaches to violence against children was circulated and children's involvement during each of the regional consultations was also secured.

The Secretary General's report was presented to the UN General Assembly (Third Committee) by Professor Pinheiro on 11 October 2006. This report provides information on the incidence of the various types of violence against children within the family, schools, alternative care institutions and detention facilities, places where children work and communities, and the study found that shocking levels of violence affect children on all parts of the globe.

Some of the key findings include that the majority of violent acts experienced by children are perpetrated by people who are part of their lives such as parents, teachers, schoolmates, employers, boyfriends or girlfriends, spouses and partners; that between 80 and 98 per cent of children suffer from physical punishment in their homes with a third or more experiencing severe physical punishment resulting from the use of implements; that 150 million girls and 73 million boys under the age of 18 experienced forced sexual intercourse or other forms of sexual violence during 2002; that harsh treatment and punishment in the family is common in both industrialized and developing countries, and children in all regions reported the physical and psychological hurt they suffer at the hands of their parents and caregivers; that violence perpetrated by teachers and other school staff includes corporal punishment, cruel and humiliating forms of psychological punishment, sexual and gender-based violence and bullying; and that institutionalized children – whether in orphanages, residential care or detention facilities – are at particular risk of violence from the staff responsible for their care, including through torture, beatings, isolation, restraints, rape and harassment (Secretary General's report 2006, 9–22).

In seeking to provide the much needed guidance for states to prevent and respond to violence against children, the report concludes with certain overarching recommendations. These recommendations include: states should strengthen their national and local commitments and actions by developing multifaceted and systematic frameworks to respond to violence against children; states must take steps to prohibit all forms of violence against children, in all settings, including corporal punishment,

---

7   In total, nine regional consultations were held of which three were convened for the African continent, namely, for West and Central Africa, Middle East and North Africa, and for Eastern and Southern Africa. These consultations brought together government ministers and officials, parliamentarians, regional and international organizations, NGOs, national human rights institutions, civil society, media, faith-based organizations and children. See Secretary General's report (2006, 6).

harmful traditional practices, sexual violence, and torture and other cruel, inhuman or degrading treatment or punishment; states must prioritize prevention strategies and must provide recovery and social integration services to children and their families when violence is detected or disclosed; states must promote non-violent values and embark on awareness-raising activities to transform those attitudes that condone or normalize violence against children; states must ensure the active engagement and participation of children in all aspects of prevention and monitoring violence against them; states must create accessible and child-friendly reporting systems for children, their representatives and others to report violence against them; states must ensure that anti-violence policies are designed and implemented from a gender perspective taking into account the different risks facing girls and boys in respect of violence; and states must improve data collection in order to identify vulnerable subgroups to inform the development of policies and programmes at all levels (Secretary General's report 2006, 25–8).

Of even greater value, the report contains specific recommendations applicable in the different settings within which violence occurs. These, among many other recommendations, include that states should support parents and caregivers to care for their children by developing education programmes that address child rearing and non-violent forms of discipline; that schools be encouraged to adopt and implement codes of conduct for staff and students; that principals and teachers use non-violent teaching and learning strategies and prevent and reduce violence in schools through specific programmes; that states prioritize reducing the rates of institutionalization of children by regularly reassessing placements and that they establish effective complaints and investigation mechanisms to deal with cases of violence in the childcare and criminal justice systems; and, to address violence within the community, states should implement prevention strategies to reduce immediate risk factors (Secretary General's report 2006, 28–32).

The report concludes with a significant remark: it is stated that while the primary responsibility for implementing these recommendations rests with the state, the participation of other actors at national, regional and international level (such as UN, civil society, national human rights institutions, community associations, educators, parents, and professional bodies such as doctors' and nurses' associations and children) is critical to assist the state in carrying out its task (Secretary General's report 2006, 32). From this it is clear that the responsibility to protect children from violence is a responsibility to be shared by all actors within a child's life and thus, no one, not even parents, shall have any defence or excuse for subjecting their children to any form of violence.

The Situation Prevailing in Africa

Like children in the rest of the world, many children in Africa are subjected to violence within the different settings mentioned above. Recent reports of the African Child Policy Forum prepared for the Second International Policy Conference on the African Child: Violence Against Girls in Africa, held during May 2006 in Addis Ababa, Ethiopia, reflect that in the African context, it is primarily girls that are victims of violence (African Child Policy Forum 2006a, 5). This is not to say that boys do not experience violence in the home, family, community, school or at work but rather, that it is girls that are often more vulnerable to violence in these settings as a result of cultural and structural factors which place girls at a severe disadvantage (African Child Policy Forum 2006a, 18). Therefore, in addressing violence against girls, it is important for interventions and programmes to target the underlying gender-related factors in order to reverse this state of affairs. Reports further highlight that it is vital for societies to acknowledge that certain forms of violence are experienced mainly by women and young girls – some of these being rape, domestic violence, incest, domestic slavery and female genital mutilation.

Furthermore, while many African countries have ratified the CRC and the ACRWC, with the result that children's human rights are increasingly a common feature and aspiration of the legal systems of African countries, at the same time, the diversity of cultures and legal systems within each territory has resulted in the retention of legal systems that are pluralistic in nature, insofar as they consist of the statutory law, religious laws and African customary laws. Culture, and cultural practices, are therefore part of the legal framework within which children's rights are enforced, and culture acts as one of the obstacles to the enforcement of children's rights on the continent (Himonga 2001). Thus, children in Africa are still subjected to harmful cultural practices such as female genital mutilation, unhygienic circumcisions, inappropriate initiation rites and also physical punishment. However, it is argued that culture is not static and these harmful practices can be overcome by understanding the reasons for the practice, providing solutions in consultation with the practising communities and by ensuring that adequate social support is given to individuals who choose to abandon these practices, for children are seen as a valuable part of society in Africa (Kaime 2005, 221).

Situational Studies

Three recent studies (Zuberi 2005; United Nations Study on Violence Against Children in West and Central Africa 2005; United Nations Study on Violence Against Children, Middle East and North Africa Region [MENA report] 2005) assessing the prevalence of violence against children in the various regions of Africa (undertaken to support and contribute to the UN Study on Violence Against Children) highlighted, *inter alia*, a number of commonalities.

Firstly, many countries are in the process of undertaking a review of their child protection legislation since what they currently have in place is not sufficient to protect children and is not in conformity with the CRC and the ACRWC. In most countries, legal provisions dealing with children are scattered throughout various pieces of legislation, which may also be outdated. In addition, many countries, such as South Africa, Zambia, Uganda, Malawi, Madagascar, Ethiopia and Comoros, have included children's rights provisions in their constitutions and this is important in ensuring the protection and promotion of the rights of children (Zuberi 2005, 15–17).[8]

---

8   See also Chapter 4 in this volume.

Secondly, it is difficult to determine the exact extent of violence against children as there is a general under-reporting of this evil. As far as violence in the home is concerned (violence in this context includes physical, sexual, emotional, neglect and harmful traditional practices), it is poorly documented and its prevalence is generally not known. The lack of reliable information regarding violence in the home is acknowledged as a gap and a problem by most of the countries and is a major concern for most governments.

With regard to sexual violence, it is noted that this occurs in and around schools, within child care institutions, within the workplace and within the family, especially against young girls. Most countries, especially within the Southern and Eastern African regions, have legislation on child sexual abuse and often it is part of the penal code insofar as an offence punishable by law is created (Zuberi 2005, 20). However, the study relating to countries in North Africa and the Middle East reveal that many countries do not have specific laws that protect children who are subjected to rape. For example, while the penalty may be a severe one if the victim is under a certain age, the rapist may be spared the penalty if he agrees to marry the victim and in many cases, victims of rape are forced to marry their rapists (MENA report 2005, 24). In addition, while there are many accounts of children, especially girls, who are victims of sexual violence, it is difficult to estimate the magnitude of sexual violence against children within the family (United Nations Study on Violence Against Children in West and Central Africa 2005, 2).

Physical punishment of children continues to be widespread within care institutions, detention facilities, at the hands of police officials at the time of arrest and during imprisonment, where children are often detained with adults. Even in countries where the use of corporal punishment in schools has been abolished by law, the practice seems to continue. This is often due to limited sanctions being imposed and few alternatives being provided to teachers. Moreover, the use of physical violence within the families as a form of a disciplinary method is widely prevalent, given that it is culturally and legally tolerated. A characteristic that is shared by almost all of the countries is the belief that children traditionally are meant to be submissive and, in accordance with this belief, physical discipline is seen to be an important and necessary element of child rearing and is not seen to be problematic (Zuberi 2005, 19). For example, in Egypt, research concerning the methods of punishment used by parents on their children indicates that the most widely used method is beating with hands (30 per cent) followed by scolding and ridicule (24 per cent) (MENA report 2005, 12).

Furthermore, it is difficult to identify the extent of psychological and mental violence caused, since the consequences can either be immediate or latent, and it varies depending upon the context and the child's age (United Nations Study on Violence Against Children in West and Central Africa 2005, 2). Thousands of children have also become vulnerable with the HIV/Aids pandemic and often suffer from psychological distress, which is made worse by the stigmatization and discrimination which results in exclusion from the community.

The MENA study (2005, 10) notes that the main factors that contribute to violence against children are: economic factors relating to the difficult economic conditions of families as a result of increased rates of poverty and unemployment; social factors such as dysfunctional families, family conflicts, marital disputes of parents, large families and polygamy; prevalent cultural beliefs which are reflected in attitudes towards raising children whereby it is accepted that some extent of physical and verbal violence may be useful; a lack of awareness regarding appropriate child rearing practices; the role of the media and programmes that encourage violence; and the lack of provisions in legislation that target the protection of children, and, in cases where these provisions do exist, inadequate enforcement. In addition, the West Africa report reveals that many countries in West and Central Africa suffer from war, poverty, illnesses and increasing urbanization which tend to increase violence against children. Therefore, in order to ensure the maximum protection of children against violence, all these underlying factors need to be taken into account.

Children's Voices

In upholding one of the four main principles of the CRC, namely, respecting the views of children and granting them the right to be heard in all matters that affect them as entrenched in article 12, various surveys have been undertaken with children to explore their views and experiences of being subjected to punishment (Clacherty et al. 2004, 2005a, 2005b).[9] What follows are children's quotes from these surveys describing the violence they experience, in the name of punishment, at the hands of their parents, teachers and care-givers.

> I was accused of breaking a tape and my mother whipped me on my hands. (Boy, 9–12, Lusaka Province A, urban area, Zambia)
>
> I was beaten because I had failed maths. Mom made me remove my shirt then she hit me with a belt. (Boy, 9–12, Lusaka Province B, urban area, Zambia)
>
> The teacher got there and wanted his homework. So when I took it out, he hit me on my finger tips with a board duster, and it was cold. (Girl, 9–12, urban area, Gauteng, South Africa)
>
> I went to show her my work and she beats with a pipe and she said I told you to stop writing wrong stuff. (Boy, 6–8, urban, Gauteng, South Africa)
>
> My grandmother beat me. She told me to clean the house and also clean the pots. Children at home played with fire and my mother blamed me for that but I was not even at home. (Girl, 9–12, Lower Manzini Region, rural area, Swaziland)

In addition, children's consultation groups have also featured at conferences in order to ensure that they are able to participate and be involved in a meaningful way in matters that affect them. For example, at the recent Second International Policy Conference on the African Child: Violence Against Girls in Africa, held during May 2006 in Addis Ababa, Ethiopia, a declaration was prepared and presented by children of the Very Important Children's Group (VIC) proposing that governments should adopt and implement laws against all forms of violence; that governments should create awareness raising programmes on violence against girls and boys; that governments and other agencies should give children a chance to participate

---

9   Also see Chapter 7 in this volume.

in all activities to fight against violence and discrimination; that governments should create awareness among the public on the consequences of violence against children by using child-friendly tools; and that governments should enable children to have access to the international and regional mechanisms; thereby informing the recommendations arising from the conference.[10]

Specific Developments

While the information detailed above highlights the plight and realities faced by many African children, various countries have taken steps to address a range of issues related to violence against children, albeit with limited impact. This conclusion reinforces the fact that throughout the African continent, physical violence within the family for purposes of discipline is culturally and legally tolerated. Moreover, despite the existence of legislation and policies seeking to protect children against violence, abuse and sexual abuse, it is noted that these are outdated and in need of reform. Even where they have been reformed, these new laws are often not enforced or implemented.

However, efforts are being made to ensure the protection of children. What follows are examples of developments concerning the more controversial issues relating to the protection of children from all forms of violence.

Efforts to Prohibit Corporal Punishment by Parents

Most countries in Africa, though not all, have taken steps to prohibit by law the use of corporal punishment in the public life of the child, such as in schools, detention facilities and child care institutions.[11] However, it has proved to be more difficult to prohibit the imposition of corporal punishment by parents, given the controversial nature of the debates. Nevertheless efforts have been made to prohibit this form of violence against children and courts have also begun to allude to the fact that this form of violence should not be accepted.

South Africa   In South Africa, initial steps to address parental corporal punishment were taken when the South African Law Reform Commission (SALRC) was requested to review and investigate the Child Care Act of 1983. During this process, the SALRC included, in the section dealing with corporal punishment contained in their proposed draft Children's Bill of 2002, a clause that abolished the common law defence of reasonable chastisement that is currently available to parents.[12] This meant that should a charge of assault be brought against a parent, then such a parent would no longer be able to rely on the defence of reasonable chastisement.

---

10 The VIC Group was comprised of children from Ethiopia, Kenya, Senegal, Somalia, Sudan and Uganda. A copy of the declaration can be accessed at <www.crin.org/violence/search/closeup.asp>.

11 A few examples are South Africa, Zambia, Kenya and Egypt.

12 In terms of the common law parents are allowed to impose reasonable and moderate chastisement on their children in the name of correction.

It should be noted that while this proposed clause did not contain an outright ban on corporal punishment by parents, it (indirectly) had the effect of banning parental corporal punishment. However, the principal Children's Act 38 of 2005, passed in 2006, and the Children's Amendment Act 41 of 2007, passed in December 2007,[13] no longer contains this clause due to parliamentary reluctance to agree on an outright prohibition. The *status quo* remains, therefore, that in South Africa, in terms of the common law parents are still allowed to impose reasonable chastisement on a child, which chastisement may include physical punishment.

Despite the fact that there is no law in place yet that abolishes parental corporal punishment, there is a strong civil society group lobbying for the prohibition of this form of violence and this network is making significant strides in capacitating other child rights organizations to lobby for a complete ban.[14] In addition, they have built strong partnerships with government departments on this issue and are consistently creating awareness on the harmful effects of corporal punishment of children as well as reminding government of its obligations. The prospect thus exists that future efforts to enact a legal prohibition may succeed.

Southern Sudan　　The Interim Constitution of Southern Sudan of 2005 includes a clause that prohibits the use of corporal punishment by parents. This development came about following the appointment, by the government of Southern Sudan, of technical drafters to draft a constitution for Southern Sudan in 2005. In order to guarantee the rights of children, the technical drafters included a particular section devoted to the rights of children. In recognizing that children need to be protected from all forms of violence even that which is imposed in the name of correction by parents and others, this section includes a clause which particularly states:

> … every child has a right to be free from corporal punishment and cruel and inhuman treatment from any person including parents, school administrations and other institutions …[15]

Southern Sudan is thus the first country in Africa to ban parental corporal punishment.[16]

13　The process by which the Bill was split and passed in two phases, and the reasons for this, are more fully described in Chapter 16 in this volume.

14　These include Resources Aimed at the Prevention of Child Abuse and Neglect (RAPCAN), Community Law Centre, Trauma Centre, Quaker Peace Centre, South African Human Rights Commission, Childline and the Centre for Child Law.

15　Section 21(f). This information was obtained from a legal expert who was part of the deliberations and drafting process.

16　Though it must be mentioned that the Children's Bill of South Sudan, which is in the process of becoming law, does not in article 20(c) include 'parents' in the category of persons that are prohibited from imposing corporal punishment on children and this omission could be seen as a retrogressive step in light of the constitutional provision. However, it could be argued that the term 'any other person in any other place …' would cover parents and thus they are also prohibited from subjecting a child to corporal punishment. The content of this draft clause is on file with the author.

Kenya   A recent case in Kenya has affirmed the child's right to be protected from torture, cruel treatment and punishment even where the perpetrator is the child's own parent (Odongo 2005). In the case of *Isaac Mwangi Wachira* v *Republic High Court of Kenya* (Nakuru), the appellant was charged and convicted in the lower court with the offence of subjecting a child to torture contrary to section 18(1) read with section 20 of the Children's Act 8 of 2001. The prosecution alleged that the appellant wilfully subjected his three-year-old daughter to torture by pinching her with fingernails on the face, ears, back and thighs, allegedly to punish her. Following his conviction and sentence, the accused then appealed to the High Court for a review of the sentence of three years imprisonment on the basis that the Children's Act provides for a maximum custodial sentence of one year.

It is of note that on review, the High Court expressly rejected the appellant's argument that he was merely a parent disciplining his child, which was argued to be a factor in mitigation of sentence. The High Court made the observation that the 'appellant had no justification in injuring the complainant, his own daughter'. Further, the Court reasoned that the appellant 'could not be said to have been disciplining a child of three years'. At the same time, 'the child could not be said to have been at fault to deserve the punishment that was meted out to her by the appellant ...'. Even though the High Court set aside the sentence of three years imprisonment that had been imposed by the lower court (replacing it with a sentence of one year of imprisonment), the Court was unequivocal in disapproving of the conduct of the appellant.

This case is significant in that even though, due to its unique facts, the High Court's judgment does not amount to a judicial ban on corporal punishment by Kenyan parents, it affirms the provisions of the Children's Act in relation to the right of children to be protected from torture, cruel and inhuman and degrading treatment (Odongo 2005). The case asserts that private individuals, including a child's own parent, can commit torture, cruel treatment or punishment under the pretext of parental discipline; it confirms the power of Kenyan courts to judicially subject the status of corporal punishment by parents to scrutiny and the case brings to the fore a need for an explicit legislative ban on corporal punishment by parents.

Other Forms of Degrading or Humiliating Treatment or Punishment

There is concern that the prohibition of corporal punishment results in its substitution with other forms of degrading or humiliating treatment or punishment such as verbal, emotional or psychological abuse or the deprivation of food. In recognizing this, countries such as South Africa have included in regulations that children should, in addition to having the right to be free from physical punishment, have the right to be protected from all forms of emotional, physical, sexual and verbal abuse.[17] Further, civil society groups have included in their advocacy and lobbying activities motivation that children be protected from these forms of punishment.

---

17 Regulations to Child Care Act 74 of 1983, Government notice R416, 31 March 1998. Regulation 30A(2) and 31A(2).

In Zambia, in a hand book entitled *How to Run a Child Care Facility* compiled by the Ministry of Community Development and Social Services Department of Social Welfare, it is stated that disciplining children should be done in accordance with the child's individual needs and development and should not include harsh, cruel or unusual treatment such as corporal punishment, shouting or threatening or abusive language (2004, 12). These examples provide evidence of a growing recognition that, even when not subjected to physical punishment, children can be abused in other ways which can have the same if not greater damaging effects and that they therefore need to be protected.

Sexual Violence

While most countries have legislation in place criminalizing sexual violence, there is recognition and acknowledgment that these are frequently outdated and in need of reform, in order to address the appalling realities of sexual violence against women and children, including boys, that occurs today. Thus, a number of countries, such as South Africa, Kenya and Namibia, have embarked on law reform processes to bring their sexual offences legislation up to date and in line with international and regional obligations. Of significance is the fact that in many jurisdictions, the common law crime of rape could only be committed by a male upon a female through sexual intercourse involving vaginal penetration. In order to grant both boys and girls equal protection of the law, the definition of rape has been amended in order to make it gender-neutral so that males are also protected against this crime and other forms of penetration, such as anal penetration, are also covered under the definition of rape.[18]

In this regard, it is noteworthy to mention how the South African courts have been proactive in protecting the rights of children even in the absence of legislation. For example, in the case of *S v Masiya*, the High Court made an order declaring the common law definition of rape to be unconstitutional. In this matter an accused was charged in a lower court for rape. The lower court found that the evidence established that the accused had had non-consensual, anal sexual intercourse with the complainant, a nine-year-old girl, but had not had vaginal sexual intercourse. Although the evidence did not support a common law charge of rape, the magistrate nevertheless convicted the accused of rape and stopped the proceedings to refer the matter to the High Court for sentencing. In convicting the accused of rape, the magistrate expressed the view that the common law definition of rape was archaic and discriminated arbitrarily with reference to which form of sexual penetration was to be regarded as most serious. Such discrimination, he found, was illogical, unjust, irrational and unconstitutional (para. 1 of the editors summary). At the High Court hearing, the judge held that the reasons given by the magistrate were cogent and that the common law ought to be developed by extending the definition of rape. The Court made an order declaring the common law definition of rape as it then stood to be unconstitutional. The definition of rape was extended to include acts

---

18 See Criminal Law (Sexual Offences and Related Matters) Amendment Act, 32 of 2007, promulgated on 16 December 2007.

of non-consensual sexual penetration of the male penis into the vagina or the anus of another person. Subsequently, this extension of the common law was confirmed in the Constitutional Court (on 10 May 2007). The above example illustrates how courts have been proactive in ensuring children are protected from all forms of violence and further illustrates their willingness to create a child rights-based set of legal precedents that ultimately gives effect to international and constitutional mandates.

Conclusion

Violence against children is a violation of their human rights and impedes their development. In order to address and combat violence against children, various measures are required. While the enactment of legislation is one way of addressing violence against children, this is not enough to eradicate all forms of violence against children. Of greater importance is the enforcement and implementation of this legislation and the need for education and awareness raising across all levels on the harmful effects of all forms of violence against children. In addition, systems for reporting incidents of violence should be established and resources must be allocated to ensure that services are provided for children who are subjected to violence. It is noteworthy in this regard that hotlines for reporting of abuse are being established in several countries in Africa, including Malawi and Kenya. It is ultimately the State's responsibility to ensure that children are protected against violence, through the drafting and implementation of adequate laws and policies and the allocation of resources to implement programmes aimed at combating violence against children. However, as indicated in the UN Study, the assistance of a range of other actors is critical in protecting children against all forms of violence, and this places duties upon the whole of society.

References

Articles, Books and Chapters in Books

Helfer, M.E., Kempe, R.S. and Krugman, R.D. (eds) (1997), *The Battered Child*, 5th edn (Chicago, IL: University of Chicago Press).
Himonga, C. (2001), 'Implementing the Rights of the Child in African Legal Systems: The *Mthembu* Journey in Search of Justice', *The International Journal of Children's Rights* 9:2, 90.
Hodgkin, R. and Newell, P. (2002), *Implementation Handbook for the Convention on the Rights of the Child* (New York: UNICEF).
Kaime, T. (2005), 'The Convention on the Rights of the Child and the Cultural Legitimacy of Children's Rights in Africa: Some Reflections', *African Human Rights Law Journal* 5:2, 221.
Ten Bensel, R.W., Rheinberger, M.M. and Radbill, S. (1997), 'Children in a World of Violence: The Roots of Child Maltreatment', in Helfer, M.E., Kempe, R.S. and Krugman, R.D. (eds).

Reports and Unpublished Documents

African Child Policy Forum (2006a), *Born to High Risk: Violence Against Girls in Africa*, prepared for the Second International Policy Conference on the African Child: Violence Against Girls in Africa.

African Child Policy Forum (2006b), *Violence Against Girls within the Community in Africa*, report prepared for the Second International Policy Conference on the African Child: Violence Against Girls in Africa.

African Child Policy Forum (2006c), *Violence Against Girls in Africa: A Retrospective Survey in Ethiopia, Kenya and Uganda*, report prepared for the Second International Policy Conference on the African Child: Violence Against Girls in Africa.

Clacherty, G., Donald, D. and Clacherty, A. (2004), *What South African Children Say About Corporal Punishment: Summary Report of a Qualitative Survey* (Commissioned by Save the Children, Sweden).

Clacherty, G., Donald, D. and Clacherty, A. (2005a), *Zambian Children's Experience of Corporal Punishment: A Quantitative and Qualitative Survey* (Commissioned by Save the Children, Sweden).

Clacherty, A., Donald, D. and Clacherty, A. (2005b), *Children's Experiences of Punishment in Swaziland: A Quantitative and Qualitative Survey* (Commissioned by Save the Children, Sweden).

CRC Committee (2006), 'General Comment No. 8: The Right of the Child to Protection from Corporal Punishment and Other Cruel or Degrading Forms of Punishment', CRC/C/GC/8 (Advanced unedited version).

Krug, E.G. et al. (eds) (2002), *World Report on Violence and Health* (Geneva: World Health Organization).

Naker, D. (2005), *Violence Against Children: The Voices of Ugandan Children and Adults* (Raising Voices and Save the Children, Uganda).

Odongo, G. (2005), 'Kenyan Law on Corporal Punishment by Parents', *Article 19* 7:1.

Secretary General's report of the independent expert for the United Nations Study on Violence Against Children (2006), 61st session, United Nations General Assembly (A/61/299).

United Nations Study on Violence Against Children, Regional Report, Middle East and North Africa Region (MENA report) (2005).

United Nations Study on Violence Against Children in West and Central Africa (2005).

Zambia Ministry of Community Development and Social Services (2004), *How to Run a Child Care Facility*, handbook extracted from UNICEF Zambia Minimum Standards of Care report.

Zuberi, F. (2005), *Assessment of Violence Against Children in the Eastern and Southern Africa Region: Results of an Initial Desk Review for the UN Secretary General's Study on Violence Against Children* (Nairobi: UNICEF/ESARO).

Cases

Isaac Mwangi Wachira v *Republic High Court of Kenya* (Nakuru) Criminal
    Application, 185 of 2004, unreported.
S v *Masiya* 2006 (11) BCLR 1377 (T).

Chapter 11

The Protection of Refugee Children Under the African Human Rights System: Finding Durable Solutions in International Law

Thoko Kaime

Introduction

At least 23 countries in Africa are either engaged in some form of armed conflict or are just emerging from one. The violence in Darfur, the never-ending lawlessness in Somalia and the on-going civil wars in the Sahrawi Republic, Uganda, Côte d'Ivoire and Chad as well as the recent history of violence in the Democratic Republic of Congo, and the Manu River states of Sierra Leone, Liberia and Guinea make Africa one of the most unstable continents on the globe. Additionally, political instability in states such as Zimbabwe, Rwanda, Burundi, Central African Republic, Ethiopia and Eritrea has caused massive social dislocation, resulting in the movement of people seeking refuge from the dangerous situations in which they find themselves. At the end of 2005, the total number of people in Africa who had sought refuge in a country other than their own was estimated at approximately 2.6 million (UNHCR 2006), whilst the total number of internally displaced persons (IDPs) numbered a little over 12 million (Internal Displacement Monitoring Centre 2006, 51). However, although these forced movements affect all the members of the population, their impact on children is disproportionate. The United Nations High Commissioner for Refugees (UNHCR) estimates that of the people who had crossed frontiers to escape, almost 45 per cent were children under the age of 18, whilst up to 60 per cent of IDPs were children.[1] Due to the factors such as their young age or, in some cases, the absence of a guardian, refugee children face a myriad of risks over and above those faced by other refugees.[2] These risks include unlawful military recruitment, sexual exploitation and abuse, child labour, denial of access to education and basic assistance, and even death.[3] Due to their heightened vulnerability, it has always been

---

1 Internal Displacement Monitoring Centre 2006. For ease of reference, refugee and internally displaced children will in this chapter be collectively referred to as 'refugee children'.

2 UNHCR 2002; see also UN General Assembly 2002 and 2000.

3 UN General Assembly 2001, para. 6. See also LeBlanc (1996, 404) who notes that '[t]hey are a group of children most likely to lack survival amenities and to have their basic rights violated. When resources are scarce, they are the first to die too.'

accepted that refugee children require a raised level of protection and assistance in order to find durable solutions for their particularly tragic situation.

However, despite the existence of multitudes of refugee children on the continent and the recognition of their vulnerable status, the African human rights system did not initially provide for a special protection regime for addressing their particular plight. Refugee protection under the African system was sourced from the Organization of African Unity (OAU) Convention Governing the Specific Aspects of Refugee Problems in Africa and the African Charter on Human and Peoples' Rights (ACHPR). But these instruments failed to provide special protection to refugee children and the result was that their protection was left to the vicissitudes of goodwill (or lack thereof) from the host states and international refugee organizations. The entry into force of the African Charter on the Rights and Welfare of the Child (ACRWC)[4] brought fundamental and profound changes in the protection of children generally and refugee children especially (see the discussion in the section below entitled 'Primary Considerations for Refugee Children'). Although the ACRWC's provisions relating to protection of refugee children are substantially similar to that of the Convention on the Rights of the Child (CRC), its strength lies in the extension of protection to internally displaced children, something which the CRC does not provide, and in the formal interrelationships that it creates between itself and other authoritative international instruments.[5]

This chapter analyses the normative framework for the protection of refugee children under the ACRWC. It examines the relevance to refugee children of the underpinning principles especially in relation to the primary responses for assisting and protecting such children. Finally, the role of complementary rights of identity, protection and support are examined. The chapter argues that whilst the ACRWC lays down an effective framework for the promotion and protection of refugee children's rights, the policy and practice at both the regional and national level lacks the sophistication demonstrated by the Charter. It is concluded that given the resource deficiencies prevalent in many African nations, effective protection of refugee children will be possible only if states ensure the rights and protections guaranteed under the Charter for their own children and if they co-operate with international organizations or other governments in assisting refugee children.

General Principles of Protection

Although the rights and duties in the ACRWC cover almost every aspect of a child's life, there are four principles that are so fundamental that they may be thought of as underpinning the entire Charter. As with the CRC, these include the rule against

---

4   Adopted 1990 (entered into force 29 November 1999) OAU Doc.CAB/LEG/24.9/49 (1990). For comparative discussions on the Charter, see Chirwa 2002, 157; Viljoen 1998, 199; Kamchedzera 1996, 549; Viljoen 2000.

5   The interpretative provision of the Charter sanctions the supervisory body (the African Committee of Experts on the Rights and Welfare of the Child [ACERWC]) to draw inspiration from international human rights law and other international instruments such as the CRC (article 46).

non-discrimination, the 'best interests' rule, the right to survival and development, and the rule requiring the child's participation.[6] Since these are crosscutting principles, they apply to all considerations relating to the protection of refugee children.

Non-discrimination

Article 3 of the ACRWC guarantees every child the enjoyment of the rights set forth in it without discrimination (see also CRC Committee 2005, para. 18). This provision obligates state parties to ensure to *all* children within their jurisdiction the rights guaranteed in the Charter. This not only implies that states must prevent discrimination, but that they must also ensure the positive enjoyment of the rights which enable children to be recognized as equally valuable members of the society. Every child within a state's jurisdiction thus holds all the rights guaranteed under the ACRWC without regard to political opinion,[7] citizenship, immigration status or any other status (Chimni 2000, 200).

In relation to refugee children, the ACRWC is even more unequivocal and obligates states to ensure that necessary measures are taken to enable refugee children enjoy the rights set forth in the Charter as well as other international human rights instruments to which the states are parties (art 23(1)). Thus, refugee children are entitled to the enjoyment of the full range of the rights contained in the Charter. (In contrast, the 1951 Refugee Convention does not provide exhaustive protection against discrimination. The preamble merely affirms 'the principle that human beings shall enjoy fundamental rights and freedoms without discrimination' (preamble para. 1). However, the substantive provisions relating to entitlements water down this affirmation and allow states to discriminate between 'citizens' and 'nationals of a foreign country' such as refugees (article 3) and since the OAU Refugee Convention was merely intended to supplement the 1951 Refugee Convention, it does not even address the issue. Thus under this framework, states were allowed to discriminate between refugee children and citizen children notwithstanding the vulnerability of the former.) By ensuring the non-discrimination of refugee children, the ACRWC has moved the level of protection to a higher plane. It is submitted that this approach takes into cognizance the vulnerability and special needs of the refugee child. Such an approach also augurs well with the 'best interests' approach.

Thus, in situations like that in Darfur where Janjaweed militias systematically rape and murder Darfuri children on the basis of ethnic affiliation, the government is clearly failing in its obligations to ensure that discrimination is not visited upon refugee children. The situation in Darfur also mirrors the 1994 Rwanda genocide where government-sponsored Hutu extremists orchestrated the mass rape of Tutsi women and girls. Clearly, where the government explicitly or implicitly supports murderous discriminatory action against individuals within its territory, it will fail its duty to provide protection for refugee children within the group.

---

6   Viljoen (1998, 219) argues that '[t]he African Children's Charter is best understood with reference to three anchoring principles: the best interests of the child, the principle of non-discrimination, and the primacy of the Charter over harmful cultural practices and customs.'

7   This ground is especially important for the protection of internally displaced children who may become victims due to their association with a particular political group.

Best Interests of the Child

Article 4 of the ACRWC provides that in all actions affecting the child, the primary consideration shall be the best interests of the child. This obligation, however, does not entail the adoption of a paternalistic attitude on the part of authorities, parents or guardians (Van Bueren 1995, 47). Since the list of factors competing 'for the core of the child's best interests is almost endless and will vary depending on each particular factual situation' (Steinbock 1996, 31), the provision requires and indeed demands that careful and objective assessment of the child's competing needs are made (Alston 1994, 7–14).

In relation to refugee children, the best interests of the child require that durable solutions be found as quickly as possible (Van Bueren 1995, 365). Durable solutions are those which positively contribute to the refugee child's survival, protection and development (Goodwin-Gill 1996, 100) and encompass considerations such as the child's need for 'bodily and mental health, normal intellectual development, adequate material security, stable and non-superficial interpersonal relationships and a fair degree of liberty' (Wolfmann 1992, 7). It requires the comprehensive assessment of the child's identity, including his/her nationality, upbringing, ethnic, cultural and linguistic particulars as well as vulnerabilities. In short, the state is bound to facilitate the quickest possible normalization of the child's situation (Goodwin-Gill 1996).

The OAU Convention and the 1951 Refugee Convention did not have any provisions requiring adherence to the best interests principle. This lacuna left the discretion of dealing with refugee children to the host state and led to inconsistent and often harsh practices in the treatment of refugee children, particularly those that were unaccompanied. By championing the best interests approach, the ACRWC has prescribed a uniform standard relating to the treatment of refugee children and African states that are parties to the Charter must ensure that they comply with this standard.

Survival and Development

Article 5(1) of the ACRWC provides that every child has an inherent right to life and that this right must be protected by law. Article 5(2) complements the recognition of this right by obliging states to ensure to the maximum extent possible the survival, protection and development of the child. Since the right to life and the right to survival are essential preconditions to the enjoyment of any of the rights protected in the ACRWC, they apply in all considerations relating to the promotion and protection of the rights and welfare of the child. In other words, the right to survival and development is a general principle that serves to reinforce the *raison d'etre* of each right enshrined in the Charter.

The survival and development principle enunciated in article 5 engenders two separate but closely related concepts, namely: the right to survival and the right to development. The right to survival encapsulates the right to life in both its civil and political as well as its social, economic and cultural aspects. In this regard, states parties are required to adopt appropriate measures aimed at increasing life expectancy and lowering infant mortality, as well as instituting prohibitions against the death penalty, extralegal, arbitrary or summary executions, and situations of enforced disappearance. States parties' actions should promote a life of human dignity. In other words, states should fully ensure the right to an adequate standard of living for children including the right to housing, nutrition and the highest attainable standard of health. By recognizing the fundamental interdependence of various aspects of the child's life, the survival and development principle highlights the unity of purpose of the ACRWC's substantive as well as procedural provisions. The principle does not create new rights for children, but merely serves to emphasize the holistic approach that must be followed. Each one of the elements of the child's survival and development is equally important, and states parties should strive to protect them all.

With regard to refugee children, guaranteeing their survival and development requires that housing, health care, food, water and other essentials are made available as quickly as possible. It also entails that arrangements for the continuation of education are made as quickly as possible (CRC Committee 2005, paras 23 and 24; UNHCR 2004). For example, the International Rescue Committee has arranged for Somali refugee children who suffered injuries such as loss of sight or hearing during the fighting in their country to attend state-funded special needs schools in Kenya.[8] Thus, instead of letting such children miss out on their education, an innovative solution ensures that their developmental rights are protected.

Participation

Implicit within the best interests approach is the requirement for individual determination of each particular child's situation and needs (Steinbock 1996; Reisler et al. 1998, 229 noting that 'individual assessments and individualised placements are required; what is truly best for a given child cannot be determined by a general formula'). The ACRWC concretizes this approach by making provision for the child's participation rights, namely the right of the child to be heard in all proceedings affecting that child (ACRWC article 4(2)) and the right of the child to freely express his or her opinions (ACRWC article 7; CRC Committee 2005, para. 25). Neither the OAU Refugee Convention nor the 1951 Convention made any provision for participation rights for refugee children. The obligation of states under the ACRWC provisions is to ensure that appropriate mechanisms for the channelling of the child's views are put in place and that interpreters are provided where necessary. Such mechanisms must be child-centred and non-threatening.

In relation to child refugees, children's participation rights require that in the determination of their status and in any aspect of providing durable solutions, the child's views should feature prominently (International Save the Children Alliance and UNHCR 1999; UNHCR 2001d, paras 46, 47 and 50). The body entrusted with the task of finding the durable solutions must solicit the views of the refugee child in determining the child's status and such views *must* be taken into account in any subsequent decisions relating to the child. The obligation also requires the state to

---

8   <http://www.theirc.org/news/irc_program_brings_special_needs_refugee_children_ into_camp_schools_in_kenya.html> (accessed 29 January 2007). See also Pigozzi 1996.

ensure that the child has a guardian or adviser who is well trained in child welfare matters and who will promote decisions in the best interests of the child and positively contribute to the quest for durable solutions (UNHCR 2001a).

An example of the effectiveness of participation as a means for normalization of refugee children's lives comes from Mozambique (McCallin 2007). In 1990, during the civil war, a UN programme officer and his local counterparts initiated a documentary project in Niassa, a northern province on the border of Malawi. The project was intended to mobilize young people, augment the limited formal schooling that was available for children, and through documentary work, increase children's appreciation of their own cultural strengths. The programme's first initiative was the development of a children's newspaper. Children were supported to organize themselves into staff positions, reporters, editors and printers. With limited materials, they began to study and report on their community, interviewing community leaders, artisans and the elderly. The children relied on a small, simple tape recorder and a manual typewriter. A simple silk-screen process was used for the actual printing of the papers. Papers were distributed free to children, while small businesses and adults who were able, were asked for small contributions. As the project evolved, a health column was included to incorporate public health messages and an 'announcements' section noted upcoming events for children in the community. A second element of the project employed two older children who began collecting and documenting traditional songs and stories. Over time, these youth were provided with support to travel to other safe areas in the province. At a later stage, they were enabled to purchase traditional instruments and gained access to the use of a camcorder to document performances of traditional musicians and dancers.

Thus, the right of participation is critical in determining the best interests of the child, and ensuring mechanisms that enable children to exercise this right is a positive step towards affording them not only effective protection and assistance, but also the realization of their developmental rights.

Primary Considerations for Refugee Children

The ACRWC provides a general direction that states parties must take all appropriate measures to ensure that a refugee child receives appropriate protection and humanitarian assistance. Article 23(1) provides specifically as follows:

> States Parties to the present Charter shall take all appropriate measures to *ensure* that a child who is seeking refugee status or who is considered a refugee in accordance with applicable international or domestic law shall, whether unaccompanied or accompanied by parents, legal guardians or close relatives, receive *appropriate protection and humanitarian assistance* in the enjoyment of the rights set out in this Charter and other international human rights and humanitarian instruments to which the States are Parties. (Emphasis supplied)

In addition, the Charter makes special provision for unaccompanied refugee children who are in an even more desperate situation. In this regard, the Charter identifies two key responses with respect to unaccompanied children, namely the 'trac[ing] of the parents or other close relatives … in order to obtain information necessary for reunification with the family' (article 23 (2)) and, where such parents or relatives cannot be found, the placement of such child in alternative care (articles 23(3) and 25(2)(b)). Decisions regarding whether to reunite the child with its family or to place him or her in alternative care must be non-discriminatory, must take into account the child's views and, above all, must be predicated on the child's best interests.

Appropriate Measures

The direction to take all appropriate measure requires states parties to deploy *all* their resources including social, economic, political, legal and diplomatic resources in ensuring that refugee children are allowed to enjoy the rights enshrined in the ACRWC and in order to alleviate the difficult situation in which such children find themselves. There are no limits to the nature and scope of such 'appropriate measures' and all child refugee situations will need to be assessed on a case by case basis and responses continually evaluated as the refugee situation unfolds. Thus, where children have moved across borders, the host country is obligated to ensure as a basic minimum that essentials such as food, adequate sanitation and shelter are made available promptly. Additionally, the host country is enjoined to ensure that children who have fled across borders have adequate security and that they are not subject to threats from elements from whom they have fled. Where the host state is unable so to do, it is a requirement to deploy its diplomatic capabilities in ensuring that international help is sourced from other regional or international partners.

Family Reunification

Where children are separated from their usual caregivers, the ACRWC makes special provision. Thus, although it gives individual rights to children, it also emphasizes relationships (Le Blanc 1996, 404). In this regard, the ACRWC proclaims the family as 'the natural unit and basis of society' and entitles every child 'to the enjoyment of parental care and protection' (article 18(1)). These affirmations are strengthened by the placement of children's rights within the context of parental rights and duties (articles 9, 11, 14, 19 and 20; Viljoen 1998, 222–3) and community responsibilities (articles 11,14 and 15). The recognition of the centrality of the family in the upbringing of a child forms the basis of the prioritization of family reunification as a primary response in situations of separation.

International law[9] and refugee policy (UNHCR 1981) also emphasize that the first priority in caring for unaccompanied children is family reunification; it has been stated that 'UNHCR and many countries consider family reunification a cornerstone of effective refugee protection and successful resettlement programs' (Canadian Council for Refugees 2002, para. 1; Hodgkin and Newell 2002, 254 noting that

---

9   Several international instruments affirm this position, for example CRC, article 22; Protocol relating to the Protection of Victims of International Armed Conflicts, adopted 10 June 1977, article 74; Protocol Relating to the Protection of Victims of Non-International Armed Conflict, adopted 10 June 1977, article 4(3)(a). See also Steinbock 1996, 24.

'preserving and restoring the child's family unity is of the highest priority in the search for durable solutions').

This is because children are generally better protected from risks such as sexual exploitation and abuse, military recruitment, child labour, denial of access to education and basic assistance and detention within the context of family protection (UNHCR 2001b). Thus, it is not surprising that the Charter advocates family reunion as the first option. However, the most important addition to the protection framework is the incorporation of the best interests standard in the resolution of the matter (Valid International 2002). Reunification is thus not an automatic response that should be dogmatically pursued. It is a factor which is subsumed under the inquiry to determine the best interests of the particular child (Steinbock 1996). This is because there will be situations where reunification may not be in the best interests of the child. In this regard, the durability of the relationship between the minor and the family must be carefully assessed to determine whether they should remain together. For example, reunification would not be advisable where the remaining parent or relatives were responsible, partly or otherwise, for the minor's flight, as was the case during the Rwandan genocide when some family members were responsible for murdering or maiming their own kin (Gourevitch 1998). Similarly, where a child flees from a social practice such as forced or early marriage or female genital mutilation, and which implicates family members, reunification must be considered with very great circumspection. Further, where a minor has developed a great degree of attachment to a foster family, the disruptive effect of ultimate family reunification must be weighed against the need for continuity and stability.

It is also important to note that reunification does not only entail returning the unaccompanied minor to his or her country of origin but may also involve organizing the reunification around the child if this is in his or her best interests. For example, during the fighting in December 2006 between Somalia's transitional federal government and Islamist guerrillas, Kenyan authorities forcibly repatriated Somalian refugees (including children) who had crossed the border even though the fighting was still raging.[10] It is clearly not in the best interests of the child to send her back to where hostilities are still going on. This principle of *non-refoulement* is also emphasized by the CRC Committee (2005, para. 26). Similarly, if minors are targeted for military recruitment by authorities or other parties in the country of origin, reunification should be organized within the host country or another third party state.

Alternative Care

Article 23(3) of the ACRWC provides that where parents or legal guardians or close relatives cannot be found, the unaccompanied refugee minor must be accorded the same protection as any other child who has been permanently or temporarily deprived of his or her family environment for any reason. The extent of the state's obligations must, therefore, be sourced from article 25 of the Charter which obligates

---

10 See *The Nation*, 'Somali border may be reopened', available at <http://allafrica.com/stories/200701081660.html> (accessed on 29 January 2007).

states to accord special protection and assistance to *any child* who is permanently or temporarily deprived of his or her family environment. Since the Charter already accords special protection and assistance to all children, the implication from this provision is that children without families are entitled to an additional level of protection and assistance above that of other children (Van Bueren 1995, 25 commenting on similar provisions in the CRC).

The obligation of states under these provisions is to ensure that children who are parentless or permanently or even temporarily deprived of their family environment must 'be provided with alternative *family* care' which may take the form of adoption, foster placement or placement in suitable institutions for the protection and care of children (ACRWC article 25(2)(a)). Further, when considering such alternative family care for the child, states are required to have the best interests of the child as the primary consideration and to pay due regard to the desirability of continuity in the child's upbringing and to the child's ethnic, religious or linguistic background.

In relation to the provision of alternative care for unaccompanied refugee children, it is noteworthy that the Charter demonstrates a preference for placements which maintain the child's previous ethnic, religious, cultural and linguistic background (article 25(3)). Furthermore, the Charter also prescribes an analogous preference to continuity in the child's upbringing. However, the most notable aspect of article 25 is that it does not prescribe an overall standard for choice of placement, leaving the ultimate choice to be predicated on the best interests of the child (Steinbock 1996, 29). Thus, the unaccompanied refugee child's ethnic, religious, cultural and linguistic background are not the *primary* consideration, but rather are 'subsumed under the larger issue whether the particular placement meets his or her best interests'.[11]

Under this obligation, states must put in place effective adoption and foster care arrangements as well as monitoring mechanisms for such arrangements (UNHCR 2002, para. 9) and must in all circumstances ensure that the process is directed at ensuring the best interests of the child and not the disposal of the affected children to their country of origin.[12] These considerations apply whether the refugee population is in camps or otherwise, and the search for durable solutions may involve the arrangement of foster placement within the host country or in third countries. In other words local integration, resettlement in a third country or inter-country adoption are all possible choices in the search for durable solutions.

---

11 This interpretation is strengthened by the requirement that 'due regard' be had to the desirability of continuity in upbringing. Obviously, 'due regard' does not preclude a determination that continuity would *not* be in the best interests of the child, for example, where the security situation in the child's own country is still unsettled.

12 This approach is a significant break from past refugee practice whereby a lot of weight was accorded to the child's background/nationality in making placement decisions. The UNHCR notes that the absence of standards applicable to unaccompanied refugee children led to the principle that children belong first to their parents and secondly to their country (see UNHCR 1994). State parties cannot now rely on this obsolete principle but must instead ensure the existence of appropriate mechanisms for ensuring that unaccompanied children are accorded treatment which guarantees their best interests.

Complementary Rights

The process of establishing durable solutions for refugee children must be informed by guarantees of the rights of identity, rights of protection and rights of support (Steinbock 1996, 34). The guarantee of these complementary rights not only takes cognizance of the vulnerability of refugee children, but also ensures the achievement of solutions which are in their best interests. Thus, in designing response systems to deal with refugee children, states must ensure that these complementary rights are observed.

Rights of Identity

Article 6 of the ACRWC guarantees every child the right to a name, the right to be registered immediately after birth, and the right to acquire a nationality (see too International Covenant on Civil and Political Rights [ICCPR], article 24(3) and articles 7 and 8 of the CRC). The obligation of states under this article is to put in place appropriate mechanisms to ensure the registration of children immediately after birth and to ensure that children are not unlawfully deprived of their names or family background.[13] It goes without saying that these rights are crucial to a child's identity because 'only by registration is it guaranteed that the existence of a [child] is legally recognised' (Nowak 1993, 432). According to Nowak, the right to identity flows from the right to privacy and the right to recognition before the law.

The preservation of a child's identity also includes within its purview the protection of the child's cultural, racial, linguistic and religious identity (Hodgson 1993, 265) and, in this regard, the ACRWC guarantees every child the right to participate freely in cultural life (article 12(1)) and the right to freedom of religion (article 9(1)).

In relation to refugee children, rights of identity are of fundamental importance. Registration of children will assist in the tracing of family members for the purpose of reunification and the protection of the child's cultural, racial, linguistic and religious identity, which in turn will inform the process of determining the child's best interests. These provisions obligate states to identify, register and document refugee children as soon as is practicable (UNHCR 1994; Steinbock 1996, 21). To this end, an active search must be undertaken to document all children, including those that are unaccompanied or living with unrelated adults. The best interests of the child and the preservation of the child's identity require that refugee children be registered and their personal history properly documented (Williams 1988, 43–52; Steinbock 1996, 21). Further, if the child's parents or relatives cannot be traced, proper mechanisms must be built into the alternative care mechanisms to ensure that children are not unlawfully deprived of their identity.

---

13 The Human Rights Committee has noted that these rights are crucial in affording children protection from abuse such as abduction, sale and trafficking. See UN Doc. CCPR/21/ Rev.1.

Rights of Protection

Due to their age or the absence of an older guardian, refugee children face a great number of risks which include sexual exploitation and abuse, forced military recruitment, child labour, and denial of access to education and health services. Consequently, to ensure the child's well-being and development by preventing the above harm, the ACRWC in article 16 protects all children from all forms of torture, physical or mental injury and abuse, neglect or maltreatment. The child also has the right to be protected from sexual exploitation (article 27) as well as economic exploitation and from performing any work that is likely to be harmful to the child's health or physical, mental, spiritual, moral or social development (article 15). Further, children under the age of 18 have protection against military recruitment and direct involvement in military hostilities (see article 22(2)).

Thus, in ensuring the best interests of the child and securing for them durable solutions, states must ensure that the protection accorded by the above provisions is extended to refugee children (UNHCR 2001c). Failure to ensure this entails failure to provide special protection and assistance to refugee children as required by the Charter.

Rights of Support

The quest for durable solutions may be described as an endeavour towards normalcy. In this respect, the guarantee of rights of support is crucial as it ensures not only the child's best interests, but also his or her rights to normal growth and development. These rights of support include the child's right to education (article 11 of the ACRWC), rest, leisure and play (article 12(1)), and to the highest attainable state of health (article 14(1)). According to the CRC Committee, protection of refugee children's right to education includes providing full access to educational facilities available to the children of the host country. It also involves the provision of formal and informal education as well as vocational training (2005, paras 41–3). Further, states must desist from measures which impact adversely on the child's right to play such as the detention of refugee children.[14] In other words, rights of support are principally aimed at helping refugee children realize their humanity and dignity despite the difficult and oftentimes dangerous situations in which they find themselves.

Conclusion

An analysis of the extent of state obligations emanating from the duty to provide protection and assistance to refugee children demonstrates just how onerous the duties assumed under these provisions of the ACRWC are. The economic and financial implications of guaranteeing these rights to refugee children by states may lead to their totally shirking their duty to protect and provide assistance to

---

14 International refugee policy sanctions detention of child refugees only as a measure of last resort and only for the shortest period of time. See UNHCR 1999.

child refugees. In many cases, African nations that host refugee and internally displaced populations have resorted to massing them in camps run by international organizations, and have not paid particular attention to the rights and welfare of the children who find themselves in these dire circumstances. For example, in Uganda and Rwanda, the state has pursued a policy of forced relocation or 'regroupement' of internally displaced persons, whereby whole communities are made to abandon their usual dwellings and live in camps where there are no or very limited social services. However, the plight of the vulnerable children caught up in problems such as this demands more creative solutions than the mass shepherding of people into camps. There is a duty on states to ensure that their security options do not cause unnecessary distress.

Problems of implementation are not only present at the national level. Despite the massive refugee problem on the African continent and the elegant rules contained in the ACRWC, the African Union (AU) does not have a central organ for co-ordinating refugee issues. The organ tasked with dealing with social issues, the Economic, Social and Cultural Council, is yet to develop management competence over refugee issues. The result is that interventions addressing the plight of refugee children on the continent are left to international non-governmental organizations, whilst regional and state initiative is kept at a minimum. However, the immediacy of the various responses required of states demonstrates the necessity of states guaranteeing these rights for their own children. Thus, the duty to protect and provide assistance to refugee children will be discharged more easily if the state already ensures the rights and the protections provided by the Charter for its own children. Where there are economic, institutional or administrative hurdles in affording protection and assistance to refugee children, it is imperative that states co-operate with other governments and international organizations (as envisaged by the Charter [article 23(2)]; Fernhout 1996, 117), instead of overlooking these duties. Unless the legal rights of refugee children are properly recognized and implemented, the only guarantee they will have is the continued hardship of their situation.

References

Articles, Books and Chapters in Books

Alston, P. (1994), 'The Best Interests Principle: Towards a Reconciliation of Culture and Human Rights', in Alston, P. (ed.) *The Best Interests of the Child: Reconciling Culture and Human Rights* (Oxford: Oxford University Press).
Chimni, B. (2000), *International Refugee Law: A Reader* (New Delhi, Thousand Oaks, CA and London: Sage Publications).
Chirwa, D.M. (2002), 'The Merits and Demerits of the African Charter on the Rights and Welfare of the Child', *International Journal of Children's Rights* 10, 157.
Davel, C.J. (ed.) (2000), *Introduction to Child Law in South Africa* (Lansdowne: Juta and Co.).
Doek, J. et al. (eds) (1996), *Children on the Move: How to Implement Their Right to Family Life* (The Hague: Martinus Nijhoff).

Fernhout, R. (1996), 'Asylum-seeking Children: How to Implement Their Right to Family Life', in Doek, J. et al. (eds).

Freeman, M. et al. (eds) (1992), *The Ideologies of Children's Rights* (Dordrecht and Boston, MA: Martinus Nijhoff).

Goodwin-Gill, G.S. (1996), 'Protecting the Human Rights of Refugee Children: Some Legal and Institutional Possibilities', in Doek, J. et al. (eds).

Gourevitch, P. (1998), *We Wish to Inform You that Tomorrow We Shall Be Killed Together with Our Families: Stories from Rwanda* (New York: Picador).

Hodgkin, R. and Newell, P. (2002), *Implementation Handbook for the Convention on the Rights of the Child* (Geneva: UNICEF).

Hodgson, D. (1993), 'The International Legal Protection of the Child's Right to a Legal Identity and the Problem of Statelessness', *International Journal of Law and the Family* 7, 255.

Kamchedzera, G.S. (1996), 'The Complementarity of the Convention on the Rights of the Child and the African Charter on the Rights and Welfare of the Child', in Verhellen, E. (ed.).

LeBlanc, V. (1996), 'The Implementation of the 1989 Convention on the Rights of the Child and the Work of the United Nations High Commissioner for Refugees', in Verhellen, E. (ed.).

Nowak, M. (1993), *UN Covenant on Civil and Political Rights: CCPR Commentary* (Kehl am Rhein: N.P. Engel).

Reisler, E.M. et al. (1998), *Unaccompanied Children: Care and Protection in Wars, National Disasters and Refugee Movements* (New York: Oxford University Press).

Steinbock, D.J. (1996), 'Unaccompanied Refugee Children in Host Country Foster Families', *International Journal on Refugee Law* 8, 6.

Van Bueren, G. (1995), *International Law on the Rights of the Child* (Dordrecht, Boston, MA and London: Martinus Nijhoff).

Verhellen, E. (ed.) (1996), *Understanding Children's Rights: Collected Papers Presented at the First International Interdisciplinary Course on Children's Rights* (Ghent: Children's Rights Centre, University of Ghent).

Viljoen, F. (1998), 'Supranational Human Rights Instruments for the Protection of Children in Africa: The Convention on the Rights of the Child and the African Charter on the Rights and Welfare of the Child', *Comparative and International Law Journal of Southern Africa* 199.

Viljoen, F. (2000), 'The African Charter on the Rights and Welfare of the Child', in Davel, C.J. (ed.).

Williams, J. et al. (1988), *Unaccompanied Children in Emergencies: A Field Guide for Their Care and Protection* (Toronto: York University).

Wolfmann, S. (1992), 'Children's Rights: The Theoretical Underpinnings of the Best Interests of the Child', in Freeman, M. et al. (eds).

General Comments, Unpublished Papers, Treaties, Declarations and Reports

African Charter on Human and Peoples' Rights, 1981, OAU Doc.CAB/LEG/67/3.
African Charter on the Rights and Welfare of the Child, 1990, OAU Doc.CAB/LEG/24.9/49.

Canadian Council for Refugees (2002), 'Proposed New Developments for Family Reunification for Refugees Resettled to Canada' <http://www.unhcr.ch> (accessed on 29 October 2006).

Convention on the Rights of the Child (CRC), 1989, UN Doc. A/RES/44/25 (1989).

CRC Committee (2005), 'General Comment no 6: Treatment of Unaccompanied Children and Separated Children outside Their Country of Origin' CRC/GC/2005/6.

Internal Displacement Monitoring Centre (2006), *Internal Displacement: Global Overview of Trends and Developments in 2005* (Geneva: Norwegian Refugee Council).

International Save the Children Alliance and UNHCR (1999), 'Statement of Good Practice' <http://www.unhcr.ch/> (accessed on 7 September 2002).

McCallin, M. (2007), 'Understanding the Psychosocial Needs of Refugee Children and Adolescents' <http://earlybird.qeh.ox.ac.uk/rfgexp/rsp_tre/student/children/toc.htm> (accessed on 29 January 2007).

Pigozzi, M.J. (1996), *Education in Emergencies and for Reconstruction: Guidelines with a Developmental Approach* (New York: UNICEF).

OAU Convention Governing the Specific Aspects of Refugee Problems in Africa 1001 U.N.T.S. 45.

UN General Assembly (2000), 'Report of the Third Committee on Assistance to Unaccompanied Refugee Minors' UN Doc.A/56/578 (2000).

UN General Assembly (2001), 'Protection and Assistance to Unaccompanied and Separated Refugee Children: Report of the Secretary-General' UN Doc.A/56/150 (2001).

UN General Assembly (2002), 'Assistance to Unaccompanied Refugee Minors' UN Doc. A/Res/56/136 (2002).

UN General Assembly Resolution 49/172 (1994), UN Doc.A/Res/49/172 (1994).

UN General Assembly Resolution 50/150 (1995), UN Doc.A/Res/50/150 (1995).

UN General Assembly Resolution 51/73 (1996), UN Doc.A/Res/51/73 (1996).

UN General Assembly Resolution 52/105 (1997), UN Doc.A/Res/52/105 (1997).

UN General Assembly Resolution 53/122 (1998), UN Doc.A/Res/53/122 (1998).

UN General Assembly Resolution 54/145 (1999), UN Doc.A/Res/54/145 (1999).

UNHCR (1981), 'Note on Family Reunification' <http://www.unhcr.ch> (accessed on 29 October 2006).

UNHCR (1994), 'Refugee Children: Guidelines for Their Protection and Care' <http://www.unhcr.ch/> (accessed on 29 October 2006).

UNHCR (1999), 'Guidelines on Applicable Criteria and Standards Relating to the Detention of Asylum Seekers' <http://www.unhcr.ch> (accessed on 29 October 2006).

UNHCR (2001a), 'Recommendations of the Berlin Conference on Children in Europe and Central Asia' <http://www.unhcr.ch> (accessed on 29 October 2006).

UNHCR (2001b), 'Summary Conclusions on Family Unity of the Geneva Expert Roundtable' <http://www.unhcr.ch> (accessed on 29 October 2006).

UNHCR (2001c), 'Recommendations from the Inter-agency Learned Conference on Prevention and Responses to Sexual and Gender-based Violence in Refugee Situations' <http://www.unhcr.ch> (accessed on 29 October 2006).

UNHCR (2001d) 'Asylum Processes (Fair and Efficient Asylum Procedures)' Doc. EC/GC/01/12 <http://www.unhcr.ch/> (accessed on 15 May 2004).

UNHCR (2002), 'Global Consultations on International Protection of Refugee Children' Doc.EC/GC/02/9 <http://www.unhcr.ch> (accessed on 29 October 2006).

UNHCR (2004), 'Education Forum Initiative: Innovative Strategic Partnerships in Refugee Education' <http://www.unhcr.org/cgi-bin/texis/vtx/home/+TwwBmftedqnwwwwnwwwwwwwhFqA72ZR0gRfZNtFqrpGdBnqBAFqA72ZR0gRfZNcFqrfNI7f20Dzmxwwwwwww/opendoc.pdf> (accessed on 29 January 2007).

UNHCR (2006), 'Global Refugee Trends (2005): Statistical Overview of Populations of Refugees, Asylum Seekers, Internally Displaced Persons, Stateless Persons and Other Persons of Concern to UNHCR' <http://www.unhcr.org/statistics/STATISTICS/4486ceb12.pdf> (accessed on 29 January 2007).

UNHCR (2006), 'Global Refugee Trends (2005): Statistical Overview of Populations of Refugees, Asylum Seekers, Internally Displaced Persons, Stateless Persons and Other Persons of Concern to UNHCR' <http://www.unhcr.org/statistics/STATISTICS/4486ceb12.pdf> (accessed on 29 January 2007).

Valid International (2002), 'Meeting the Rights and Protection Needs of Refugee Children: An Independent Evaluation of the Impact of UNHCR's Activities' <http://www.unhcr.ch> (accessed on 29 October 2006).

Chapter 12

Children at Both Ends of the Gun: Child Soldiers in Africa

Benyam D. Mezmur

Introduction

If one assesses the three main factors that mar the life of the African child at present, the answers that would spring to mind would arguably be poverty, HIV/Aids and armed conflict. The implementation of children's rights in Africa has to contend with, amongst other things, the common occurrence of armed conflicts in which children are often the most severely affected. This chapter is concerned with children's rights in the context of armed conflict and the involvement of children in it.

While the participation of children in armed conflict has been evident for some time, international community mobilization on the issue is fairly recent. In 1993, the General Assembly of the UN adopted resolution 48/157 in response to a request by the Convention on the Rights of the Child (CRC) Committee.[1] It is evident that, while the use of child soldiers is a worldwide problem, it is particularly acute in Africa (Human Rights Watch 2004a). In recent years, the use of child soldiers by both government forces and insurgent groups in African countries such as Angola, Burundi, the Democratic Republic of Congo, Sierra Leone and Sudan has been witnessed and harshly condemned by the international community. For example, the UN Security Council (UNSC) has passed a number of resolutions condemning the use of child soldiers.[2]

Due to the obviously clandestine nature of child soldiering, global and regional statistics are hard to gather. However, in 2006, the UN estimated that more than 250,000 children were actively involved in armed conflict in government armed forces, government militias and in a range of armed opposition groups (Human Rights Watch 2004a). Of the estimated 250,000 child soldiers in the world, 120,000 can be found in Africa alone.[3] The areas most affected by the use of children in armed conflicts in Africa include Algeria, Angola, Burundi, Congo-Brazzaville, Cote D'Ivoire, the Democratic Republic of Congo (DRC), Liberia, Rwanda, Sierra Leone, Sudan and Uganda.

---

1   The General Assembly requested the Secretary General to appoint an expert to head a study on children in armed conflicts (including combatants). G. Machel was appointed in 1994 and her report was submitted in 1996.

2   These include resolution no. 1261 (1999), 1314 (2000) and 1539 (2004).

3   For instance in Northern Uganda, the Lord's Resistance Army (LRA) has abducted at least 20,000 children during the 19-year conflict with the government, with at least 5,000 children taken since June 2002.

These young combatants participate in all aspects of contemporary warfare. They wield AK-47s and M-16s on the front lines of combat. Apart from enlisting them as direct combatants, both governments and armed groups use children as messengers, lookouts, porters, spies able to enter small spaces, and even use them as suicide bombers and human mine detectors (Human Rights Watch 2004a). Children are forced to kill or are themselves killed, sexually assaulted, raped, forced to become wives of commanders, and are exposed to drugs and forced labour. This shows the cross-cutting nature and magnitude of the problem of child soldiers, and illustrates the malleability and susceptibility of children caught up in armed conflict.

There are a variety of international legal standards which give guidance on the protection of child soldiers. In spite of these, much remains to be done as the problem is continuing on a large scale and new challenges keep cropping up.

This chapter will first explore the existing legal framework relevant to the protection of child soldiers. Following this is an elaboration of some of the main issues surrounding child soldiers. In an attempt to be comprehensive, ways of dealing with child soldiers who have allegedly committed atrocities during armed conflict also forms part of the discussion. All the issues raised will be addressed within the context of Africa.

The Legal Framework for the Protection of Child Soldiers

Over the past few decades, the international child rights movement has undertaken an expansive development of international law, policies and programmes for the protection of children. As part of this, legal devices have been created which address the involvement of children in armed conflict. The areas of law covering this include humanitarian law, human rights law, international criminal law and international law on child labour.

The four Geneva Conventions of 1949 and their two Additional Protocols together make up the body of international humanitarian law. In the four Geneva Conventions, children are protected as members of the civilian population and therefore, by definition, as non-participants in armed conflict. The first three Geneva Conventions deal with combatants and prisoners of war. No specific provisions on children are included. Under the Fourth Geneva Convention on the Protection of Civilians, specific provisions were drawn up to ensure special treatment for children with regards to material relief, distribution of food, medical care, as well as family reunification (see, for example articles 14, 17, 23, 24 and 132 of the Fourth Geneva Convention). Clearly these provisions fall short of addressing the protection of child soldiers specifically. It also needs to be noted that application of the Geneva Conventions is limited to international armed conflicts.

However, turning to the two Additional Protocols, Additional Protocol I of 1977 provides for the protection of victims of international armed conflict. Article 77 of Additional Protocol I, also applicable only to international armed conflicts, states that '[T]he Parties to the conflict shall take all feasible measures in order that children who have not attained the age of fifteen years do not take a direct part in hostilities and, in particular, they shall refrain from recruiting them into their armed forces.' Moreover, Additional Protocol II of 1977 provides for similar protections except that it is geared towards non-international armed conflicts (articles 4, 6, 78 and 79). While article 4(3)(c) of Additional Protocol II specifically prohibits the recruitment of children under 15 years of age and their participation, whether direct or indirect, in hostilities, article 4(3)(d) provides that children under 15 who do take direct part in hostilities and whom enemy forces capture do not lose the special protections guaranteed under article 4. There is some evidence to suggest that the states participating in the Diplomatic Conference – the gathering of state representatives that negotiated the instrument – indeed intended to impose a stricter standard on parties involved in an internal armed conflict than on those involved in international armed conflict (Institute for Security Studies 1997).

Moreover, although Additional Protocol II is relevant to child soldiers, its failure to establish any measures of implementation or supervision to ensure compliance with its provisions (Ramcharan 1983, 99) and the requirement of a higher degree of intensity for its application (as it does not apply to riots or to isolated and sporadic acts of violence which have not reached the level of internal armed conflicts) are weaknesses. Most current conflicts involving child soldiers in Africa are internal and below the Additional Protocol II minimum threshold.[4] Last, it is worthy of note that both Additional Protocols, as with the Rome Statute, prescribe 15 as the minimum age for recruitment and participation in hostilities (article 77 of Additional Protocol I and article 4 of Additional Protocol II).

As the most comprehensive children's rights instrument, the CRC has created an opportunity to address explicitly the problem of child soldiers. As Fontana (Institute of Security Studies 1997) observes,

> [w]hen the UN embarked on the drafting of a convention that would solely address the rights of the child, the inclusion of a provision addressing the situation of armed conflicts was considered essential. Some states and non-government agencies hoped it would be the perfect opportunity to improve the provisions of International Humanitarian Law on the question of age, type of recruitment, and type of participation.

Accordingly, article 38 of the CRC provides that state parties undertake to respect, and to ensure respect for, relevant rules of international humanitarian law; to ensure that children under 15 do not take a direct part in hostilities; to refrain from recruiting those under 15 and to give priority to the oldest among those under 18; and, in accordance with international humanitarian law, to ensure protection and care of children affected by armed conflict. The recognition by the CRC, in article 38, of humanitarian law makes it an unusual treaty (Van Bueren 1995, 349), indicating that, at least in relation to children in armed conflict, the two can no longer be seen as distinct bodies of law.

However, in relation to article 38, what comes as a surprise at first reading is that, even though article 1 defines a child as 'any person under the age of 18 unless under the law applicable to the child, majority is attained earlier', in the same document

---

4 Article 22(3) of the ACRWC provides that it does not only apply to children caught up in international and internal armed conflict, but also to lower levels of violence described as 'tension and strife'.

it provides for a minimum age of recruitment at 15. The 'straight 18' position could not be adopted as it faced a serious challenge from countries like the United States. It is actually reported that article 38 remained one of the four most difficult issues to resolve until the final draft was completed (Hackenberg 2000, 428). Ultimately, the failure to adopt the 'straight 18' position led to the commencement of the drafting and subsequent adoption of an optional protocol (Optional Protocol on the Involvement of Children in Armed Conflict 2000).

Following the CRC, the African Charter on the Rights and Welfare of the Child (ACRWC) was adopted. One of the reasons that motivated its need was the use of children as soldiers and the required establishment of a compulsory minimum age for military service (see generally, Gose 2002). Under article 22(2), the ACRWC prohibits the recruitment and use of children under 18 in both international and internal armed conflicts and requires states to '… take all necessary measures to ensure that no child shall take a direct part in hostilities and refrain in particular, from recruiting any child'. Unlike the CRC, it adopts a 'straight 18' position, compliant with the overall definition of a child. It therefore sends a clear message that the participation of children in conflict is unacceptable and will not be tolerated on the continent.

Child soldiers have also found protection within the discourse of international criminal law. The Rome Statute of 1998, which establishes the international criminal court, in its definition of war crimes, prohibits 'conscripting or enlisting children under the age of 15 years into national armed forces or using them to participate actively in hostilities' (article 8(2)(b)(xxvi)). It also provides that, in the case of an internal armed conflict, 'conscripting or enlisting children under the age of 15 years into armed forces or groups or using them to participate actively in hostilities' is a war crime (article 8(2)(e)(vii)).

When drafting the above treaty, a footnote was inserted providing guidance for the interpretation of the concepts of 'use' and 'participation'.

> The words 'using' and 'participate' have been adopted in order to cover both direct participation in combat and also active participation in military activities linked to combat such as scouting, spying, sabotage and the use of children as decoys, couriers or at military checkpoints. (Draft statute report 1998)

The implication of this is a 'child soldier' is not only one who has combatant status. It affords a wider protection by proscribing as a war crime the situation whereby children also recruited or enlisted to play an active role linked to combat. In addition, in regard to the notion of 'to enlist', it is submitted that this comprises both the act of recruiting and the act of conscripting (Dormann 2003, 377). It is argued, therefore, that the term to 'enlist' encompasses every act – formal or *de facto* – of including persons in the armed forces.

To date, there are 29 states parties in Africa to the Rome Statute. In a recent development, on 28 August 2006, the Prosecutor of the International Criminal Court (ICC) officially charged Thomas Lubanga with enlisting and conscripting children under the age of 15 and using them to participate actively in hostilities in the DRC. In what could become the first case for the ICC, the hearing for the confirmation of charges against Lubanga started on 9 November 2006 in The Hague. In addition, it is to be noted that the ICC indictments against five senior members of the armed group, the Lord's Resistance Army (LRA) in Uganda, involving charges of conscripting, enlisting or using children in hostilities are in preparation.

In 1999, all 174 Member States of the International Labour Organization (ILO) unanimously adopted ILO Convention 182.[5] It commits each state which ratifies it to 'take immediate and effective measures to secure the prohibition and elimination of the worst forms of child labour as a matter of urgency' (article 1). The term 'child' applies to all persons under the age of 18 years and the worst forms of child labour include, among others, forced or compulsory recruitment of children for use in armed conflict (article 3(a)). However, conspicuously absent from the list of the worst forms of child labour is a total ban on the use of children as soldiers in armed conflict. While taking an important step, the Convention's language only covers the most horrific examples of the use of child soldiers, such as forced abductions by the LRA in Uganda and the Revolutionary United Front (RUF) in Sierra Leone. Thousands of children who are 'voluntary' recruits would not be protected by the ILO Convention.

During the drafting of the CRC, there was concern that article 38 was inadequate and the proposal for an optional protocol to the CRC arose from the first Day of General Discussion held by the CRC Committee, on 'Children in armed conflicts' (Hodgkin and Newell 2002, 642). By 2000, international campaigning by NGOs, notably the Coalition to Stop the Use of Child Soldiers, led to the adoption of the Optional Protocol which significantly strengthened legal norms regarding the use of child soldiers.

The Optional Protocol, under article 1, raises the minimum age of direct participation in hostilities from 15 years to 18 years. However, the Optional Protocol retained 15 years as the minimum age for voluntary enlistment (article 3(3)). Article 2 provides that governments 'shall ensure that persons who have not attained the age of 18 years are not compulsorily recruited into their armed forces'. Article 4(1) forbids rebel or other non-governmental armed groups from recruiting persons under the age of 18 years or using them in hostilities under any circumstances. Under article 4(2), governments are required to take all feasible measures to prevent the recruitment and use of children by such groups, including the criminalization of such practices. Importantly, the Optional Protocol also recognizes the vital need for proper disarmament, demobilization and reintegration (DDR) (article 7).

Admittedly, although not a solution in and of itself, a comprehensive legal framework is the starting point towards alleviating the problem of child soldiers in Africa. A good number of the existing provisions of the relevant legal frameworks, although progressive in some respects, nonetheless fall short of addressing the needs of the child soldier in Africa adequately. The next section explores these weaknesses, but also highlights strengths and consequently the most appropriate ways and means towards addressing the problem specifically in the context of Africa.

---

5 See Chapter 18 in this volume, in which child labour and ILO Convention 182 is elaborated further.

Opportunities and Challenges in Protecting Child Soldiers in Africa

Although humanitarian law, international criminal law and labour law also have a role to play in protecting child soldiers, human rights law and more specifically children's rights law is the part of international law that is predominantly at play. Therefore, the Optional Protocol calls for more emphasis because of its particular importance in addressing the issue of child soldiers. However, where appropriate, reference is also made to the CRC and ACRWC. With this background, the next sub-sections look into thematic issues on opportunities and challenges in protecting child soldiers in Africa.

Why the Need for a 'Straight 18' Position?

Unlike article 2 of the ACRWC, which allows for no exceptions, article 1 of the CRC establishes that a 'child means every human being below the age of eighteen years, unless under the law applicable to the child, majority is attained earlier'. The only restriction placed on this principle in the CRC itself is to be found in article 38 on recruitment and participation in hostilities. The Optional Protocol makes reference to article 1 of the CRC for its definition of the 'child' (paragraph 7 of Preamble).

According to Alston, the CRC's drafters chose 18 as the age limit in order to maximize the protection offered by the CRC and to ensure that the rights would uniformly apply to as large a group as possible (Alston 1992, 3). Therefore, setting the cut-off age for recruitment and use as child soldiers at 18, as opposed to 15, is the best way of achieving the CRC's and the ACRWC's protective aims. From a practical point of view as well, for recruitment and participation purposes, the 'straight 18' position offers an advantage. This is because, for instance, in cases where children do not possess birth certificates, which is usually the case in Africa, it is easy for their superiors to pass them off as being older than they really are. A good example is Southern Sudan where the physical appearance of the children is relatively larger than their real age, and birth certificates are very difficult to come by. However, if the age limit were fixed at 18 years, the recruitment of very young children could certainly be avoided, as their reduced physical appearance would speak for itself.

The Nature of State Obligations

The Optional Protocol is a compromise (Revaz 2001, 13). As a result, the nature of the state obligation suffers from some degree of vagueness. In this regard, article 1 of the Optional Protocol stipulates that states 'shall take all feasible measures to ensure that members of their armed forces who have not attained the age of 18 years do not take a direct part in hostilities'. However, it is also notable that, for instance, the obligations under article 2 of the Optional Protocol place a stronger obligation 'to ensure' that persons who have not attained the age of 18 years are not compulsorily recruited into armed forces. The employment of the phrase 'all feasible measures' could be considered as a lesser and more imprecise obligation on the part of the state. Therefore, although article 1 is the most important provision of the Optional Protocol, the scope of the obligation contained in it is one of conduct rather than of result.

Under the ACRWC, however, the obligation that a state undertakes is 'to take all necessary measures to ensure' that no child takes a direct part in hostilities and to refrain in particular, from recruiting any child (article 22(2)). This obviously accords a better standard for the protection of children and is commendable.

Direct and Indirect Participation in Hostilities

The CRC under article 38(2), the Optional Protocol under article 1 and the ACRWC under article 22(2) all prohibit children taking a 'direct part' in hostilities. 'Direct' seems to imply a combatant position and to exclude supplementary roles (serving as scouts, porters and the like) which also involve a great risk for the life, survival and development of the child.

During the drafting of the CRC, the phrase 'direct part in hostilities' had faced considerable challenge and criticism from a number of delegations (Detrick 1999, 652–6). In order to provide children with the maximum level of protection, as Van Bueren rightly argues, a combination of the terms 'to take part in hostilities' (which includes supplementary roles such as serving as scouts, porters and the like) as incorporated in article 4(3) of Additional Protocol II and the obligation 'to take all the necessary measures to ensure that children under 18 would not participate' as incorporated in article 22(2) of the ACRWC is important (Van Bueren 1995, 335). Otherwise, children who are involved in a non-combatant status but in the meantime are at the risk of imperilling their life, survival and development would not be able to benefit from the protection that is called for.

Voluntary Recruitment?

The Optional Protocol allows for voluntary recruitment into a state's armed forces at a younger age, despite the fact that other provisions raise the minimum age of compulsory recruitment to 18 (article 3(1)). This provision also establishes that upon ratification of the Optional Protocol, governments must deposit a binding declaration stating their minimum recruiting age (article 3(2)).

However, to ensure that recruitment is voluntary, the Optional Protocol (under article 3) mandates four safeguards. These safeguards require that: (i) the recruitment is genuinely voluntary; (ii) the recruitment is carried out with the informed consent of the potential recruit's parents or legal guardians; (iii) the potential recruit is fully informed of the duties involved in such military service; and (iv) the recruit provides reliable proof of age prior to acceptance (article 3(3)).

The safeguards built into the provision are commendable as they can play a significant role in screening out those children who do not fulfil the minimum requirements. However, for a number of reasons, the practicality of applying them in the context of Africa is questionable. For instance, in Africa, many child soldiers come from poor families and are often children without parental care, or refugees or internally displaced persons or orphans. Thus, it sounds impractical to expect these vulnerable groups of children to register voluntarily with the consent of parents or legal guardians. In the same vein, the safeguard requiring children to '… provide reliable proof of age prior to acceptance' is not of much practical help in Africa. It is reported that in sub-Saharan Africa, 55 per cent of children are not registered by their fifth birthday (UNICEF 2005). This clearly shows that it will often be difficult to prove a child's age when the child volunteers; governments might just continue their recruitment in the face of lack of the proof of age.

In the UN Study on the Impact of Armed Conflict on Children, Machel dismisses the idea of 'volunteerism' completely in African context, arguing that when the only options are survival or poverty, the choices of the children can hardly be called free and fair (Machel 1996). For children in some parts of the world, the army serves as a substitute family. They are drawn to gangs or the military because the social structure has collapsed. In some instances, joining the military is crucial for their survival, as many of them have had their relatives killed in armed conflicts. The experience of child soldiers in Sierra Leone testifies to this fact. It is clear that the degree of real choice varies from situation to situation. Vandergrift correctly argues,

> [o]ne of the problems is that young people can easily be forced to say they joined voluntarily; we witness this in many places. Is it truly voluntary when there are immense pressures to join armed forces and there are few options for those who do not join? (Vandergrift 2004, 550)

However, the possibility of a genuine volunteerism, at least in exceptional circumstances, cannot be ruled out. In this regard, therefore, a tension is created with the right of the child to participation, to freedom of association and freedom of expression on the one hand, and the right to protection on the other. Accordingly, the so-called protection versus participation debate ensues. This debate may need consideration on its own merit. However, for the purpose of this chapter, it would suffice to note that the protection accorded to child soldiers, particularly under article 22(2) of the ACRWC (against voluntary enlistment), is an appropriate humanitarian gesture although its underlying philosophy may conflict with regard to, for instance, freedom of expression. Van Bueren is also of the view that the argument for protection is more convincing than the one based on the right to freedom of association (Van Bueren 1995, 816).

Finally, a question that needs to be posed in connection with voluntary recruitment is contained under article 4(1) of the Optional Protocol which explicitly provides that '[a]rmed groups that are distinct from the armed forces of a State should not, under any circumstances, recruit or use in hostilities persons under the age of 18 years.' In effect, therefore, while article 3 allows for voluntary recruitment by government forces, article 4(1) of the Optional Protocol prohibits the same right from being exercised by armed groups. At face value, this is a commendable step because the recruitment and use of child soldiers is more rampant among armed groups than within government forces.[6] For instance, the RUF of Sierra Leone and LRA of Uganda have recruited more child soldiers than their respective government forces. In the LRA it is reported that minors make up 80 per cent of its forces (*Washington Times* 2005). But, equally, this double standard sets a wrong precedent and the likelihood that

---

6   Out of the 38 parties in 12 countries that recruit or use children in situations of armed conflict listed in the October 2006 report of the UN Secretary-General on Children and Armed Conflict, 24 are non-state armed groups.

armed groups will treat it as a legal obligation is minimal. It will also put in question the impartiality of the whole instrument from the point of view of armed groups, and the general application of the Optional Protocol could be undermined.

Disarmament, Demobilization and Reintegration (DDR)

The Optional Protocol addresses post-conflict issues, including demobilization and reintegration of child soldiers. Accordingly, article 6 of the Optional Protocol provides that persons 'recruited or used in hostilities' are to be demobilized and accorded 'all appropriate assistance for their physical and psychological recovery and their social reintegration' (article 6(3)).

However, a number of factors militate against the realization of this right. At times, because children are not thought to be a threat and of not much importance, DDR programmes might overlook their involvement in the process.[7] In addition, particularly in Africa, DDR programmes are generally marred by financial constraints. For instance, the majority of former fighters interviewed who had participated in the 2000–2003 UN-sponsored Sierra Leonean DDR programme received only partial benefits, were kept out of the skills training component of the programme or failed to receive any benefits at all (Amnesty International 2005). Of the 21,000 children recruited by both rebel and government forces during the Liberian civil war – some as young as six years old – only 4,300 were demobilized (Amnesty International 2005). A severe funding shortage of US$39 million in the Liberian disarmament programme not only left some 40,000 combatants at risk of missing out on job training and education, but appeared to make them more vulnerable for re-recruitment to fight in future armed conflicts. The lack of a gender sensitive approach by DDR programmes to girl child soldiers (discussed in the ensuing section) is another challenge. In accordance with article 7 of the Optional Protocol which obliges '[s]tate parties to co-operate in the implementation of the Protocol ...', the issue of DDR for child soldiers is an area in which a great deal of international co-operation can be sought to help child soldiers on the journey back to their childhood.[8]

Girl Soldiers

There was a time when the prevailing opinion was that all child soldiers were boys. This is because war has traditionally been considered a male preserve, and this remains predominantly true. But we now know that child soldiers include girls as well as boys. Women and girls participate in warfare to a far greater degree than is generally recognized (Brett 2002). In addition to armed combat, girl soldiers are often forced to serve as sexual slaves of armed groups. The experience of girl soldiers in

---

7   Governments tend to consider adult soldiers more of a threat than child soldiers and prefer to see the DDR of adult soldiers first.

8   Because DDR programmes often fail due to financial constraints, states should co-operate to meet the resources required to optimize the effect DDR can have on child soldiers.

Sierra Leone is just one example.[9] Girl soldiers have also been used to augment the number of rebel fighters in supplementary roles, such as cooks, domestic workers and porters, and are sometimes given positions of power as spies or commanders (McKay et al. 2004, 11). Therefore, the experience of girl soldiers defeats the assumption that child soldiers constitute a monolithic category of children who possess the same characteristics and needs.

Regrettably, international laws including the CRC and Optional Protocol which prohibit the use of child soldiers do not specifically cater for these experiences, and many programmes designed to prevent the recruitment of child soldiers and aid in their rehabilitation offer insufficient assistance to girls (Leibig 2005, 6). At the continental level, although the ACRWC emphasizes the girl child in general, article 22 which deals with child soldiers does not provide for a way in which the specific concerns of girl soldiers are to be dealt with. The lack of specific legal provisions catering for the needs of girl soldiers has adversely affected the best interests of this group of children. If any child rights instrument is to be complete and gender neutral, it should protect the rights of boys and girls in a manner that promotes substantive equality.

Cross-border Recruitment

Cross-border recruitment has become endemic to Africa. It arises whenever there is a conflict occurring in different countries within a region, and children are recruited from one territory to fight conflicts in other territories. For instance, Human Rights Watch reports that Liberian commanders have admitted that they were actively involved in recruiting other Liberians, including children, most of whom had fought in the recently ended Liberian civil war (1999–2003), for the conflict in Côte d'Ivoire (Human Rights Watch 2005a). Gliding back and forth across the borders of Guinea, Burkina Faso and Sierra Leone is a migrant population of young fighters – regional warriors – who view war mainly as an economic opportunity (Human Rights Watch 2005b). Moreover, in the case of the rebel-held territories in the eastern portion of the Congo, cross-border forced child soldier recruitment is all too common (Refugee International 2004). As the economic activity in parts of the Great Lakes region of Africa have virtually ceased, more and more youngsters are becoming prey to the only viable employer in the region: war (Human Rights Watch 2005a).

The Optional Protocol is of limited use in addressing cross-border recruitment, if any at all. Paragraph 11 of its Preamble, provides '[c]ondemning with the gravest concern the recruitment, training and use within and *across national borders* of children in hostilities by armed groups distinct from the armed forces of a State ...' (emphasis added). However, this lead is not followed in any substantive provisions. Cross-border recruitment also frustrates DDR programmes, and makes the applicability of the existing provisions of the Optional Protocol difficult. Therefore, the phenomenon of cross-border recruitment of child soldiers has not been clearly addressed by human rights instruments and calls for a more concerted response.

---

9 The Prosecutor of the Special Court for Sierra Leone (SCSL) has filed the crime of 'bush wives' as a war crime against six defendants.

Enforcement

In the words of Otunnu, the former Special Representative of the Secretary General of the UN for Children and Armed Conflict, 'words on paper cannot save children in peril.' Political willingness to adhere to already existing obligations, as well as readiness to think along new lines, are both necessary prerequisites for improved enforcement.

The words of Cohn (2004, 531) capture the bigger enforcement failure of the CRC:

> The main problem in enforcement, however, is that the enforcement mechanisms of the Convention on the Rights of the Child are incredibly weak. Consider that the main mechanism for accountability is reporting ... And a report may or may not be taken seriously as an enforcement vehicle by the receiving government.

Unfortunately, the Optional Protocol is vulnerable to the same problems concerning the procedure of reporting (article 8). Partly motivated by the need to address this enforcement gap, there are five Security Council (UNSC) resolutions to date devoted to the protection and rehabilitation of children affected by armed conflict. Resolution 1261 (1999) affirms that the protection and well being of war-affected children constitutes a fundamental peace and security concern that belongs on the agenda of the UNSC. Resolution 1314 (2000) sets out specific action-oriented measures such as tackling the illicit trade in conflict diamonds, ending impunity for war crimes against children, and securing the release of abducted children. Resolution 1379 (2001) strengthens the measures provided for in resolution 1314 (2000) and makes them more targeted. Resolution 1460 (2003) broadens the scope for monitoring and reporting, stipulating that all country-specific reports should include sections on children, and endorses the call for an era of application. In respect of these four resolutions, each one has been stronger than the last and each of them has enforced an important principle: violations of the security and rights of children are in themselves a threat to international peace and security.

Resolution 1612 (2005) was voted on unanimously by all 15 members of the UNSC (UNSC Resolutions S/Res/1612/2005). It calls for a series of measures to be taken, including the establishment of a mechanism for monitoring and reporting violations, a UNSC Working Group to monitor progress and oversee implementation of these measures, and a demand to offending parties to prepare and implement concrete action plans for ending violations against children. Under the new mechanism, UN-led task forces are established in phases, to monitor the conduct of all parties and transmit regular reports to a central task force in New York.

Through the established UN-led task forces, signs of some success are already being recorded. For instance, in Burundi, positive developments have been undertaken by the government pursuant to the previous conclusions and recommendations of the Security Council Working Group. In the DRC, significant progress is said to be made by the Congolese Government to address grave violations against children, but great concern remains about the impunity for crimes against them, in particular in Ituri Province and the Kivus. Undoubtedly, ending the culture of impunity can contribute a great deal towards alleviating the problem of child soldiers. As already pointed out, one of the major successes of the Rome Statute has been the inclusion, as a crime, of the recruitment of children under the age of 15 as soldiers. The Special Court for Sierra Leone (SCSL) has also shed some light on the international criminal law accountability aspect of those who recruit and use children as soldiers.[10] In fact, in June 2007, Alex Tamba Brima, Brima Bazzy Kamara and Santigie Borbor Kanu were found guilty on 11 counts of war crimes and crimes against humanity, including the conscripting or enlisting of children under 15 years of age into armed forces or groups, or using them to participate actively in hostilities. Currently, the referrals under investigation by the Prosecutor of the ICC relate to Sudan, DRC and Uganda, conflicts that have engaged the use of child soldiers. Consequently, increasing ratification numbers to the Rome Statute within the continent is necessary. In addition, the Rome Statute allows the ICC to address the issue of reparations to victims, establishing general rules for 'restitution, compensation and rehabilitation' (Christopher 2003, 303–10); orders for such reparations could, for instance, be used for reintegrating child soldiers back to normal life.

There are some indications that protections for child soldiers could be better enforced at the regional level. The African Committee of Experts on the Rights and Welfare of the Child (ACERWC) established under the ACRWC, with the necessary financial and technical support, can prove itself to be a major tool for alleviating the problem of child soldiers in Africa. The African Court Protocol under article 5(1)(e) explicitly provides that the African Committee has standing and can bring a case before the Court. Bringing a case before the Court would be advantageous as the decisions of the African Court are binding and final (article 28(2)).

In the absence of robust UN action, stronger efforts by regional organizations like the African Union (AU) and individual governments are critical. This includes developing resolutions which have tangible repercussions for those who continue to violate the rights of these children. In addition, for instance, the Peace and Security Council of the AU, which is the body with the primary mandate for conflict prevention, management and resolution, offers a suitable platform for addressing the problem of child soldiers.

Apart from the AU, an opportunity that could be explored is through the New Partnership for Africa's Development (NEPAD). Although the main concerns of NEPAD are economic issues, the African Peer Review Mechanism (APRM) could possibly address issues of human rights under its 'democracy and political stability' focus, as democratic governance should necessarily incorporate human rights promotion and protection of children from armed conflict.

Children's issues have been incorporated into peace negotiations and peace accords, such as the 1999 Lomé Peace Accord on Sierra Leone, the 2000 Arusha Accords on Burundi, and the Accra Peace Agreement on Liberia of 2003; the latter provides for the protection and rehabilitation of war-affected children and calls upon the Special Representative and UNICEF to assist in mobilizing resources for the DDR of child soldiers. These are also positive developments that need to be harnessed.

---

10 A recent contribution in the area of international criminal law pertains to the decision of the SCSL in the Norman Case in which the Court held that the recruitment of child soldiers below the age of 15 had become a crime under customary international law by 1996. See SCSL <http://www.sc-sl.org/summary-childsoldiers.html> (accessed 24 April 2005).

Calling Child Soldiers to Account

It is argued that child soldiers are not always victims (Arzoumanian and Pizzutelli 2003, 852). This is because they also commit some of the worst atrocities during armed conflict. Therefore, the accountability of child soldiers and how they should be dealt with as perpetrators is discussed next. However, this is one of the most controversial issues surrounding their use in armed conflict. It poses complex questions of culpability, justice and impunity, as well as individual and social healing. Accountability inevitably poses both moral and legal questions. There remain many unanswered questions about what should happen to children who participate in the commission of atrocities in armed conflict.

On the one hand are those who argue that such child soldiers are solely victims, and consequently only those who forcibly recruited the children must face prosecution (Davison 2004, 147). On the other, some argue that if child soldiers commit criminal deeds themselves, there should be consequences (Amnesty International 2000). The latter substantiate their arguments on the ground of ending the culture of impunity towards perpetrators, as well as on the right to a remedy for victims (Amnesty International 2000). In relation to the Rwandan genocide of 1994, Reis (1997, 634–5) articulated this position:

> Rwandans say that if a child was able to kill, if a child was able to discriminate between two ethnic groups, to decide who was a Hutu moderate and who was not, and was able to carry out murder in that way, why should that child be considered differently from an adult? And therefore, the punishment should be the same.

This author believes that child soldiers should be held accountable for their participation in the commission of atrocities, sad though it is that children scarcely able to dribble a soccer ball may take up arms and commit unthinkable atrocities. In order to provide some sort of respite from grief for the victims and the local community, and to aid in the assimilation of these children back into society, there may need to be accountability for these acts. The question, rather, should be how the accountability of these children should be established while continuing to regard them as beneficiaries of special protections attributable to their vulnerable status.

Under international law, the prosecution of children is not prohibited. Although not necessarily directly addressed to the prosecution of child soldiers, both the CRC and the ACRWC envisage the prosecution of children. In international criminal law, neither the International Criminal Court for the former Yugoslavia (ICTY) nor the International Criminal Tribunal for Rwanda (ICTR) Statutes have explicitly given jurisdiction to the tribunals to try juveniles. The Rome Statute explicitly prohibits the prosecution of individuals less than 18 years of age at the time of the commission of the offence (article 26). The decision to exclude juveniles from ICC jurisdiction rested on the inability to set an age range for which jurisdiction would apply, combined with member countries evaluating maturity differently. However, the Statute of the SCSL is the first international document that expressly provides for the prosecution of children for international crimes (article 7), setting a precedent. Obviously, by implication, it also indicates the possibility of child soldiers being tried under national jurisdictions. For instance, in 2000, six child soldiers were arrested in the DRC and while five were convicted for conspiracy to overthrow the government, the other was convicted of murder; the court sentenced all six to death (Coalition to Stop the Use of Child Soldiers 2001). Child soldiers have also faced closed and unfair trials before military courts with no legal representation, and some have been sentenced to death and executed (Coalition to Stop the Use of Child Soldiers 2001).

If prosecution is to be considered as an option for holding child soldiers accountable, both in international and national courts, certain minimum standards should be met to cater for their vulnerable positions. Among these minimum standards, those of great importance relate to the age of criminal responsibility, fair trials, sentencing and detention.

If the age of criminal responsibility is fixed too low or if there is no lower age limit at all, the notion of responsibility for child soldiers would become meaningless. In Africa, where the CRC Committee has expressed the concern that a significant number of countries including Liberia, Sudan and DRC have an age of criminal responsibility that is too low, prosecuting child soldiers under such situations would not be compliant with international law. During any trial, child soldiers should, as rightly incorporated in the Statute of the SCSL '[b]e treated with dignity and a sense of worth, taking into account his or her young age and the desirability of promoting his or her rehabilitation, reintegration into and assumption of a constructive role in society' (article 7). To belabour the obvious, rights including the right to be heard, presumption of innocence, the right to be notified of charges, the right to remain silent, the right to counsel, the right to the presence of a parent or guardian, the right to confront and cross-examine witnesses, and the right to appeal to a higher authority at all stages of proceedings should be upheld for child soldiers (Beijing Rules, Rule 7.1, CRC article 40(2)).

The surrounding circumstance in which child soldiers became involved and continue to be soldiers should also be taken into account as a defence or a mitigating factor. For instance, the defence of duress may arise because of threats of death or serious bodily injury to the child or to another (see, for instance, article 31(1)(d) of the Rome Statute), and the defence of superior orders should be employed when appropriate. Moreover, child soldiers are frequently drugged to commit atrocities. In Liberia, it was reported that children are doped up – on amphetamines, marijuana and palm wine (MSNBC 1999). In Sierra Leone, the RUF exploited natural teenage recklessness by drugging teenage boys and sending them into battle (Bald 2002, 53). This intensifies the diminished capacity of children to distinguish between right and wrong and should serve either as a complete defence or as a mitigating factor.

If found guilty, in recognition of normative international standards, child soldiers should not face the death penalty, or be sentenced to life imprisonment without parole (article 37(a) of CRC). And, according to article 37(b) of the CRC '[t]he … detention or imprisonment of a child … shall be used only as a measure of last resort and for the shortest appropriate period of time.'

Finally, the SCSL Statute offers some guidance in the sentencing of child soldiers. Instead of ordering imprisonment as a penalty, the SCSL is limited to ordering one of the following rehabilitative measures: care, guidance, and supervision orders; community service orders; counselling; foster care; correctional, educational, and vocational training programmes; approved schools; and, as appropriate, any disarmament, demobilization and reintegration programmes of child protection agencies (article 7(2)).

But accountability mechanisms can take many forms, and there are alternatives to prosecution. In the context of child soldiers, the purpose of holding them accountable should primarily be for their rehabilitation and reintegration into society, keeping the best interest of the child at the heart of the process. Therefore, depending on their availability, alternatives to prosecution could play a major role in holding child soldiers to account. Although the best-known alternative to prosecution is the truth and reconciliation commission (TRC), a court-like body whereby victims and perpetrators alike can come forward and be heard, it is not the only alternative; other options include reports by international delegations, civil liability, reparations and historical inquiry (see, for instance, Bassiouni 1996, 20–22). As Zarifis (2002, 21) argues, in relation to child soldiers and the TRC in Sierra Leone:

> The unique position of the child combatant, first victim then perpetrator, would best be served by truth telling before the TRC to facilitate effective social rehabilitation and reintegration.

Indeed, in conclusion, prosecution should not be the first port of call in holding child soldiers accountable. In situations where alternatives to prosecution like TRC and traditional dispute resolution procedures exist, the possibility of exhausting these alternatives should first be sought. As long as these alternatives put in place safeguards to ensure the best interest of the child and their purpose is restorative justice,[11] they could offer an appealing form of accountability for child soldiers.

Conclusion

In the words of Kofi Annan, former Secretary General of the UN, 'conflict and violence rob children of a secure family life, betray their trust and their hope.' Machel's report has had a significant impact and was followed by major initiatives such as the Optional Protocol, the ICC and ILO Convention 182.

But what is the consequence of war today? Ten thousand children are victims of landmines, 2 million children dead, 6 million children maimed; 13 million are internally displaced, 10 million children are refugees, 300,000 to half a million children are forced and used as child soldiers, a number which exceeds the level 10 years ago (Secretary General Report 2000, 2). In October 2007, a new UN report that reviews progress since the groundbreaking 1996 study on children in armed conflict by Machel highlighted that dozens of conflicts around the world are still robbing children of their childhood.

The unfortunate share of African children in this is great. And, as Stephen Lewis, the former UN Special Envoy for HIV/Aids in Africa, says, this comes 'after a definitive report, after the appointment of a special representative internationally on Children and War, after heightened international awareness, and after the emergence

---

11 See Chapter 8 in this volume for further discussion on restorative justice in African context.

of a vast panoply of norms and standards around the rights and needs of vulnerable children in conflict. An exercise in international criminal delinquency' (Lewis 2004).

Measured against the ideal, the reality in sub-Saharan Africa leaves much to be desired. However, although the situation may seem bleak, it is not completely so. Therefore the existing legal framework needs to be improved and a great amount of energy needs to be exerted to concretize the implementation of standards. Political will, regulation of arms, effective utilization of existing structures for protection, and rights based programmes for child soldiers need to form part of the solution. With these efforts and others, war would no longer be child's play.

References

Articles, Books and Chapters in Books

Alston, P. (1992), 'The Legal Framework of the Convention on the Rights of the Child', *UN Bulletin of Human Rights: The Rights of the Child* 91, 2.
Arzoumanian, N. and Pizzutelli, F. (2003), 'Victims and Perpetrators: Issues of Responsibility Relating to the Problem of Child Soldiers in Africa', *International Review of the Red Cross* 852, 827.
Bald, S. (2002), 'Searching for a Lost Childhood: Will the Special Court of Sierra Leone Find Justice for its Children?', *American University International Law Review* 18, 537.
Bassiouni, M.C. (1996), 'Searching for Peace and Achieving Justice: The Need for Accountability', *Law and Contemporary Problems* 59, 9.
Christopher, M. (2003), 'Reparation to Victims', in Lattanzi, F. and Schabas, W. (eds).
Cohn, I. (2004), 'Progress and Hurdles on the Road Preventing the Use of Children as Soldiers and Ensuring their Rehabilitation and Reintegration', *Cornell International Law Journal* 37, 531.
Davidson, M.G. (2001), 'The International Labour Organization's Latest Campaign to End Child Labour: Will it Succeed Where Others Have Failed?', *Transnational and Contemporary Problems* 11, 209.
Davison, A. (2004), 'Child Soldiers: No Longer a Minor Incident', *Willamette Journal of International Law and Dispute Resolution* 12, 147.
Detrick, S. (1999), *A Commentary on the United Convention of the Rights of the Child* (The Hague: Marthinus Nijhoff).
Dormann, K. (2003), *Elements of War Crimes under the Rome Statute of the International Criminal Court; Sources and Commentary* (Cambridge: Cambridge University Press).
Gose, M. (2002), *The African Charter on the Rights and Welfare of the Child: An Assessment of the Legal Value of its Substantive Provisions by Means of a Direct Comparison to the Convention on the Rights of the Child* (Bellville: Community Law Centre, University of the Western Cape).

Hackenberg, M.L. (2000), 'Can the Optional Protocol for the Convention on the Rights of the Child Protect the Ugandan Child Soldier?', *Indiana International and Comparative Law Review* 10, 417.

Hodgkin, R. and Newell, P. (2002), *Implementation Handbook for the Convention on the Rights of the Child* (fully revised edition) (New York: UNICEF).

Lattanzi, F. and Schabas, W. (eds) (2003), *Essays on the Rome Statute* (St Paul, MN: West Publishing).

Leibig, A. (2005), 'Girl Child Soldiers in Northern Uganda: Do Current Legal Frameworks Offer Sufficient Protection?', *Northwestern University Journal of International Human Rights* 3, 6.

Lewis, S. (2004), *Conflict and AIDS – Nails in the Coffin of Childhood* (Addis Ababa: African Child Policy Forum).

McKay, S., Burman, M. and Worthen, M. (2004), 'Known but Invisible: Girl Mothers Returning from Fighting Forces', *Child Soldiers Newsletter* 11.

Ramcharan, S. (1983), 'The Role of International Bodies in the Implementation and Enforcement of Humanitarian Law and Human Rights Law in Non-international Armed Conflicts', *American University Law Review* 33, 99.

Reis, C. (1997), 'Trying the Future: Avenging the Past: The Implications of Prosecuting Children for Participation in Internal Armed Conflict', *Columbia Human Rights Law Review* 28, 629.

Revaz, C.R. (2001), 'The Optional Protocols to the UN Convention the Rights of the Child on Sex Trafficking and Child Soldiers', *Human Rights Brief* 9:1, 13.

Van Bueren, G. (1995), *The International Law on the Rights of the Child* (The Hague: Marthinus Nijhoff).

Vandergrift, K. (2004), 'International Law Barring Child Soldiers in Combat: Problems in Enforcement and Accountability: Challenges in Implementing and Enforcing Children's Rights', *Cornell International Law Journal* 37, 550.

Zarifis, I. (2002), 'Sierra Leone's Search for Justice and Accountability of Child Soldiers', *Human Rights Brief* 9:3, 20.

Reports, Treaties, Documents and Unpublished Work

African Charter on the Rights and Welfare of the Child of 1990, OAU Doc CAB/LEG/24.9/49 (entered into force 29 November 1999).

Draft Statute for the ICC, Report of the Preparatory Committee on the Establishment of an International Criminal Court, Addendum, Part One, A/Conf.183/2/Add.1 (14 April 1998).

Geneva Convention for the Amelioration of the Condition of the Wounded and Sick in Armed Forces in the Field of 12 September 1949, 75 UNTS 31 (First Geneva Convention) (entry into force 21 October 1950).

Geneva Convention for the Amelioration of the Wounded, Sick and Shipwrecked Members of Armed Forces at the Sea of 12 September 1949, 75 UNTS 85 (Second Geneva Convention) (entry into force 21 October 1950).

Geneva Convention Relative to the Protection of Civilian Persons in Time of War of 12 September 1949, 75 UNTS 135 (Third Geneva Convention) (entry into force 21 October 1950).

Geneva Convention for the Protection of Prisoners of War of 12 September 1949, 75 UNTS 287 (Fourth Geneva Convention) (entry into force 21 October 1950).

ILO Convention on the Worst Forms of Child Labour of 17 June 1999 (entry into force 19 November 2000).

Machel, G. (1996), *Report to the Secretary General on the Impact of Armed Conflict on Children* (New York: UNICEF).

Optional Protocol to the Convention on the Rights of the Child on the Involvement of Children in Armed Conflict, GA Resolution A/RES/54/263 of 25 May 2000 (entry into force 12 February 2002).

Protocol Additional to the Geneva Conventions, and Relating to the Protection of Victims of International Armed Conflicts (Additional Protocol I) of 12 August 1949, 1125 UNTS 3 (entry into force 7 December 1978).

Protocol Additional to the Geneva Conventions Relating to the Protection of Victims of Non-International Armed Conflicts (Additional Protocol II), 1125 UNTS 609 (entry into force 7 December 1978).

Protocol to the African Charter Establishing the African Court on Human and People's Rights of 1998 (entry into force January 2004).

Rome Statute on the International Criminal Court of 17 July 1998 (entry into force 1 July 2002).

Secretary General Report (2000), 'Children and Armed Conflict', UN doc. S/2000/712, 19 July 2000.

Internet Sources

African Union <http://www.africa-union.org/home/Welcome.htm> (accessed 3 July 2005).

Amnesty International (2000), 'Child Soldiers: Criminals or Victims' <http://web.amnesty.org/library/Index/ENGIOR500022000?open&of=ENG-364> (accessed 22 July 2005).

Amnesty International (2003), 'Democratic Republic of Congo: Children at War' <http://web.amnesty.org/library/index/engafr620342003> (accessed 13 September 2005).

Amnesty International (2005), 'Côte D'Ivoire: Cross-border Child Soldiers' <http://www.amnesty.ca/take_action/actions/cote_divoire_child_soldiers.php>(accessed 22 August 2005).

BBC News (2003), 'DR Congo "awash" with child soldiers' <www.news.bbc.co.uk/2/hi/africa/2772575.stm> 17 February 2003 (accessed 13 July 2005).

Brett, R. (2002), *Girl Soldiers: Challenging the Assumptions* <http://www.geneva.quno.info/pdf/Girl_Soldiers.doc.pdf> (accessed 23 July 2005).

Coalition to Stop the Use of Child Soldiers (2001), <http://www.childsoldiers.org/cs/childsoldiers.nsf/fffdbd058ae1d99d80256adc005c2bb8/bb1c00f3effdae4d80256c6a00611d4e? OpenDocument&Highlight=0> (accessed 16 Sept 2005).

Human Rights Watch (2004a), 'Facts about Child Soldiers'<www.humanrightswatch.org/campaigns/crp/facts.htm> (accessed 27 July 2005).

Human Rights Watch (2004b), 'More than 120,000 Child Soldiers Fighting in Africa' <http://hrw.org/english/docs/1999/04/19/africa852.htm> (accessed 22 March 2005).

Human Rights Watch (2005a), 'Recruitment of Ex-child Soldiers in Cote d'Ivoire' <http://hrw.org/english/docs/2005/03/30/cotedi10402.htm> (accessed 18 August 2005).

Human Rights Watch (2005b), 'Youth, Poverty and Blood: The Lethal Legacy of West Africa's Regional Warriors' <http://hrw.org/reports/2005/westafrica0405/westafrica0405text.pdf> (accessed 22 July 2005).

Institute for Security Studies (1997), 'Child Soldiers and International Law' <http://www.iss.co.za/Pubs/ASR/6No3/Fontana.html> (accessed 17 March 2005).

MSNBC (1999), 'Child Soldiers Add to Liberian Tragedy' <http://www.msnbc.com/news/945577.asp> (accessed 13 August 2005).

Refugee International (2004), 'Child Soldiers: Promising Commitments in the Congo' <http://www.refugeesinternational.org/content/article/detail/1322/> (accessed 12 July 2005).

Special Court for Sierra Leone <http://www.sc-sl.org/summary-childsoldiers.html> (accessed 24 April 2005).

UN Security Council (UNSC) Resolutions S/Res/1612/2005 <http://www.un.org/Docs/sc/unsc_resolutions05.htm> (accessed 4 September 2005).

UNICEF (2005), 'The "Rights" Start to Life: A Statistical Analysis of Birth Registration' <http://www.unicef.org/publications/files/BirthReg10a_rev.pdf> (accessed 3 August 2005).

Washington Times (2005), 'Africa's Forgotten War' by S. Brownback and R.E. Stearns <http://washingtontimes.com/op-ed/20050308-094129-9853r.htm> (accessed 22 August 2005).

Chapter 13

Implementing the Girl Child's Right to Education in Selected Countries in Africa

Lea Mwambene

Without achieving gender equality for girls in education, the world has no chance of achieving many of the ambitious health, social and development targets it has set for itself.[1]

Introduction

Education is a fundamental human right. It is also an enabling right[2] that permits the exercise of other fundamental rights. Thus the right to education functions as a multiplier – it enhances the fulfilment of all other rights and freedoms when it is guaranteed (Sloth-Nielsen and Mezmur 2007). Equally, though, it jeopardizes them all when it is violated. Thus, the role of education, and in particular girls' education, in the advancement of a nation's general well-being cannot be overstated.

This chapter discusses the extent to which selected African governments are implementing the right to education of the girl child through an examination of, among others, constitutions, policies and legislative measures. As noted by several writers (Nduru 1999) the problems and difficulties faced by the African girl child, to enjoy her right to education, are multifarious. They include exploitative child labour, sexual abuse (Naylor 2002), early pregnancies (Kadzamira), discrimination,[3] culture and religious practices (Chamblee 2004, 1073), violence[4] and poverty (Mlama 2006, 1). The intention of this chapter is not, however, to identify and detail the problems.

---

1 United Nations Secretary-General, Kofi Annan (published online 3 March 2005) <http://www.66.102.9.104/search?q=cache:r501EUsEm5wJ:www.campaignforeducation. org/resources/Mar2005/b10_brief_final.doc+Implementing+the+right+to+education+of+a+g irl+child+in+Kenya&hl=en,&gl=za&ct=clnk&cd=9> (accessed on 14 June 2006).

2 The right to education is also sometimes described as an empowerment right, as it has an enormous liberating potential and makes it possible for the individual to take charge of his or her life. See Beiter 2006, 28.

3 For example, Togo's education statistics for 2003 show that the enrolment of girls was at 42.1 per cent whereas boys' enrolment was at 62.2 per cent.

4 For example, from mid-2005, Plan Togo commissioned research into violence and abuse in schools (Plan Togo 2006). This included a joint study with Forum for African Women Educationalists (FAWE). In the FAWE research, children in their last three years of primary school were interviewed: 88 per cent of the girls and 87 per cent of the boys reported experiencing physical violence at school; 52 per cent of girls and 48 per cent of boys reported experiencing threatening behaviour or physical violence. Sixty-seven of the 750

Rather, it will analyse the practical steps taken towards the realization of the girl's right to education through a review of the trends in the recognition of this right at both international law level and domestically in selected countries in Africa.

The chapter is divided into five sections. The first section gives a brief discussion of some of the international instruments that are available for the protection of the right to education of the girl child. The main aim is to show the role and influence of international standards on the implementation of the girl child's right to education by African governments. The second section looks at the constitutionalization, legislation and policy initiatives that have been taken by selected African governments towards the implementation of the right to education. This part also includes efforts made by some non-governmental organizations (NGOs) as partners in the implementation of the right to education in Africa. Following this, in the third section, is an examination of the progress made towards the implementation of policies and legislations by governments. The fourth section looks at how some African governments are responding towards realizing the right to education of the African girl child faced with armed conflicts or who are refugees. Before concluding, an examination of the constraints experienced by the selected African governments in the implementation of the right to education is undertaken.

International Framework for the Right to Education

Education is a human right recognized by several international human rights instruments. For example, article 26 of the Universal Declaration on Human Rights (UDHR, 1948), provides that '[e]veryone has the right to education'. Education shall be free, at least in elementary stages. Following from the UDHR, the United Nations Educational, Scientific, and Cultural Organization (UNESCO) Convention against Discrimination in Education (Convention) was adopted in 1960. The Convention is the oldest global treaty guaranteeing the right to free and compulsory education (Chamblee 2004, 1074). Like the UDHR, the Convention recognized parents' right to choose freely their children's educational institution. However, unlike the UDHR, the Convention also allows parents to ensure the religious and moral education of their children. In addition, and possibly conflicting with the parents' convictions, parties to the Convention agreed to eliminate discriminatory educational practices and to 'ensure that the standards of education are equivalent in all public educational institutions of the same level, and that the conditions relating to the quality of education are also equivalent'. The Convention expanded the right to education by encouraging nations to ensure that elementary education shall be compulsory. After the Convention, in 1966, the International Covenant on Economic Social and Cultural Rights (ICESCR) also recognized the right to education (article 13). General Comment no. 13[5] provides details on implementation of this fundamental right.

---

girls interviewed and 15 of the 250 boys said they wanted to stop going to school because of violence they were experiencing.

5 Substantive issues arising in the implementation of the ICESCR, E/C.12/1999/10, CESCR (General Comment) (published 8 December 1999) <http://cesr.org/generalcomment1 3?PHRSESSID=91...978f9969da61bd9> (accessed on 24 October 2006).

The General Comment refers to several UNESCO standard-setting instruments, notably the Convention and World Declaration on Education for All, adopted in Jomtien, Thailand in 1990. The ICESCR is the most comprehensive article on the right to education in international human rights law (Lithur 2003). The language in the UDHR, the Convention and the ICESCR has been argued to have laid the groundwork for subsequent international standards for the protection of the girl's right to education (Chamblee 2004).

The Convention on the Rights of the Child (CRC) makes an important rallying point for governments with regard to education policies and interventions. All countries in Africa, with the exception of Somalia, have ratified the CRC; thus, it provides a good framework for action on behalf of the girl child in Africa (Ewelukwa 2005). Article 28 of the CRC provides for education as a basic right, and for free and compulsory primary education as a matter of urgent priority. It encourages the development of different forms of secondary education, including general and vocational education, stating that they should be available and accessible to all children (article 28(1)(b)). Higher education is to be accessible to all on the basis of capacity (article 28(1)(c)). Measures to encourage school attendance and reduce dropout rates are also envisaged (article 28(1)(e)). Furthermore, article 29 of the CRC calls on governments to ensure that education leads to the fullest possible development of each child's ability and to respect for child's parents, cultural identity and for human rights.

General Comment no. 1 of the CRC Committee provides details on the aims of the right to education as provided in article 29 of the CRC. Under this General Comment, the aims of education are to promote, support and protect the core value of the Convention: the human dignity innate in every child and his or her equal and inalienable rights. These aims, set out in the five subparagraphs of article 29(1) of the treaty, are all linked directly to the realization of the child's human dignity and rights, taking into account the child's special developmental needs and diverse evolving capacities. It is further stated under General Comment no. 1 that article 29(1) not only adds a qualitative dimension to the right to education recognized in article 28, one which reflects the rights and inherent dignity of the child, it also insists upon the need for education to be child-centred, child-friendly and empowering, and it highlights the need for educational processes to be based upon the very principles it enunciates. The education to which every child has a right is one designed to provide the child with life skills, and which helps to strengthen the child's capacity to enjoy the full range of human rights and to promote a culture which is infused by appropriate human rights values. The goal is to empower the child by developing his or her skills, learning and other capacities, human dignity, self-esteem and self-confidence. 'Education' in this context goes far beyond formal schooling to embrace the broad range of life experiences and learning processes which enable children, individually and collectively, to develop their personalities, talents and abilities and to live a full and satisfying life within society. It should be noted that General Comment no. 1 refers to several standard-setting guidelines (for example, General Comment no. 13 (1999) of the ICESCR) and it also refers to the general guidelines regarding the form and content of periodic reports to be submitted by states parties under article 44(1)(b) of the CRC.

Although the term 'girl child' does not appear anywhere in the CRC, several provisions of the CRC speak to the situation of the girl child and can be used as an agenda for action to identify persistent forms of inequality and discrimination against the girl child in all fields, including education (Ewelukwa 2005, 144). Furthermore, articles 28 and 29 of the CRC are buttressed by four other articles that assert overarching principles of law on this right. All have far-reaching ramifications, particularly in terms of what is needed to mould an education system. These are article 2, on non-discrimination; article 3 on the best interest of the child; article 6 on the child's right to life, survival and development; and article 12 on the views of the child (UNICEF 1999, 11). The non-discrimination principle has been argued to be key in combating gender discrimination. Schools must ensure that they are responsive to girl's needs in every possible way, from physical location to classroom curriculum and practice (UNICEF 1999).

The need for a special focus on girl's education, however, was first established in the 1979 Convention on the Elimination of all forms of Discrimination against Women (CEDAW). According to an NGO summary report, presented at the Sixth African Regional Conference on African Women, between 22 and 26 November 1999 in Addis Ababa, Ethiopia, 46 countries in Africa had, as of 1999, ratified CEDAW.[6] Parties to the treaty are called upon to take all appropriate measures to eliminate discrimination against women in order to ensure for them equal rights with men in the field of education (article 10). Of particular importance to the realization of the right to education of a girl child is article 10(f), which calls for states parties to take appropriate measures for the reduction of female student dropout rates and the organization of programmes for girls and women who have left school prematurely. This provision is very important in an African context, where the dropout rate for the girl child is significantly higher than for boys.

At regional level, the African Charter on Human and Peoples' Rights (ACHPR) also establishes education as a fundamental right. Article 17(1) provides that '[e]very individual shall have the right to education'. It provides further that the right to education must be guaranteed without distinction as to gender. Apart from the ACHPR, the African Charter on the Rights and Welfare of the Child (ACRWC) also provides a good framework for the protection of the right to education of the African girl child. The right to education is provided in article 11 of the ACRWC. Most provisions of the ACRWC are similar to the CRC with regard to the protection of the right to education. In addition, article 11(3)(e) of the ACRWC seems to have taken a step further in the protection of the girl's right to education than the CRC. It specifically mentions that state parties shall '... take special measures in respect of *female*, gifted and disadvantaged children, to ensure equal access to education for all sections of the community ...' (emphasis added). Article 11(6) of the ACRWC, which provides for states parties to take all appropriate measures to ensure that 'children who become pregnant before completing their education shall have an opportunity to continue with their education on the basis of their individual ability' is obviously

---

6   NGO Summary Report, at <http://www.uneca.org/eca-resources/Major-ECA-Websites/6thregionalconference/html/conference/ngos-summary-report.htm> (accessed on 20 October 2006).

intended to protect girls because, biologically, females fall pregnant. This is also a departure from the CRC which does not specifically mention the protection of pregnant girls. So, in terms of the strengths and weaknesses of the two instruments in the protection of the right to education of the African girl child, the ACRWC, it is argued, seems to offer more protection than the CRC.

Apart from the ACHPR and ACRWC as discussed above, the Protocol to the ACHPR on the Rights of Women in Africa (the Protocol, in force from 24 November 2005) also covers a broad range of issues and advances human rights for African women through creative, substantive and detailed language.[7] Article 12 of the Protocol addresses the right to education and training. The Protocol obligates state parties to eliminate all forms of discrimination against women[8] and guarantee equal opportunity and access in the sphere of education and training (article 12(1)(a)). Article 12(c) of the Protocol obligates state parties to protect women, especially the girl child, from all forms of abuse, including sexual harassment in schools and other educational institutions and provide for sanctions against perpetrators of such practices. This provision is extremely important in the sense that many girls are denied their right to education because of the sexual harassment that they experience in schools (Naylor 2002). Examples of this would be South Africa and Togo. According to a report by Human Rights Watch (2001), South African girls suffer great harm at the hands of their male teachers and classmates. Similarly, a recent report by Plan Togo (2006) shows that sexual abuse and harassment of girls in schools is common and contributes to the dropout rate.

The UN Millennium Development Goals (MDGs) target ensuring that all boys and girls complete a full course of primary schooling. MDG 2 aims at achieving universal primary education by 2015, whilst MDG 3 aims to eliminate gender disparities in primary and secondary education (this target was supposed to have been achieved by 2005, but was not met). Considerable momentum has built up in support of the commitments expressed by the MDGs, and for developing countries there is pressure to develop good quality plans and transparent means of achieving education for all (EFA).

The need for a special focus on women and girls' education has also been reconfirmed at various international conferences. Some of these conferences include the 1985 3rd World Conference on Women (Nairobi), where education was declared the basis for improving the status of women; and the 4th World Conference on Women in 1995, where representatives from 189 countries voted unanimously to adopt the Beijing Declaration and the Plan for Action (PFA), reflecting a new institutional commitment to the goals of gender equality and development. The PFA states that specific action should be taken by governments to ensure equal access to education and that the gender gap in elementary education be closed by 2005. When 189 heads of states signed the Millennium Declaration in 2000, they recognized that educating girls is a powerful and necessary first step towards ending poverty and achieving human rights (Annan 2005). They also agreed to achieve gender equality at all levels

---

7   Of the 53 member states of the African Union 43 have signed the Charter.

8   According to article 1 of the Protocol, 'women' means persons of female gender, including girls.

of education by 2015 with a focus on ensuring girl's full and equal access to and achievement in basic education of good quality. All these international conferences were well attended by African governments.

From the above, it is clear that most African countries are formally committed, internationally, to improve the girl's right to education as enunciated in international human rights instruments. International law thus requires that a state providing education to its citizens must assure equal access to education for all its citizens. However, international commitment to improve girl's right to education is not going to help the girl child if it cannot be translated into national laws and policies, as the first step towards implementation. It is, therefore, important to look at the practical implementation of the right to education by selected African governments. In the following section, an examination of some constitutional provisions on the right to education, policy and legislative initiatives is made.

Constitutionalization, Legislation and Policy Initiatives by Selected African Governments

Many African countries have undertaken a number of constitutional, policy and legislative reforms to realize the right of the girl child to education. Although not very common, the issue of children's access to socio-economic rights is mentioned in some African constitutions.[9] One notable socio-economic right that often finds its way into African constitutions and legislation is indeed the right to education, and particularly the right to free and compulsory primary education, as contemplated by articles 28(1)(a) of the CRC and 11(3)(a) of the ACRWC. According to a report by Action Aid,

> [f]irst, education is an entitlement that is sanctioned by states, through legislation and national constitutions – twenty-seven sub-Saharan African countries have a constitutional guarantee of free basic education for all children ... and therefore education is a justiciable right.

The following is a consideration of such reforms by selected countries in Africa, chosen because of the author's familiarity with developments concerning girl's access to education, or because activities surrounding implementation of girl's rights to education appear to be good practice.

South Africa

Section 29 of the South African Constitution, Act 108 of 1996 provides that every citizen has the right to education, including adult basic education. It has been argued that the right to education is afforded to all its citizens irrespective of age, sex, race or class (Vilakazi-Tselane 1998). The South African Schools Act (84 of 1996) defines

---

9   See for instance, Constitution of the People's Democratic Republic of Algeria (article 59), Constitution of the Republic of Angola (article 31), Constitution of the Republic of Burundi (article 39). For further discussion see Chapters 4 and 6 in this volume.

the right to basic education as compulsory education for all children aged 7–15 years (or in Grades 1–9). The first White Paper (1995) formed the principal reference point for subsequent policy and legislative reform in the education system after apartheid. Some important legislative developments include the National Education Policy Act (1996) and the South African Schools Act (1996). On admission to a school or educational institution, the Schools Act bans unfair admission policies and discriminatory educational practices in public schools. The Schools Act also makes provision for a school fee exemption process and stipulates that no child may be refused admission to a public school because of non-payment. However, all parents are liable to pay a fee agreed upon by a school governing body, unless exempted. In 2007, government introduced for the first time some 'fee free' schools, targeting the poorest school communities.

Some important recent education campaigns in relation to South Africa include a focus on expanding the role of schools in the community, expanding education coverage for youth and adults in response to development needs, and addressing HIV/Aids through the education and training system. Among other things, the Department of Education has identified the problems related to gender equality as important gaps within the proposed implementation of the Ministerial *Tirisano* plan, which establishes priorities for the sector. There is also a National Policy on HIV/Aids for Learners, Educators in Public Schools and Students in Further Education and Training which aims to increase learner knowledge about HIV/Aids through schools and the curriculum design, to reduce discrimination against those affected by HIV/Aids, and to introduce universal precautions for the safety of learners and educators at education institutions. Implementation has been supported by the development of resources and materials, together with a plan to monitor progress.[10]

Other measures taken by the South African government include the establishment of the Committee on Gender Equity. This Committee was established by the Minister of Education in October 1996 (Human Rights Watch 2001), and has contributed to the development of Curriculum 2005 to ensure that gender sensitivity is reflected in the learning outcomes. All curriculum development work is sensitive to gender, race and disability. This Committee is also responsible for reviewing practices within the department of education and within schools that negatively influence the participation of girls and women in formal education. The elimination of gender disparity in South Africa is evident in the fact that more girl children than boys successfully completed formal schooling in 2007.

Malawi

Malawi has ratified a number of international instruments aimed at the protection of the right to education of the girl child and has taken several initiatives that are aimed at implementing the right to education. For instance, the Malawi Constitution of 1994 recognizes the right to education (section 25). Section 25 provides that 'all

---

10 See <http://66.102.9.104/search?q=cache:t78q-wnUg8wJ:web.uct.ac.za/depts/ci/pubs/pdf/poverty/resrep/rapid/chapter5.pdf+Implementing+the+right+to+education+of+a+girl+child+by+African+governments&hl=en&gl=za&ct=clnk&cd=42/> (accessed on 15 June 2006).

persons are entitled to education'. 'All persons' would, arguably, include girls, boys, women and refugees. While applauding Malawi for the constitutional recognition of the right to education, it has been noted that the formulation of this provision is problematic in that it does not spell out the content of the right to education (Chirwa 2006). This is particularly so considering that the right to education is also included as a principle of national policy, which is not justiciable by courts of law. According to Chirwa, as a principle of national policy, the right to education has more detailed content. It obligates the state to 'provide adequate resources to the education sector and devise programmes' in order to 'eliminate literacy in Malawi', to 'make primary education compulsory and free to all citizens of Malawi', to 'offer greater access to higher learning and continuing education', and to 'promote national goals such as unity and the elimination of political, religious, racial and ethnic intolerance' (section 13(f) of the Malawian Constitution). If these principles were to be construed to be justiciable as rights to education under section 25, Malawi would come close to complying with the requirements of the right to education in both the CRC and the ACRWC as far as constitutional recognition is concerned (Chirwa 2006).

At the domestic level, Malawi has undertaken a number of policy changes. For example, the Malawi Education Policy has been said to be gender sensitive and has put several measures in place to reduce the gender gap in education. At primary level, all children had to have an equal access to quality primary education without discrimination due to gender, colour, race, religion or ethnic background. To ensure full participation of girls at secondary level, the Malawi government intended to increase constantly the quota for girls' enrolment from 33 per cent towards 50 per cent as the pool of girls increase. It was reported that, by 1995, the spread of children attending day urban secondary schools was 50 per cent boys and 50 per cent girls. Further, at tertiary education level, the policy of the Ministry of Education was to give special attention to the enrolment of women and make deliberate efforts to encourage women to enrol in courses that have traditionally been dominated by men. Additionally, a review of a pregnancy policy had been done to allow pregnant girls to be enrolled at school after delivery. If the boy responsible for the pregnancy was in school, he was also supposed to be withdrawn and be readmitted after one year (Swainson et al. 1998).

In October 1994, the Malawi government introduced a Free Primary Education (FPE) policy, one of the first African countries to do so. Just prior to that, the government had brought in tuition waivers, in phases, from Standard 1, but parents were still expected to pay book fees and to contribute to school funds (Riddell 2003). It was a top-level dynamic political initiative that triggered FPE implementation, and a mass media campaign mobilized the population on FPE. However, enrolment rose over 78 per cent in eight years following the introduction of FPE, leading to 'access shock'. Nevertheless, a result of the FPE was that gender disparities in enrolment were greatly reduced (Swainson et al.). Furthermore, the Girls Attainment in Basic Literacy and Education (GABLE) school fee waiver programme for non-repeating girls from standard 2 to 8 also increased the girls' access and persistence in school. In 1992/1993 and 1993/1994 school years, it was estimated that half a million girls benefited from the programme each year. Net enrolment prior to FPE had been 58 per cent for both boys and girls; by 1999/2000, male and female gross enrolment rates were comparable, at 157 per cent and 158 per cent respectively (Sloth-Nielsen and Mezmur 2007). Early childhood programmes and day care centres have been established in some places as they facilitate access to school for girl children who are entrusted with the care of babies (Sloth-Nielsen and Mezmur 2007).

Uganda

According to section 30 of the 1995 Ugandan Constitution, 'all persons have a right to education'. The understanding of some writers is that section 30 entails that each child be entitled to basic education. However, as is the case with Malawi, the provision lacks clear normative content of what exactly is the entitlement conferred. But following on the 1995 Constitution, the 1996 Ugandan Children's Statute (6 of 1996) has gone a step further in defining what the content of the right to education is. For example, in defining parental responsibility to maintain children, the Act adds that this parental duty gives the child the right to education (Tomasevski 1999). Furthermore, the Education Strategic Investment Plan (ESIP) 1998–2003 commits government to assuring universal access to primary education as the highest priority, points to the removal of financial impediments, and pays particular attention to gender and regional equality. In 1997, Uganda also launched a Universal Primary Education policy (UPE). Additionally, the Ministry of Education in Uganda resolved to address the sexual abuse of girls in schools (Hyde et al. 2005). This resolution led to the dismissal and imprisonment of some teachers and male students who had had intercourse with under-age girls. Successful legal cases coupled with media drawing attention to the issue, encourages other girls to speak out (Hyde et al. 2005). This in turn has a potential of reducing sexual misconduct and violence in schools.

Ghana

Article 25(1) of the 1992 Constitution of Ghana guarantees the right to equal educational opportunities and facilities. Article 38 of the same constitution provides for educational objectives under the Directive Principles of State Policy. The government of Ghana's determination to ensure equity by the year 2005 and equality by the year 2015 in education is reinforced in several of its policies. For example, the Education Strategic Plan Policy (2003–2015) is gender sensitive in its allocation of funds for the education of girls. There is also the Adolescent Sexual and Reproductive Health (ASRH) policy that includes the Population Policy of 1994 and the Youth Policy (Lithur 2003).

All these policies contain linkages with the Ministry of Education (MOE) as an institution and roles are carved out in these policies for the MOE in relation to ASRH issues. In the Youth Policy, the Ministry of Youth and Sports identifies health problems and challenges facing the youth to include sexuality and reproductive health, teenage pregnancy, early marriage and parentage. Priority areas for action in the Policy include the strengthening linkages between education and training. The Population Policy identifies the issue of sexually transmitted diseases (STDs) and HIV/Aids and puts forward the objective to educate the youth on population matters directly affecting them such as sexual relationships, fertility regulation, adolescent health and so on.

Other African Countries

As already mentioned, quite a number of African countries have incorporated the right to education either in their constitutions, other national legislation or a combination of both. For instance, article 20 of Namibia's Constitution provides that all people should have access to education and basic education shall be free and compulsory.[11] The Constitution of 2005 of Southern Sudan provides that '[e]ducation is a right for every citizen'[12] and that '[p]rimary education is compulsory and the State shall provide it free'.[13] Article 17 of the Malian Constitution, and articles 35(2) and (4) of the Constitution of Chad express a similar sentiment. Similarly, subordinate national legislation declaring free and compulsory primary education is also not in short supply. Examples include section 7 of the Kenyan Children's Act, 2001, the Education Act of 2004 of Sierra Leone, Act No. 99-046 of 28 December 1999 containing the Education Policy Act of Mali, the Act on the general organization of education (Act No. 16/96) of Gabon, sections 4(3) and 9 of Act No. 016/PR/06 of Chad,[14] article 11 of the Finance Act in Cameroon,[15] and section 8 of the Children's Act of Ghana coupled with the Education Act 87 of 1961.

Beyond the realm of the black letter of the law, certain policies and practices that promote girls' education exist on the continent. For instance, well placed individuals with a commitment to gender equality in education have been noted to champion girls' education.[16] For example, in Ethiopia, a woman filled the post of Minister of Education from 1992 to 2005. As a female minister, she consistently drew the attention of politicians and policy makers to girls' education. In Benin, abolition of school fees for girls in rural areas coupled with a network of parents, teachers, NGOs, students and community leaders set up to change family schooling practices in relation to girls, has helped to increase girls primary education.[17] The

---

11 Article 20 states:

* All persons shall have a right to education.
* Primary education shall be compulsory and the State shall provide reasonable facilities to render effective this right for every resident within Namibia, by establishing and maintaining State schools at which primary education will be provided free of charge.
* Children shall not be allowed to leave school until they have completed their primary education or have attained the age of sixteen (16) years, whichever is the sooner, save in so far as this may be authorized by an act of Parliament on grounds of health or other considerations pertaining to the public interest.

12 Article 44(1) of Constitution.

13 Article 44(2) of Constitution.

14 Act No. 016/PR/06 of 13 March 2003 that provides directives and orientation for primary and elementary education. See <www.juriafrica.com/?base=jort&action=viewDoc&iddoc=1278&highlight=false&position=0> (accessed 23 November 2007).

15 Finance Act No. 2000/08 of 30 June 2000, as referred to in Heyns (2004, 946).

16 Oxfam GB, 'Making it Happen: Political Will for Gender Equality', December 2005.

17 EFA/UNESCO 'Global Monitoring Report 2006: Literacy for Life' (2006) <http://unesdoc.unesco.org/images/0014/001416/141639e.pdf> (accessed 23 February 2007).

experience of Sudan through the establishment of a girls' basic education service and of an education service for nomadic children has helped improve the situation of marginalized children.[18] In addition, Ethiopia's policy has resulted in the reduction of travel time to and from schools, as well as the minimization of risks associated with distance, which has had a positive effect on girls' education.[19]

Another important innovation comes from Chad, where the state has the additional burden to ensure access to quality education, to promote schooling/education of girl children by combating stereotypes, and to create structures adapted to the needs of handicapped children as well as children living in rural areas, especially children from nomadic groups.[20]

Additionally, some countries have recognized that traditional and religious leaders are crucial advocates of reform. In Guinea and Mauritania for example, religious leaders were called upon to help create public awareness on the importance of educating girls. The success of this strategy showed that gaining the trust and support of prominent community members ought to be the starting point for any initiative to change negative attitudes towards girl's schooling (Kane 2004).

Non-Governmental Organizations (NGOs) Working in African Countries

Apart from governments, NGOs such as UNICEF work with partners such as the South African Girl Child Alliance and the Girls Education Movement (GEM) to advocate for development of national policy and legislation on violence against women and children (UNICEF South Africa 2006). At community level, UNICEF is working with organizations like Crime Reduction in the Schools Project (CRISP) to facilitate community level action in reducing violence, and to declare 200 schools as 'safe schools' for boys and girls in South Africa (UNICEF South Africa 2006).

Furthermore, UNICEF's West and Central Africa Regional Office supports UNICEF Country Offices in implementing a diverse range of activities to help ensure that all girls get into school, that all girls stay in school and that all girls learn what they need to succeed later in life.[21] Some activities include: launching the '25 x 2005' initiative on accelerating girls' education, targeting eight countries in the region (Benin, Burkina-Faso, Central African Republic, Chad, Guinea-Conakry, Democratic Republic of the Congo [DRC], Mali and Nigeria); supporting 'back to school' programmes in Liberia and Côte d'Ivoire; assisting in the expansion of the satellite school programme in Burkina-Faso; initiating a volunteer 'young professional female role model' campaign as part of the integrated approach to accelerating girls' education in the DRC; implementing teacher orientation activities

---

However, this by no means should be read to imply that the practice of not abolishing school fees for boys is legally sound under international law.

18 CRC Committee, 'Concluding Observations on the Periodic Report of Sudan' (2002) para. 53.

19 CRC Committee, 'Periodic Report of Ethiopia' (2005) para. 196.

20 Sections 15(1), 15(5) and 21(2) of Act No. 016/PR/06.

21 United Nations, 'Girls Education: West and Central Africa Region (published on 8 January 2004) <http://www.reliefweb.int/rw/RWB.NSF/db900SID/OCHA-64D96E?OpenDocument> (accessed on 19 July 2006).

and conducting a needs assessment for the reconstruction of the education sector by providing emergency education classes for children displaced and affected by regional conflict; participating in national education gender reviews; supplying 'school-in-the-box' education kits and other essential teaching and learning supplies; advocating for the right of all children to go to school and for the abolition of primary school fees that prevent many girls and boys from going to school.

In conclusion, this part has outlined the contribution of constitutional protection, policy initiatives and legislation passed by selected African governments towards the realization of the girl's right to education. What has been observed, as a common feature, is the domestication of the CRC and other international standards in many country's constitutions after ratification of the CRC.[22] This, obviously, highlights the important role that the international standards have played in the implementation of the right to education of an African girl child. It has also been observed that legislation and educational policies that have been put in place to achieve the right to education are gender neutral. Additionally, it has further been observed that in some cases deliberate steps (affirmative action) have been taken in order to realize the right to education of a girl child. However, the realization of the African girl child's right to education will only be achieved by the actual implementation of the policies and laws. Therefore, the next part will examine the progress made by some African governments in order to see the effectiveness of the legislation and policies that have been put in place.

Progress Made by some African Governments Towards the Implementation of the Right to Education

Rapid progress on girl's education, on a scale needed to achieve gender parity in Africa within the next few years, is eminently possible (Annan 2005). Many African countries have made remarkable progress. For example, in January 2003, when Kenya's plan for FPE was adopted, over a million children came to school and enrolment shot up from 5.9 to 7.2 million in a week (Department of International Development 2005). It was also noted that gender disparities in primary education in Kenya practically disappeared. The ratio of girls to boys remains among the best in the region, with 94 girls enrolled for every 100 boys (Fleshman 2005). It is also stated that Kenya is among the few African countries where a greater population of all school-aged girls, 73 per cent enrol in primary education than do boys, 71 per cent of whom attend classes. With families no longer forced to choose which children they can afford to educate, millions of girls now have access to an education in Kenya (Bouchane 2006). Equally impressive has been Kenya's success in reducing dropout rates from 4.9 per cent in 1999 to just 2 per cent in 2003 (Fleshman 2005). Although these statistics on the dropout rate do not give the ratio of boys to girls, a presumption can be made that the dropout rate has also been reduced for girls because of the high

---

22 Despite the fact that most African countries have ratified the international conventions, it should be noted that there are some African countries such as Ethiopia, Burundi, Angola, Botswana, Kenya and Swaziland that have no constitutional guarantee of the right to education in their constitutions.

attendance rate of girls referred to earlier. Most significantly, the Kenyan Education Ministry has said that the average household living is much improved because the money previously earmarked for school fees can now be spent on other things such as food. Awareness of HIV/Aids and other issues is also now greater. The importance of educating girls in relation to HIV/Aids can be seen in a study that was conducted in Zambia, which, according to Bouchane, found that HIV/Aids spread twice as fast among uneducated girls as among educated girls (Bouchane 2006).

Mauritania, which also made a commitment to free and compulsory primary education, increased the ratio of girls to boys from 67 per cent to 93 per cent between 1990 and 1996. Mali cut a steep gender gap by more than 10 percentage points in the 1990s, at the same time raising primary completion rates among both boys and girls by more than 20 percentage points (Bouchane 2006). After Uganda abolished fees, girls' enrolment increased by 20 percentage points almost overnight; between the poorest fifth of girls, it went from 46 per cent to 82 per cent. Additionally, in 1996, Uganda abolished user fees for up to four children from each family (two of whom should be girls), and for all orphans (Deininger 2003). This led to an increase of more than 70 per cent in total enrolments overnight – an increase of over 2 million children in education. The share of education in the overall national budget rose from 22 per cent in 1995 to 31 per cent in 1999. In Malawi, the introduction of FPE has helped to raise enrolment rates from 1.9 million to 3.2 million in 1994 (Swainson et al. 1998) but school dropouts have been increasing, especially among girls, and interventions by UNICEF, the World Food Programme (WFP), the United Nations Development Programme (UNDP) and the United Nations Fund for Population Activities (UNFPA) have aimed to stem the tide. Other countries including Côte d'Ivoire, Morocco and Togo also saw an increase in primary school enrolment of more than 20 per cent between 1990/91 and 2000/01. In these countries, improvements were attributed mainly to an increase in girl's enrolment.[23]

In Tanzania, because of debt relief, the government was able, in 2001, to abolish the user fees families had to pay to send their children to school; enrolments in primary education increased by 50 per cent as a result. It is estimated that 1.6 million children returned to school after these changes.[24] However, Tanzania now spends over $150 million more on schools and teachers than before and debt relief has provided predictable financing which has enabled the government to implement a long-term plan for universal primary education. The country is now on track to get every child into primary school by 2006 – nine years ahead of target – and to achieve the goal of gender equity as well. In South Africa, 2003 saw more girls enrolled in schools than boys, a continuing trend despite the fact that in the early grades, boys make up the majority of enrolment (51–52 per cent in grades 1–4) (UNICEF South Africa 2006). In grade 5, boys constitute 50.5 per cent of enrolment, but thereafter, girls outnumber the boys and by grade 12, boys make up 45 per cent enrolment. Gross enrolment has improved over the last decade moving closer to 100 per cent in primary schools.

---

23 'Progress towards the Millennium Development Goals, 1990–2005', at <http://unstats. un.org/unsd/mi/mi_coverfinal.htm> (accessed on 05 July 2006).

24 UNICEF 'Debt Relief and Girls' Education' (published online October 2003), <http:// gbgm-umc.org/umw/action-Girlsedu.html> (accessed on 6 September 2006).

Overall, across sub-Saharan Africa the primary school enrolment rate increased from 74 per cent in 1990 to 87 per cent in 2001. Thirty million more children have enrolled in primary school since 1990. And secondary enrolment in the least developed countries has increased from 18 per cent in 1990 to 30 per cent in 2000. Over 90 per cent of reporting member states to CEDAW (including Chad, Central African Republic, Eritrea, Ethiopia, Liberia, Mauritania, Rwanda, Tanzania, Uganda and Zimbabwe) have developed national action plans that address, among other things, women's empowerment. Among other things, these plans advocate the enrolment of all school-age girls as well as the readmission of such girls who have dropped out of school due to pregnancy. It should, however, be noted, that despite the considerable progress realized, the advancement of girl children in schools remains low in Africa.[25] According to the State of the World's Children Report, 2004, girl's primary school completion rates lag way behind that of boys, at 76 per cent compared to 85 per cent. This gender gap means that millions more girls than boys are dropping out each year. As a result, the majority of the children not in school are girls. It is also reported that the most worrying figures come from sub-Saharan Africa where the number of girls out of school rose from 20 million in 1990 to 24 million in 2002.

Addressing the Educational Needs of an African Girl Child in Armed Conflicts and as a Refugee

The right to education is often lost in countries at war.[26] However, conflicts have been argued to provide no exception to the CRC and the ACRWC that elaborates in articles 28 and 11, respectively, the right of the child to education (Roger 2002). The CRC Committee's General Comment no. 6 (2005) on the Treatment of Unaccompanied and Separated Children outside their Country of Origin offers some guidance to states parties on what should be done to ensure that access to education is maintained during all phases of the displaced cycle, irrespective of status.[27] It is also important to note that there is specific guidance with regard to separated and unaccompanied girls, namely that they should have equal access to formal and informal education, including vocational training at all levels. Though it is acknowledged that schooling can be all the more important for children and families in times of crisis (Richardson 2000), the challenge to maintain schools during and after war is huge. Schools have often been targets of attack (Roger 2002; Sommers 2002).

Despite difficulties, some African countries and communities have risen to the challenge of implementing the right to education for both boys and girls during and after conflicts. For example, in Tanzania, after the influx of half a million refugees from Rwanda in 1994, an emergency education system was set up. Makeshift schools

---

25 The United Nations Girls Initiative, at <http://ungei.org/news/index_270.html> (accessed on 05 July 2006).

26 Examples of African countries that have been affected are Sierra Leone, Mozambique, Northern Uganda, Somalia, Liberia, Sudan and Angola. For a discussion of war and education, and in particular the challenges posed for education in reconstruction efforts after war, see Save the Children 2007.

27 See further on displaced and refugee children, Chapter 11 in this volume.

were built hastily with rocks and logs, enabling 65 per cent of refugee children to have access to a minimum level of education (Roger 2002). Eritrea is another example; in the 1980s, Roger records that classes were held under trees, in caves or in camouflaged huts. In Liberia, United Nations High Commissioner for Refugees (UNHCR) and Save the Children provided psychosocial support to ex-child soldiers among refugees from Sierra Leone. They offered remedial courses as well as vocational training. UNHCR also trained teachers and community leaders to improve their ability to meet educational needs in Kenya and Guinea. Schools for refugee children provide classes on peace and life skills, as well as teacher training on these matters.

Article 38 of the CRC makes special note of the obligation of states parties to respect and ensure respect for international humanitarian law as it applies to children, as well as to take all feasible measures to ensure the protection and care of children affected by armed conflict. Article 39 of the CRC focuses on the treatment, recovery and social reintegration of children who are victims of conflict. Education has a special role to play in the fulfilment of both of these articles, since it can be an important medium of protection and also of recovery and social reintegration in the context of conflict (Boyden and Ryder 1996). The importance of providing education to girl children faced with war cannot be overemphasized. Otherwise, they are at risk of becoming sex workers or face unwanted pregnancies, as happened in Sierra Leone. After the war, organizations such as the Forum for African Women Educationalists (FAWE) was one such organization established in 1995 to address the educational needs of these girl survivors. FAWE Sierra Leone opened a primary school for war-affected girls in the western area. It catered mostly for internally displaced girls in Freetown. Their next target was the establishment of Skills Training and Vocational centres for teenage and girl mothers in Freetown. After the January 1999 invasion of the city of Freetown, FAWE again intervened by organizing programmes for girls affected by the invasion, especially rape victims. It is said that by 1999, FAWE had established eight institutions for girls to access primary level education and ten skills training centres for young war affected girls nationwide.

Apart from FAWE, organizations like the Council of Churches in Sierra Leone (CCSL), Family Homes Movement (FHM), Christian Children's Fund (CCF), and a host more have come to the aid of girl children, though many more girl children continue to suffer silently. Government has now implemented a primary education scheme for all children.[28] This will assist parents send all their children to school and not to discriminate against the girl child because of poverty. In 2002, the government also established an umbrella National Commission for War Affected Children (NACWAC) to cater for the needs of war affected boys and girls in the country. To commemorate the day of the African Child, the NACWAC opened a centre that caters for war-affected children, with girls constituting a good number of these children. In doing all this, the government is collaborating with other child protection agencies to support these young boys and girls. This idea has been commended as a good approach, as these children also need care and love, apart from the education that they gain.

---

28 See <http://66.102.9.104/search?q=cache:HLhkc82qq8sJ:www.isis.or.ug/docs/2003_ conflict_consq.doc+Implementing+the+right+to+education+of+a+girl+child+by+African ı g overnments&hl=en&gl=za&ct=clnk&cd=46> (accessed on 15 June 2006).

Another example is Uganda,[29] where girls who had been abducted and raped, and returned as child-mothers, faced specific hardships.[30] War Child, through Ancholi Education Initiative, supports child-mothers by providing scholarships for education, and materials such as school uniforms, books and pens for the duration of their three-year secondary school programme. Child mothers are given access to psychosocial support, counselling services and support to meet their basic needs such as food, shelter, childcare and health care. Emphasis is placed on increasing child mothers' access to basic education, including by means of a community-based outreach initiative and social support programme.

CCF[31] has also come to the rescue of Ugandan children affected by war. In that country, CCF is providing psychosocial support through non-formal education and youth group activities and works with the community to reduce the vulnerability of children to sexual and gender-based violence.[32] Apart from CCF, To Love Children (TLC) is said to be working towards the realization of the right to education of girls affected by war in northern Uganda. TLC is reported to be presently building a resource centre and library for the girl children affected by 20 years of insurgency and war in Uganda (Waldam 2006). To achieve this, TLC has created partnerships with UNICEF, private business in the United States, as well as the government of Uganda to see that this first effort is replicated all over the north of Uganda and Africa. By creating a concrete library in a war zone, a message is sent to the girls that there is optimism for their future. Waldam further argues that by providing education, violence and discrimination are reduced or eliminated.

This section has demonstrated that, regardless of whether the girl child's right to education is affected by being a refugee or due to armed conflicts, it is certainly the case that far more could be done to support the girl child achieve her right to education. Having looked at what governments are doing in order to implement the right to education of an African girl child, a discussion on the overall constraints faced by governments in implementing this right is obviously necessary. The following section looks briefly at some of these.

Constraints

An obvious common constraint is, firstly, a financial one. Countries that have abolished school fees and have opened the doors of learning to all are spending 20

---

29 In 1986, a brutal civil war began raging in northern Uganda between government forces and the Lord's Resistance Army (LRA), displacing 1.5 million people. UN sources estimate that 75 per cent of the LRA fighting force consists of abducted children and that approximately 26,000 children have been abducted in the course of the 18-year conflict.

30 Ugandan Girl's Education Initiative Project (2005), at <http://www.warchild.org/projects/WC-Canada?Uganda/uganda.html> (accessed on 21 October 2006).

31 Christian Children's Fund (CCF), which is working in Sierra Leone, is also working in Uganda.

32 'Child Soldiers' (published February 2006) <http://www.christianchildrensfund.org/uploadedFiles/Public_Site/news/Relief_professionals/ChildSoldiers_Brief.pdf> (accessed on 27 July 2006), 2.

per cent or more of their budgets on education (Annan 2005). For example, since Kenya's introduction of FPE in 2003, education spending has risen to 40 per cent of the government budget. Overall, it is reported that the government's spending on education and training reached an estimated $420 million. Similarly, in Gambia, education spending increased by 10 per cent annually during that period, and primary education absorbed nearly half of its budget.[33]

Secondly, it has been argued that there is a lack of political will in some governments towards implementation of the right to education. This is reflected in the budgetary allocations. For example, despite longstanding commitments to increase education spending to 6 per cent of GDP, countries in Africa still devote an average of less than 3.5 per cent of GDP to spending on all levels of education. Primary education receives less of their GDP, on average, than military spending (Annan 2005). Most countries still levy fees and charges of various kinds for primary education. Very few countries have a comprehensive national scheme of cash stipends, free school meals or other incentives to support attendance by girls and the poorest pupils (Tomasevski 2006).

Thirdly, it is evident that implementation of the policies has been problematic. Because of this, well intended policies may become diluted. For example, when the government of Malawi changed its policy to permit young mothers to re-enter school after giving birth, implementation of this policy met with considerable resistance. School personnel, among others, were concerned that it would encourage promiscuity. They also felt that young mothers would be a bad influence on the young girls in school (Semu 2005).

Conclusion

This chapter has looked at the commitment of African countries to achieve gender equality and universal access to education, expressed through the ratification of international instruments, the passing of legislation and the adoption of policies that have been put in place by the governments. Most of these offer equitable opportunities (measures to address formal equality) for both boys and girls to advance up the educational ladder, to secondary and even tertiary level. It has, however, been noted that in some countries these measures to eradicate the educational disadvantage facing poor girls stop at the primary school level. Other countries, however, provide opportunities up to tertiary level, which can be regarded as good practice. This chapter has also looked at some policies and legislative measures that have an indirect impact on the right to education, and address substantive inequality that persists for girl's access to education. Some of these proceed from an awareness of the fact that girls' education is also achievable if they are freed from the threat of sexual harassment, they are adequately fed, and they are free from gender-biased assumptions of what and how children should learn. Finally, the specific concerns relating to girl's education during armed conflict and specific challenges emerging in implementing progressive policies to further girl's education are provided.

---

33 This position had a dramatic impact on girls' enrolment. It doubled from 36 per cent in 1980 to 75 per cent in 2000.

References

Articles, Books and Chapters in Books

Beiter, K.D. (2006), *The Protection of the Right to Education by International Law* (Boston, MA: Martinus Nijhoff).

Boyden, J. and Ryder, P. (1996), *The Provision of Education to Children Affected by Armed Conflict* (Oxford: Oxford University Press).

Chamblee, L.E. (2004), 'Rhetoric or Rights: When Culture and Religion Bar Girls' Right to Education', *Virginia Journal of International Law* 44, 1073.

Deininger, K. (2003), 'Does Cost of Schooling Affect Enrolment by the Poor? Universal Primary Education in Uganda', *Economics of Education Review* 22, 291.

Ewelukwa, U.U. (2005), 'The Girl Child, African States, and International Human Rights Law: Towards a New Framework for Action', in Ezeilo J. and Nnaemeka O. (eds), *Engendering Human Rights: Cultural and Socio-Economic Realities in Africa* (New York: Palgrave Macmillan).

Ezeilo, J. and Nnaemeka, O. (eds) (2005), *Engendering Human Rights: Cultural and Socio-Economic Realities in Africa* (New York: Palgrave Macmillan).

Heyns, C. (ed.) (2004), *Human Rights Law in Africa*, vol. 2 (Leiden: Martinus Nijhoff).

Nicholson, H.J. and Maschino, M.F. (2001), 'Strong, Smart, and Bold Girls: The Girls Incorporated Approach to Education', *Fordham Urban Law Journal* 29, 561.

General Comments, Unpublished Papers, Treaties, Declarations and Reports

Annan, K. (2005), 'Girls Can't Wait: A Briefing Paper for the UN Beijing + Review Appraisal' <http://www.campaignforeducation.org/resources/Mar2005/bio-brief-final.doc> (accessed 16 June 2006).

Bouchane, K. (2006), 'Basics: Global Education For All Campaign' <http://www.irinnews.org/images/301243.JPG> (accessed 27 July 2006).

CESCR Committee (1999), 'General Comment no. 13: Substantive Issues Arising in the Implementation of the ICESCR' (E/C.12/1999/10).

Child Soldiers (2006), <http://www.christianchildrensfund.org/uploadedFiles/Public_Site/news/Relief_professionals/ChildSoldiers.Brief.pdf> (accessed 27 July 2006).

Chirwa, D.M. (2006), 'Harmonization of National and International Laws to Protect Children's Rights: The Malawi Report' (African Child Policy Forum, unpublished).

CRC Committee (2001), 'General Comment no. 1: The Aims of Education' (CRC/GC/2001/1).

CRC Committee, (2006), 'General Comment no. 6: The Treatment of Unaccompanied and Separated Children Outside their Country of Origin' (CRC/GC/2006/1).

Department of International Development (2005), 'Girls' Education: Towards a Better Future for All' <http://www.ohchr.org/english/issues/development/docs/girlseducation.pdf> (accessed 8 June 2006).

Education For ALL/UNESCO (2006), 'Global Monitoring Report 2006: Literacy for Life' <http://unesdoc.unesco.org/images/0014/001416/141639e.pdf> (accessed 23 February 2007).

Fleshman, M. (2005), 'Giant Steps for Kenya's Schools' <http://www.un.org/ecosocdev/geninfo/afrec/vol19no2/192-pg10.htm> (accessed 23 October 2006).

Human Rights Watch (2001), 'National and Provincial Government Response' <http://www.hrw.org/reports/2001/safrica/ZA-FINAL-o8.htm> (accessed 23 October 2006).

Hyde, K., Ekatan, P., Kiaye, P. and Basara, C. (2005), 'The Impact of HIV/AIDS on Formal Schooling in Uganda', as cited in Oxfam GB (2005).

Kadzamira, E.C., 'Affirmative Action Policies for Girls Education: A Strategy that Works' <http://www.osisa.org/files/openspace/1-1-p35-esme-chipo-kadzamira.pdf> (accessed 23 October 2006).

Kane, E. (2004), 'Girls Education in Africa: What Do We Know about Strategies that Work?' (Washington DC: World Bank).

Lithur, N.O. (2003), 'Ghana's Education Policy Framework and Adolescent Reproductive Health: A Perspective' <http://www.ayaonline.org/CDWebDocs/AYAResources/Toolbox/AYA-Countries/Ghana/GH-Edupolicy-ASRH.pdf> (accessed 23 October 2006).

Mlama, P. (2006), 'Annual Report, Forum for African Women Educationalists (FAWE)' <www.fawe.org> (accessed 26 May 2008).

Naylor, N. (2002), 'Prohibiting the Ongoing Sexual Harassment of and Sexual Violence against Learners' <http://www.erp.org.za/htm/issue4-2.htm> (accessed 23 October 2006).

Nduru, M. (1999), 'Africa: Urged to Invest in Education of Girls to Reduce Poverty' (22 March 1999) <http://www.twnside.org.sg/title/edu-cn.htm>.

NGO Summary Report (1999), Presented at Sixth African Regional Conference on African Women, Addis Ababa, Ethiopia <http://www.uneca.org/eca-resources/Major-ECA-Websites/6thregionalconference/html/conference/ngos-summary-report.htm> (accessed 23 October 2006).

Okuni, A., 'EFA Policies, Strategies and Reforms in Uganda: Assessment of the Current Potential for Sustainable Progress Towards Achieving the EFA Goals by 2015' <http//portal.unesco.org/education/en/file_download.php> (accessed 23 October 2006).

Oxfam GB (2005), 'Making it Happen: Political Will for Gender Equality' <http://www.oxfam.org.uk/what_we_do/issues/education/downloads/edPaper5.pd> (accessed 26 December 2007).

Plan Togo (2006), 'Suffering to Succeed? Violence and Abuse in Schools in Togo' <http://www.crin.org/docs/plan ed togo.pdf > (accessed 23 October 2006).

Progress Towards the Millennium Development Goals (1990–2005), <http://unstats.un.org/unsd/mi/mi_coverfinal.htm> (accessed 23 October 2006).

Richardson, A. (2000), 'Social Injustice: The Irony of African Schooling Disruption', cited in Warsame, F. (2003), 'Barriers and Constraints to Education in Sub-Saharan Africa: A Case Study of Somalia', MA Thesis, University of Alberta <http://action.web.ca/home/somalicanadians/attach/education-war.pdf.> (accessed 28 July 2006).

Riddell, A. (2003), 'The Introduction of Free Primary Education in Sub-Saharan Africa', (paper commissioned for the EFA Global Monitoring Report 2003/4, The Leap to Equality) <http://unesdoc.unesco.org/images/0014/001469/146914e.pdf> (accessed 28 July 2006).

Roger, I. (2002), 'Education for Children during Armed Conflicts and Post-Conflict Reconstruction' <http://www.unidir.org/pdf/articles/pdf-art1731.pdf> (accessed 28 July 2006).

Save the Children (2007), 'Last in Line, Last in School: How Donors are Failing Children in Conflict Affected Fragile States' <http://www.savethechildren.org.uk/en/docs/last_in_line_long.pdf> (accessed 23 July 2007).

Semu, L. (2005), 'Malawi Country Study', (Background Paper for the Global Campaign for Education) cited in Oxfam GB (2005).

Sloth-Nielsen, J. and Mezmur, B.D. (2007), 'Free Education is a Right for Me: A Report on Free and Compulsory Primary Education' (Save the Children, Southern Sudan Office).

Sommers, M. (2002), 'Children, Education and War: Reaching Education For All (EFA) Objectives in Countries Affected by Conflict' (CPR Working Paper No. 1) (Washington DC: World Bank).

Swainson, N., Bendera, S., Gordon, R. and Kadzamira, E. (1998), 'Promoting Girls' Education in Africa: The Design and Implementation of Policy Intervention', (Education Research Paper No. 25) <http://www.dfid.gov.uk/pubs/files/promgirledafricaedpaper25.pdf> (accessed 28 July 2006).

Tomasevski, K. (1999), 'Report Submitted to the Commission on Economic, Social and Cultural Rights' <http://www.unhchr.ch/Huridocda/Huridoca.nsf/0/e100916 8ab9018aa8025683100351e0c?Opendocument> (accessed 28 July 2006).

Tomasevski, K. (2006), 'The State of the Right to Education Worldwide: Free or Fee: Global Report 2006' <http://www.katarinatomasevski.com/images/Global_Report.pdf>.

UNICEF (1999), 'The State of the World's Children: Education' <http://www.unicef.org/sowc99/>.

UNICEF (2004), 'The State of the World's Children' <http://www.unicef.org/sowc04/files/sowc-africa.doc > (accessed 21 July 2006).

UNICEF South Africa (2006), 'Girls Education' <http://www.unicef.org/southafrica/education.html> (accessed 21 July 2006).

United Nations (2004), 'Girls Education: West and Central Africa Region' <http://www.reliefweb.int/rw/RWB.NSF/db900SID/OCHA-64D96E?OpenDocument> (accessed 15 July 2006).

'United Nations Girls Initiative' <http://ungei.org/news/index_270.html> (accessed 15 July 2006).

Vilakazi-Tselane, L. (1998), 'A Situational Analysis of the Girl Child: A Research Report for NIPILAR – South Africa' (Pretoria: NIPILAR).

Waldam, D.K. (2006), 'Sustainable Educational Development' <http://esaconf.un.org/NB/default.asap?action=a&bordid=518read=2729&fid=47> (accessed 15 July 2006).

War Child (2005), 'Ugandan Girl's Education Initiative Project' <http://www.warchild.org/projects/WC-Canada?Uganda/uganda.html> (accessed 21 July 2006).

Chapter 14

Trafficking of Children in Africa: An Overview of Research, International Obligations and Existing Legal Provisions

Jacqui Gallinetti and Daksha Kassan[1]

Introduction

Trafficking is widely regarded as a global scourge. It affects both children and adults alike, with women and girl children being the most vulnerable, as one of the primary purposes of trafficking is commercial sexual exploitation. However, people are also trafficked for various other purposes such as exploitative labour, removal of organs and slavery.

In particular, child trafficking is a deadly evil on account of the fact that children are the most vulnerable to this 'hidden crime'. Victims of trafficking rarely have the opportunity to report their ordeals to the authorities and children in this regard are the most disempowered. It is therefore incumbent on states to provide practical as well as legal assistance to children. However it has been noted that the magnitude of child trafficking globally makes it clear that many states have been quite ineffectual in protecting children from this particular phenomenon (Grover 2006, 242).

In recent years there has been increased activity in Africa to increase awareness on the issue as well as to enact comprehensive anti-trafficking legislation that not only addresses investigations and prosecutions, but also rehabilitation and repatriation services to victims of trafficking.

In this chapter, the realities relating to trafficking in Africa will be discussed, international instruments will be examined and the extent to which the domestic laws of certain African countries seek to address the problem will be investigated.

Realities on the Ground: Child Trafficking in Africa

Prior to examining whether African countries are fulfilling their international obligations in domestic law, it is necessary to understand the extent of the problem in Africa at the grass-roots level. This will provide an insight into what would be required by legislation to combat and criminalize the phenomenon, the realities of trafficking in and outside of the countries involved, the reasons for the dilemma,

1 The authors wish to thank the Ford Foundation for their support in the compilation of this chapter.

the purposes for which children are trafficked and the means used. Without this information, it is difficult to draft laws that would comprehensively deal with the crime as well as provide for procedures that would effectively assist in their implementation and enforcement.

There is little research available that quantifies the problem and, in any event, it has been noted that it is notoriously difficult to measure the number of children trafficked worldwide (Beyrer 2004). However, what is available does provide an insightful snapshot of the child trafficking phenomenon.

In relation to the Southern African region, the International Organisation for Migration (IOM) has produced a report detailing some of the trafficking trends that prevail (Martens et al. 2003, 13). The IOM report highlights nine distinct trafficking operations that have been identified in the Southern African region, namely, trafficking of women from refugee-producing countries to South Africa; trafficking of children from Lesotho to towns in the eastern Free State of South Africa; trafficking of women and girls from Mozambique to Gauteng and KwaZulu-Natal; trafficking of women from Malawi to Northern Europe; trafficking of women and girls from Malawi to South Africa overland; trafficking of girl and boy children from Malawi to Northern Europe; trafficking of women from Thailand to South Africa; trafficking of women from China to South Africa; and trafficking of Eastern European women to South Africa (Martens et al. 2003, 79).

As far as South Africa is concerned, there appears to be no published research on the trafficking of persons from South Africa to other parts of the world; however, there have been news reports mentioning the trafficking of children from African countries, including South Africa, to Britain to be used in slave-like practices and in the sex industry (South African Law Reform Commission 2004, 11–12). Research by a non-governmental child rights organization in Cape Town shows that the causal factors that give rise to the increase in the phenomenon lie primarily in the economic situation in South Africa coupled with factors such as the breakdown in extended and nuclear families and changes in cultural attitudes and practices (Molo Songololo 2000, 31–5).

Another aspect of this problem that manifests itself in South Africa is the trafficking of refugees and Cape Town[2] has been singled out as the principal destination point for trafficked victims of refugee producing countries (Martens et al. 2003, 13). The report by the IOM notes that war, civil strife and natural disasters have caused the displacement of millions of Africans. For many of them South Africa is seen as an ideal country in which to seek asylum because of its relative economic prosperity and its proximity to many conflict zones (Martens et al. 2003, 13).

The Molo Songololo Report states that the trafficking of South African children is predominantly an in-country phenomenon, with girl children being the primary targets, and parents and local criminal gangs being the primary traffickers (Molo Songololo 2000, 2). The report notes that such in-country trafficking of children takes place both between and within provinces and that the primary provinces of origin are the Eastern Cape and KwaZulu-Natal (considered to be more rural provinces) while the primary provinces of destination are Gauteng and the Western Cape (considered to be more urban provinces) (Molo Songololo 2000, 38).

---

2   One of the major cities in South Africa.

Apart from the trafficking of children for purposes of sexual exploitation, the phenomenon of trafficking children for domestic labour has arisen in South Africa. Evidence for the link with the trafficking of children for this purpose comes from a study undertaken by *terre des hommes schweiz* (tdh-ch) (Koen and Van Vuuren 2002). The tdh-ch report notes that child domestic workers in the Western Cape are generally recruited from impoverished rural areas by an agent who usually promises them work as shop assistants, office workers or domestic workers. The report goes on to note that the conditions of employment can include slave-like conditions, sexual violence and debt bondage.

According to the Molo Songololo report, the cross border trafficking of children in South Africa involves the traffic of children from South East Asia to escort agencies in Cape Town and Gauteng and the main perpetrators of such trafficking have been identified as foreign (Molo Songololo 2000, 37). It has also been noted that South Africa is a transit point for trafficking operations between developing countries and Europe, the United States and Canada because it has direct flights and shipping routes to most countries in the developed world (South African Law Reform Commission 2004, 11).

In relation to North Africa, the fourth report on the implementation of the Agenda for Action adopted at the World Congress against Commercial Sexual Exploitation of Children held in Stockholm, Sweden, August 1996 provides some information on the situation. The report notes that there is very limited information on the trafficking of children for sexual purposes in the North African region as a result of under-reporting and taboos surrounding such issues (ECPAT 2000, 11). The ECPAT 2000 Report relates some of the trafficking trends for the region including reports of Algerian young women trafficked to Europe, especially Italy where they are forced to marry residents of North African origin. In Egypt, young girls from poor rural and underdeveloped areas of Cairo are married off to men in the oil rich Gulf states (this practice was also confirmed by two UNICEF Cairo case studies on early and temporary marriage of young Egyptian women to Arabs) (ECPAT 2000, 11).

The ECPAT 2000 Report states that there is also evidence of trafficking in general rather than the trafficking of children specifically for sexual purposes. The routes identified include: nomadic cattle men from Cameroon and Chad trafficking boys to the Central African Republic; in war torn Sudan, young women and children are considered to be the most profitable war bounty and are taken to East Africa and other North African countries and sometimes to the Middle East; there are also unconfirmed reports of trafficking in young girls from the Horn of Africa to North Africa (ECPAT 2000, 11).

The ECPAT 2000 Report also deals with Central and East Africa and again notes that very limited information has been received on the trafficking of children for sexual purposes in Central and East Africa and as a result it is quite difficult to determine the state of the problem (ECPAT 2000, 25). This observation in the Report is echoed in a recent conference report on trafficking in East Africa, where it is noted that while the problem of human trafficking and forced labour is well documented in some regions, notably in West Africa, South East Asia and Eastern Europe, very little information exists in East Africa and the Horn of Africa (Report of the Eastern and Horn of Africa Conference on Human Trafficking and Forced Labour 2005).

The general trafficking trend in the region, particularly in Central Africa, is the trafficking of children for cheap child labour and not sexual purposes. Most trafficking is characterized by the in-country trafficking of children from rural to urban areas to work as domestic helpers for prosperous families. Some examples cited by the Report include reports from Cameroon indicating that poor parents sell their children abroad as domestic servants where they are treated like slaves and sexually exploited and similarly, reports that children as young as seven are being trafficked for cheap labour between Gabon and Benin where most of the victims are girls who are subjected to harsh living and working conditions (Report of the Eastern and Horn of Africa Conference on Human Trafficking and Forced Labour 2005, 25).

As far as West Africa is concerned, it has been noted that there is a high awareness of the trafficking phenomenon due to international attention paid to slave ships carrying child labourers to markets and plantations in the region (Fitzgibbon 2003, 82). Some examples of trafficking in the region include: between 10,000 and 15,000 West African children working on cocoa plantations in the Ivory Coast sold by middlemen to farm owners; between 1995 and 1999, 3,000 Beninese children being trafficked within the region; and approximately 25,000 foreign children working in markets and on farms in Gabon, of whom 7,000 are likely to have been trafficked (Fitzgibbon 2003, 83).

A recent study reveals that trafficking in persons (TIP) occurs both within Senegalese borders and internationally to, through, and from Senegal. The main victims of human trafficking in Senegal are women and children who are trafficked for prostitution, sex tourism, domestic labour or organized begging. The report states that a minimum of about 142,000 children in Senegal have been trafficked for exploitative domestic labour and forced begging (Moens et al. 2004).

As a possible reason for the problem in the region, Fitzgibbon further notes that civil unrest, internal armed conflict and natural disasters have destabilized and displaced populations, thereby increasing their vulnerability to exploitation, abuse and trafficking (2003, 83).[3] She also lists various factors that have contributed to the increase in trafficking in the regions, namely, the promise of a better life, the market or demand for commercial sexual exploitation and high profits at low risk – as African traffickers face a low risk of arrest, prosecution or other negative consequences (Fitzgibbon 2003, 83–6).

Despite the above discussion, the exact nature and extent of the problem remains unquantified. The hidden nature of the phenomenon militates against an accurate assessment of the numbers of children trafficked, their profiles, the perpetrators involved, the means used for trafficking and the resultant profits. Notwithstanding this, the fact remains that trafficking is a clear and present danger to the children of Africa. Therefore there is a pressing need for all states to ensure that this problem is addressed, through legislation, policies and programmes, to guarantee protections to children who fall prey to traffickers.

---

3   Beyrer also suggests that another driver of child trafficking is the increasing use of children by armies, militias and paramilitary organizations in global conflict zones – for example forced child soldiers used in recent and ongoing civil conflicts in Burma, Uganda, Liberia, Côte d'Ivoire and Sierra Leone (the last mentioned being highlighted in the recent film *Blood Diamond*).

International Law

There are a number of international instruments governing the issue of trafficking and the exploitation of children. These international treaties have placed various obligations on ratifying states to ensure that national laws are enacted in order to give effect to their provisions.

As far as children are concerned, the United Nations Convention on the Rights of the Child of 1989 (CRC) and the African Charter on the Rights and Welfare of the Child (ACRWC) are two seminal documents protecting the rights of children in the region.

There are a number of provisions in the CRC that aim to protect children against exploitative labour practices, sexual exploitation and sexual abuse. For example, article 32 protects children against exploitative or harmful work, article 34 protects children from their use in the sex trade and article 36 protects children from all other forms of exploitation. Article 35 specifically refers to the issues of trafficking and sale of children and obliges states to take all appropriate national, bilateral and multilateral measures to prevent these actions against children. Article 35 acts as a 'fail safe' protection for children at risk of abduction, sale or trafficking and is seen as a safety net to ensure that children are safe from being abducted and not procured for these purposes or for any other purpose (Hodgkin and Newell 2002, 521). While the other provisions mentioned above deal with the main forms of trafficking, article 35 provides a double protection for children in that it provides 'blanket-action' on abduction, sale or traffic of children for any purpose or in any form (Hodgkin and Newell 2002, 523). Unfortunately, the CRC deals very broadly with the sale and trafficking of children and fails to give any guidance on what constitutes trafficking and sale of children.

Similarly to article 35 of the CRC, the ACRWC (in article 29) deals with the sale, trafficking and abduction of children. It has been noted that the inclusion of the words 'by any person including parents or legal guardians of the child' in article 29(a) adds a conceptual clarification to the issue of sale, trafficking and abduction that translates into a higher level of protection for the child (Gose 2002, 66).

Following the CRC, a further Optional Protocol to the Convention on the Rights of the Child, namely, on the Sale of Children, Child Prostitution and Child Pornography was adopted in 2000. While the Optional Protocol does not specifically mention trafficking it does seek to clarify what constitutes sale of children. Furthermore article 3 enumerates certain minimum core acts and activities that states must ensure are criminalized in their domestic legislation in relation to the sale of children whether committed within the jurisdiction of the state party or transnationally and whether committed by an individual, organized group(s) of individuals or juridical persons.[4]

In relation to child labour, the International Labour Organization (ILO) Convention Concerning the Prohibition and Immediate Action for the Elimination of the Worst Forms of Child Labour of 1999 (Convention no. 182) deals with child trafficking. This instrument obliges member states, as a matter of urgency, to take

---

4 This provision can be seen as setting out what the substantive provisions of laws relating to the sale of children should contain.

immediate and effective measures to secure the prohibition and elimination of the worst forms of child labour. The Convention further stipulates that one of the worst forms of child labour is all forms of slavery or practices similar to slavery, such as the sale and trafficking of children (article 3).

Apart from the above, by far the most relevant international instruments relevant to trafficking are the UN Convention Against Transnational Organized Crime of 2000 and its Optional Protocol to Prevent, Suppress and Punish Trafficking in Persons, Especially Women and Children (the Palermo Protocol).

While the UN Convention Against Transnational Organized Crime does not specifically deal with trafficking *per se*, it does criminalize participation in organized criminal groups. However, it is noted, from the preamble to the Palermo Protocol, that while the mother Convention was not adequate to address trafficking because of its broader focus on organized crime, an instrument specifically dealing with trafficking was required. So while this Convention sets out the general international obligations regarding transnational organized crime, the specific details relating to trafficking are dealt with in the Palermo Protocol.

The Convention has numerous provisions requiring states parties to adopt procedural provisions and measures in order to combat transnational organized crime. These include the criminalization of, and measures to combat, money laundering (articles 6 and 7), criminalization of and measures against corruption (articles 8 and 9), confiscation and seizure of proceeds of crime (article 12), extradition (article 16), mutual legal assistance (article 18), protection of witnesses (article 24) and assistance to and protection of victims (article 25). These provisions form the foundation of any states' attempt to combat all forms of organized crime and therefore adoption of this Convention is an important step in the fight against the transnational offence of trafficking.

The Palermo Protocol is one of three Protocols to the Convention (the others being on smuggling of migrants and trafficking in firearms). The preamble to this Protocol notes that the states parties to the Protocol were convinced that it would be useful to supplement the Convention Against Transnational Organized Crime with an international instrument to prevent, combat and punish trafficking in persons, especially women and children.

It has been noted that, collectively, the Vienna Process (whereby the Vienna-based UN Commission on Crime Prevention and Criminal Justice led the initiative in the adoption of the Convention and Protocols) represents the first serious attempt by the international community to combat organized crime (Gallagher 2001, 976). Further, the fact that trafficking was incorporated into a separate agreement highlights its priority position on the political agenda and, further, indicates that sovereignty and security issues are the main drivers for such specific attention being accorded the phenomenon (Gallagher 2001, 976).

The overarching purposes of the Protocol are to prevent and combat trafficking in persons (especially women and children), to protect and assist victims of trafficking (article 6), and to promote co-operation amongst state parties to meet the above objectives.

The Protocol serves a very useful purpose in that it provides a comprehensive definition of trafficking, namely:

the recruitment, transportation, transfer, harbouring or receipt of persons, by means of the threat or use of force or other forms of coercion, of abduction, of fraud, of deception, of the abuse of power or of a position of vulnerability or of the giving or receiving of payments or benefits to achieve the consent of a person having control over another person, for the purpose of exploitation. Exploitation shall include at a minimum, the exploitation of the prostitution of others or other forms of sexual exploitation, forced labour or services, slavery or practices similar to slavery, servitude or the removal of organs. (Article 3(a))

However, in respect of children who are trafficked, article 3(c) states, 'the recruitment, transportation, transfer, harbouring or receipt of a child for the purpose of exploitation shall be considered "trafficking in persons" even if this does not involve any of the means set forth in sub-paragraph (a) of this article.' Therefore child trafficking can occur when a child is transferred, recruited, harboured and so forth, for the purposes of exploitation alone, and proof of threats, force or other forms of coercion (and so on) is not necessary to establish the crime of trafficking in children. It is noted that the initial deliberations did not specifically deal with trafficking in children and that the above definition was only produced after a submission made by the International Organisation for Migration (IOM), UNICEF, the Office of the UN High Commissioner for Human Rights and the UN High Commissioner for Refugees (UNHCR) (Gallagher 2001, 988–9). However, the submission called for far greater protections for children than those that were finally included in article 3(c) and a further submission to expand the list of end-purposes of trafficking to include the worst forms of child labour as defined in ILO Convention 182 was not successful (Gallagher 2001, 989). It is unfortunate that the Protocol does not go further in creating a special protective environment for children.

The Protocol sets out specific measures that states parties need to include in their domestic legal and administrative systems to assist and protect victims of trafficking (articles 6(1) and (2)). In addition the Protocol deals with measures to provide for the physical, psychological and social recovery of victims of trafficking (article 6(3)). Provision is made that, in appropriate cases, states parties shall provide *appropriate* housing, counselling and information in a language that the victim can understand, medical, psychological and material assistance and employment, educational and training opportunities. However these measures are left to the discretion of each state party in relation to their implementation. The Protocol has, however, been criticized for containing very little in the way of hard obligations requiring states to protect victims of trafficking (Gallagher 2001, 990). While there are a range of protection provisions, these provisions are formulated in weak terms such as: each state party *shall ensure* that its domestic legal or administrative system contains measures that provide to victims information on procedure and a platform to ensure that their views are presented and considered at appropriate stages of the criminal proceedings against offenders (article 6(2)); or each state party *shall consider* implementing measures to provide for the physical, psychological and social recovery of victims (article 6(3)); or each party *shall endeavour* to provide for the physical safety of victims while in their territory. They therefore do not place clear mandatory obligations on the ratifying state party.

It is also important to note that the Palermo Protocol requires states to adopt legislative or other appropriate measures in relation to border controls (article 11), travel or identity documents (articles 12 and 13) and repatriation of victims of trafficking (article 8), however again not differentiating between the needs of children and adults who have been trafficked.

The extensive provisions of the Protocol and recognition it gives to the transnational nature of trafficking highlights the need for international and regional co-operation and mutual assistance to successfully investigate and prosecute the crime. Effective and efficient law enforcement is a critical component in the eradication of trafficking. While the international instruments provide a comprehensive framework to prohibit trafficking, law reform, policy development, cross-border policing, mutual legal assistance, programmatic development and services are key in fulfilling the provisions of the Convention and Protocol and ensuring their implementation.

International and Foreign Policy and Programmes

Many countries across Africa have taken steps to combat trafficking. In addition, various international programmes also address the issue. In this regard, the ILO can be said to have taken the lead in assisting African states in combat trafficking as a worst form of child labour. Generally, on a global scale the ILO has been, since 2000, trying to influence the debate on trafficking by stressing its forced labour dimension, after having focused in the early years on commercial sexual exploitation of girls and boys as an outcome of trafficking (ILO 2006, 41). Accordingly there has been resource mobilization in this area, with seven donor countries collaborating with the ILO in 2005 to implement projects to combat trafficking of children (ILO 2006, 41). As a result, the International Programme for the Elimination of the Worst Forms of Child Labour (IPEC) has become a significant force for influencing policy agendas towards incorporating the labour dimension of trafficking which leads to child labour exploitation (ILO 2006, 41). In addition, an inter-agency Memorandum of Understanding has been entered into between the ILO and the IOM to provide for collaboration on the issue (ILO 2006, 41). With specific regard to Africa, the ILO has singled the continent out for specific action in relation to worst forms of child labour.[5] In particular, IPEC is working on strengthening various areas of its work in Africa in relation to worst forms of child labour, including trafficking, such as increasing the knowledge base on child labour, the development of national child labour policies, mainstreaming child labour concerns in development and poverty reduction strategies, and developing sectoral policies in areas such as education, agricultural and rural development. The promotion of universal primary education is seen as a crucial pillar of a strategy to eliminate child labour as well as strengthening the technical and organizational capacity of social partners, including government and other stakeholders (ILO 2006, 65–6).

---

5   This is discussed in more detail in Chapter 18 of this volume on worst forms of child labour.

It has been noted that the United States, and more recently the European Commission, are the largest funders of the ILO programmes to fight child labour currently run in 86 countries (ILO 2006, vii). The United States has made concerted efforts to tackle the trafficking phenomenon by enacting the Trafficking Victims Protection Act of 2000. In terms of this legislation, an annual report by the US Department of State must be submitted to the US Congress that describes the nature and extent of severe forms of trafficking in persons with respect to each foreign, non-US country and an assessment of the efforts made by the government of that country to combat trafficking (section 104). Section 108 of the Act sets out minimum standards that need to be complied with for the elimination of trafficking and countries are then assessed to determine whether they fully comply with the minimum standards (Tier 1) or do not yet fully comply but are making significant efforts to bring themselves into compliance (Tier 2) or whether they do not comply and have not made any efforts to comply (Tier 3) (section 110(b)). For example, in the 2002 report to US Congress, South Africa was placed in the second category as a 'tier 2' country (US Department of State 2002). However, in the 2006 report South Africa was placed on the 'tier 2 watch list' for not showing any increased efforts to combat trafficking in the past year (US Department of State 2006, 226). In terms of section 110, the United States will not provide non-humanitarian, non-trade related foreign assistance to the government of a country, for the subsequent fiscal year, until such government complies with the minimum standards or makes significant efforts to bring itself into compliance.

While possibly established in good faith, it is argued that this law unduly pressurizes countries to bring their laws into compliance with standards set by the United States of America, by means of threats to withhold certain foreign financial assistance. In the context of South Africa, it has been argued that this should not be one of the reasons why South Africa should enact comprehensive anti-trafficking legislation (Leggett 2004). The authors argue that such foreign pressure by one state should not be the reason to enact anti-trafficking legislation, but that international obligations following the ratification of relevant treaties as well as a recognition that the rights of children to be protected should be the underlying reason for enacting such laws.

Country Specific Responses to Combating Child Trafficking

As stated above, there have been concerted efforts to deal with the issue of trafficking by African states. These efforts include national plans on trafficking, child labour programmes of action, law reform initiatives and the enactment of laws. What follows is a discussion of developments undertaken in selected West, Southern and Eastern African countries.

In Southern Africa, a recent study on six countries (Thompson 2006, 5–6) noted that South Africa is the only country that has a specific legal provision criminalizing 'child trafficking' as contained in the Children's Act 38 of 2005 (only partially in operation).[6] According to section 1 of the Act, trafficking is defined as follows:

'trafficking', in relation to a child –

(a) means the recruitment, sale, supply, transportation, transfer, harbouring or receipt of children, within or across the borders of the Republic –

(i) by any means, including the use of threat, force or other forms of coercion, abduction, fraud, deception, abuse of power or the giving or receiving of payments or benefits to achieve the consent of a person having control of a child; or
(ii) due to a position of vulnerability, for the purpose of exploitation; and

(b) includes the adoption of a child facilitated or secured through illegal means.

Likewise, exploitation is defined in the same section as:

'exploitation', in relation to a child, includes –

(a) all forms of slavery or practices similar to slavery, including debt bondage or forced marriage;
(b) sexual exploitation;
(c) servitude;
(d) forced labour or services;
(e) child labour prohibited in terms of section 141; and
(f) the removal of body parts.

Previously it has been thought that a fundamental problem in responding to the issue of trafficking is the lack of a precise and coherent definition; hence the tendency is to rather define trafficking as broadly as possible (South African Law Reform Commission 2001, 1125). In so far as the definition contained in the Children's Act is similar to that contained in article 3(a) of the Palermo Protocol as detailed above, the Act goes a long way to achieve certainty in South African law in that the definition provides clarity as to what constitutes exploitation. However, it is argued that there are nevertheless a few problems with the definition.[7]

---

6   It is somewhat ironic that since South Africa has enacted new legislation criminalizing child trafficking, it has also been 'downgraded' by the United States of America to a 'tier 2 watch list' country – possibly illustrating the difficulties with such legislation, particularly if the information upon which the grading is done is inaccurate.

7   It should be noted that the definition as contained in the Palermo Protocol refers to trafficking in persons and in article 3(c) the Protocol states that the means listed in article 3(a) do not need to be involved if there is the recruitment, transfer harbouring or receipt of a child for the purposes of exploitation. Therefore the definition as contained in the Children's Act has arguably created a greater evidential burden than necessarily required by the Palermo Protocol. Secondly, the Children's Act extends the definition of trafficking to include 'the adoption of a child facilitated or secured through illegal means' irrespective of whether the child is exploited or not by the 'adoptive' parents. It is submitted that, since the international law defines trafficking in relation to the objective that there must be some form of intended exploitation of the victim, the adoption of a child facilitated or secured through illegal means is better referred to as an 'illegal adoption' and not trafficking. An 'illegal adoption' amounts to

In addition, South Africa is currently embarking on various law reform processes relevant to trafficking; notably, the South African Law Reform Commission (SALRC) is investigating the possibility of drafting comprehensive legislation regarding trafficking in persons. The SALRC has released an Issue Paper and Discussion Paper to serve as a basis for the Commission's deliberations on the topic, to elicit comment and suggestions from relevant stakeholders and to disseminate information on the issue of trafficking in persons to the public at large. Submissions on the Issue and Discussion Papers, coupled with further intensive research, will form the basis for the SALRC's preliminary proposals for law reform and draft legislation.[8]

The study by the IOM examining the laws of six Southern African countries has noted that virtually all of the countries in the region have provisions in their criminal law relating to prostitution and sexual offences, although only a few specifically prohibit the commercial sexual exploitation of children, child pornography or child prostitution (Thompson 2006, 6). The study determined that the laws varied from weak (Mozambique) to strong provisions (Tanzania and Zimbabwe) to address, among other issues, commercial sexual exploitation. However, the research found that while some sexual offence/prostitution laws in the region could be used to prosecute certain aspects and types of sex trafficking, there are many gaps and weaknesses (Thompson 2006, 6).[9]

The research did find that of the six countries examined, the new Zambian statute (Employment of Children and Young Persons Act (Laws of Zambia, 2004), sections 4 and 17) was the most promising for deterring and punishing more serious forms of child labour, including child trafficking, as it specifically prohibits employment of any child under 18 in 'any type of employment or work which by its nature or the circumstances in which it is carried out, constitutes a worst form of [child] labour'(Thompson 2006, 4).The statute incorporates the definition of worst forms of child labour contained in ILO Convention no. 182.

In addition, the research sets out what some of the obstacles to effective prosecution of the worst forms of child labour (including child trafficking) are. These include the fact that labour departments in the region do not have sufficient human and financial resources to combat child labour effectively; child labour is not an enforcement priority; the lack of awareness and training on new legislation or amendments can create practical obstacles; and many police officers consider child

---

an exploitation of the adoption system and laws and not the exploitation of the adopted child. This should therefore be criminalized in terms of adoption laws and not trafficking laws.

8   The Criminal Law (Sexual Offences and Related Matters) Amendment 38 Act of 2007, promulgated on 16 December 2007, contains transitional provisions which criminalize trafficking of persons.

9   These gaps and weaknesses include, for example, the fact that some laws against 'procurement for prostitution' only apply to females, or are restricted to young people under a certain age. Some carry a corroboration requirement, which alone is sufficient in many cases to render prosecution for commercial sexual exploitation impossible. In addition, with a few exceptions, sexual offences relating to prostitution tend to be misdemeanours carrying very low penalties.

labour and other forms of labour exploitation to fall outside their jurisdiction or mandate, despite them constituting criminal offences (Thompson 2006, 10–14).[10]

On the other hand, Malawi is a Southern African country that has exhibited real commitment to combating trafficking both in law and in practice. The existing Malawian law covers the full scope of trafficking in persons and in 2006, the Malawian Law Commission submitted a draft law that specifically criminalizes child trafficking to the Ministry of Justice (US Department of State 2006, 171–2). In addition, the government has embarked on specialized training for judges on the issue of child trafficking; in 2005 border patrol and police officials throughout the country received anti-trafficking training from government and NGOs; and the government has also opened a drop-in centre to provide counselling medical care, legal assistance, shelter, food and vocational training to victims of trafficking and sexual violence (US Department of State 2006, 171–2).

Finally, a manual on investigating and prosecuting trafficking in persons has been under development since 2005 in Southern Africa. The manual is a joint undertaking by the United Nations Office on Drugs and Crime (UNODC) and Southern African Police Chief's Cooperation Organization (SARPCCO). The manual aims at developing a standardized training curriculum for the training of police and prosecutors on trafficking in human beings in Southern Africa. The project will also organize a pilot training course for one police and one prosecutor per country in the identification, investigation and prosecution of cases of trafficking in persons. This Manual is based on the UNODC 'Assistance for the Implementation of the ECOWAS Plan of Action against Trafficking in Persons: Training Manual', developed for the Economic Community of West African States.

Initiatives such as the last-mentioned are extremely valuable in relation to this type of transnational offence. The fact that SARPCCO recognized the need for a standardized and uniform approach to the investigation and prosecution of trafficking indicates the keen commitment by the police to bring offenders to book through mutual co-operation and assistance.

It has been noted that one of the challenges facing West Africa in developing appropriate responses to child trafficking is the fact that there is a lack of a clear and publicly accepted definition of child trafficking in the region, where the terms 'trafficking', 'abduction' or 'sale of children' have different meanings in different countries (UNICEF 2002, para. 1.1).

Apart from law reform efforts, plans of action and policy development are crucial in ensuring a comprehensive strategy to combat trafficking. In 2002 it was reported that there were various National Plans and Draft National Plans underway in certain West African states to combat the trafficking phenomenon (see UNICEF 2002): Burkina Faso had a Draft National Plan against Child Trafficking that was under discussion; Cameroon had a Draft National Plan to Fight against Child Labour that was being amended to integrate child trafficking; Côte D'Ivoire had a National Plan to Fight Against Child Trafficking but which was not yet in operation; Gabon had a Draft National Plan to Fight against Child Labour; Mali had a National Emergency

---

10 These are dealt with in more detail in Chapter 18 of this volume on worst forms of child labour.

Plan to Fight against Child Trafficking that was adopted on 24 March 2000; Nigeria had a National Plan of Action for Combating Child Labour, but this was not yet operational; and Togo had a National Plan to Fight against Child Labour and Child Trafficking. A short four years later, some progress had been achieved.

In 2006, the Trafficking in Persons Report released by the United States provides the following information on the status of West African states' law reform efforts. The Report indicates that in December 2005, Cameroon enacted a statute that prohibited child trafficking. In addition, the country plans to strengthen its fight against trafficking by drafting a Child Protection Code and finalizing a Family Code that increases the minimum marriage age for girls to 18. Furthermore, other initiatives have included bilateral collaboration with Gabon to repatriate Cameroonian trafficking victims from Gabon; collaboration with the ILO on education projects for child labour victims; and the General Delegate for National Security signed an order in December 2005 creating an anti-trafficking vice squad within the National Office of Interpol (US Department of State 2006, 85–6).

As far as Côte D'Ivoire is concerned, despite the fact that a law to prohibit trafficking, drafted in 2002, still awaits adoption, the National Committee for the Fight against Trafficking and Child Exploitation has taken the lead in drafting a regional multilateral anti-trafficking agreement with eight other countries in 2005 (US Department of State 2006, 97–8). Benin adopted a new law on child trafficking in 2006 (Kamidi 2007).

Since 2004 the Gabonese law has prohibited child trafficking for labour exploitation, but has not enacted specific general criminal law provisions to outlaw trafficking. In addition, while the government has not provided specialized training on recognizing, investigating or prosecuting trafficking, such training has occurred through NGOs and international organizations (US Department of State 2006, 120–21).

Child trafficking is prohibited under Malian law, which provides a sanction of up to 20 years' imprisonment for child traffickers. In addition in 2005, Mali entered various multilateral and bilateral anti-trafficking agreements (US Department of State 2006, 174–5).

Nigeria has a federal law prohibiting trafficking that was amended in 2005 to allow for forfeiture and seizure of trafficker's assets. In addition, the country has embarked on numerous initiatives to further combat trafficking through, for example, providing training for investigators and prosecutors, maintaining a computerized trafficking crime database, and establishing an anti-trafficking network covering 11 states (US Department of State 2006, 193–4).

Togo adopted anti-child trafficking legislation in July 2005, and it is noted that Burkina Faso's law does prohibit child trafficking but there is no law prohibiting the trafficking of adults. Furthermore, the US TIP Report has stated that the government has not complied with the minimum standards for the elimination of trafficking as set out by the US Protection of Victims Act, but that it is making significant progress to do so. For example, out of 44 traffickers detained by police, local vigilance committees and other security forces in 2005, six were prosecuted and convicted (US Department of State 2006, 79–80).

From the above, it is clear that the issue of trafficking is being actively addressed in numerous ways by various African states. While the adoption of law on the matter is critical, the practical implementation of the law in order for it to be effective in realizing children's rights is dependent on a range of other actions. In this regard it is promising to note that the West African countries have recognized the need, *inter alia*, of training, multilateral and bilateral co-operation with neighbouring countries, investigation and prosecution of traffickers and the importance of information gathering by means of electronic databases. Significant advances have been made through regional agreements such as the Multilateral Co-operation agreement to Combat Child Trafficking in West Africa of July 2005 (Kamidi 2007). On the other hand, Southern African countries (with certain exceptions such as Malawi) have only recently started concerted efforts to draft appropriate laws to combat trafficking and the finalization and implementation of these laws still present a challenge to realizing the rights of children to be protected against exploitation and trafficking.

Challenges Facing the Continent

There appear to be many developments underway to address the trafficking phenomenon in Africa. These include law reform efforts, policy development, law enforcement initiatives and research. However, there still remain challenges. What follows is a very brief and superficial attempt to highlight some of these.

On one level, these challenges include the need for greater co-operation between role-players – domestically and cross-border. Trafficking is a crime that requires numerous disciplines to become involved, such as the police, prosecutors, social workers and service providers at the very least. The response, therefore, should be one that is co-ordinated across these professions. One example of such an approach is evident from the various regional training initiatives that are being developed by police in Southern and Western Africa. However, they still fall short of including all role-players. Granted, specific training is different depending on roles and responsibilities, but there are issues common to all working in the field, such as victim assistance, that require mutual knowledge and co-operation.

On another level, law enforcement becomes involved as an 'end-product' of trafficking. Primary prevention that addresses the root causes of trafficking is a vital component to any trafficking strategy, whether domestic or regional. Prevention initiatives also need to have various facets in that they need to address the social causes of trafficking such as, among others, poverty, unemployment and family disintegration. Likewise, health is a great challenge facing Africa and diseases such as HIV/Aids, tuberculosis and malaria result in increasing numbers of African orphans who become vulnerable to a wide range of risks, including trafficking. Therefore a comprehensive social policy should recognize the range of causes of trafficking and what risk factors feed the phenomenon in order to address them. In addition, focused crime prevention itself, entailing, *inter alia*, awareness raising, community mobilization and co-ordinated activities between local stakeholders, is obviously a key part of any undertaking by government to address organized crime of this nature.

Finally, placing the needs of victims on the same footing as that of law enforcement initiatives is a continuing challenge. This is even evident from the wording of the Palermo Protocol insofar as protection provisions for victims are couched in discretionary terms and are not mandatory. It might be argued that limited resources ultimately trump definitive victim assistance, however, services such as family reunification, repatriation, counselling and the like represent the 'life after' for trafficking victims and are, as such, often decisive in the rehabilitation and recovery of victims of trafficking, especially children.

Conclusion

Children's rights are realized in a number of ways. In order for there to be proper legal protection and appropriate responses, an understanding of the practical dimensions regarding trafficking of children is essential. Following such understanding at country level, policy and legislative developments should follow, coupled with implementation plans that include resource allocation, training and the allocation of rights and responsibilities to the relevant role-players. In addition, monitoring and evaluation is a critical means of ensuring that the particular issues are being adequately addressed through the implementation of law and policy. It is noteworthy that all of these considerations in the fight against child trafficking are manifested in one form or another throughout Africa. Research on child trafficking, the formulation of law and policy as well as general measures of implementation of such law and policy are evident in many countries. However, there are still numerous problems in the development of law and policy and African countries are at different stages of addressing the issue. On a continent where children are trafficked across borders within the region, the lack of a unified approach can be seen as an obstacle to progress towards a comprehensive regional strategy to combat child trafficking.

On another level, community awareness is also crucial to ensuring that children are protected from the dangers of trafficking and in this regard governments and civil society play a key role.

Therefore, in order to address the phenomenon of child trafficking in Africa adequately, a single, comprehensive approach across countries on the continent and between regions is required to provide the African child with the maximum protection against this global scourge.

References

Articles, Books and Chapters in Books

Fitzgibbon, K. (2003), 'Modern-Day Slavery? The Scope of Trafficking in Persons in Africa', *African Security Review* 12, 81.
Gallagher, A. (2001), 'Human Rights and the New UN Protocols on Trafficking and Migrant Smuggling: A Preliminary Analysis', *Human Rights Quarterly* 23, 975.
Gose, M. (2002), *The African Charter on the Rights and Welfare of the Child* (Bellville: Community Law Centre, University of the Western Cape).
Grover, S. (2006), 'Denying the Right of Trafficked Minors to be Classed as Convention Refugees: The Canadian Case Example' *International Journal of Children's Rights* 14, 235.

Hodgkin, R. and Newell, P. (2002), *Implementation Handbook for the Convention on the Rights of the Child* (New York and Geneva: UNICEF).

Koen, K. and Van Vuuren, B. (2002), *Children in Domestic Services: The Case of the Western Cape* (Basel: Terres des Hommes, Switzerland).

General Comments, Unpublished Papers, Treaties, Declarations and Reports

Beyrer, C. (2004), 'Global Child Trafficking', *Medicine, Crime and Punishment*, vol. 364, available at <www.thelancet.com> (accessed 22 February 2007).

ECPAT International (2000), 'Looking Back: Thinking Forward' (The fourth report on the implementation of the Agenda for Action adopted at the World Congress against Commercial Sexual Exploitation of Children held in Stockholm, Sweden, August 1996) (Bangkok: ECPAT International).

International Labor Organization (ILO) (2006), 'The End of Child Labour: Within Reach' (Global Report under the follow up to the ILO Declaration on Fundamental Principles and Rights at Work, International Labour Conference, 95th Session, Report 1(B)) (Geneva: ILO).

Kamidi, R., (2007), 'A Legal Response to Child Trafficking in Africa: A Case Study of South Africa and Benin' (unpublished LLM dissertation, Pretoria: University of Pretoria).

Leggett, T. (2004), 'Hidden Agenda's? The Risk of Human Trafficking Legislation', *Crime Quarterly* 9 (2004), available at <www.iss.org.za/Pubs/CrimeQ/No.9/Leggett.htm> (accessed 3 February 2007).

Martens, J., Pieczkowski, M. and Van Vuuren-Smythe, B. (2003), *Trafficking in Women and Children for Sexual Exploitation in Southern Africa* (International Organisation for Migration).

Moens, B., Zeitlin, V., Bop, C. and Gaye, R. (2004), *Study on the Practice of Trafficking in Persons in Senegal* (Senegal: USAID).

Molo Songololo (2000), *The Trafficking of Children for Purposes of Sexual Exploitation: South Africa* (Cape Town).

Report of the Eastern and Horn of Africa Conference on Human Trafficking and Forced Labour (5–7 July 2005), Nairobi Safari Club, hosted by ANPPCAN and Anti-Slavery International.

South African Law Reform Commission (2001), 'Review of the Child Care Act' (Discussion Paper 103) (Project 110).

South African Law Reform Commission (2004), 'Trafficking in Persons' (Issue Paper 25) (Project 131).

Thompson, J. (2006), 'Legal and Practical Obstacles to Prosecution of Child Labour Exploitation in Southern Africa', paper presented at the RECLISA Conference, South Africa, July 2006.

UNICEF (2002), *Child Trafficking in West Africa: Policy Responses* (Florence: Innocenti Research Centre).

US Department of State (2002), 'Victims of Trafficking and Violence Protection Act 2000' (Washington DC: US Department of State).

US Department of State (2006), 'Trafficking in Persons Report' (Washington DC: US Department of State).

Legislation

South Africa (2005), Children's Act 38 of 2005.
South Africa (2007), Criminal Law (Sexual Offences and Related Matters) Amendment Act 38 of 2007.
The Employment of Children and Young Persons Act (Laws of Zambia), 2004.

Chapter 15

Intercountry Adoption
from an African Perspective

Trynie Davel

Introduction

The Convention on the Rights of the Child (CRC) clearly states that children who are deprived of their family environment,[1] or in whose own best interests cannot be allowed to remain in that environment, are entitled to special protection (article 20(1)). States parties are obliged to provide alternative care for these children in accordance with their national laws (article 20(2)). In recent times various factors, such as civil wars, have contributed to increase the number of destitute children, especially on the African continent (Stark 2003, 275). The HIV/Aids pandemic alone has left millions of Aids orphans behind.[2] On the other hand, lower birth rates and the growing social acceptance of single motherhood has dramatically decreased the number of children available for adoption in some countries, for instance in the United States (Stark 2003, 276). Globalization has opened up national borders and ease of travel, worker mobility and the breaking down of cultural barriers have all led to a situation where adoption and, in the above context, especially intercountry adoption, is viewed as a viable option for children in need of alternative care (article 20(3)).

Article 21 of the CRC, which deals with adoption and also intercountry[3] adoption in more detail, provides:

> State Parties that recognize and/or permit the system of adoption shall ensure that the best interests of the child shall be the paramount consideration and they shall:
>
> (a) Ensure that the adoption of a child is authorized only by competent authorities who determine, in accordance with applicable law and procedures and on the basis of all pertinent and reliable information, that the adoption is permissible in view of the child's status concerning parents, relatives and legal guardians and that, if required, the persons concerned have given their informed consent to the adoption on the basis of such counselling as may be necessary;

---

1   Placement in the wider/extended family should be considered before looking for alternatives (Hodgkin and Newell 2002, 259).

2   There are 7.7 million double orphans (children who have lost both parents) in sub-Saharan Africa. The number of double orphans is estimated to increase to 9 million in 2010, largely due to Aids: Joint Report by UNAIDS, UNICEF and USAID 2004, 3–11. See for further details about the impact of HIV/Aids on African children, Chapter 16 of this volume.

3   The preferred spelling of the term for purposes of this chapter is 'intercountry'. The hyphenated version of the term will only be used when quoting verbatim from other sources.

(b) Recognize that inter-country adoption may be considered as an alternative means of care, if the child cannot be placed in a foster or an adoptive family or cannot in any suitable manner be cared for in the child's country of origin;

(c) Ensure that the child concerned by inter-country adoption enjoys safeguards and standards equivalent to those existing in the case of national adoption;

(d) Take all appropriate measures to ensure that, in inter-country adoption, the placement does not result in improper financial gain for those involved in it;

(e) Promote, where appropriate, the objectives of the present article by concluding bilateral or multilateral arrangements or agreements, and endeavour, within the framework, to ensure that the placement of the child in another country is carried out by competent authorities or organs.

The thrust of article 21 could be summarized as follows:

- States which recognize adoption have to ensure that the best interests of the child shall be the paramount consideration.[4]
- States parties are required to ensure that the adoption of a child is authorized only by competent authorities in accordance with legislation regulating both its national and international forms (Hodgkin and Newell 2002).
- States parties are required to ensure that any required consent to adoption has been given, that the consent is informed and that it has been given on the basis of such counselling as may be necessary.[5]
- Intercountry adoption may only be considered if there is no suitable alternative for the child in his or her country of origin.[6]
- States parties are required to ensure that the child concerned by intercountry adoption enjoys safeguards and standards equivalent to those existing in the case of ordinary/national adoption.[7]
- States shall take all appropriate measures to ensure that an intercountry adoption does not result in improper financial gain for any party involved in it.
- States parties shall ensure that the placement of the child in another country is carried out by competent authorities or organs.

---

4   Implementing one of the three basic or guiding principles of the CRC, namely the 'best interest' standard set out in article 4 (Hodgkin and Newell 2002, 272; Hamilton 1999, 19; Van Bueren 2000, 203–5).

5   Linking to the second basic principle of the CRC, namely participation of the child as set out in article 12(1) (Hodgkin and Newell 2002, 273–4; Hamilton 1999, 19; Van Bueren 2000, 205–7; Duncan 2006, 2).

6   As a measure of last resort, consonant with article 20(3), and requiring due regard and continuity in a child's ethnic, religious, cultural and linguistic background; see also articles 7 and 8 of the CRC (Hodgkin and Newell 2002, 275).

7   If 'safeguards and standards' are interpreted as applying both to procedures before an adoption order is made and to the status of the child following the order, this embodies the basic principle against discrimination set out in article 2(1) of the CRC (Hamilton 1999, 19; Van Bueren 2000, 204; Duncan 2006, 2).

Article 30 of the CRC could also be of relevance in the context of intercountry adoption. It aims at preserving the cultural identity of a child, which includes the right to enjoy his or her own religion and language.

The African Charter on the Rights and Welfare of the Child

On the continent of Africa, the African Charter on the Rights and Welfare of the Child (ACRWC) is an important international human rights law instrument (Thompson 1992, 433; Arts 1992, 144; Lloyd in Chapter 3 of this volume). This regional instrument was drafted because of the need to deal with issues pertinent to children in Africa – specific issues omitted from the CRC (Viljoen 2000, 219). One of those issues relates very closely to the subject of intercountry adoptions, namely the fact that the CRC has been regarded as negating the role of the family (also in its extended sense) in the upbringing of the child and in matters of adoption (and fostering) (Viljoen 2000, 219; Chirwa 2002, 167).

Adoption and specifically intercountry adoption is dealt with in article 24 of the ACRWC, which provides:

States parties which recognize the system of adoption shall ensure that the best interests of the child shall be the paramount consideration and they shall:

(a) Establish competent authorities to determine matters of adoption and ensure that the adoption is carried out in conformity with applicable laws and procedures and on the basis of all relevant and reliable information, that the adoption is permissible in view of the child's status concerning parents, relatives and guardians and that, if necessary, the appropriate persons concerned have given their informed consent to the adoption on the basis of appropriate counselling;

(b) Recognize that inter-country adoption in those States who have ratified or adhered to the International Convention on the Rights of the Child or this Charter, may, as the last resort, be considered as an alternative means of a child's care, if the child cannot be placed in a foster or an adoptive family or cannot in any suitable manner be cared for in the child's country of origin;

(c) Ensure that the child affected by inter-country adoption enjoys safeguards and standards equivalent to those existing in the case of national adoption;

(d) Take all appropriate measures to ensure that in inter-country adoption, the placement does not result in trafficking or improper financial gain for those who try to adopt a child;

(e) Promote, where appropriate, the objectives of this Article by concluding bilateral or multilateral arrangements or agreements, and endeavour, within this framework to ensure that the placement of the child in another country is carried out by competent authorities or organs;

(f) Establish a machinery to monitor the well-being of the adopted child.

A comparison between article 24 of the ACRWC and article 21 of the CRC highlights the following features in the African context: the ACRWC, like the CRC, promotes the best interests of the child in the context of adoption, as states parties have to ensure that the best interests of the child shall be the paramount consideration.[8] The ACRWC explicitly states that intercountry adoption is a 'last resort' if the child cannot be placed in a foster or an adoptive family or cared for in any suitable manner in the child's country of origin. Although not in so many words, the same concept also underlies the CRC's provision in this regard (Gose 2002, 110; Stark 2003, 276).

The ACRWC mentions states that 'recognize' a system of adoption, while the CRC speaks of states that 'recognize and/or permit' adoption. It is submitted that this slight difference in the wording is meaningless, because it is unlikely that a state would permit the system of adoption without recognizing it (Gose 2002, 107).

The ACRWC provides for a special obligation on a state to 'establish competent authorities' while the CRC seems to take the existence of such authorities for granted. It is submitted that it constitutes a special safeguard in states where no suitable administrative infrastructure exists for handling adoption cases, and this could well be the case in many African countries (Gose 2002, 107).[9] The ACRWC also omits the word 'legal' when referring to the child's guardian. This could be interpreted as setting a higher level of protection for the child if it is recognized that retaining the *status quo* could be in the best interests of the child, that is, remaining where he or she is actually cared for, although without the care-giver having a legal relationship towards him or her (Gose 2002, 108).

The ACRWC requires the consent of the 'appropriate persons concerned' whereas the CRC only mentions 'persons concerned' in this context. It is submitted that inserting 'appropriate' could be meaningful if there is a variety of persons that are concerned, but out of those persons, only the ones that are nearest to the child should have the right to deny consent to the adoption.

There is a very interesting addition of the words 'in those states who have ratified or adhered to the International Convention on the Rights of the Child or this Charter' in the ACRWC, words not in the original text of the CRC. It is submitted that the clause could be understood as a special safeguard for the rights of the child, which could be threatened if the child is removed from the ambit of applicability of the CRC or the ACRWC by way of intercountry adoption (Gose 2002, 109). The ACRWC introduces the notion of 'trafficking' (in article 24(d)), which should be welcomed as a further clarification of the CRC approach (Gose 2002, 110).

Unfortunately, the ACRWC narrows the wording of the CRC when stipulating that intercountry adoption may not result in financial gain 'for those who try to adopt a child'. The CRC calls on states parties to ensure that intercountry adoptions do not result in financial gain 'for those involved in it'. It is submitted that the wording of the CRC should have been followed to ensure that agents are not tempted into effectuating intercountry adoptions for financial gain (Gose 2002, 110–11).

---

8   But the ACRWC contains the more powerful statement in article 4(1), namely that the best interests of the child shall be *the* primary consideration whereas the CRC articulates the standard as *a* primary consideration in article 3(1) (Viljoen 2000, 224).

9   It is on this level where the Hague Conference on Private International Law (HCCH) has been a pioneer in developing systems of international co-operation at both administrative and judicial levels. Central Authorities established under the Hague Conventions constitute the core of a global network of inter-state co-operation for the protection of children.

The ACRWC introduces an obligation for states to provide for the appropriate monitoring of the well-being of the adopted child in article 23(f). The provision will only benefit children if the receiving state has also ratified the ACRWC, since an equivalent protection does not appear in the CRC. Gose argues, however, that African states will in reality be the 'suppliers' of children and that Western countries will normally be the 'receiving' countries, in which case this provision seems well-intended but useless if not interpreted to include the conclusion of international co-operation agreements or treaties relating to monitoring and enforcement of the ACRWC's provisions (Gose 2002, 111–12). Chirwa (2002, 168) opines on a more positive note that this provision would operate to curb problems that accompany intercountry adoptions due to the lack of an international obligation by states to exercise a continuous duty regarding the welfare of the adopted child.

The ACRWC does not contain a provision (similar to article 30 of the CRC) aimed at preserving the cultural identity of the adoptive child (Gose 2002, 112). This is surprising because the ACRWC's overall emphasis is on enhancing African traditional cultural values (Davel 2002, 282).

The Hague Convention on the Protection of Children and Co-operation in Respect of Intercountry Adoption

Introduction

The Hague Convention on the Protection of Children and Co-operation in Respect of Intercountry Adoption of 29 May 1993 (hereafter the Hague Convention) is one of the three modern Hague children's conventions.[10] Although 75 states have either ratified or acceded to this Convention to date,[11] there are only six countries on the African continent among them, that is, Burkina Faso, Burundi, Kenya, Madagascar, Mauritius and South Africa. But the Hague Conference on Private International Law and the Hague Forum for Judicial Expertise have embarked on a project, 'The Hague Project for International Co-operation on the Protection of Children in the Southern and Eastern African Region', which is, amongst other things, aimed at introducing practical legal structures to support co-operation in terms of the Hague Child Protection Conventions. The participants (judges from most southern and eastern African countries as well as some from central Africa) at the 'Judicial Seminar on the Role of the Hague Child Protection Conventions on the Practical Implementation of the CRC and the ACRWC', which was held in the Hague from

---

10 The other two being the Hague Convention on the Civil Aspects of International Child Abduction of 25 October 1980, and the Hague Convention on Jurisdiction, Applicable Law, Recognition, Enforcement and Co-operation in Respect of Parental Responsibility and Measures for the Protection of Children, of 19 October 1996.

11 January 2008. Information on the status of the Convention can be found on the internet: <http://hcch.e-vision.nl/index-en.php?act=conventions.statusccide=68>. For a comprehensive commentary on the Convention, see the *Explanatory Report on the Convention on Protection of Children and Co-operation in Respect of Inter-country Adoption* by G. Parra-Aranguren, Hague Conference on Private International Law, May 1994.

3 to 6 September 2006, recommended that the African Union (AU) should raise and promote awareness among Member States of the ACRWC, the Hague Child Protection Convention, and the CRC. A similar seminar was convened for judicial officers from Western and Central African states in 2007. It is submitted that these endeavours could also raise the number of contracting states to these particular conventions on the African continent.

Objectives of the Hague Convention

Intercountry adoption is a worldwide phenomenon. However, the geographic relocation of children over long distances cutting across cultural, religious and racial differences and environments has the potential to create and aggravate serious problems and human rights abuses. Thus the objective of this Hague Convention is not to encourage intercountry adoptions, but rather to ensure that where such adoption takes place it will be regulated to secure the best interests of the child concerned while respecting his or her fundamental rights (article 1(a)). In order to achieve this goal, the Hague Convention creates a system of co-operation amongst states to ensure that safeguards are respected, and to prevent various abuses within the process of intercountry adoption, such as abductions and the sale of, and trafficking, in children (article 1(b)). A further aim of the Hague Convention is to secure recognition of international adoptions under the Convention (article 1(c)).

Scope of the Convention

The Convention will apply between contracting states in circumstances in which a child who is the habitual resident of one state, the state of origin, has been, is being, or will be moved to another state, the receiving state, as a consequence of his or her adoption in the state of origin by a person or persons who are habitually resident in the receiving state (article 2(1); Nicholson 2000, 248). The Convention covers only adoptions which create a permanent parent–child relationship (article 2(2); Nicholson 2000, 248). It shall apply in every case where an application has been made after the Convention has entered into force in both the receiving state and the state of origin (article 41).

The Convention contains a mixture of substantive and procedural requirements. They include the division of responsibilities in respect of the adoption process between the state of origin and the receiving state involved in the adoption.

The Subsidiarity Principle

The CRC specifies that intercountry adoption may be considered as an alternative form of child care in circumstances where the child cannot be cared for in any suitable way in the child's country of origin (article 21(c) and Nicholson 2000, 247–8), which characterizes intercountry adoptions as being subsidiary by nature. The principle of subsidiarity is also enshrined in article 24(b) of the ACRWC, in somewhat stronger terms (*AD and Another* v *DW and Others (Centre for Child Law as Amicus Curiae)* 2007 (5) SA 184 (SCA) par 12). This important subsidiarity principle finds concrete expression in the Hague Convention in the requirement of article 4(b) that the competent authorities of the state of origin must determine, 'after possibilities for placement of the child within the state of origin have been given due consideration', that an intercountry adoption is in the child's best interests. The Hague Convention departs slightly from the CRC formula in that its preamble recognizes that intercountry adoption 'may offer the advantage of a permanent family to a child *for whom a suitable family cannot be found* in his or her state of origin' (own emphasis). This suggests that there are circumstances in which intercountry adoption may be preferable over institutional care in the country of origin (Duncan 1995, 221). However, it is for the state of origin to decide what constitutes appropriate possibilities for placement in the home country (Duncan 1995, 221).

It is also for the state of origin to decide what form 'due consideration' of alternatives should entail. Duncan suggests that the subsidiarity principle should not be applied in an inflexible manner. He explains that it could be in the best interests of a child to be placed with parents abroad rather than with prospective adopters in the country of origin if, for example, the child's roots are in fact in that foreign country (Duncan 1995, 222). He also warns against the application of the subsidiarity principle leading to excessive delay in the placement of the child, for example by the adoption of rigid administrative practices. Thus, the subsidiarity principle should always be applied in the context of the best interests principle.[12] The successful operation of the subsidiarity principle therefore also requires that the placing agency in the country of origin has the capacity to explore the alternatives to intercountry adoption (see further Duncan 1995, 222).

Responsibilities of the Competent Authorities of the State of Origin

The Hague Convention imposes minimum standards. It does not require a state to assist in or approve an intercountry adoption where that adoption is regarded as inappropriate (Duncan 1995, 219). Individual states are free to apply more stringent safeguards where these are deemed appropriate, for instance by limiting intercountry adoptions strictly to situations where there is absolutely no alternative family placement in the child's country of origin.

The competent authorities of the state of origin determine the adoptability of the child (article 4(a)). In doing so, the child's age and status will have to be considered.[13] It is suggested that these issues will normally be decided in accordance with the internal law of the state of origin or in accordance with its conflicts rules (Duncan 1995, 220). It is important that the legal criteria as well as medical, psychological and social aspects of adoptability, which may be relevant, are addressed in implementing legislation and procedures.

---

12 See the linkage of these two principles in article 4(b) of the Hague Convention.

13 Unfortunately not every child deprived of parental care is adoptable. In considering whether there are any factors or conditions, such as those relating to health or age, which may render a child 'unadoptable', it is important to bear in mind the basic principle of non-discrimination.

It could also be appropriate to consider the child's adoptability under the law of the receiving state because in the end the Central Authorities in both these states have to agree that the adoption may proceed (article 17(c)).

The competent authorities of the state of origin apply the subsidiarity principle to establish whether or not intercountry adoption is appropriate (article 4(b)). In doing so the best interests of the child standard has to be adhered to and therefore they are at liberty to find that the intercountry adoption is the preferable alternative.

The competent authorities of the state of origin control the consent procedures. They must ensure that the necessary consents are informed consents given after suitable counselling (article 4(c)(1)). The person or body whose consent is required must be informed of its effects, and in particular whether or not an adoption will result in the termination of the legal relationship between the child and his or her family of origin. The consent must be expressed or evidenced in writing (article 4(c)(2)). The necessary consent must be given freely, that is voluntarily and not induced by financial gain or compensation (article 4(c)(2)–(3)).[14] In order to ensure this, the Convention specifically prohibits contact between the prospective adoptive parents and the child's parents or caregivers until the consents have been obtained (article 29; Duncan 1995, 225–6; Nicholson 2000, 249). The only exception to this will be in the case of a family adoption.

If the consent of the mother is required, that consent must be given after the child's birth apparently to eliminate any possible duress (article 4(c)(4); Nicholson 2000, 249).

The authorities in the state of origin must also ensure, with due regard to the age and maturity of the child, that he or she is appropriately counselled and informed of the effects of the adoption before obtaining his or her consent where such consent is required (article 4(d)(1)). They will also have to ensure that the wishes and opinions of the child are duly considered (article 4(d)(2)). As with the other consents, the child's consent must be in writing and freely given (article 4(d)(3)), that is without financial or any other inducement (article 4(d)(4)).

Once again, apart from the mandatory provisions in the Convention, the norm to be applied by the state of origin will be its own domestic rules relating to consent (Duncan 1995, 221). However, the possibility should be considered that the receiving state may refuse to agree to the adoption if its own fundamental principles relating to consent have been violated (article 17).

Responsibilities of the Competent Authorities of the Receiving State

The competent authorities of the receiving state are responsible to ensure that the prospective adoptive parent(s) are both eligible and suited and that they have been appropriately counselled.[15] The Convention uses both 'eligible' and 'suited' to clarify

---

14 The competent authorities in the state of origin also have to ensure that the required consents have not been withdrawn.

15 Article 5(a)–(b). A receiving state must decide which authority or body shall receive applications from, and perform evaluations of, the prospective adoptive parent(s) to determine if the parent(s) are 'eligible and suited to adopt'.

two distinct categories of evaluation: 'eligible' referring to the fulfilment of all legal requirements, and 'suited' referring to the fulfilment of socio-psychological criteria. The competent authorities of the receiving state determine whether or not the child will be permitted permanent resident status in the receiving state after the adoption has been finalized (article 5(c)).

Central Authorities and Accredited Bodies

Central Authorities are established in contracting (both sending and receiving) states to carry out the duties created by the Convention.[16] Central Authorities engender co-operation between contracting states to protect children and achieve the objectives of the Convention (article 7(1)). These authorities bear responsibility for the free flow of information on adoption in general and on the operation of the Convention in a specific adoption (article 7(2)(a)–(b)). Their activities are also directed towards eliminating any obstacles to the proper implementation of the Convention (article 7(2)(b)). Central Authorities are specifically required to take appropriate measures to prevent trafficking in children.[17]

Articles 9(a)–(e) of the Convention require Central Authorities (or public authorities or duly accredited bodies) to:

- collect, preserve and exchange information necessary to an adoption;
- facilitate the process to secure and expedite a successful adoption;
- promote adoption counselling and post-adoption services in that particular state;
- prepare and exchange evaluation reports on intercountry adoption; and
- respond to justified requests for information pertaining to a particular adoption.

These specific functions may be delegated to 'accredited bodies' such as approved adoption agencies, if they demonstrate their competence in this regard (article 9 read with article 22(1); article 10; Duncan 1995, 219). Central Authorities may also utilize other bodies that are not accredited.[18]

Competent authorities supervise accredited bodies in that particular contracting state as to their composition, operation and finances (article 11(c)). Accredited bodies must be staffed by suitably qualified persons with experience in the field of intercountry adoptions (article 11(b)). These bodies shall pursue only non-profit objectives (article 11(a)). Accredited bodies from one contracting state will only be

---

16 Chapter III: Article 6(1). In certain circumstances one state may designate more than one Central Authority: Article 6(2).

17 Article 8; Nicholson 2000, 250. See also the prohibition on improper financial gain in article 32; Nicholson 2000, 254–5. In this regard, the Hague Convention follows the ACRWC, Article 24(d).

18 In terms of an article 22(2) declaration. There is thus the possibility for individuals such as lawyers or doctors to be involved, but subject to requirements of supervision and special qualifications, and then only where this is permitted by the two states concerned (Duncan 1995, 219, and see 'Independent adoptions' at 224–5).

entitled to operate in another state if duly authorized by the competent authorities in both the states concerned (article 12). Contracting states are required to furnish details of all designated Central Authorities and their functions, as well as the names and addresses of accredited bodies or other bodies or persons permitted to perform central authority functions to the Permanent Bureau of the Hague Conference on Private International Law (article 13 read with article 22(3)).

Procedural Requirements under the Convention

The procedural requirements in Chapter IV of the Convention are of particular importance. It will be indicated below that other procedures, like guardianship orders, should not be used to avoid compliance with the procedural requirements under the Convention.

Once persons who are habitually resident within a contracting state decide to adopt a child who is habitually resident in another contracting state, they apply to the Central Authority in their country of habitual residence, that is, the receiving state (article 14). If the Central Authority of the receiving state is satisfied that the applicants are eligible and suitable adopters, it will prepare a comprehensive report including, *inter alia*, information relating to the background, family and medical history of the prospective adoptive parents, as well as the characteristics of the children they would be qualified to care for (article 15(1)). The Central Authority in the receiving state then submits the report to the Central Authority in the state of origin of the child to be adopted (article 15(2)). The Central Authority in the state of origin has to take a decision on the adoptability of the child and then prepare a comprehensive report on the child, *inter alia*, his or her background, social environment, family and medical history and any special needs the child might have (article 16(1)(a)). This Central Authority has to consider the child's upbringing and his or her ethnic, religious and cultural background (article 16(1)(b)). It also has to ensure that all the necessary consents have been obtained (article 16(1)(c), in terms of article 4). The Central Authority of the state of origin will then determine, on the basis of the reports on both the child and the prospective adoptive parents, whether the placement would be in the child's best interests (article 16(1)(d)). The Central Authority of the state of origin will notify the Central Authority of the receiving state of its decision and transmit all the documentation on which the decision was taken to the Central Authority in the receiving state (article 16(2)). Care will be taken not to reveal the identity of the mother and father if these identities may not be disclosed in the state of origin.[19] The Central Authority in the state of origin may only decide to entrust[20] the child to the prospective adoptive parents, in accordance with articles 17(a)–(d), if:

---

19 The Central Authority of the receiving state may request a certified translation of the documentation (article 34). The cost of this translation will be borne by the prospective adoptive parents.

20 Duncan (1995, 222) indicates that the concept of 'entrustment' is used to denote the physical transfer of the child to the prospective adoptive parents.

- the Central Authority of the receiving state has secured the agreement of the prospective adoptive parents;
- the Central Authority of the receiving state has approved of the determination;[21]
- the Central Authorities of both states agree that the adoption should proceed; and
- the adoptive parents have been found eligible and suitable to adopt and the child will be permitted to enter the receiving state and to take up permanent residence there.

Article 17 is of central importance in that it enables the Central Authorities in either the state of origin or the receiving state to stop the adoption process before the child has been placed, where the adoption is deemed inappropriate (Duncan 1995, 222). Duncan submits that it should help to avoid an unfortunate legal 'limbo' which may arise if a child is placed with prospective adoptive parents and it later proves impossible for legal or other reasons, to complete the adoption process (1995, 223; also see article 19(1)).

The Central Authorities of both states must take the necessary steps to secure the transfer of the child from the state of origin to the receiving state and to arrange for the child's permanent residence in the receiving state (article 18). It is the responsibility of the Central Authorities of both states to ensure that the transfer only takes place in secure and appropriate circumstances and preferably in the company of the prospective adoptive parents.[22]

Central Authorities are required to keep each other informed of progress throughout the adoption process and any probationary period that may be required (article 20).

The Central Authority of the receiving state may take measures, set out in articles 21(1)(a)–(c), to protect a child if the continued placement of the child is not in the best interests of the child concerned, in particular:

- place the child in temporary care;
- arrange a new placement or long-term care in consultation with the Central Authority of the state of origin; or
- as a last resort, return the child to the state of origin if that appears to be in the best interests of the child.

The child's wishes will be taken into account in making new arrangements where appropriate (article 21(2)).

---

21 Although the primary responsibility for 'matching' the child with suitable adoptive parents lies with the state of origin, article 17(b) means that the approval of the Central Authority of the receiving state will have to be obtained where it is required by the law of either state (Duncan 1995, 223).

22 Article 19(2). Article 19(1) emphasizes that the transfer of the child to the receiving state can only be carried out if the requirements of article 17 have been met.

Recognition and Enforcement of Adoptions under the Convention

Once an adoption has been certified as an adoption in accordance with the Convention, the adoption will automatically be recognized *ex lege* in all other contracting states.[23] No state is, however, required to give recognition to any certified adoption order that is manifestly contrary to its public policy, taking into account the best interests of the child (article 24). Recognition of an adoption means recognition of the legal effects of that adoption (Nicholson 2000, 253). In terms of the Convention's articles 26(1)(a)–(c), it entails recognition of:

- the legal parent–child relationship between the child and his or her adoptive parents;
- the parental responsibilities of the adoptive parents for the child; and
- the termination of the parent–child relationship between the child and his or her natural parents, where that is the effect in the state of origin.

If the adoption terminates the parent–child relationship between the child and his or her natural parents in the state of origin, the relationship will also be regarded as terminated in the receiving state and in any other contracting state.[24]

In the event that an adoption is not recognized in the state of origin as terminating the pre-existing legal parent–child relationship, the receiving state (or other contracting state called upon to recognize the adoption) may convert the adoption into a full adoption (article 27).

Preservation of, and Access to, Information

Competent authorities of contracting states are obliged to preserve the information held by them concerning the child's origin, in particular information on the identity of the child's biological parents and medical history (article 30(1)). The adoptive child or his or her representative is to have access to such information to the extent permitted by the law of the state where the information is held.[25] Duncan (1995, 226) explains that the child's right to have access to information concerning origins may be made subject to legal limitations in the state where the information is held. The reason for this is the potential for disaster when the identity of the parent of a child born out of wedlock becomes known in certain cultures.[26]

---

23 Article 23(1) and the certificate will reflect that the authorities in the two states agreed that the adoption should proceed.

24 Article 26(2). Article 26(3) provides that if a contracting state has legal provisions that are more favourable to the child than those of the state of origin it will be permitted to give the adoption the more favourable effect.

25 Article 30(2). It should be noted, however, that information gathered for the purpose of the reports on the prospective adoptive parents and the child (in terms of articles 15 and 16) may only be used for the purpose for which it was gathered (article 31).

26 See article 16(2) for a similar provision for exactly the same reason.

Other General Provisions

Any competent authority of any contracting state which believes that there is a serious risk that any provision of the Convention is not being or will not be complied with is obliged to inform the Central Authority of its state immediately. The Central Authority is then required to take appropriate steps (article 33).

The Convention does not affect any other international instrument to which contracting states are parties save where the provisions of such instruments are contrary to the Convention (article 39(1)). Contracting states are free to enter into agreements amongst themselves regarding adoption and may, for the purpose, derogate from certain provisions of the Convention (article 39(2)). Other contracting states may, however, notify the depository of the Convention that it will not automatically recognize adoptions that are made in compliance with such an agreement between states (article 25; Nicholson 2000, 255). States which have concluded agreements in terms of article 39 must transmit a copy to the depository of the Convention. Article 40 is to the effect that no reservation to the Convention is permitted.

Africa is by and large a sending, rather than receiving, continent. The Hague Convention on Intercountry Adoption places a heavy burden of responsibility on sending countries. The concluding remarks of the Deputy Secretary General of the Hague Conference on Private International Law have to be endorsed. He said:[27]

> It is the state of origin which will have the major responsibility in regulating the process of 'matching', in ensuring that the rights of the child and the biological family are protected, in exploring alternative placements for the child in the country of origin and in combating illicit practices. The effective discharge of these responsibilities will require a level of supervision, a degree of administrative control and a range of services, which for many countries of origin – with their scarce resources and sometimes vast geographical areas – will be difficult to achieve. There will also naturally be a desire in many such countries to concentrate limited resources on the development of domestic family support and child placement services. If the Convention is to work, these basic facts of life will have to be recognized, especially by the wealthier receiving states, who may have to consider whether they are contributing sufficiently to the development of such services in the poorer countries.

Intercountry Adoption on the African Continent

There is very little information available on intercountry adoption in Africa. The fact that only Burkina Faso, Burundi, Kenya and South Africa (and Madagascar and Mauritius) have either ratified or acceded to the Hague Convention on Intercountry Adoption has also been mentioned. The question could be asked why the African continent has thus far shown so little interest in the Hague Convention in the context of intercountry adoptions and more than one reason could perhaps be given.

The first reason links to the remarks of the Deputy Secretary General of the Hague Conference on Private International Law already mentioned above. African countries will normally be the sending country or the state of origin carrying the primary responsibility in the matching process. These countries have to bear the

---

27 Duncan (1995, 227), quoting himself in Bainham, A. and Pearl, D.S. (eds) (1993, 60).

burden of supervision, administrative control and provide a wide range of services to ensure successful placement. This additional financial obligation is perhaps out of reach for many developing countries with their scarce resources.

The second reason could be the fact that 'adoption' as it is known in common law rarely, if ever, occurs in African communities (in Southern Africa). A childless couple would not, for instance, adopt a child merely for the sake of having a child. Nor would somebody adopt a child for charitable reasons to give the child a home. According to Bennett (1991, 375–6):

> Adoption is a common-law concept that is sometimes loosely applied in the context of customary law. It is doubtful, however, whether there is an exact correspondence. The customary law institution resembles early Roman Law *adoptio*, the main purpose of which was the perpetuation of the bloodline.[28]

The related institution in customary law is, what may more accurately be called, the institution of an heir. A man who has no son may adopt a nephew or close kinsman as his successor. It may take different forms, but the child concerned will always be a member of the adopter's bloodline (Bennet 2004, 319–29). The different forms are not relevant for present purposes. However, the absence of the common-law concept of adoption may account for the failure of African countries to adopt the Hague Convention on Intercountry Adoption.[29] Adoption outside the African conception of children as belonging to or being affiliated to a particular family moreover would not make sense. In addition, it cuts across the African practice of ancestor worship. A child who is deprived of its roots would lose contact with the patrilineal ancestors. However, culture is not stagnant. Individual African families may have different views about adoption and succession, but Bennett's view still prevails.[30]

Third, the institution of adoption is not accepted in the *Sharia* law states and therefore intercountry adoptions will remain rare in the Islamic states on the African continent. In Muslim countries, if a child's parents are unable to take care of him or her, a relative assumes responsibility for the child through an informal system known as *kafala* (Stark 2003, 276).

The reluctance of African countries about intercountry adoption could also relate to the argument that it is a new form of liberalism and that African countries value cultural identity. Stark (2003, 277) quotes international adoption experts Alstein and Simon, pointing out that what most viewed as charitable, humane and even noble, has been defined as imperialistic, self-serving and even a form of colonialism by developing countries. The lack of information on intercountry adoption in Africa could perhaps also be explained against this backdrop. The developments on this topic could however be traced in the following countries.

---

28 See also *Helela* v *Maxinana* 1921 NHC 52, where it was held that adoption was unknown to customary law.

29 Note that according to the ACRWC institutionalization is preferred over intercountry adoption (Stark 2003, 276).

30 In an interview with J.C. Bekker, Emeritus Professor formerly Dean of Faculty of Law, Vista University and expert witness on customary law, see, for example, *Metiso* v *Padongelukkefonds* 2001 3 SA 1142.

Uganda

Uganda has not ratified or acceded to the Hague Convention on Intercountry Adoptions, but it has ratified or acceded to the African Charter on the Rights and Welfare of the Child and in 1996 adopted a Children's Statute. The Statute provides for adoptions in Part VII, sections 44 to 55. Intercountry adoptions are in a very limited sense provided for in section 46.[31] It stipulates that foreigners may only in *exceptional circumstances* adopt a Ugandan child, that is *inter alia* if the non-citizen of Uganda has stayed in Uganda for at least three years and has fostered the child for at least six months under supervision. The circumstances under which an intercountry adoption can take place in Uganda are therefore very restricted.[32]

Kenya

Kenya has ratified the ACRWC and most recently (12 February 2007) also the Hague Convention on Intercountry Adoption. Their Children's Act (8 of 2001) provides in section 162 for 'international' adoptions in very broad terms:

1. An adoption order may be made in respect of a child upon the joint application of two spouses who are not Kenyan citizens and not resident in Kenya (in this Act referred to as an 'international adoption') if they –

   (a) have obtained the consents specified in paragraph (e) of subsection 4 of section 158;[33] and

---

31 Section 46:

(1) A person who is not a citizen of Uganda may in exceptional circumstances adopt a Ugandan child, if he or she –

   (a) has stayed in Uganda for at least three years;
   (b) has fostered the child for at least thirty-six months under the supervision of a probation and social welfare officer;
   (c) does not have a criminal record;
   (d) has a recommendation concerning his or her suitability to adopt a child from his or her country's probation and welfare office or other competent authority; and
   (e) has satisfied the court that his or her country of origin will respect and recognize the adoption order.

(2) For the purpose of an application to which this section applies, the probation and social welfare officer referred to in subsection (1)(b) shall be required to submit a report to assist the court in considering the application; and the court may, in addition, require some other person or authority to make a report in respect of the application.

(3) The restrictions and conditions in section 45, other than subsections (4) and (5), apply to an application to which this section relates.

32 See Hodgkin and Newell (1998, 274) to the effect that intercountry adoption was illegal in Namibia in 1998 because one of the applicants had to be Namibian or at least applying to become a Namibian.

33 Section 158(4)(e): 'in the case of two spouses who are not Kenyan citizens and who are not resident in Kenya, with the consent of the court of competent jurisdiction or of a government authority situated in the country where both or one of the spouses is ordinarily resident, permitting the spouses to adopt a foreign child.'

(b) have satisfied the court that the country where they ordinarily reside and where they expect to reside with the child immediately after the making of the adoption order will respect and recognize the adoption order and will grant resident status to the child; and

(c) have been authorized and recommended as persons who are suitable (including being morally fit and financially capable) to adopt a foreign child by a competent government authority or court of competent jurisdiction in the country immediately after the making of the adoption order.

Malawi

The world's attention recently focused on Malawi when the pop star Madonna whisked the 13-month-old David Banda to her English home in contravention of Malawian law.[34] Malawi, like Uganda, has ratified the ACRWC but not the Hague Convention on Intercountry Adoption. Adoption is regulated by the Adoption of Children Act (Cap. 26:01 laws of Malawi) and intercountry adoptions are prohibited under the Act.[35] The Law Commission of Malawi published a report on the *Review of the Children and Young Persons Act* (Cap. 26:03) dated 8 October 2005 and recommended fundamental changes to the law relating to intercountry adoptions. This report explains (at 97) that intercountry adoptions were prohibited because of the difficulties involved in monitoring the placement in the receiving state. The Commission notes that the 'best interests of the child' standard could also entail that an intercountry adoption should be considered as an alternative means of caring for a child if the child cannot be placed in an adoptive family or in any other suitable manner in the country of the child's origin (article 26(1) of the CRC). The Commission also notes the adoption of the Hague Convention on Intercountry Adoption and the objectives thereof and concludes (at 98) that in view of these developments, the blanket prohibition on intercountry adoptions should be removed. The Commission expresses itself in favour of a system where intercountry adoptions should be allowed if the prospective adoptive parents reside in a country that is a signatory to the Hague Convention and has already implemented the provisions of the Convention. The Commission therefore recommends that section 3(5) of the Adoption Act should be deleted and replaced by the following section:

3A (1) Subject to the provisions of this Act, a court may grant an inter-country adoption order as an alternative means of care and protection of a child who cannot be placed under foster care or in an adoptive family or who cannot in any suitable manner be cared for, in Malawi.

---

34 American actress Mia Farrow is recognized as starting the celebrity trend for foreign adoptions in 1973 and is now the mother of 14. Hollywood star Angelina Jolie is perhaps the most famous exponent, having adopted two children from the developing world: a daughter from Ethiopia and a son from Cambodia.

35 Section 3(5) requires the adoptive parents and the child to be resident in Malawi for a minimum of 18 months. Madonna was in Malawi for about nine days and a temporary order to adopt the child was granted. On the one hand the adoption was met with resistance from the Human Rights Consultative Committee (HRCC), but on the other hand it also highlighted the need to review adoption laws: <http://www.usatoday.com/life/people/2006-10-23-madonna-opera-x.htm>.

(2) A court shall not grant an inter-country adoption order unless the Minister, after consultation with the competent authorities of the receiving country, determines that –

    (a) the applicants are eligible to adopt the child;

    (b) the applicants have been counselled as may be necessary;

    (c) the child is or will be authorized to enter and reside permanently in the receiving country;

    (d) the applicants or one of the applicants, if not a relative of the child, has, while in Malawi, fostered the child for a period of one year; and

    (e) the receiving country is a signatory to and has implemented the United Nations Convention on Protection of Children and Co-operation in Respect of Inter-Country Adoption.

(3) For the purpose of this section, inter-country adoption means an adoption in which the applicant intends to take the adopted child outside Malawi within a period of one year from the date of the application.

Zambia

Zambia, unlike Uganda and Kenya, has not ratified the ACRWC yet. It is only a signatory to this regional document. Adoption in Zambia is governed by the Adoption Act (Cap. 54 of the Laws of Zambia). Mushota (2005, 387) explains that adoption is a creation of statute because under customary law children belong to everybody in the extended family and therefore do not have to be formally adopted. She confirms the notions of customary law as explained above and concludes, '[t]he concept of adoption or inalienability of rights does not exist.'

The Zambian Adoption Act does not prohibit intercountry adoptions. It provides that the child must be resident in Zambia (section 4(5)) and that the child assumes the nationality of the adoptive parents (Mushota 2005, 391).

South Africa

South Africa is one of the very few African countries that have acceded to the Hague Convention on Intercountry Adoption (on 1 December 2003). South Africa has also gone a long way to enact the said Hague Convention in domestic law, although the Children's Act (38 of 2005) has not become effective in full.[36] While the Convention has not formally been incorporated into domestic law, its provisions are, in terms of section 231 of the Constitution of the Republic of South Africa, 1996 unenforceable in the courts. There has very recently been a case dealing with the Hague Convention and other related issues and it deserves to be discussed in more detail.[37]

The applicants were an American couple who resided in the State of Virginia in the United States. They wished to adopt an abandoned child that was being fostered by the first and second respondents. Judge Goldblatt had some reservations when

---

36 An interim Central Authority in the Chief Directorate: Children, Youth and Families in the Department of Social Development has been established in the meantime.

37 *AD and Another* v *DW and Others (Centre for Child Law, University of Pretoria, amicus curiae)* 2006 (6) SA 51 (WD); 2007 (5) SA 184 (SCA); [2007] ZACC 27.

the case served in front of him (52B–D in the WLD) and requested the Centre for Child Law at the University of Pretoria to enter as *amicus curiae*. The applicants applied for a guardianship and custody order in the High Court with a view to later adopting the child outside of South Africa, while the normal route for undertaking an intercountry adoption would be by using the children's court and the provisions prescribed in chapter 4 of the Child Care Act (74 of 1983). The application was dismissed and Goldblatt J opined that the High Court should not be placed in the position of having to fulfil the functions of a commissioner of child welfare, who is better trained and more experienced in adoption matters than High Court judges (at 54G–H, 66E). He relied on the decision of *Minister of Welfare and Population Development* v *Fitzpatrick* (2000 (3) SA 422 (CC)) where the Constitutional Court *inter alia* emphasized that the religious and cultural background of the child and his or her parents as against that of the adoptive parents should be considered (Louw 2006, 503). The judgment also linked this consideration to the subsidiarity principle discussed above. However, the case was taken on appeal and the Supreme Court of Appeal was sharply divided. The majority held that adoption falls under the exclusive jurisdiction of the children's court and that granting the order sought by the applicants would result in sanctioning an alternative route to intercountry adoptions. This alternative route via a custody and guardianship order in the High Court would be without the internationally sanctioned standards and safeguards (see para. 15 of the Supreme Court of Appeal judgment). The majority also held that the appeal should fail because of the principle of subsidiarity. In their view subsidiarity required that preference be given to domestic measures over intercountry adoption (para. 12 at 191D–192C). The minority held that the High Court as upper guardian is both empowered and obliged to enquire into all matters concerning the best interests of the child and therefore has jurisdiction to make an order of sole custody and sole guardianship whenever such an order is appropriate (para. 36 at 201).

The Constitutional Court heard the matter during September 2007. An agreement reached between the parties was made an order of court in terms of which the children's court was directed to hear the matter within 30 days while the parties agreed that adoption is in the best interests of the child and that the principle of subsidiarity is not a bar to the adoption. However, this agreement did not resolve all the underlying issues and Sachs J handed down judgment in December 2007.

The Constitutional Court held that the Child Care Act should not be interpreted to dispossess the High Court of its inherent jurisdiction as upper guardian (para. 31), but that the children's court procedure should not have been by-passed in the present case (para. 34). According to the court, the subsidiarity principle itself must be seen as subsidiary to the paramountcy of the best interest principle (para. 55). The court supported the view of the Supreme Court of Appeal that the matter should have been pursued in the children's court, but this should not have resulted in simply dismissing the appeal without referring the matter to the children's court for speedy resolution (para. 56).

In considering the current position in South Africa, some reference could also be made to the fact that the new Children's Act (38 of 2005), which was passed by parliament on 13 December 2005, contains extensive provisions on intercountry adoption in Chapter 16. Section 25 of the new Act makes it clear that when a non-

South African citizen applies for guardianship of the child, the application must be regarded as an intercountry adoption in terms of the Hague Convention on Intercountry Adoption and Chapter 16 of the Act. Section 254 spells out that the purpose of Chapter16 is *inter alia* to give effect to the Hague Convention. Section 257 further states that the Director-General of the Department of Social Development is the Central Authority in relation to intercountry adoption. The Hague Convention is set out in full as Schedule 1 to the Act.

Conclusion

On the African continent, both customary law and Islamic law fail to recognize formal legal adoption and therefore also intercountry adoption. Intercountry adoption in Africa is a measure of last resort, that is, only if the child cannot be placed with relatives or a foster family or institutionalized (Stark 2003, 276). Under the ACRWC, intercountry adoption is further limited to those countries that are either signatories to the ACRWC or the UN CRC (article 24(b)). Countries which have adopted recent children's laws provide for intercountry adoptions on more or less restricted terms. But even in countries where the Hague Convention has been acceded to and national law aims at enforcing the Convention, difficult issues are still being resolved in the courts.

The Hague Conference on Private International Law embarked on 'The Hague Project for International Co-operation and the Protection of Children in the Southern and Eastern African Region' and participating judges and experts at a 'Judicial Seminar on the Role of the Hague Child Protection Conventions' agreed *inter alia* that there is a need to develop an effective inter-state structure among African countries to facilitate co-operation, and that measures should be taken to ensure that national, regional and international instruments concerning child protection are fully and effectively implemented in African countries. Attention was drawn to the potential value of using the 'Central Authority' model, as developed in the Hague Child Protection Conventions, in achieving inter-state co-operation. It was recommended that further work be done to consider adapting this model to the needs of African countries and establishing a database of Central Authorities in Africa. The importance of monitoring and of reviewing the practical operation of the international instruments was also recognized. The Deputy Secretary General of the Hague Conference on Private International Law mentioned that inclusion of Islamic states within the sphere of international co-operation is a major challenge. The participants recommended *inter alia* that the African Union should raise and promote awareness among Member States of the Hague Child Protection Conventions. It is also recognized that the African Union can mobilize regional and international efforts for child protection. There is thus much potential for further embedding of children's rights principles in intercountry adoption practice in Africa.

References

Articles, Books and Chapters in Books

Arts, K.C.J.M. (1992), 'The International Protection of Children's Rights in Africa: The 1990 OAU Charter on the Rights and Welfare of the Child', *African Journal on International and Comparative Law* 5, 139–61.

Bennett, T.W. (1991), *A Sourcebook of African Customary Law for Southern Africa* (Cape Town: Juta and Co.).

Bennett, T.W. (2004), *Customary Law in South Africa* (Lansdowne: Juta and Co.).

Chirwa, D.M. (2002), 'The Merits and Demerits of the African Charter on the Rights and Welfare of the Child', *The International Journal of Children's Rights* 10, 157–77.

Davel, C.J. (ed.) (1999), *Children's Rights in a Transitional Society* (Pretoria: Protea Book House).

Davel, C.J. (ed.) (2000), *Introduction to Child Law in South Africa* (Lansdowne: Juta and Co.).

Davel, C.J. (2002), 'The African Charter on the Rights and Welfare of the Child, Family Law and Children's Rights', *De Jure* 2, 281–96.

Duncan, W. (1993), 'Regulating Intercountry Adoption', in Bainham, A. and Pearl, D.S. (eds) *Frontiers of Family Law* (London: John Wiley and Sons).

Duncan, W. (1995), 'The Hague Convention on the Protection of Children and Co-operation in Respect of Intercountry Adoption 1993. Some Issues of Special Relevance to Sending Countries', in Jaffe, E.D. (ed.).

Duncan, W. (2006), 'Fundamental Principles of the Hague Convention of 29 May 1993 on Protection of Children and Co-operation in Respect of Intercountry Adoption', paper presented at the Hague Conference on Private International Law on 'The Role of the Hague Child Protection Conventions in the Practical Implementation of the United Nations Convention on the Rights of the Child and the African Charter on the Rights and Welfare of the Child', 3–6 September 2006, The Hague.

Gose, M. (2002), *The African Charter on the Rights and Welfare of the Child* (Bellville: Community Law Centre, University of the Western Cape).

Hamilton, C. (1999), 'Implementing Children's Rights in a Transitional Society', in Davel, C.J. (ed.).

Hodgkin, R. and Newell, P. (1998/2002), *Implementation Handbook for the Convention on the Rights of the Child* (UNICEF).

Jaffe, E.D. (1995), *Intercountry Adoptions* (Netherlands: Jaffe and Kluwer Academic Publishers).

Louw, A.S. (2006), 'Intercountry Adoption in South Africa: Have the Fears Become Fact?', *De Jure* 503.

Mushota, L. (2005), *Family Law in Zambia: Cases and Materials* (Lusaka: UNZA Press for the School of Law, University of Zambia).

Nicholson, C. (2000), 'The Hague Convention on the Protection of Children and Co-operation in Respect of Inter-country Adoption 1993', in Davel, C.J. (ed.).

Stark, B. (2003), 'Lost Boys and Forgotten Girls: Intercountry Adoption, Human Rights, and African Children', *St. Louis U. Pub. L. Rev.* 22, 275.

Thompson, B. (1992), 'Africa's Charter on Children's Rights: A Normative Break with Cultural Traditionalism', *International and Comparative Law Quarterly* 41, 432–44.

UNAIDS, UNICEF and USAID (2004), *Children on the Brink 2004.*

Van Bueren, G. (2000), 'The United Nations Convention on the Rights of the Child: An Evolutionary Revolution', in Davel, C.J. (ed.).

Viljoen, F. (2000), 'The African Charter on the Rights and Welfare of the Child', in Davel, C.J. (ed.).

Chapter 16

HIV/Aids and Children's Rights in Law and Policy in Africa: Confronting Hydra Head On

Julia Sloth-Nielsen and Benyam D. Mezmur

Introduction

The scourge of HIV/Aids which is ravaging Africa, and most particularly sub-Saharan Africa, has especially dire effects for children and the fulfilment of their rights. Despite a slow start, policy makers and legal systems are beginning to respond to provide a more protective and enabling framework in the context of the rapidly changing demographics of our societies being brought about by the disease. Indeed, the rise of HIV/Aids and its impact on children has spawned an entirely new children's rights 'language': the 'orphan generation', OVCs (orphaned and vulnerable children), MTCT (mother-to-child-transmission) and child-headed households have long since entered the everyday lexicon in policy and programming on the continent.

This chapter will review some of the key challenges for children thrown up by the HIV/Aids pandemic, but will also point to some positive, if possibly unintended, developments that have emerged of late in effort to confront the many tentacles produced by the disease. The chapter will focus mainly on the legal consequences pertaining to children deriving from the HIV/Aids phenomenon, and point to the influence that HIV/Aids is having on legislative reforms for children's rights.

The Scale and Impact of HIV/Aids

Since the first clinical evidence of HIV/Aids was reported some two decades ago, HIV/Aids has spread to every corner of the world. It is truly a global epidemic, imposing a burden on all countries and regions, leaving none immune from its devastating impact. The virus has spread at alarming rates, particularly in sub-Saharan Africa, a region which can least afford the sickness, death, and the loss of productivity associated with the epidemic. The epidemic is at its peak in sub-Saharan Africa. This region has just over 10 per cent of the world's population, but more than two thirds (68 per cent) of all people who are HIV-positive live in this region, a region where more than three quarters (76 per cent) of all Aids deaths in 2007 occurred (UNAIDS/WHO 2007, 15). It is reported that, in 2007, Aids killed approximately

330,000 children under the age of 15, and an estimated 2.1 million additional children under age 15 were living with the HIV virus (UNAIDS/WHO 2007, 1). In 2004, an estimated 3.1 million people in the region became newly infected, while 3.3 million died of Aids (UNAIDS/WHO 2006). This number decreased in 2006 to an estimated 2.8 million adults and children (2.4–3.2 million) who became infected, which still is a higher figure than in all other regions of the world combined (UNAIDS/WHO 2006), before dropping further to 1.7 million (1.4–2.4 million) in 2007 estimates (UNAIDS/WHO 2007, 15).

> Adult HIV prevalence in the region has been roughly stable in recent years, but this does not necessarily mean that the epidemic is slowing. On the contrary, it can disguise the worst phases of an epidemic, when roughly equally large numbers of people are being newly infected with HIV as are dying of Aids. (UNAIDS 2004)

HIV/Aids is the leading cause of death among adults aged 15–59 in sub-Saharan Africa (UNICEF 2003, 2). But of greater concern, perhaps, is that the Aids epidemic has already orphaned millions of children. According to a joint Report of UNICEF and the Government of Kenya produced in 2004 on the number of orphans in Kenya, 1.7 million children between 0 and 14 years old (that is, 12 per cent of all Kenyan children) have lost one or both parents, and 50–60 per cent of these have lost one or both parents due to HIV/Aids. In Kenya it has been found, too, that there are insufficient human and financial resources to meet the needs of orphaned and vulnerable children, despite various OVC programmes being in place, including financial assistance programmes (Save the Children UK 2006). Approximately 100,000 Kenyan children were at that stage HIV positive themselves, mostly children aged under five due to mother-to-child-transmission of the virus. The data for other countries in Southern Africa is equally disturbing; in Swaziland, for instance, more than a quarter of the country's children are now orphans (Whitehead 2007; Gallinetti 2006). Noting that the Joint United Nations Programme on HIV/AIDS (UNAIDS), UNICEF and the United States Agency for International Development (USAID) estimate that 17 per cent of the total child population of Lesotho is already orphaned, and that half of these are orphaned as a result of HIV/Aids, with a recent figure of 91,844 orphaned children, it is asserted that the numbers continue to swell (Kimane 2005). Similar figures have been raised in the context of Botswana, with the highest prevalence rate in the world for some years (at 37.3 per cent of the population infected with the virus). Nigeria, Ethiopia and Uganda have the largest number of orphans in the continent. In Malawi, it is estimated that there are more than 700,000 orphans in the country.[1] Further, a recent costing of the South African Children's Act 38 of 2005 (not yet fully in operation), legislation which contains elaborate care and protection provisions, including the whole gamut of alternative care possibilities, has projected that, due to the impact of HIV/Aids, close to a million South African orphans will require some form of social work services and alternative care placement by 2009 (Cornerstone Economic Research 2006).

---

1 <http://www.msf.org/msfinternational/invoke.cfm?component=article&objectid=630E 7F3A-41D2-468C-98ACB06C728CCBAE&method=full_html> (accessed 22 August 2005).

[A]lthough the total number of orphans from all causes in Asia and in Latin America and the Caribbean since 1990 has been decreasing, the number of orphans from all causes has risen by more than 50 per cent in sub-Saharan Africa, where an estimated 12 million children aged 0–17 have lost one or both parents to Aids. (UNICEF 2003, 2)

This makes the region home to 80 per cent of all the children in the developing world who have already lost a parent to the disease. Moreover, it is estimated that by 2010, an estimated 15.7 million children – 30 per cent of the 53 million anticipated orphans from all causes in sub-Saharan Africa – will have lost at least one parent due to Aids.

It is now known that even where HIV prevalence stabilizes or begins to decline, the number of orphans will continue to grow or at least remain high for years, reflecting the time lag between HIV infection and death. It has been said that even if prevention campaigns become more successful and HIV infections drop dramatically, most people already infected with HIV are expected to succumb to Aids-related illnesses, absent wide-scale ongoing treatment, which most countries are struggling to provide on the requisite scale (Aids and Human Rights Research Unit 2007).

Hence, UNICEF rightly ranks HIV/Aids as one of the three greatest threats to childhood today (UNICEF 2006 and 2008). Children and young people are at the frontline of the epidemic's advance, bearing the brunt of its impact. The human rights of the child placed at risk in the context of HIV/Aids include: the right to life; the right to the highest attainable standard of mental and physical health; the right to non-discrimination, equal protection and equality before the law; the right to privacy; the right to freedom of expression and opinion and the right to freely receive and impart information; the right to equal access to education; the right to an adequate standard of living; the right to social security, assistance and welfare; and the right to parental care. In the words of the Convention on the Rights of the Child (CRC) Committee, 'the HIV/Aids epidemic has drastically changed the world in which children live. The epidemic impacts on the daily life of younger children, and increases the victimization and marginalization of children, especially those living in particularly difficult circumstances' (General Comment no. 3, para. 1). In addition, the structures and services that exist for their benefit are often strained by the consequences of the HIV/Aids epidemic. For example, in countries that are severely affected, the loss of health professionals and the magnitude of the burden of HIV/Aids on health, education and social systems that are already lacking in resources can become overwhelming. The diverse effects of HIV/Aids on children can include being orphaned, growing up in incapacitated and low capacity households, dropping out of school, being forced into child labour, failing to access health services, facing severe emotional burdens occasioned by the illness and death of kin, and social stigma. Thus it is clear that, for large parts of Africa, 'Aids is beginning to reverse decades of steady progress in child survival' (UNAIDS 2001, 11).

In families affected by HIV/Aids, children start to carry the burden of being heads of households even before the death of their parents. The phenomenon of child-headed households is taking a harsh toll on families, communities, nations and, most important, on children themselves (Tsegaye 2006, 1). Orphans are less likely to attend school, which compromises their abilities and future prospects. HIV/

Aids orphans in Ethiopia tend to have minimal access to social services, particularly education. A baseline survey conducted by the World Food Programme found that an estimated 75 per cent of HIV/Aids orphans were not attending school (Rapid Country Response Analysis: Ethiopia 2004). Teachers may also become ill, disrupting education services. Frequently, orphans become engaged in hazardous work, or take to the streets to beg, to feed themselves and their siblings. The likely long term emotional and psychosocial consequences of being rendered an orphan are alarming. Empirical evidence suggests that when children have to assist to tend to their dying care-givers, it may have a long lasting psychological impact on their lives, especially when they are not prepared for this role, or are not assisted by other adults. Not only material security is threatened by the parent's death, but love and emotional security, a most important need of a child, also disappears.

Until recently, international children's rights law was devoid of any specific provisions applicable to the legal and other problems which may be faced by children in an era of HIV/Aids. However, the CRC Committee has now released two General Comments dealing either directly or indirectly with the issue, and providing an analytical framework within which to assess both the application of children's rights, and the responsibilities of governments and communities. This framework forms the basis of the discussion in the next section.

International and Regional Law Framework Surrounding HIV/Aids

The international law framework surrounding children affected by the HIV/Aids crisis can only be described as relatively weak. Neither the CRC nor the African Charter on the Rights and Welfare of the Child (ACRWC) refer expressly to HIV/Aids at all, although it must be conceded that both instruments were being drafted at a time when the pandemic was in its infancy, its relevance to Africa not yet visible, and its disproportionate impact upon children not yet experienced (Sloth-Nielsen 2004, 2005). There is much improvement in the regulatory framework in the form of the CRC Committee's General Comment no. 3, entitled 'HIV/Aids and the Rights of the Child' (2003). General Comment no. 4 'Adolescent Health and the Rights of the Child' is also of some relevance. At the regional level, the Protocol to the African Charter on Human and Peoples' Rights on the Rights of Women (AWP) (adopted as an Optional Protocol to the African Charter on Human and Peoples' Rights [ACHPR] in Maputo 2004), is of some relevance, particularly insofar as the girl child is concerned. Substantively, therefore, discussions of the myriad of legal and policy issues raised for children by HIV/Aids have to be founded by and large on the general rights articulated in the main children's rights treaties. This indeed appears to be how General Comment no. 3 approaches the issue.

General Comment No. 3 on HIV/Aids and the Rights of the Child

The Comment commences with the assertion that whilst initially children were thought to be only marginally affected by HIV/Aids, the realization has taken root that in fact children are at the epicentre of the disease, and for several reasons. The highest number of new infections is occurring amongst adolescents and young people, on the one hand, but on the other, MTCT during the birthing process renders infants especially vulnerable to acquiring it. Making the oft-overlooked point that HIV/Aids must be viewed as having an impact far beyond the health dimensions, and that children's civil, political and socio-economic rights may all be implicated, the General Comment advocates for a rights-based approach to the issue, building on the four 'pillars' of the CRC to guide measures and interventions at all levels. The potential for discrimination in various forms is particularly acute in the context of HIV/Aids, given social stigma and cultural taboos that are manifest. This extends from discrimination against children who are themselves infected, to discrimination against children on account of the HIV/Aids status of their family members and care-givers. Moreover, there is discrimination evident in children's access to health and other services, for example between children in rural areas and those living in better resourced urban settings. The girl child is especially vulnerable to discrimination. Judgmental attitudes to female sexual activity can limit the access of girl children to preventive and other services, for instance (General Comment no. 3, para. 9), and states are urged to give careful attention to the sexuality and lifestyles of teenagers, and to take steps to prevent early or forced marriage which can exacerbate vulnerability.

As an overall strategy, the General Comment motivates for the adoption of measures which stress the mutual reinforcement of prevention, care, treatment and support on a continuum of responses. Particular attention is paid in the General Comment to health services and to education. As regards the latter, the General Comment highlights that a crucial aspect of prevention is children's access to appropriate sex education and information about sexuality so that they can equip themselves to take measures against the acquisition of infection, even where this is not the cultural norm (General Comment paras 13 and 14). Empowering children via educational measures to make informed choices is, according to the General Comment, a key objective. As regards health services, the CRC Committee notes that generally these are not responsive to the needs of adolescents, and advocates for health services that are accessible, affordable, confidential, non-judgmental, do not require parental consent and do not discriminate. The suggested package of services for children includes voluntary counselling and testing,[2] confidential sexual and reproductive health services, free or low-cost contraception, as well as HIV/Aids care and treatment, including treatment for opportunistic infections, such as tuberculosis.

In order to uphold the rights of the child, the General Comment eschews mandatory testing of children for HIV/Aids, requiring that states parties ensure that children are protected against compulsory testing. Insofar as consent to HIV testing has to be obtained, it is the evolving capacities, age and maturity of the child, according to the General Comment, that will determine whether consent is obtained

---

2 Although in recent times, regional policies in some places – for example Botswana – have moved away from voluntary counselling and testing (VCT) to provider-initiated counselling and testing: see Tadesse, 2007; Chingore 2007. This policy shift has occurred due to low take up rates of VCT regimes, and because of the attempts to scale up treatment.

directly from a child, or from a parent or guardian. The outcomes of HIV tests must remain completely confidential, however, to the point where the General Comment maintains that disclosure may not occur in health and social welfare settings, nor even to parents, without the consent of the child.

The most critical area of concern for Africa in the HIV/Aids context is arguably around the issue of the child's rights to parental or family care, or to alternative care when deprived of a family environment, due to the growing number of orphaned children. In relation to alternative care and OVCs, the stance adopted in the General Comment is that communities (and not governments alone) are at the forefront of the fight against the epidemic, and hence that community absorption of orphans is the preferred and first response. '[O]rphans are best protected and cared for when efforts are made to enable siblings to remain together, and in the care of relatives or other family members' (General Comment no. 3, para. 31). There is but a limited place for institutional care in the philosophy of the General Comment – only when family- or community-based care is not available and as a last resort – and limits should be set on the period of time that children spend in institutions, with the eventual reintegration of orphans into the community being the overall goal.

The General Comment breaks new ground insofar as it accords recognition at the international law level to the phenomenon of child-headed households (Sloth-Nielsen 2005, 76). Whilst the General Comment does not define the concept of a 'child-headed household', it must be assumed that it refers to a household containing younger siblings where the oldest care-giver is himself or herself below the age of 18 years (the age set by article 1 of the CRC for the end of childhood). It has previously been noted that this conception is not necessarily on all fours with international programming, which (certainly until the early 2000s) defined OVCs, and by implication child-headed households, as those headed by children 15 years and younger (Sloth-Nielsen 2004). However, the recent South African legislation adopts the position that a child-headed household is one in which 'a child over the age of 16 years has assumed the role of care-giver in respect of the children in the household (section 137(1) of the Children's Amendment Act 41 of 2007),[3] which clearly contemplates protection for households headed by older children as well. The position that protection should extend to all children living in households headed by persons younger than 18 years appears to have taken root at the policy level as well (Save the Children UK 2006).

Of note is that the General Comment requires not only that social and economic protection and support must be accorded children growing up in child-headed households, but also that *legal protection* (emphasis inserted) must be developed, specifically regarding protection of inheritance and property rights, access to education, and birth registration, which is regarded as essential (para. 28).[4] It has

---

3   The age of 16 years mirrors the age at which a child may apply for an official identity document in South Africa, which is a requirement for being able to access any available social grants, such as the child support grant, which would be an important source of social assistance for younger siblings in the household.

4   It may be worth noting, though, that there is little in the way of precedent or international best practice that is relevant to the African context as to how to address the

previously been argued (Sloth-Nielsen 2005) that the legal recognition of autonomous and independently functioning child-headed households stands in odd juxtaposition to the overall increasing recognition in international law of the need to standardize the definition of a child at 18 years in other spheres for maximum protection (such as with respect to marriage and recruitment into the armed forces [African Child Policy Forum 2007]). However, the recognition of the autonomy of households headed by children aged below 18 does accord with the evident functional independence of these family structures in practice (Children's Institute 2005), and gives unusually trenchant effect to the philosophy underlining respect for the evolving maturity of children (article 12 of CRC).

As regards the right to education, the General Comment requires states parties to make adequate provision to ensure that children affected by HIV/Aids can stay in school; also, states are required to ensure the qualified replacement of sick teachers so that children's regular attendance at schools is not affected, so that the right to education of all children living within affected communities is fully protected (General Comment no. 3, para. 18).

General Comment No. 4 on Adolescent Health and Development

This General Comment reaffirms many of the principles covered in General Comment no. 3, including the obligation to safeguard the right of the adolescent to medical treatment without parental consent; the need to ensure respect for the privacy and confidentiality of medical information; and the need to provide access to adequate information essential for adolescent health and development. Complementary requirements concern ensuring access to sexual and reproductive information concerning contraception; raising the minimum age for marriage; encouraging changing cultural perceptions about adolescent's need for contraception; and addressing taboos surrounding adolescent sexuality. At the core lies the principle (and lived experience) of children's evolving autonomy and sexual development, which in turn, in the era of HIV/Aids, entails contemplating expansive legal provisions to ensure that they are able to be afforded the fullest possible protection from transmission. This underlies some of the (controversial) new legal provisions in African context, discussed below, which are arguably reshaping the legal construction of childhood in notable respects.

African Women's Charter (AWP)

The African Women's Charter (AWP), which entered into force on 25 November 2005, is unique insofar as it explicitly refers to HIV/Aids, notably in connection with ensuring that the right to health of women, including sexual and reproductive health, is respected and promoted (article 14). The right encompasses the right to self protection and to be protected specifically against sexually transmitted infections,

---

rights of children vulnerable to HIV/Aids in legal instruments. For many countries, it is still a question of taking the first tentative steps. Some of these efforts will be detailed in the themes covered in the section 'Some Implications of HIV/Aids for Children's Legal' below.

including HIV/Aids, the right to choose any method of contraception, and to have family planning education (article 14, 10(e), (c) and (f)). Reinforcing the provisions of the ACRWC, and recognizing the link between early marriage and vulnerability to HIV/Aids transmission, the AWP sets the minimum age for marriage at 18. Amollo argues, though, that despite the clear jeopardy posed by the intersection of age and gender in the context of HIV/Aids, the Protocol does not comprehensively or specifically address the situation of adolescents (2006, 49).

Some Implications of HIV/Aids for Children's Legal Rights

Implications for Children's Rights to Family Life

Such is the threat to children's rights to family life brought about by HIV/Aids on the subcontinent, that violation of this right is arguably the most severe consequence for children of the pandemic. The escalating number of orphans prompted the following statement by the chairperson of the Child Law Reform Committee of the Lesotho Law Reform Commission:

> For countries such as Lesotho, orphaning has reached crisis levels in the recent years. While there have always been orphaned children, it is believed that the HIV/Aids pandemic has fuelled the numbers beyond proportion. The HIV sero-prevalence rate for Lesotho is estimated at 29 per cent. This puts her as the number three of countries most ravaged by the pandemic in the world. Like elsewhere in the world, the HIV/Aids pandemic in Lesotho has also turned into the greatest humanitarian, social, economic and developmental challenge of today. (Kimane 2005)

Some existing legislation, and developing policy, highlights the desirability of community placement, or kinship care in the extended family setting for orphaned children, in any event the characteristic response in Africa to the loss of care-givers. An instance in this regard is section 7(2) of Uganda's Children's Act, which provides that, where the natural parents of a child are deceased, parental responsibility may be passed on to relatives of either parent. However, the capacity of communities, themselves ravaged by HIV illness and deaths, to cope with added childcare responsibilities has been significantly diminished. The consequences for children who are orphaned or vulnerable (due to their care-givers' HIV status) of the devastation of their right to family life is severe (Foster, Levine and Williamson 2005; Bessler 2008, 82). They may lack care and supervision, and require moral guidance or bereavement counselling, not to mention that basic socio-economic necessities such as food, access to education, and health care become elusive (Sloth-Nielsen 2004). Numerous studies have pointed to the overall decline in access to financial and other resources that more often than not besets a family with members who have full blown Aids anyway, as those with the illness consume resources and can no longer contribute to production or earning (Human Sciences Research Council 2006). For children, the end result can be dire, and exacerbated should they fall prey to property grabbing upon the death of their care-giver, an issue discussed further in the section below titled 'Vital Registration and Inheritance'.

As mentioned, a new phenomenon, directly linked to the HIV/Aids pandemic, has been the emergence of child-headed households, brought about by the fact that the greatest impact of the virus is being experienced by women of child-bearing (and child-rearing) age. Research indicates that child-headed households frequently reflect the child members' own care preferences: an articulated desire to maintain independence and sibling cohesion (Foster, Levine and Williamson 2005, 33). South Africa has arguably been the first country in Africa to recognize the child-headed household as a legal entity, via certain provisions in the Children's Act 38 of 2005, but is by no means the only country to have considered legal recognition, as the Malawi and Lesotho Law Reform Commissions have proposed similar provisions as part of their overhaul of child protection law. The South African legislation[5] uniquely provides for formal legal recognition of the household as an independent family form (by the provincial department of social development [section 137]), provided this is in the best interests of all the children living in the household. The recognition can occur even before the death of adult guardians or care-givers where the applicable person is already terminally ill (section 137(1)(a)).

Further to this, the protective nature of the recognition entails that the household should function under the general support of an adult, designated as such by the children's court or an organ of state, or a member of a non-governmental organization determined by social welfare authorities (section 137(2)). This 'supervising adult' (or mentor) must perform such duties as are to be prescribed in regulations, but do not include overriding the decision-making capabilities of the child heading the household (section 137 (6)), nor taking the day-to-day decisions related to the functioning of the household, which remains the task of the child heading the household and the other children in the home. The kind of support that the supervising adult is supposed to provide is evident in the regulations setting this out (though these have not been finalized and are still in draft form). They include providing psychological, social and emotional support to members of the household, ensuring school attendance, supervision of homework, assistance with health care requirements and obtaining official documentation, where possible reconnecting the household with parents or relatives, assisting the household to procure provisions to meet basic needs, and ensuring that household chores are fairly allocated between members of the child-headed household (draft regulations to the Children's Act, 2007). There are specific provisions contemplated relating to the administration of money (notably social grants received for any members of the households), to facilitate proper control by the children's court, organ of state or non-governmental organization who has designated that particular adult as a supervisor.

---

5   The parts of the Children's Act dealing with national competencies were passed in 2006 as the Children's Act 38 of 2005. The parts which affect provincial competencies and provincial budgeting processes were dealt with as an amendment to the principal Act, and passed in December 2007 as the Children's Amendment Act 41 of 2007. Parts of Act 38 of 2005 were put into operation on 1 July 2007, but significant areas require that regulations be drafted, and the Act cannot be operationalized until this is completed. Draft regulations were prepared in 2007 and have been submitted to the Department of Social Development.

As regards the functioning of child-headed households themselves, the Act newly requires that minimum norms and standards for such households be prescribed. The Act proceeds from the premise that, whilst the fact of being resident in a home headed only by a child may be a ground for the institution of welfare proceedings, this is not mandatory; hence the minimum norms and standards provide some indication as to when formal state intervention and alternative care arrangements may be required, or conversely, are not required. Criteria such as the need to keep siblings to together, where practicable, the need to promote children's right to family life, and preference for the provision of support to enable independent functioning (rather than removal of children to the alternative care system), are examples of the norms envisaged (see draft regulations, Annexure C(k)(i)). Further, a set of specific standards concerning the survival and optimal development of all the children in this type of family unit are proposed, and their right to participate in decisions about the course of any welfare investigation confirmed.

The South African legislative example raises several issues for reflection. First, it illustrates an approach that grapples with the multitude of problems thrown up for children affected by HIV/Aids head on, controversial though it may be to acknowledge that children are oftentimes better off with their siblings than in any alternative living arrangement. Second, underlying the approach of legal recognition of child-headed households is an implicit endorsement of the centrality of family in African society, and, at the same time, a possible preference for family type arrangements over fostering and adoption. Third, the legislation and its accompanying draft regulations give a 'front of stage' role to child participation and the exercise of autonomous decision making about how they wish to regulate their 'family life', and this in a way that is probably unprecedented elsewhere in the world. Finally, the charge may be levelled that legal recognition of child-headed households represents both an irreversible loss of faith in the ability of communities and extended families to absorb and care for the orphaned amongst them, as well as abandonment of these children by the state and by the authorities, rather than the state stepping into the default care position (as the South African constitution contemplates at face value).[6] Refuting this, however, are provisions for mentors (supervisors) and those who seek to ensure basic support for the fulfilment of children's basic needs, which rather point to the role of the state as a subsidiary one in order to buttress and sustain such households.

In Namibia, the Children's Status Act, 2006 (not yet in operation) also contains provisions directly linked to the practical difficulties of dealing with children who lose their care-givers. So, for example, the existing procedure entailing an application to the High Court for the appointment of a replacement guardian in the capital city, Windhoek, will be replaced by a simpler procedure for application for a guardianship order or for the award of custody in the local children's court (section 12 and section 13 read with section 1), and such application may be brought, amongst others, by any person who is acting as the primary caretaker of the child. Indeed, an entire chapter, chapter 5, headed 'Custody and guardianship on death of

---

6   Section 28(1)(b) of the Constitution provides for the child's right to parental or family care, or to state care when otherwise deprived of family environment.

custodian or guardian' provides explicitly for various scenarios. These range from testamentary disposition of a replacement custodian, to revival of a surviving non-custodian parents' powers, and, failing that, the appointment of a person 'with a genuine interest in a child, whether or not related to the child', but with preference given to 'close family member of a child, or to a person who is the custodian or primary caretaker of the child' (section 21(5) read with section 21(11)). Malawi's draft Child (Care, Protection and Justice) Bill (2005) was similarly predicated on a lengthy discussion of the impact of HIV upon children in the Law Commission's Review and Report (Aids and Human Rights Research Unit 2007, 117), and the elaboration in the draft Bill of a raft of care options for affected children. Swaziland has been encouraged by the CRC Committee (CRC/C/SWA/CO/(2006)) to develop a comprehensive policy for addressing the needs of children without parental care due to the ravages of HIV/Aids, which is likely to form the backbone of the pending law drafting process.[7]

Health and HIV Testing

There is an indefinite array of issues relating to children's health rights that have emerged from the onset of the HIV/Aids pandemic, few of which have been explored in any depth from a legal angle. To a great extent, these traverse new territory in the children's rights field, more especially when the African context – of poverty, overwhelming dependence on state health care at a primary level, illiteracy, nutritional deprivation and cultural beliefs and taboos – is considered (Fombad 2005).

One of the starting points concerns the thorny question of HIV testing of children, which precedes any form of treatment, and is often a pre-cursor to placement in many forms of alternative care, including adoption and foster care. Here a number of examples derived from law and policy can be adduced, many being of very recent origin. The trend is to provide for children's evolving capacity by specifying an age for consent, which may be lower than the age of consent provided for in relation to other matters, for example, consent to medical treatment or to surgical interventions.

In Ethiopia, the 2007 Federal HIV/Aids Prevention and Control Council/Federal Ministry of Health *Guidelines for HIV Counselling and Testing in Ethiopia* accord children at the age of 15 the capacity to give informed consent to HIV testing.[8] However, children aged 13 and above in certain situations are regarded as mature minors, able to furnish consent to testing without parental consent (Tadesse 2007, 46). These are children who are commercial sex workers, street children, children heading families, sexually active adolescents, or those who are married or pregnant. However, the Guidelines guarantee confidentiality of results (with insignificant

---

7   A review of existing child law in Swaziland has been undertaken (Gallinetti 2006), and drafting of a comprehensive new Children's Act will commence soon (personal communication, Save the Children, Swaziland office).

8   HIV testing for children aged under 15 shall only be done for the benefit of the child, and with the parents' or guardians' consent. Hence, parents cannot rely on this provision to require a child to submit to a HIV test purely for the purposes of satisfying curiosity.

exceptions), in accordance with acknowledged universal human rights principles. In Uganda, children of 12 years may furnish independent consent to HIV testing, provided they have the capacity to understand the implications of the results of the HIV test (Tadesse 2007, 51). Further, it is provided that when children aged below 12 are brought for testing by parents or guardians, the HIV test must be done only to facilitate the medical care of the child: it must be clinically indicated or a risk of infection must be evident. It is spelt out that HIV testing on children may not be carried out for screening purposes, or for the sake of parental curiosity.

South Africa's Children's Act 38 of 2005 takes full cognizance of the impact of HIV upon children and its role in exacerbating vulnerability. It is of some significance that the law even uses HIV in the headings to sections 130–33 (Sloth-Nielsen 2007). These deal comprehensively with HIV testing, and provide for the testing of a child (who, for the purposes of the Act is a person aged below 18 years) for HIV only where this is in the best interests of the child, the required consent has been given, or where such a test is necessary to protect a health worker or other person who may be at risk of having contracted HIV through contact with bodily fluids.

As far as consent is concerned, a child who is aged 12 years or older may consent to his or her own test, and a child even below this specified age is also authorized to consent, provided that the child is of sufficient maturity to understand the benefits, risks, and social implications of an HIV test. In cases where that child is aged below 12 and is not able to furnish valid consent, parents or caregivers (who need be neither parents nor guardians, but could be the person in charge of the day-to-day care of the child) are empowered to give consent to the test, and failing this, the provincial head of social development may be approached (Sloth-Nielsen 2007; Aids and Human Rights Research Unit 2007, 259). Various other possible consent givers are also enumerated, including a children's court, which is established at each magisterial jurisdiction. Section 132 of the Children's Act contains the well-accepted policy that no HIV test should be performed without pre-test and post-test counselling, and it is further provided that this 'must be provided by an appropriately trained person'. Children's rights to confidentiality are also provided for, insofar as the results of an HIV test may not be disclosed without consent (see in general African Child Policy Forum 2008 [forthcoming]).

These new legal provisions proceed from the policy goal that children (as with all potential victims of the virus) should be placed in the best possible position to become acquainted with their sero-status, and that providing for their capacity to consent independent of their parent's assent (or even knowledge) facilitates this objective, as well as catering to the situation that, increasingly, children may not have parents due to HIV/Aids. The new legal rules are fully consistent with current international law as suggested by the General Comments of the CRC Committee discussed above.

Mention must be made of a further provision in the South African Children's Act, one which has met with a heated and adverse public response. This relates to a new provision contained within the sub-part dealing with HIV/Aids which states that no person may refuse to sell or provide free condoms to a child aged 12 or more, even without the consent of care-givers (section 134, in operation as at 1 July 2007). Access to other reproductive devices, subject to proper medical advice and medical examination ensure that there are no medical reasons why a specific contraceptive should not be provided to the child, is also guaranteed (section 134). This provision links directly to the policy goal of scaling up prevention efforts aimed at reducing the spread of HIV/Aids amongst youth (Sloth-Nielsen 2007); it is therefore characterized as aimed at increasing protection for those who are sexually active, even though, at the same time, this age is well below the formal legal age for consent to sexual intercourse (and its promulgation widely castigated publicly as an invitation to premature youth sexual promiscuity).[9] From another vantage point, though, it may be conceded that this does not mesh well with notions of childhood as a state of innocence and dependency.

Vital Registration and Inheritance

The Lesotho Children's Protection and Welfare Bill, 2004, makes several important innovations in respect of children without parental care. First, it provides for the right of orphaned and vulnerable children to vital registration. Registration of orphans also appears to be a response adopted in Botswana, and the point is to be able to target services to such vulnerable children. Thus in Botswana, registered orphaned and vulnerable children are also registered with the name of a care-giver, who is then eligible to receive assistance in the form of monthly food baskets. There is also, in some cases, the possibility of free school uniforms, waiver of school fees and housing assistance (Save the Children UK 2006; Aids and Human Rights Research Unit 2007, 27). At a policy level, many countries have been encouraged to establish OVC forums at district level, whose task it is to identify vulnerable children and channel donor aid and resources to them (Zambia, Zimbabwe and Mozambique, for example).

Second, the HIV/Aids pandemic has serious implications for the rights of children to access property. Property rights are a critical issue for children infected or affected by HIV/Aids 'as the common practice of property grabbing after the death of an adult means widows, widowers and children can be thrown out of the family home by relatives of the deceased and are frequently left destitute' (Save the Children Sweden 2006, 20). A similar view is articulated by Csete who highlights that 'property grabbing' has been widely documented against children orphaned by Aids and widows of Aids sufferers (Csete 2002). Few people in Africa develop official wills, increasing the risk that a deceased person's property will be grabbed by other family or community members.

In the context of Aids, land is a vital asset that can generate cash crops, provide security, and ward off poverty for surviving family members. But legislation is sometimes silent as regards the protection of children in this regard or is explicit, but inadequately enforced. In Côte d'Ivoire, although there is a civil law (no. 64-379, 7 October 1964) protecting inheritance rights for children, these rights are difficult to claim and are barely enforced. Apart from inadequate and discriminatory laws, challenges to will writing form part of the problem, illiteracy being an obvious

---

9 Part XXV (clause 245) of the Lesotho Child Care and Protection Bill contains identical provisions to the South African model (Sloth-Nielsen 2006).

problem, but cultural beliefs too play a role: for instance in Uganda, there is a widespread belief that making a will and 'preparing for death' will itself cause death (UNICEF 2003, 21). In general in Africa, even where the inheritance rights of women and children are spelled out in law, such rights are difficult to claim and are poorly enforced (UNICEF 2003, 20), and projects such as 'Justice for Widows and Orphans in Zambia', established to assist women and children to get their property returned need to be adapted and duplicated where the need exists.

Despite the above, there is nevertheless scope for legislative reform to address this dimension of HIV/Aids and its impact upon children, as African law-makers have recognized. So, the Lesotho draft legislation gives children, whether or not born in wedlock or orphaned, rights to reasonable access to the estate of their parents (clause 38 et seq.). There is an intentional emphasis in the Bill that both boy and girl children should enjoy similar rights in respect of family property (Kimane 2006). Duties are placed on a range of role players in this regard, including employers, the Master of the High Court and financial institutions. This is intended to ensure that orphaned children are not dispossessed of family property, and that the customary law rule that reserves inheritance right to the eldest male relative (the rule of primogeniture) does not result in orphaned children being left destitute. In Swaziland, steps have been taken to mitigate the effects of dispossession that occurs under customary law when property passes out of the hands of orphaned children, but these have not yet been concretized in legislative form.[10]

In Malawi, the Wills and Inheritance Act was amended in 1998 to provide better protection to orphans, vulnerable children and widows, and to mitigate against the adverse effects of property grabbing; this was revisited by the Law Commission in 2005, and comprehensive new legislative provisions await approval. Instead of a 'nebulous network of extended family members' (Aids and Human Rights Research Unit 2007, 117) sharing in a deceased estate under customary law, the proposed Bill designates only two categories of beneficiaries: the spouse and children (immediate family category) or dependants (draft Deceased Estates (Wills, Inheritance and Protection) Bill, section 17). Far reaching proposals for improved enforcement of these provisions accompanies the Law Commission report.

Education

Children's right to education appears in all of the major international human rights instruments, including the Universal Declaration of Human Rights (UDHR), the International Covenant on Economic, Social and Cultural Rights (ICESCR), the CRC and the ACRWC. Under the CRC and the ACRWC, states parties have the obligation to ensure that primary education is available (free and compulsory) to all children, whether infected, orphaned or otherwise affected by HIV/Aids. In the words of the Special Rapporteur on Education, education should be 'available, accessible, acceptable and adaptable' (See Sloth-Nielsen and Mezmur 2007, 15).

The role of education in the fight against HIV/Aids is a crucial one. The CRC Committee believes that 'education plays a critical role in providing children with

---

10 Aids and Human Rights Research Unit (2007, 300).

relevant and appropriate information on HIV/Aids, which can contribute to increased awareness and better understanding of this pandemic and prevent negative attitudes towards victims of HIV/Aids' (General Comment no. 3, para. 18). Furthermore, education should empower children to protect themselves from the risk of HIV infection, through sex education to youth, including confidential counselling and testing and the promotion of contraceptive use, and provision of training to health workers, teachers and education personnel on teaching about HIV/Aids and sex education. Criticisms abound where policies that fail to inform the youth about HIV/ Aids and sex education are adopted, such as in Uganda (See Human Rights Watch 2005). Therefore, education should have an element of reproductive health and an HIV/Aids component in order to be complete.

It is now well established that the pandemic is significantly affecting the supply of, demand for, and quality of education. Countries heavily affected by HIV/Aids are experiencing severe losses in their teaching forces due to teacher illness or death, to care for family, or through transfers to other government or private sectors to replace personnel lost to Aids (UNAIDS IATT on Education 2002). The impact of HIV/AIDS on the entire education system – seen primarily in the deterioration of educational services and the deaths of teachers – adversely affects orphans, as it does all children. Children and adolescents are finding it more difficult to attend and remain in school for the same reasons, and because they may be needed to help with household chores or to supplement family labour or income. These dynamics place enormous strain on learning achievement. All educators need to ensure that education reduces risk and vulnerability while providing all learners with a quality education that is meaningful in the twenty-first century (UNAIDS IATT on Education 2006). 'Staying in school offers orphaned children the best chance of escaping extreme poverty and its associated risks. Thus, everything possible needs to be done to keep them in school' (UNAIDS 2004).

There are different types of missed opportunities in education, including lack of enrolment, interrupted schooling and poor performance while in school (UNICEF 2003, 21). In Côte d'Ivoire, for instance, the school attendance rate for non-orphans who live with at least one parent is 67 per cent but for double orphans it is 56 per cent. Children in sibling-headed households were also at risk of low enrolment compared to those headed by a parent (Rapid Country Response Analysis: Cote d'Ivoire 2004). A baseline survey in Ethiopia conducted by the World Food Programme found that an estimated 75 per cent of HIV/Aids orphans were not attending school (Rapid Country Response Analysis: Ethiopia 2004). In terms of continuity of schooling and appropriate grade for age, orphans are found to be at a disadvantage in some countries. An analysis of data from eastern Africa shows that double orphans aged 6–10 are half as likely to be at the correct educational level as non-orphaned children; double orphans aged 11–14 are two thirds as likely to be at lower levels. Longitudinal evidence from South Africa shows that maternal orphans are at lower education levels than other children of the same age and also compared to other non-orphans with whom they live (UNICEF 2003, 21).

In addition, in Ethiopia, since the mid-1980s, close to 10,000 teachers and teacher's aides have died, most likely from HIV/Aids. In Zambia, where 40 per cent of teachers are HIV-positive, they are dying at a faster rate than they can be replaced by new graduates (UNICEF 2003, 27–9). In the United Republic of Tanzania, the school attendance rate for non-orphans who live with at least one parent is 71 per cent but for double orphans it is only 52 per cent (UNICEF 2003, 27).

There is an array of reasons that orphans and vulnerable children are struggling to access their right to education. These include:

> ... inability to afford fees and school-related costs such as books, materials, uniforms or shoes; parents or caregivers who do not value or understand the importance of education, particularly for girls; long distances to schools; lack of awareness of the fee exemption regulations and how to access the exemptions; poor performance related to lack of support in the home environment and lack of adequate nutrition affecting children's ability of children to concentrate in class. (Save the Children UK 2006, 43–4)

Apart from legislation concerning access to education, the role of national policies and strategic plans on education and HIV/Aids in order to address the education gap for children infected or affected by HIV/Aids has been significant in Africa. In Mozambique, the Ministry of Education Strategic Plan for the fight against HIV/Aids (2003–2005) addressed support for people living with HIV/Aids in the education system. The HIV/Aids Strategic Plan 2001–2005 of Zambia and the Strategic Plan 2000–2006 of the Ministry of Education of Zimbabwe looks at ways in which orphans will be able to have a decent education and ensure non-discriminatory environment in the education process.

So what should education systems do for orphans and HIV/Aids affected children? The first imperative is to ensure through legislation and practice that every child can attend a conventional school and complete the relevant education cycle. Here, key interventions would include the abolition of all learner costs and the provision of support to enable poor families and child-headed households to cope without the labour of scholars. The second imperative for the education sector is to establish conditions in schools that enable every child to experience real and relevant learning. Finally legislation should facilitate strengthening partnerships, in regard to issues relating to physical health, psychological and emotional well being, and family difficulties that affect students (Foster, Levine and Williamson 2005, 87).

Conclusions

Despite the very serious plight into which the HIV/Aids epidemic has plunged the fulfilment of children's rights in Africa, there may be some positive developments to record. First, some countries are starting to see a decline in infection rates, indicating that the growth of the disease appears to have peaked. In Kenya, a welcome development has been a decline in the HIV prevalence rate nationally from 13 per cent estimated in 1999 to 9.4 per cent in 2004. Other countries are also beginning to report declining prevalence rates, such as Uganda and Burkina Faso, likely to be the success of prevention programmes finally starting to bear fruit.

Second, there has been an unprecedented surge in research on HIV/Aids with respect to children particularly. This research spans any number of disciplines apart from those associated with the medical and health aspects of the virus – sociology, psychology, law, occupational therapy, dietetics, social work and education to name but a few. A case in point could be the role of male circumcision as a preventive intervention, as alluded to by the former UN Special Envoy for HIV and AIDS in Africa Stephen Lewis during the 16th International Aids Conference in 2006. This surge of research has raised trenchant questions relating to the ethics of research with and upon children, the relevance of which has assumed heightened significance because of the stigma and discrimination associated with disclosure of HIV status, not to mention the difficulties associated with obtaining informed consent in respect of children. Knowledge of, and concern about, research ethics where children are concerned have arguably been considerably advanced.

Third, studies of the experiences of children orphaned or infected and affected by HIV/Aids have taken child participation in research to new levels of significance. Studies with child-headed households have revealed that although their situation is far from ideal, children living in this type of arrangement prefer this to 'enforced' kinship or community care in many instances (Children's Institute 2005). Similarly, children have been granted unparalleled space to articulate their most pressing needs in the context of HIV/Aids, shaping ensuing policy and programme responses.

Fourth, as hinted at in the section on education above, the intersection between education and HIV/Aids has arguably played a crucial role in the continent-wide massification of primary education that has intensified since the turn of the millennium, resulting in millions of children enrolling in schools. Debates around costs in education, vulnerability to dropping out or to exclusion, and access by marginalized groups have been sharpened by the reality of children's evolving experience of the HIV/Aids crisis, and these in turn have significantly influenced education policies and laws to overcome *de facto* discrimination in access to education (Sloth-Nielsen and Mezmur 2007; Aids and Human Rights Research Unit 2007; African Child Policy Forum 2007).

Finally, as this chapter has endeavoured to show, legal responses to accommodate HIV/Aids implications for children have, of necessity, had to be creative and home grown – no precedent for the appropriate legal framework exists, and policy is rapidly shifting with the advent of treatment, improved knowledge of risk and of stigma, and the development of a globalized research community evaluating support services, programme interventions and public health initiatives. Yet amidst the concern for children that HIV/Aids carries with it, most especially in African context, there are clear signs that the pandemic has brought with it a last positive benefit: that it has entailed a form of 'coming of age' for African children, whose autonomy, participation rights and evolving capacities are now explicitly being brought to the fore.

References

Articles, Books and Chapters in Books

Aids and Human Rights Research Unit (2007), *Human Rights Protected? Nine Southern African Country Reports on HIV/Aids and the Law* (Pretoria: Pretoria University Law Press).

Bessler, J.D. (2008), 'In the Spirit of Ubuntu: Enforcing the Rights of Orphans and Vulnerable Children Affected by HIV/Aids in South Africa', *Hastings International and Comparative Law Review* 31, 33.

Chingore, N. (2007), 'Routine Testing of Individuals at Public Health Facilities: Are SADC Countries Ready?', in Viljoen, F. and Precious, S. (eds).

Csete, J. (2002), 'Several for the Price of One: Right to AIDS Treatment as Link to Other Human Rights', *Connecticut Journal of International Law* 17, 263.

Davel, C.J. and Skelton, A. (eds) (2007), *A Commentary on the Children's Act* (Lansdowne: Juta and Co.).

Fombad, C.M. (2005), 'Children and Informed Consent to HIV/Aids Testing in Botswana', *University of Botswana Law Journal* 2, 33.

Foster, G., Levine, C. and Williamson, J. (eds) (2005), *A Generation at Risk: The Global Impact of HIV/AIDS on Orphans and Vulnerable Children* (Cambridge: Cambridge University Press).

Kelly, C. (2004), 'Conspiring to Kill: Gender Biased Legislation, Culture and Aids in Sub-Saharan Africa', *Journal of Law and Family Studies* 439.

Sloth-Nielsen, J. (2005), 'Of Newborns and Nubiles: Some Critical Challenges to Children's Rights in Africa in the Era of HIV/Aids', *International Journal on Children's Rights* 13, 73–85.

Sloth-Nielsen, J. (2007), 'Child Protection', in Davel, C.J. and Skelton, A. (eds).

Viljoen, F. and Precious, S. (eds) (2007), *Human Rights under Threat: Four Perspectives on HIV/Aids and the Law in Southern Africa* (Pretoria: Pretoria University Law Press).

Reports, Unpublished Documents and Internet Sources

African Child Policy Forum (2007), *In the Best Interests of the Child: Harmonising laws in Eastern and Southern* (Addis Ababa: African Child Policy Forum).

African Child Policy Forum (2008, forthcoming), *Child Friendly Laws and Policies in Africa* (Addis Ababa: African Child Policy Forum).

Amollo, R. (2006), 'A Critical Reflection on the African Women's Protocol as a Means to Combat HIV/Aids among Women in Africa' (unpublished LLM thesis, Pretoria: University of Pretoria).

Children's Institute (2005), 'Child Gauge 2005', available at <www.ci.org.za/depts/ci/pubs/pdf/general/SA20%child20%guage20%2005.pdf>.

Cornerstone Economic Research (2006), *Costing the Children's Bill* (Pretoria: Department of Social Development).

CRC Committee (2003), 'General Comment no. 3: HIV/Aids and the Rights of the Child' (CRC/GC/2003/1).

CRC Committee (2004), 'General Comment no. 4: Adolescent Health and the Rights of the Child' (CRC/GC/2003/4).

CRC Committee (2006), 'Concluding Observations: Swaziland Country Report on the Convention on the Rights of the Child' (CRC/C/SWA/CO).

Gallinetti, J. (2006), 'Report on Harmonization of Law, Policy and Programmes: Swaziland' (Addis Ababa: unpublished).

Human Rights Watch (2005), 'The Less They Know, the Better: Abstinence-Only HIV/Aids Programs in Uganda', *Human Rights Watch Report* vol. 17, no. 4, available at <http://hrw.org/reports/2005/uganda0305/uganda0305.pdf> (accessed 28 December 2006).

Human Sciences Research Council (2006), *A Situational Analysis of Orphans and Vulnerable Children in Four Districts of South Africa* (Pretoria: Human Sciences Research Council).

Kimane, I. (2005), 'Protecting Orphaned Children through Legislation: The Case of Lesotho', unpublished paper presented at the IVth World Congress on the Rights of Children and Youth, Cape Town.

Kimane, I. (2006), 'The Lesotho Child Protection and Welfare Bill 2005: Why the Delays in Enacting the Children's Law?', unpublished paper presented at the University of the Western Cape/Miller Du Toit conference 'The Globalization of Child and Family Law'.

Rapid Country Response Analysis: Côte d'Ivoire (2004).

Rapid Country Response Analysis: Ethiopia (2004).

Save the Children, Sweden (2006), 'Children's Rights in Kenya: An Analysis Based on the CRC Reports' (Nairobi: Save the Children Sweden).

Save the Children, UK (2006), *Legal and Policy Frameworks to Protect the Rights of Vulnerable Children in Southern Africa* (Pretoria: Save the Children UK).

Sloth-Nielsen. J. (2004), *Realising the Rights of Children Growing Up in Child-headed Households: A Guide to Laws Policy and Social Advocacy* (Bellville: Community Law Centre, University of the Western Cape).

Sloth-Nielsen. J. (2006), 'Report on Harmonization of Law, Policy and Programmes: Lesotho' (Addis Ababa: unpublished).

Sloth-Nielsen, J. and Mezmur, B.D. (2007), *Free Education is a Right for Me: A Report on Free and Compulsory Primary Education* (Nairobi: Save the Children, Sweden, Southern Sudan office).

Tadesse, M. (2007), 'HIV Testing from an African Human Rights System Perspective: An Analysis of the Legal and Policy Framework of Botswana, Ethiopia and Uganda' (Pretoria: University of Pretoria, unpublished LLM thesis).

Tomasevski, K. (2001), 'Human Rights Obligations: Making Education Available, Accessible, Acceptable and Adaptable', available at <http://www.right-to-education.org/content/primers/rte_03.pdf> (accessed 13 January 2007).

Tsegaye, S. (2006), 'HIV/AIDS and the New Face of Orphanhood in Africa: The Emerging Challenge of Children Heading Households', unpublished paper delivered at the 3rd Annual World Conference on Children without Parental Care.

UNAIDS (2001), *Children and Young People at a World of AIDS* (New York: UNAIDS).

UNAIDS (2004), *Report on the Global AIDS Epidemic* (New York: UNAIDS).

UNAIDS Inter-Agency Task Team on Education (2002), 'HIV/AIDS and Education: A Strategic Approach' (Paris: UNESCO IIEP), available at <http://www.unesco.org/education/just_published_en/pdf/hiv_approach_english.pdf> (accessed 23 December 2006).

UNAIDS Inter-Agency Task Team on Education (2006), 'Quality Education and HIV and Aids', available at <http://unesdoc.unesco.org/images/0014/001461/146115e.pdf> (accessed 12 November 2007).

UNAIDS/WHO (2006), *AIDS Epidemic Update* (Geneva: UNAIDS).

UNAIDS/WHO (2007), *AIDS Epidemic Update* (New York: UNAIDS).

UNICEF (2003), *Africa's Orphaned Generation* (New York: UNICEF).

UNICEF (2006), *The State of the World's Children* (New York: UNICEF).

UNICEF (2008), *The State of the World's Children* (New York: UNICEF).

USAID, UNICEF, UNAIDS (2002), *Children on the Brink 2002: A Joint Report on Orphan Estimates and Program Strategies* (New York: USAID, UNICEF, UNAIDS).

Whitehead, A. (2007), presentation at a workshop on HIV/Aids hosted by the Rockerfeller Brothers Foundation, Cape Town.

Legislation and Policy

Côte d'Ivoire (1964), Law on inheritance, no 64-379.

Ethiopia Federal HIV/Aids Prevention and Control Council/Federal Ministry of Health (2007), *Guidelines for HIV Counselling and Testing in Ethiopia*.

Lesotho (2004), draft Children's Protection and Welfare Bill.

Malawi (2005), draft Child (Care, Protection and Justice) Bill.

Malawi (2005), draft Deceased Estates (Wills, Inheritance and Protection) Bill.

Namibia (2006), Children's Status Act.

South Africa (2005), Children's Act 38 of 2005.

South Africa (2007), Children's Amendment ct 41 of 2007.

Uganda (1996), Children's Act 1996.

Chapter 17

The Hidden Ones:
Children with Disabilities in Africa
and the Right to Education

Helene Combrinck

Introduction

> Education is both a human right in itself and an indispensable means of realizing other
> human rights ... But the importance of education is not just practical: a well-educated,
> enlightened and active mind, able to wander freely and widely, is one of the joys and
> rewards of human existence. (Committee on Economic, Social and Cultural Rights
> 1999, para. 1)

It is currently estimated that there are 500–650 million persons living with
disabilities[1] in the world (approximately 10 per cent of the world population), 150
million of whom are children (CRC Committee 2006, para. 1). More than 80 per
cent of disabled persons live in low-income or middle-income countries where they
often have difficulty accessing services (World Health Organization 2006, 39). This
includes education, evident in the fact that 98 per cent of children with disabilities
in developing[2] countries remain out of school (Richler 2005, 39).[3] UNESCO reports
that in Africa specifically, fewer than 10 per cent of disabled children are in school
(2006, 74).

The right to education is said to be both the most important right for children with
disabilities and the right most frequently denied (Kilkelly 2002, 123). Historically,
excluding disabled children from education was based on the assumption that these
children were inferior and unable to benefit from education (Balescut and Eklindh
2005, 1).

Recent years have seen the development of an international and regional
framework for the rights of persons with disabilities,[4] culminating in the adoption
of the Convention on the Rights of Persons with Disabilities (hereafter Disability

---

1   This chapter employs the phrases 'person/child with disabilities' and 'disabled child/
person' interchangeably.

2   The terms 'developing/developed' countries are not unproblematic – see, for example,
Stubbs 2004, 4. However, they are used here for ease of reference.

3   Girls with disabilities have even more limited access to education than their male
counterparts, and accordingly, higher levels of illiteracy (see Rousso 2003, 2; Richler 2005, 39).

4   For an overview of this development, see Quinn and Degener 2002, 19–26.

Convention) by the UN General Assembly on 13 December 2006. Another landmark development was the issuing of a General Comment on the rights of disabled children by the Convention on the Rights of the Child (CRC) Committee in September 2006. This chapter accordingly aims to examine the norms that have evolved in international and regional human rights documents relating to the right to education of disabled children, and how these should find practical application in the African context.

The chapter commences by providing an understanding of 'disability', and considering the notion of education for disabled children. The chapter then builds a picture of the normative or macro-level outline by examining a number of international and regional instruments. Having established the current standards regarding the right to education of children with disabilities, and concomitant state duties to ensure the realization of this right,[5] we scrutinize three examples of national legislation and policy from African countries and progress in implementing these provisions. (The scope of this chapter does not permit an exhaustive survey of African jurisdictions.) In conclusion, arguments for countries to approach this issue with urgency are set out.

It should be noted that the right to education is a composite right consisting of various aspects.[6] In addition to its guarantee in article 26 of the Universal Declaration on Human Rights (UDHR), it is also dealt with in article 13 of the International Covenant on Economic, Social and Cultural Rights (ICESCR) and various regional instruments. However, this chapter focuses on two specific aspects of this right, viz. the right to *free primary education*, on a basis of *equality of opportunity*. The chapter concentrates on instruments that have a specific focus either on children's rights or disability rights.

Understanding 'Disability'

Models of Disability

In order to understand the notion of disability, three theoretical models can be distinguished.[7] The *medical* model focuses on persons' impairments (Quinn and Degener 2002, 10) and concentrates on individualized cures, treatments and rehabilitation for what are considered abnormalities or 'defects' (Heyer 2002, 726; Kanter 2003, 246). This view has the effect of locating the 'problem' of disability

---

5   Currie and De Waal (2005, 636) point out that education rights are essentially rights to positive action, since they can only be assured by collective action – 'by society assuming the task of promoting education'.

6   For example, the right to early childhood care and education, the right to free primary education, the principle of compulsory education, the right of access to secondary and tertiary education, the provision of technical and vocational education, the right of children to be educated in accordance with their convictions, equal access to education, and so on (see Van Bueren 1995, 233–55).

7   Certain authors view the social model and the human rights or civil rights model as one (see Heyer 2002, 726–7; Kanter 2003, 247). However, in line with the approach taken by Quinn and Degener (2002a, 10), they have been treated as two distinct models here.

within the person. The medical model therefore encapsulates a broader and deeper social attitude: a tendency to view the individual person as an object for clinical intervention (Quinn and Degener 2002, 10).

The medical understanding of disability gave rise to a social welfare approach to policy, which traditionally provides for the different needs of persons with disabilities in segregated settings such as special schools (Heyer 2002, 726). The assumption is that rather than making mainstream institutions accessible, the needs of disabled people are better accommodated in separate facilities that can be constructed to meet very specialized needs. The exclusion of people with disabilities is not seen as discriminatory, but as a necessary outcome of their medical limitations, and is deemed just because these persons are believed incapable of coping with society at large and all or most major life activities (Degener 1999, 180). One of the corollaries of the medical model was that persons with disabilities were depicted not as subjects of legal rights but as objects of welfare, health and charity programmes.

The *social* model of disability developed in reaction to the shortcomings of the medical model.[8] It locates the problem outside the individual and in society, and posits that human difference is not innate but something socially constructed and applied through labels such as 'the disabled' (Quinn and Degener 2002a, 10). The principal aim is to replace the medical model's focus on the disabled individual with a focus on disabling environments and social structures (Heyer 2002, 726). Social exclusion is not an inevitable consequence of disability; rather, it is a result of discriminatory attitudes and a history of exclusion from institutions that have failed to adapt to the needs of people with disabilities in the same ways that they routinely adapt to the needs of the majority. For example, inaccessibility problems result not so much from the individual's mobility impairments, but instead are a corollary of a political decision to build steps rather than ramps (Degener 1999, 180).

The development of the social model constituted an important paradigm shift. Instead of disability being seen as a shortcoming on the part of the individual, the focus has moved to the environment and society as a whole and to the lack of consideration for human differences (Degener 1999, 180; Heyer 2002, 726). On a policy level, this model replaces segregation with integration, and 'parallel tracks' with equal opportunity and the prohibition of discrimination (Heyer 2002, 726). Persons with disabilities are therefore transformed from passive patients and welfare recipients to holders of rights that are enforceable by law. Law reforms in this area have accordingly been aimed at providing equal opportunities for persons with disabilities and to combat disability-based discrimination, with a shift from welfare law towards civil rights or civil rights law, such as the Americans with Disabilities Act (Degener 1999, 180–81).

A powerful link exists between the social model and the *human rights approach* to disability (Quinn and Degener 2002a, 10). In terms of this model the problem of disability stems from a lack of responsiveness by the state and civil society to the difference that disabilities represent. It follows that the state has a responsibility to address socially created obstacles in order to ensure full respect for the dignity and equal rights of all persons.

---

8   See Quinn and Degener 2002a, 10 for a more comprehensive explanation.

The human rights perspective emphasizes that society has ignored or discounted the difference of disability in regulating the terms of entry into and participation in the mainstream, thus excluding (or effectively excluding) 10 per cent of any given population (Quinn and Degener 2002a, 10). This is not merely irrational from an economic point of view; it also violates the inherent dignity of all human beings. The end goal of the human rights approach to disability is therefore to build societies that are genuinely inclusive, that value difference and respect the dignity and equality of all human beings regardless of difference.

Social Attitudes Towards Children with Disabilities

Once we accept that disability is socially constructed, the question is what value contemporary society attaches to disability, and how children with disabilities are perceived (Basser and Jones 2002, 256). The CRC Committee (2006, para. 31) has noted that some cultures still view a child with any form of disability as a bad omen that may 'tarnish the family pedigree'. In its extreme form, this prejudice results in infanticide or the systematic killing of children with disabilities.

Kisanji (1995, 195) cautions that certain literature on disability in developing countries may over-emphasize the presence of negative attitudes towards persons with disabilities. He asserts that the general pattern of overt community reaction has been one of sympathy and acceptance, providing basic needs such as shelter, food and clothing at the extended family level, and allowing persons with disabilities to participate in community institutions and activities.[9]

However, he notes that attitudes towards people with disabilities in African communities do vary according to the type, cause and severity of the disability.[10] Because of the spiritual meaning attached to the birth of a child in traditional African belief systems, a mother may be blamed when a child is born with disabilities.[11] Significantly, a disproportionate number of children with disabilities live in single-parent families because of fathers abandoning the family when the child is born (Lansdown 2003, Section 1). The CRC Committee (1997, para. 328) has observed that behind the denial of many of the rights of disabled children lay attitudes that viewed the life of a disabled child as being of less worth, less importance and less potential than that of an able-bodied child.

Definition of 'Disability'

The term 'persons with disabilities' is a very broad one. According to Basser and Jones (2002, 255–6), this concept includes people whose activity is limited by physical

---

9   Certain responses on the part of parents and caregivers may also be misinterpreted. For instance, hiding away disabled children may be ascribed to overprotection rather than shame or guilt (Kisanji 1995, 195).

10   For example, certain diseases or conditions such as leprosy or albinism have been regarded as a curse or bad omen and attributed to witchcraft or sorcery (Kisanji 1995, 185–7).

11   Kisanji 1995, 194. See also 'Disabled children embattled by education policy', *IRIN (PLUSNEWS)* dated 15 October 2006.

disabilities, those with visual or hearing disabilities, those with chronic illness, mental health and communication disorders, those with intellectual disabilities, genetic disorders and disfigurement, and those with problems associated with aging or with delay in achieving developmental milestones. Unlike sex or race, disability can be acquired at any point in a person's life.

Degener (2004, 4) explains that while the legal definitions of categories such as sex, ethnic background and sexual orientation also raise questions of demarcation, disability is even harder to define because it encompasses such a broad range of conditions and also because the boundary between ability and disability seems to be less clear. Legal definitions of disability may also vary in relation to different legal purposes. For example, a social welfare law providing personal assistance benefits may have a different target group to a discrimination law (and accordingly, a different definition of disability).

The CRC Committee adopts the definition from the (then) draft text of the Disability Convention for purposes of its General Comment on the rights of children with disabilities:

> Persons with disabilities include those who have long-term physical, mental, intellectual, or sensory impairments which in interaction with various barriers may hinder their full and effective participation in society on an equal basis with others. (2006, para. 7)

This definition will also be relied on for purposes of this chapter (though it is a contested area [Lawrence 2004, 11–12; Filmer 2005, 1]).

Causes of Disability

Although the causes of disability are multiple (UNICEF 2002, 327), there are a number that are closely associated with circumstances in developing countries. These include the prevalence of communicable diseases such as poliomyelitis, meningitis and cerebral malaria, and poor nutrition, for example, blindness caused by vitamin A deficiency (CRC Committee 2006, para. 53; Zinkin 1995, 10–11).[12] Inadequate prenatal, childbirth and neonatal health care services also play an important role. Armed conflicts and their aftermath, for example, unexploded landmines, remain a major concern in certain parts of Africa (CRC Committee 2006, para. 54).

It is now well-recognized that poverty is both a cause and a consequence of disability (Kanter 2003, 244–5; CRC Committee 2006, para. 3). Kanter reports that people with disabilities throughout the world are more likely to live below the poverty level than the rest of the population in any given country (2003, 245). Not only does disability add to the risk of poverty, but conditions of poverty add to the risk of disability (Kanter 2003, 245; Filmer 2005, 7, 15) – for example, where children are exposed to poor nutrition.

Poverty further limits access to basic health services, including rehabilitation services (World Health Assembly 2005, Preamble), thus exacerbating the secondary

---

12 An estimated 4 million children under age 5 are affected by xerophthalmia, a serious eye disorder that can be caused by moderate to severe [vitamin A] deficiency and can lead to blindness (UNICEF 2007).

impacts of disabilities. As regards education, studies in Ethiopia and Peru documented that the majority of poor families could not afford the mobility aids that could make it easier for children with (physical) disabilities to attend school, so many were simply kept at home (Lawrence 2004, 7).

Education of Children with Disabilities

Development of 'Inclusive Education'

When considering the right to education of children with disabilities, one of the primary (and most controversial) questions is what this education should entail. Advocates of inclusive education argue that children with disabilities do better in mainstream settings rather than in separate ones (UNESCO 2006, 75). Another view is that for children with some types of disabilities (for example, those with deafness, blindness or both), small specialized units and schools are required in order to guarantee their right to education in the medium of sign language and access to deaf culture (UNESCO 2006, 75; Stubbs 2004, 18).

The significance of the latter position becomes clear when one looks at the findings from research recently conducted in three districts in Malawi. The study found that the teaching method for deaf children and children with hearing impairments was 'the oral method', that is, teaching through lip-reading. Sign language is not used. The report notes that where these learners are integrated into mainstream schools, major communication difficulties exist between educators and learners (Salmonsson 2006, 17–20).

Historically, the education of children with disabilities consisted of 'specialized' education in segregated institutions (Balescut and Eklindh 2005, 2; Kisanji 1999, 4; Richler 2005, 32).[13] This approach is rooted in the medical model of disability. Towards the end of the 1950s, questions began to arise about the wisdom of segregating children with disabilities (Kisanji 1999, 4–5),[14] and the approach shifted to one of *integration* (Balescut and Eklindh 2005, 2).

Integration (also called 'mainstreaming') entails the process of bringing children with disabilities into a mainstream school (Stubbs 2004, 24). It can take many forms: in some instances it was limited to children with disabilities sharing the same dining hall with other children, and in others it consisted of teaching children with disabilities together with other children for several hours per week (Balescut and Eklindh 2005, 2). Small units (special classrooms or buildings attached to a mainstream school with special teachers) are also occasionally cited as examples of integration.[15]

---

13 While separate education, integration and inclusive integration are discussed here are in terms of historical progression from one to the next, the three approaches (and variations thereof) are all currently being implemented (see Stubbs 2004, 23).

14 Kilkelly (2002, 123) explains that children in so-called 'special schools' frequently fail to enjoy the same range of academic and leisure activities and the needs of individual learners are not met in a comprehensive or dedicated manner; see also Heyer 2002, 730–32.

15 However, Stubbs (2004, 24–5) points out that these separate units are often just 'segregation in closer proximity'.

Integration has been criticized for focusing on the individual child and her or his 'deficits' rather than on the broader education system.[16] This approach implies that learners with disabilities need to change or become 'ready' for accommodation in the mainstream (Balescut and Eklindh 2005, 3; Stubbs 2004, 24–5). The 'integrated' child will either just be left to cope with a rigid mainstream system with no support, or will receive individual attention that separates him or her out from peers.

The perceived shortcomings of integration led to a call for the reconceptualization of education for children with disabilities and the development of the notion of *inclusive education* (Balescut and Eklindh 2005, 3). This approach acknowledges that all children can learn, and recognizes and respects differences in children: age, gender, ethnicity, disability, HIV status and so forth.[17] It enables education structures, systems and methodologies to meet the needs of all children.

The basic principles of inclusive education entail that all children have a right to attend their local community school – this does not depend on the characteristics of the child or the preferences of the teacher (Stubbs 2004, 21). The system should be changed to fit the child, not vice versa. Appropriate support should be provided to enable children to access learning (for example, Braille or sign interpretation). Porter (2001, 10) notes that while inclusive education is considered an innovation, it is in fact in many cultural circumstances also the traditional way to educate children.[18]

These principles are illustrated in the following example. Waddembere Yasin attends a primary school in Uganda (UNESCO 1999, 15). He has a visual impairment, and his teacher modifies his programme by providing raised maps, teaching in Braille and teaching mobility and orientation skills in the classroom and playroom. She also ensures that there is sufficient light in the classroom. Waddembere's teacher further receives support from a specialist teacher for learners with visual impairments and involves parents in the learning programme. Waddembere, who spends his days with his classmates and follows the same curriculum, is one of 37 learners with special needs at this school.

State Commitments Regarding Inclusive Education and 'Education for All'

Since the early 1990s, governments have undertaken a number of commitments on the international level regarding the education of disabled children. These commitments have taken shape around three world conferences on education, that is the World Conference on Education for All held in 1990 in Jomtien, Thailand, the World Conference on Special Needs Education convened by UNESCO in Salamanca, Spain, in 1994 and the World Education Forum that was convened in Dakar, Senegal, in 2000 to present the evaluation of the Decade of 'Education for

---

16 This approach conforms with the medical model discussed above.

17 This forms part of the definition that was agreed on by the participants in the Agra seminar in 1998 (primarily from developing countries); see Stubbs 2004, 21. This definition was later adopted practically unchanged in the South African Department of Education's *White Paper on Inclusive Education*, which is discussed below.

18 While Porter makes this statement in relation to the Latin-American context, it also appears to hold true for African settings (see Stubbs 2004, 17–18 and the authorities cited there).

All' begun with the Jomtien Conference (Stubbs 2004, 12). The resulting documents set out undertakings regarding 'Education for All' and education for children with disabilities that were endorsed by all countries participating in these conferences.

Also noteworthy was the UN Millennium Summit in September 2000, where world leaders endorsed eight Millennium Development Goals (MDGs) in order to combat hunger, poverty, disease, illiteracy and environmental degradation on a global scale. The first two Development Goals are the eradication of extreme poverty and hunger and the achievement of universal primary education respectively (see also Chapter 13 in this volume). The second MDG is to ensure that by 2015, children everywhere will be able to complete a full course of primary schooling and that girls and boys will have equal access to all levels of education. Current progress in meeting this target is discussed below.

International Instruments

Introduction

In this section, the provisions of the CRC on the rights of children with disabilities are examined, and it looks at how the CRC Committee has shaped the contours of interpretation of the Convention. Subsequently, the section investigates (in overview), amongst others, the newly-adopted Disability Convention. The exposition focuses on substantive provisions rather than procedural arrangements for implementation.

Convention on the Rights of the Child

Provisions of the Convention   The CRC, in addition to being the first binding instrument in international law to deal with the rights of children, was also the first such document to include a dedicated disability provision (Kilkelly 2002, 119). Article 23 deals specifically with the rights of children with disabilities, and in addition, article 2 explicitly includes disability in its prohibition of discrimination.

Article 23 consists of four paragraphs. Paragraph 1 provides that states parties recognize that a child with mental or physical disabilities 'should enjoy a full and decent life, in conditions which ensure dignity, promote self-reliance and facilitate the child's active participation in the community'. Paragraph 2 deals with the right of children with disabilities to special care. States parties must ensure that assistance is extended to children with disabilities and their caregivers. However, this assistance is subject to several qualifiers: children must be eligible for assistance, application must be made for the assistance, the assistance must be 'appropriate to the child's condition' and to the circumstances of the parents or caregivers. Significantly, provision of assistance is made subject to available resources.

Paragraph 3 of article 23 recognizes that children with disabilities have special needs, and requires that the assistance provided in accordance with paragraph 2 must be provided free of charge, and must be designed to ensure that children with disabilities have effective access to and receive services, including education, 'in a manner conducive to the child's achieving the fullest possible social integration and individual development'. Again, the provision of assistance is qualified: 'whenever possible' and 'taking into account the financial resources of the parents or others caring for the child'.

The fourth paragraph deals with international co-operation to improve the skills and widen the experience of states parties. Particular account must be taken of the needs of developing countries.

Commentators have been strongly critical of article 23. For example, Kilkelly (2002, 120) explains that children with disabilities have no absolute right to assistance under this article: access to services is made subject to conditions such as whether children are eligible and apply for such services. She also voices concerns about the qualifications and limitations with regard to resources included in paragraphs 2 and 3.[19] The same criticism applies to paragraph 3, where again there is no clear need-based entitlement or right to have access to or benefit from such services.

Because of these weaknesses, Kilkelly (2002, 120) is of the opinion that the other provisions of the CRC hold more promise for the vindication of the rights of children with disabilities. Article 2 is specifically important, since its explicit prohibition of discrimination on the ground of disability means that the 'general rights' in the CRC apply equally to children with disabilities. Stubbs (2004, 10) agrees that because of the limitations of article 23, the article needs to be considered in the context of the four general principles – viz. non-discrimination, best interests, right to survival and development, and participation – underpinning all other articles, as well as articles 28 and 29 on education. With a view to achieving the right to education progressively and on the basis of equal opportunity, article 28(1)(a) requires states parties (*inter alia*) to make primary education compulsory and available free to all. Article 29 sets out the aims of education, which include the development of the child's personality, talents and mental and physical abilities to their fullest potential.

Monitoring of implementation by the Committee on the Rights of the Child   The CRC Committee has consistently paid attention to the rights of disabled children in its monitoring functions (UNICEF 2002, 322). In terms of the general reporting guidelines issued by the Committee, states parties are required to provide information on children with disabilities in their initial as well as periodic reports.

In 1996, the Committee provided a report to the Sub-Commission on Prevention of Discrimination and Protection of Minorities,[20] summarizing the general concerns arising from its examination of states parties' reports. The Committee reported that it was struck by the widespread discriminatory attitudes towards these children, and expressed concern about the low number of disabled children enrolled in schools (Kilkelly 2002, 134). It pointed out that budgetary reductions have also affected disabled children who are particularly disadvantaged in their access to adequate health and educational facilities. More recently, the Committee reiterated in its General Comment that in reviewing state party reports, it found

---

19 See also Van Bueren's (1995, 359) robustly worded commentary. Detrick (1999, 385–9) provides background information on the inclusion of these phrases in articles 23(2) and (3).

20 A subsidiary body of the Commission on Human Rights, since renamed the Sub-Commission on the Promotion and Protection of Human Rights (Kilkelly 2002, 134).

that in the overwhelming majority of countries some recommendations had to be made specifically for children with disabilities (CRC Committee 2006, para. 3).

On 6 October 1997, the Committee devoted a Day of General Discussion to the rights of children with disabilities. The issues that were outlined for consideration included the right of disabled children to inclusive education (CRC Committee 1997, para. 313). The discussion culminated in 14 recommendations for further action, one of which was that the Committee should work in co-operation with UNESCO, UNICEF and other relevant agencies to ensure that inclusive education remains an integral part of the debate on education.

General Comment on the Rights of Children with Disabilities   Potentially the most significant step taken by the Committee is the General Comment on the rights of children with disabilities, issued on 29 September 2006. Its purpose is to provide guidance and assistance to states parties in their efforts to implement the rights of children with disabilities 'in a comprehensive manner which covers all the provisions of the Convention' (para. 5). This statement may allay some of the concerns expressed by Kilkelly and other commentators.

The Committee highlights paragraph 1 of article 23 as the leading principle of the implementation of the CRC for children with disabilities (para. 11). The core message of this paragraph is that children with disabilities should be included in society, and measures taken for the implementation of the rights in the Convention, for example in the areas of education and health, should explicitly aim at the maximum inclusion of such children. Paras 12–13 further set out what is expected of states parties in order to meet the requirements of article 23.

As regards general measures of implementation,[21] it is necessary for states parties to set up and develop data gathering mechanisms to reflect accurately the situation of children with disabilities (para. 19; Filmer 2005, 15). This aspect is often overlooked, in spite of the fact that accurate data is essential for the distribution of the resources that are needed to fund programmes. Extra efforts are often required to collect data on children with disabilities, because their parents and caregivers may hide them away (para. 19).

Under article 4, states parties must undertake measures 'to the maximum extent of their available resources'. This provision implies that services and programmes for children should be a priority in resource allocation (para. 20). The Committee expresses its concern about the fact that many states parties not only do not allocate sufficient resources, but have also shown a decline in the budget allocated to children over the years. This has serious implications for children with disabilities, who often rank quite low, or not at all, on priority lists. For example, if a state party is failing to allocate sufficient funds to ensure compulsory and free quality education for all children, it will be unlikely to allocate funds for training of teachers for children with disabilities or for providing necessary teaching aids and transportation for children with disabilities. The Committee reminds that states parties are responsible for ensuring that adequate funds are allocated to children with disabilities along

---

21   These measures include, for example, legislation, national plans of action and policies, international co-operation and monitoring systems.

with strict guidelines for service delivery. Specific reference is made to funding for programmes necessary for including children with disabilities into mainstream education (such as renovating schools to render them physically accessible).

The right to education is dealt with at some length. It is reiterated that children with disabilities have the same right to education as all other children and must enjoy this right without any discrimination and on the basis of equal opportunity as stipulated in the Convention (para. 62). Primary education has to be provided for children with disabilities free of cost (para. 65). In order to fully exercise this right, many children need personal assistance, in particular, teachers trained in methodology and techniques (such as appropriate languages and other forms of communication) for teaching children with a diverse range of abilities, and appropriate and accessible teaching materials, equipment and assistive devices, which should be provided to the maximum extent of available resources.

The Committee notes that the movement towards inclusive education has received much support in recent years (para. 67), and emphasizes this should be the goal of educating children with disabilities (para. 66). It cautions that placement and type of education must be dictated by the individual educational needs of the child, since the education of some children with disabilities requires a kind of support that the regular school cannot offer.

Convention on the Rights of Persons with Disabilities (The Disability Convention)
On 13 December 2006, the UN General Assembly adopted the Disability Convention, the first legally binding international instrument to deal with the rights of persons with disabilities, and hailed as 'the dawn of a new era' for persons with disabilities worldwide (UN News Centre 2006).

Article 3 sets out the general principles underpinning the Convention. These include the principle of respect for the evolving capacities of children with disabilities and for the right of children with disabilities to preserve their identities (article 3(h)). In terms of article 4, states parties undertake to ensure and promote the full realization of all rights and freedoms for all persons with disabilities. Article 7 specifically deals with children with disabilities, and provides that states parties must take all necessary measures to ensure the full enjoyment by children with disabilities of all human rights and fundamental freedoms on an equal basis with other children (para. 1).

The right to education is recognized in article 24. With a view to realizing this right without discrimination and on the basis of equal opportunity, states parties must ensure an inclusive education system at all levels (article 24(1)). Article 24(2) sets out the obligations of states parties in realizing the right to education: to ensure that children with disabilities are not excluded from free and compulsory primary education on the basis of disability (article 24(2)(a)), and to be able to access an inclusive, quality and free primary education (and secondary) education on an equal basis with others in the communities in which they live (article 24(2)(b)). Reasonable accommodation of the individual's requirements must be provided, and persons with disabilities must receive the support required, within the general education system, to facilitate their effective education. States parties are further required to provide effective individualized support measures in environments that maximize academic and social development, consistent with the goal of full inclusion (subarticles (c)–(e)).

The theme of full and equal participation, both in education and as members of the community, is carried further in subarticle 3, which sets out the measures to be taken by states parties to enable persons with disabilities to learn life and social development skills to facilitate such full and equal participation. These measures include (*inter alia*) facilitating the learning of Braille and sign language and the promotion of the linguistic identity of the deaf community (article 24(3)(a)–(c)).

In addition, states parties are required to take appropriate measures to employ teachers, including teachers with disabilities, who are qualified in sign language and/ or Braille, and to train professionals and staff who work at all levels of education (art 24(4)). Such training shall incorporate disability awareness and the use of appropriate augmentative and alternative means of communication, educational techniques and materials to support persons with disabilities.

The Convention opened for signature and ratification on 30 March 2007; 81 states signed on that day, the highest number of signatures of any human rights convention on its opening day. It will enter into force after it has been ratified by 20 countries: currently 17 member states have ratified it. It is hoped that the Convention will be ratified speedily: the fact that it is the most rapidly negotiated human rights treaty in the history of international law (UN News Centre 2006) does create some basis for optimism in this regard.[22]

Regional Instruments

Introduction

From a specialized children's rights perspective, the African human rights framework consists first and foremost of the African Children's Charter (ACRWC), considered in this section, along with the provisions of the Continental Plan of Action for the African Decade of Persons with Disabilities, which is a non-binding document.

African Charter on the Rights and Welfare of the Child[23]

Article 3 of the African Charter on the Rights and Welfare of the Child (ACRWC) sets out the principle of non-discrimination and is the counterpart of article 2 of the CRC, although the African Charter omits to mention 'disability' as a prohibited ground for discrimination. Gose (2002, 47–8) remarks that it is doubtful that this means that discrimination against children with disabilities is allowed under the ACRWC, given the fact that the first part of this article confers the rights to 'every child'. However, he observes (correctly) that this omission is unfortunate, since the Charter in this way misses an opportunity to reaffirm the rights of children with disabilities.

Article 13 of the ACRWC, which deals with the rights of disabled children, reads:

---

22 The Convention entered into force on 3 May 2008.
23 See further, Chapter 3 in this volume.

1. Every child who is mentally or physically disabled shall have the right to special measures of protection in keeping with his physical and moral needs and under conditions which ensure his dignity, promote his self-reliance and active participation in the community.
2. States Parties to the present Charter shall ensure, subject to available resources, to a disabled child and to those responsible for his care ... assistance for which application is made and which is appropriate to the child's condition and in particular shall ensure that the disabled child has effective access to training, preparation for employment and recreation opportunities in a manner conducive to the child achieving the fullest possible social integration, individual development and his cultural and moral development.
3. The States Parties to the present Charter shall use their available resources with a view to achieving progressively the full convenience of the mentally and physically disabled person to movement and access to public highways, buildings and other places to which the disabled may legitimately want to have access to.

Article 13(2) of the Charter thus contains special measures that the state has to undertake, but is shorter and less detailed than the CRC equivalent (Gose 2002, 90). Both instruments subject the rights of the child with disabilities to the availability of resources. However, assistance under the Charter is not dependent on the circumstances of the parent or caregiver (as is the case under paragraph 2 of article 23 of the Convention). Commentators posit that this could be to the advantage of a disabled child in need: in this way, states are allowed to take into account only the circumstances of the child's special situation and not those of his or her parents. This could translate into a higher level of protection, since it widens the circle of persons eligible for state assistance.

Regarding the list of facilities and services to which the child with disabilities should have access, the list contained in the African Charter leaves out 'education', 'health care services', and 'rehabilitation services' as provided for in the CRC. Although education is dealt with in terms of article 11 of the Charter, Gose comments (correctly) that since the educational needs of disabled children are different from those of children without disabilities, the omission of the word 'education' from article 13(2) is regrettable (2002, 91).

Paragraph 3 of article 3 is a new addition to the formulation outlined in the CRC. It aims to guarantee mobility for children with disabilities and their access to public institutions and facilities. The state's obligation could include different measures, such as the construction of public buildings with easy access for persons with disabilities (for example, stairs must be supplemented by ramps, doors must be wide enough to allow passage for wheelchairs, and so on) and could extend to the availability of public transport for persons with disabilities (Gose 2002, 92). This paragraph is especially noteworthy in the context of education and the accessibility of public school buildings.

For the sake of comparison, it is useful also to look briefly at the right to education as set out in article 11 of the African Charter. Paragraph 1 of article 11, which is the counterpart to articles 28 and 29 of the Convention, provides that every child has the right to education (para. 1). States must take all appropriate measures with a view to achieving the full realization of this right and must in particular provide free and compulsory basic education (para. 3(a)).

Although the direct operation of the ACRWC has been weakened by the well-documented shortcomings in its implementation mechanisms,[24] this does not detract from the fact that the norms set out in the Charter can contribute to the evolving body of international human rights principles on the rights of children with disabilities. In addition, African courts on the national level may be able to draw on this body of principles as an interpretive aid.

African Decade of Persons with Disabilities (African decade)

In July 1999, the Organization of African Unity (OAU) Heads of State and Government adopted a resolution to declare the period 1999–2009 as the African Decade of Persons with Disabilities. This initiative arose from the UN Decade of Persons with Disabilities (1983–92), which had been criticized for adopting global solutions without taking into consideration the political, social and economic context of developing countries and emerging democracies. It was hoped that regional Decades would allow for a proper contextual analysis and understanding and for appropriate approaches and solutions to emerge.

The goal of the African Decade is the full participation, equality and empowerment of people with disabilities in Africa. To this end, a Continental Plan of Action was adopted in 2002. Objective 6 of the Plan is to ensure and improve access to (*inter alia*) education. In order to achieve this objective, member states should take a number of measures, including the establishment of policies to ensure that girls and boys with disabilities have access to relevant education in integrated settings at all levels, paying particular attention to the requirements of children in rural areas (para. 30(i)(a)). Where integrated education is not possible, special education should be provided (para. 30(i)(b)). Specific budgets should be allocated for the education of children with disabilities (para. 30(i)(c)).

Progress in commencing with African Decade activities has been painfully slow. The first two years passed without implementation of any programme of activities due to lack of financial resources, and the Secretariat was established in Cape Town only in 2004 (Chalken et al. 2006, 93–8). However, a partnership meeting held in Addis Ababa, Ethiopia, in September 2005 to discuss future initiatives holds promise for accelerated action.

Expansion of the Rights of Children with Disabilities

The principles that have emerged in international and regional human rights law are clear. Founded on articles 2 and 23 of the Convention, these principles have been significantly expanded on in the CRC Committee's General Comment. Firstly, discrimination based on disability is unmistakably prohibited under article 2 of the CRC, which obviously implicates the field of education. Secondly, in the sense that article 23 of the Convention has been criticized for not going far enough in setting

---

24 See Chapter 3 further in this regard.

out the entitlements of disabled children or the concomitant state duties, General Comment no. 9 has gone some way to clarify the ambit of the article.

Article 28 of the CRC confirms that all children are entitled to education on the basis of equal opportunity, and states parties must make free and compulsory primary education available to all children. General Comment no. 9 endorses the notion of inclusive education, although subject to the caveat that placement and type of education must be dictated by the individual needs of each child.

The Standard Rules on the Equalization of Opportunities for Persons with Disabilities confirms the Convention's foundational premises of free and compulsory primary education. However, it expands on the CRC provisions, and unequivocally moves away from a model of separate education to one of integrated education.[25]

The Disability Convention elevates the right to education of disabled persons and accompanying state duties to a new level. Lansdown (2006) remarks the new Convention shifts the focus from addressing the 'special needs' of children with disabilities (as in the CRC) to one of realizing their rights.

The document accordingly sets out state obligations in considerable detail. Article 24, dealing with education, is a case in point: it emphasizes a number of key principles, including equal opportunity, community-based education, reasonable accommodation of individual learning requirements and facilitating the learning of sign language. Governments should move speedily to ratify and implement the Convention.

In the African context, one should also take note of the Continental Plan of Action for the African Decade of Persons with Disabilities. Although this is not a binding document, it does again expand on the standards of the African Charter regarding state obligations. It is suggested that it is essential that the African Committee of Experts on the Rights and Welfare of the Child (ACERWC) draws specific attention to the right of children with disabilities to education.

Legislative and Policy Frameworks

Introduction

An examination of legislation and policies on the national level brings us one step closer to the question of whether children with disabilities are in practice enjoying the benefits of the rights guaranteed under the international, regional and constitutional frameworks. It should be noted from the outset that cross-country comparisons on education for children with disabilities are made difficult by variations in definitions of disability (see Filmer 2005, 14), as well as by a lack of reliable, current information (Lawrence 2004, 7).

While examples of 'good practice' case studies abound in the literature on inclusive education (Stubbs 2000; Karangwa 2003; Peters 2004, 29), these are virtually all illustrations of innovative practices at a micro (school or community)

---

25 It is interesting to note that the Standard Rules makes use of the language of 'integration' rather than 'inclusion'.

level. Their importance should never be discounted, but it is clear that what is required from governments are well-designed, sustainable national policies (fitting into an enabling legislative framework) for providing children with disabilities with education that go well beyond ad hoc interventions.

In this section, the question is posed whether African governments have made adequate progress in developing the required legislation and policy frameworks to ensure realization of the right to education of children with disabilities. The fleeting overview provided below is by no means a comprehensive response.

South Africa

South Africa represents an instructive case study on the level of legislation and policy. The enabling legislation in the context of education is the South African Schools Act of 1996, which provides that public schools must admit learners and serve their educational needs without unfairly discriminating in any way (s. 5(1)).[26] In 2001, the Department of Education published a White Paper on special needs education, which sets out a 20-year plan for developing an inclusive education and training system in South Africa.[27]

The White Paper describes how during the apartheid regime, segregation of learners on the basis of race was extended to incorporate segregation on the basis of disability. Special schools were thus organized according to two segregating criteria, race and disability. In accordance with apartheid policy, schools that accommodated white disabled learners were extremely well-resourced, whilst the few schools for black disabled learners were systematically under resourced (Department of Education 2001, 9).

In order to address the historical inequities and to establish an inclusive education system, a number of measures are set out in the White Paper. These include the qualitative improvement of the 378 existing special schools and their phased conversion to resource centres that provide professional support to neighbourhood schools and are integrated into district-based support teams (Department of Education 2001, 21, 47). Within mainstream schooling, approximately 500 out of 20,000 primary schools will be designated and converted (incrementally) to full-service schools. Full-service schools will be provided with the necessary physical, material and human resources and professional development of staff in order to accommodate the diverse range of learning needs among all learners.

---

26 See also sections 12(4) and (5), dealing with provision of education for learners with 'special education needs' at ordinary public schools and physical accessibility of public schools to learners with disabilities respectively. Section 6(4) provides that a recognized Sign Language has the status of an official language for purposes of learning at a public school. See also the relevant provisions of the Children's Act 38 of 2005, which amplifies section 28 of the Constitution in respect of children's rights. Section 11 of the Act focuses on disabled children, and provides that in any matter concerning a child with a disability, due consideration must be given to making it possible for the child to participate in (amongst others) education activities, recognizing the special needs that the child may have (section 11(1)(b)).

27 See Soudien and Baxen (2006, 153–61) for a thought-provoking critique of the White Paper and its proposed strategies.

The Department of Education has established a Directorate for Inclusive Education and is currently in the process of putting into practice the measures set out in the White Paper.[28] In this regard, pilot projects have been conducted from which valuable lessons can be drawn (Da Costa 2003, 55–90). Realistically, it is too early to evaluate the impact of the policy.

However, a study recently conducted in Orange Farm near Soweto emphasized the urgency of ensuring that policy commitments are translated into reality for children with disabilities. The research aimed to assess whether children with disabilities in this disadvantaged peri-urban township had access to education, health, rehabilitation and other services (Salojee et al. 2006, 2). Of the 92 children in the research sample who were of compulsory school-going age (that is, between 7 and 15 years), 40 (44 per cent) were attending a school or specialized institution. Of these children, 55 per cent were attending mainstream schools, and 45 per cent attended a special school, training centre or day-care centre. Thirty (42 per cent) children of school-going age with motor impairments and 28 (44 per cent) children with intellectual impairments were not attending school at all (Salojee et al. 2006, 4).

The explanations provided by caregivers for non-attendance at school included the family's financial difficulties, refusal on the part of schools to accept the child, and the caregiver's perception that the child will not cope at school. Researchers also identified inadequate and inaccessible transport as well as poor administration of services as explanations for the low utilization of available services (Salojee et al. 2006, 5). In the context of education, the researchers noted ignorance of policies and a lack of empathy from teachers and principals when caregivers tried to place a child with disabilities at a school.

The conclusion reached by the researchers, namely that children with disabilities in Orange Farm are not enjoying the rights and services to which they are entitled under the South African Constitution and current legislation, appears unavoidable. It is this 'implementation gap' between legislation and policy and the practical experience of disabled children that needs to be addressed.

Further Examples

The implementation gap described above does not exist in South Africa alone, as the following cursory examination reveals.[29] Kenya, one of the jurisdictions that has adopted progressive legislation on children's rights,[30] states in its 2004 conference report that out of an estimated 750,000 children of school-going age with disabilities,

---

28 In June 2005, the Department of Education's Directorate for Inclusive Education published guidelines on full service schools and on special schools as resource centres, as well as draft guidelines for inclusive learning.

29 Information for this section was drawn *inter alia* from the national education reports presented at the 47th Session of the International Conference on Education convened by UNESCO in 2004. The Conference was attended by 100 ministers and deputy ministers of education from 137 UNESCO Member States.

30 Children Act 8 of 2001, which includes 'disability' in its prohibition of discrimination (section 5). Section 12 provides that a disabled child has the right to be accorded education and training free of charge or at a reduced cost whenever possible. The right to education,

approximately 90 per cent are either at home or in regular schools with little or no specialized assistance (Ministry of Education, Science and Technology 2004, 6). The report states that a special policy is required to cater for the schooling needs of children with disabilities. It also calls for awareness programmes to eradicate taboos and beliefs associated with disabilities, the development and implementation of a flexible child-centred curriculum and the inclusion of children with disabilities in 'regular' schools.

A recent UNESCO assessment confirms that special needs education in Kenya suffers from inadequate funding, lack of a clear policy framework, low progress in assessing and placing children with disabilities, few qualified teachers and lack of teaching and learning resources (UNESCO Nairobi Office 2006, 28–9). Further constraints are a lack of clear legal guidelines on the implementation of inclusive education and a lack of reliable data on children 'with special needs' (UNESCO Nairobi Office 2006, 33; Ministry of Education, Science and Technology 2005, 37). However, the Kenyan government has embarked on a number of strategies to address the current situation.

In neighbouring Uganda, the implementation gap appears to have been narrowed considerably.[31] Uganda was the first country in East Africa to introduce 'Universal Primary Education' in 1997, offering free schooling for four children in every family (UNESCO Nairobi Office 2006, 55). This policy drastically increased school enrolment, and has also benefited children with disabilities (Ministry of Education and Sports 2004, 10).

Before the introduction of Universal Primary Education, the few schools for children with disabilities were over-stretched and the majority of children with disabilities were excluded from school. The situation has subsequently improved in two respects. Firstly, specialized schools benefit from Universal Primary Education funding, and secondly, children with disabilities are being enrolled in mainstream schools as a result of a shift to a policy of inclusion (Ministry of Education and Sports 2004, 11; UNESCO 2001, 31).

The Ugandan government has expanded programmes for assessing children with learning difficulties and has also trained teachers on special education (UNESCO Nairobi Office 2006, 57). However, challenges remain in the form of high enrolments against limited facilities at both primary and secondary school levels (Ministry of Education and Sports 2004, 14; UNESCO Nairobi Office 2006, 62–3). These high enrolments have created the need for additional physical facilities, teachers and teaching materials.

It is disconcerting to note that one of the countries that is in the process of developing children's legislation expressly guaranteeing the rights of children with

---

set out in section 7, includes the right to free basic education. Section 18 of Act 14 of 2003: Persons with Disabilities is also relevant to the right to education.

31 Uganda enacted its Children's Statute in 1996. Section 10 makes specific provision for the rights of children with disabilities, and guarantees them equal opportunities to education (sections 10(1)(c)). In terms of section 11, local government councils must keep a register of disabled children within their areas of jurisdiction and give assistance to them whenever possible.

disabilities, that is Mozambique,[32] made little reference to the education of children with disabilities in its 2004 report (Ministry of Education, Mozambique 2004, 11).

Conclusion: Looking Ahead

> The truth is, all countries are developing countries when it comes to disability rights. (Quinn 2005, 520)

For a number of reasons, it is important for African governments to approach the education of disabled children with a sense of urgency. According to the 2007 MDG Report, the net enrolment rates in primary education in the school year 2004/5 primary education in developing regions increased to 88 per cent, up from 80 per cent in 1990/91. Although the sub-Saharan region has made significant progress since 1990/91, in Burkina Faso, Djibouti, Eritrea, Ethiopia, Mali and Niger, fewer than half the children of primary-school age are enrolled in school. Therefore, according to the report, sub-Saharan Africa still trails behind other regions, with 30 per cent of its primary school aged children out of school. The report does not disaggregate the data to indicate the number of disabled children included in the net enrolment rates.

With seven years to go before the target date of 2015, it is now imperative for African countries to heed the frequently quoted warning of James Wolfensohn, former president of the World Bank. He stated in 2003 that unless disabled people were brought into the development mainstream, it would be impossible to cut poverty in half by 2015 or to give every girl and boy the chance to achieve a primary education by the same date.

Another reason for urgency: a recent situational analysis of HIV and young people with disabilities in Uganda and in Rwanda found that participants from both countries raised concerns about the majority of disabled people in their countries who had little education or who did not attend school because these people were perceived as not having access to information about HIV/Aids (Yousafzi and Edwards 2004, 65; Lawrence 2004, 18). In sub-Saharan Africa, a lack of access to information about HIV/Aids could well have fatal consequences.

Commentators are, however, cautiously optimistic that inclusive education is gaining momentum across the African continent. For example, Richler (2005, 38) points out that this momentum is now supported by the various complementary initiatives that are contributing to education reform: the 'Education for All' initiative, the New Partnerships for Africa's Development (NEPAD), and the Decade of Persons with Disabilities. All of these require governments to make new investments in education to ensure that all children, including disabled children, attend and complete, primary school.

---

32 Article 29(1) of the draft Bill on Child Protection (dated December 2005) guarantees children the right to education, and in particular, 'equality of condition in access to and remaining at school' (subarticle (a)). In terms of article 30, the state has the duty to guarantee to children basic, compulsory and free education. In addition, the state must ensure specialized educational care for disabled children, preferably in inclusive classes.

The adoption of the Disability Convention will add further impetus. As Richler so compellingly notes, a lack of education is a life sentence to poverty and exclusion (2005, 32). However, ensuring that children with disabilities enjoy the full benefits of the right to education is at the same time part of the broader project underpinning the human rights approach to disability: a society that is genuinely inclusive, that values difference and respects the dignity and equality of all human beings regardless of difference. This ideal can also be expressed as *ubuntu* – a truly African value.

References

Articles, Books and Chapters in Books

Basser, L.A. and Jones, M. (2002), 'The Disability Discrimination Act 1992 (CTH): A Three-Dimensional Approach to Operationalising Human Rights', *Melbourne University Law Review* 26, 254–84, reproduced in Blanck, P. (ed.).

Blanck, P. (ed.) (2005), *Disability Rights* (Aldershot: Ashgate).

Chalken, S. et al. (2006), 'Setting up the Secretariat for the African Decade of Persons with Disabilities', in Watermeyer, B. et al. (eds).

Currie, I. and De Waal, J. (2005), *Bill of Rights Handbook*, 5th edn (Lansdowne: Juta and Co.).

Da Costa, M. (ed.) (2003), *Opening Schools for All Children in South Africa: The Experience of Inclusive Education in Mpumalanga and Northern Cape Provinces* (Institute of Education: University of Warwick).

Degener, T. (1999), 'International Disability Law: A New Legal Subject on the Rise: The Interregional Experts' Meeting in Hong Kong, December 13–17, 1999', *Berkeley Journal of International Law* 18, 180–95, reproduced in Blanck, P. (ed.).

Detrick, S. (1999), *A Commentary on the United Nations Convention on the Rights of the Child* (The Hague: Kluwer Law International).

Filmer, D. (2005), *Disability, Poverty and Schooling in Developing Countries: Results from Eleven Household Surveys* (Washington DC: World Bank).

Gose, M. (2002), *The African Charter on the Rights of the Child* (Bellville: Community Law Centre, University of the Western Cape).

Heyer, K.C. (2002), 'The ADA on the Road: Disability Rights in Germany', *Law and Social Inquiry* 27, 723–62, reproduced in Blanck, P. (ed.).

Kanter, A.S. (2003), 'The Globalization of Disability Rights Law', *Syracuse Journal of International Law and Commerce* 30, 241–69, reproduced in Blanck, P. (ed.).

Kilkelly, U. (2002), 'Disability and Children: The Convention on the Rights of the Child (CRC)', in Quinn, G. and Degener, T. (eds).

Kisanji, J. (1995), 'Growing Up Disabled', in Zinkin, P. and McConachie, H. (eds).

Kisanji, J. (1999), 'The Historical and Theoretical Basis of Inclusive Education', keynote paper read at the conference on 'Inclusive Education in Namibia: The Challenge for Teacher Education', Windhoek, Namibia, 23–25 March 1999.

Lansdown, G. (2003), *What Works? Promoting the Rights of Disabled Children* (London: Disability Awareness in Action).

Murray, R. (2004), *Human Rights in Africa: From the OAU to the African Union* (Cambridge: Cambridge University Press).

Peters, S.J. (2004), *Inclusive Education: An EFA Strategy for All Children* (Washington DC: World Bank).

Quinn, G. (2005), 'Closing: Next steps – Towards a United Nations Treaty on the Rights of Persons with Disabilities', in Blanck, P. (ed.), 519–41.

Quinn, G. and Degener, T. (eds) (2002a), *Human Rights and Disability* (Geneva: United Nations).

Quinn, G. and Degener, T. (2002b), 'The Moral Authority for Change: Human Rights Values and the Worldwide Process of Disability Reform', in Quinn, G. and Degener, T. (eds).

Quinn, G. and Degener, T. (2002c), 'The Application of Moral Authority: The Shift to the Human Rights Perspective on Disability through Human Rights "Soft" Law', in Quinn, G. and Degener, T. (eds).

Rousso, H. (2003), *Education for All: A Gender and Disability Perspective* (Washington DC: World Bank).

Salmonsson, A. (2006), *Disability is Not Inability* (Stockholm: Institute of Public Management).

Salojee, G. et al. (2006), 'Unmet Health, Welfare and Educational Needs of Disabled Children in an Impoverished South African Peri-Urban Township', *Child: Care, Health and Development* (Published online on 15 June 2006) doi:10.1111/j.1365-2214.2006.006454.x.

Soudien, C. and Baxen, J. (2006), 'Disability and Schooling in South Africa', in Watermeyer, B. et al. (eds).

Stubbs, S. (2004), *Inclusive Education Where There Are Few Resources* (Oslo: Atlas Alliance).

UNICEF (2002), *Implementation Handbook for the Rights of the Child*, 2nd edn (New York and Geneva: UNICEF).

UNICEF (2005), *Excluded and Invisible: The State of the World's Children 2006* (New York: UNICEF).

UNICEF (2007), *Vitamin A Supplementation: A Decade of Progress* (New York: UNICEF).

Van Bueren, G. (1995), *The International Law on the Rights of the Child* (Dordrecht: Martinus Nijhoff).

Watermeyer, B. et al. (eds) (2006), *Disability and Social Change: A South African Agenda* (Cape Town: HSRC Press).

Yousafzi, A.I. and Edwards, K. (2004), *Double Burden: A Situation Analysis of HIV/ AIDS and Young People with Disabilities in Rwanda and Uganda* (London: Save the Children).

Zinkin, P. (1995), 'Framework: Priorities', in Zinkin, P. and McConachie, H. (eds).

Zinkin, P. and McConachie, H. (eds) (1995), *Disabled Children and Developing Countries* (London: Mac Keith Press).

International and Regional Documents

African Charter on the Rights and Welfare of the Child, OAU Doc CAB/LEG/24.9/49 (1990).

Continental Plan of Action for the African Decade of Persons with Disabilities, endorsed by the seventy-sixth ordinary session of the OAU Council of Ministers, held at Durban (28 June–6 July 2002) by Decision CM/DEC.676 (LXXVI).

Convention on the Rights of Persons with Disabilities, GA Res A/61/611 dated 6 December 2006.

UN Millennium Declaration, A/Res/55/2 (dated 18 September 2000).

UN Standard Rules on the Equalization of Opportunities for Persons with Disabilities, GA Resolution 48/96 of 20 December 1993.

Universal Declaration of Human Rights, GA Res 217A (III) UN Doc A/810 (10 December 1948).

Reports, Papers and Other Documents

Balescut, J. and Eklindh, K. (2005), 'Literacy and Persons with Developmental Disabilities: Why and How', paper commissioned for the *EFA Global Monitoring Report 2006, Literacy for Life*, Reference Number 2006/ED/EFA/MRT/PI/9.

Committee on Economic, Social and Cultural Rights (1999), 'General Comment on the Right to Education (No 13)'.

CRC Committee (2006), 'General Comment on the Rights of Children with Disabilities'.

Degener, T. (2004), 'Definition of Disability', paper produced under the European Community Programme to combat discrimination.

Department of Education, South Africa (2001), *White Paper on Special Needs Education* (Pretoria: Department of Education).

Karangwa, E. (2003), 'Challenging the Exclusion of Blind Students in Rwanda', *EENET Newsletter* Issue 7 (Manchester: University of Manchester).

Lawrence, J. (2004), 'The Right to Education for Persons with Disabilities: Towards Inclusion', conceptual paper prepared for the World Bank; Reference Number ED/BAS/EIE/2004/1 REV.

Lehtomaki, E. (2002), 'Inclusive Schools in Mozambique: From Policy to Strategy', *EENET Newsletter* Issue 6 (Manchester: University of Manchester).

Ministry of Education, Mozambique (2004), *Education Sector Strategic Plan II (ESSP II) 2005–2009*.

Ministry of Education, Science and Technology (2004), *Development of Education in Kenya*, report presented at the 47th Session of the International Conference on Education convened by UNESCO in 2004.

Ministry of Education, Science and Technology (2005), *Kenya Education Sector Support Programme 2005–2010: Delivering Quality Equitable Education and Training to All Kenyans*.

Ministry of Education and Sports, Uganda (2004), *National Report on the Development of Education in Uganda at the Beginning of the 21st Century*, report presented at the 47th Session of the International Conference on Education convened by UNESCO in 2004.

Porter, G.L. (2001), 'Disability and Inclusive Education', paper prepared for the InterAmerican Development Bank.

Richler, D. (2005), 'Mainstreaming Disability in Development Programmes of African Countries: Promoting Inclusive Education' in Secretariat of the African Decade of Persons with Disabilities, *International Partners Meeting Addis Ababa, 21–22 September 2005*.

Secretariat of the African Decade of Persons with Disabilities (2005), *International Partners Meeting Addis Ababa, 21–22 September 2005* (Conference papers) (Cape Town: Secretariat of the African Decade).

Stubbs, S. (2000), 'Facilitating Education in Mali', *EENET Newsletter* Issue 4 (Manchester: University of Manchester).

UNAIDS (2006), *2006 Report on the Global AIDS Epidemic* (Geneva: UNAIDS).

UNESCO (1999), *Welcoming Schools: Students with Disabilities in Regular Schools* (Paris: UNESCO).

UNESCO (2001), *Including the Excluded: Meeting Diversity in Education – Example from Uganda* (Paris: UNESCO).

UNESCO (2006), *Education For All Monitoring Report 2007 Strong Foundations: Early Childhood Care and Education* (Paris: UNESCO).

UNESCO Nairobi Office (2006), *Fact Book on Education For All* (Nairobi: UNESCO).

Wolfensohn, J.D. (2002), 'Poor, Disabled and Shut Out', *Washington Post* (3 December 2002).

World Health Assembly (2005), *Resolution on Disability, Including Prevention, Management and Rehabilitation*, WHA58.23 dated 25 May 2005.

World Health Organization (2006), *Injuries, Violence and Disabilities: Biennial Report 2004–2005* (Geneva: World Health Organization).

Cases

Ephrahim v *Pastory and Kaizingele* (1990) 87 LLR 106; (1990) LRC (Const) 757 (HC of Tanzania).

Internet Sources

Country information for Uganda <http://uganda.disabilityafrica.org>, accessible through website for African Decade of Persons with Disabilities <http://www.africandecade.org> (accessed on 22 December 2006).

CRC Committee (1997), 'Day of General Discussion on Children with Disabilities' <www.unhchr/html/menu2/6/crc/doc/days/disabled.pdf>.

Dakar Framework for Action (2000), <http://www.unesco.org/education/efa/ed_for_all/dakfram_eng.shtml>.

'Disabled children embattled by education policy', dated 15 October 2006, IRIN (PLUSNEWS) <http://www.irinnews.org> (accessed 27 October 2006).

Jomtien World Declaration on Education for All (1990), <http://www.unesco.org/education/efa/ed_for_all/background/jomtien_declaration.shtml>.

Lansdown, G. (2006), 'The New Disability Convention and the Protection of Children', dated 8 December 2006 <http://www.crin.org/resources> (accessed 20 December 2006).

Salamanca Statement on Principles, Policy and Practice in Special Needs Education (1994), <http://www.unesco.org/education/information/nfsunesco/pdf/SALAMA _E.PDF>.

UN News Centre (2006), 'Lauding disability convention as "dawn of a new era", UN urges speedy ratification', dated 13 December 2006 <http//un.org/ga/61/news> (accessed on 20 December 2006).

Chapter 18

Worst Forms of Child Labour: A View from Out of Africa

Jacqui Gallinetti[1]

Introduction

Child labour, strictly defined, is work that affects the child's enjoyment of his or her fundamental rights: civil, political or economic, social and cultural – particularly the broad right to survival and development of the child. The relevant International Labour Organization (ILO) Conventions, the UN Convention on the Rights of the Child (CRC) and a number of domestic laws call for the elimination of child labour (with priority being given to its worst forms). According to the ILO's International Programme on the Elimination of Child Labour (IPEC), not all work performed by children is child labour: '[child labour] depends on multiple factors, including, but not restricted to, the age of the child, the duration for which the activity is performed, the nature of the activity, the conditions of work, or a combination of these and other factors' (IPEC 2003, 12). Thus, while the relevant ILO Conventions and the CRC call for the elimination of child labour, this does not mean the elimination of every type of work performed by children.

A relevant issue in relation to child labour concerns household chores and non-economic activities like domestic work. This is more so in the context of cultures and traditions where child domestic work may be taken for granted as normal. Thus IPEC has identified a contemporary additional challenge in the elimination of child labour as being the focus on this type of child work. It correctly observes that while household chores and other non-economic activities are usually considered a normal part of a child's upbringing, they can be potentially harmful to the child and a violation of his or her rights. This would be the case, for example, where a child is required to help around the house or care for younger siblings to an extent that schoolwork suffers or she or he drops out of school (IPEC 2003, 12). This is especially relevant in the African context where various types of hazardous work or worst forms of child labour are justified through cultural arguments, for example in the case of herdboys in Lesotho (Ministry of Employment and Labour, Kingdom of Lesotho 2005, viii). As pointed out by Ncube (1992, 22):

1   The author wishes to thank the Ford Foundation for its support to the author in the compilation of this chapter.

Although the main objective underlying the engagement of children in various economic activities was to train them for future adult roles, there is no doubt that tangible economic benefits accrued to parents and the household members from the work of children.

The different types of child labour in different countries and regions have been well documented over the last century and as a result there is a vast litany of accounts of child labour (see, for instance, Bass 2004; Bequele and Boyden 1988; Boyden, Ling and Myers 1998; Gomango 2001; Isaacman and Allman 2006; Kielland and Tovo 2006; Mendelievich 1979; Myers 1991; and Weston 2005).

More specifically, there are many documented accounts of the extent of child labour in Africa. The Global March Against Child Labour has issued country fact sheets on child labour which have shown the extent of the problem quite succinctly. For instance in Angola, a country that has ratified ILO Convention no. 182 on the worst forms of child labour, children constitute more than 50 per cent of the population and, in 2000, the ILO estimated that 431,000 children were economically active. It was also reported that worst forms of child labour in the country including child slavery, child prostitution and child soldiers were prevalent. Likewise in Benin, also a country that has ratified Convention 182 and one where children similarly constitute more than 50 per cent of the population, the ILO estimated that in 2000, 223,000 children were economically active and that worst forms of child labour such as child trafficking and child prostitution were rife. In Ghana, also a signatory to Convention 182, children are trafficked, sold into slavery for sexual exploitation, forced into prostitution, and 80 per cent of girls who are domestic servants are between the ages of ten and 14 years.

A survey has shown that 83 per cent of Ethiopian children aged between five and 14 years are engaged in either a productive activity or the performance of household chores. In relation to children aged 15–17 years, 97 per cent are engaged in either a productive activity or the performance of household chores. More revealing of the extent to which children are engaged in economic activities is the fact that 62 per cent aged 10–14 years and 39 per cent of children aged 5–9 years are engaged in at least one type of employment besides household chores. The survey revealed that all in all, 15.5 million of the 18.13 million children in Ethiopia are working either in the household or in an outside context. In other words, only 14 per cent of the Ethiopian children in the age cohort of 5–17 are not working (African Child Policy Forum 2007).

In South Africa, Statistics South Africa conducted the first national survey of child work in 1999, entitled the *Survey of Activities of Young People* (SAYP). In 1999 there were an estimated 13.4 million children in South Africa between the ages of five and 17 years. Some of the key findings of the SAYP were that of the children engaged in economic activities, 59 per cent said they were working because they had a duty to help their family, and a further 15 per cent said they worked to assist the family with money. In addition, children aged 5–14 years who appear to be working (in contravention of the law) accounted for more than 30 per cent of the children working in economic activities.

In 2005, the Ministry of Employment and Labour in Lesotho released a report on worst forms of child labour in that country. The report notes that the 1999 labour force survey estimated that there were approximately 68,250 children aged between ten and 14 years who were economically active (projections based on the 1996 population census indicated there were approximately 284,000 children aged between ten and 14 years in 2001 in Lesotho) (Ministry of Employment and Labour, Kingdom of Lesotho 2005, 1). The report identified herdboys, street workers, domestic workers and child sex workers as particular sites for intervention in the fight against the worst forms of child labour in Lesotho. The findings of the study indicated that more than half the herdboys were unpaid family workers ordered by parents or guardians to supplement family labour; that the main reasons for children becoming involved in sex work were to provide for themselves, support siblings and to support the family; and that all of the children across the four categories had low levels of education and school drop-out rates were high for these children. This study clearly showed the important need for education in the fight against child labour.

In 2006, the ILO released a study that assesses the problem of child labour globally (ILO 2006). In 2000, the ILO had provided a set of statistics that would allow in future for the reliable assessment of the extent of the child labour problem and, four years later, a further set of statistics were released that illustrated the changing trends (ILO 2006, vii). Overall, the analysis illustrated that globally there was a reduction in the numbers of economically active children, child labourers and children involved in hazardous work from 2000 to 2004 (ILO 2006, 6). On a regional analysis, however, the report noted that the numbers of economically active children aged 5–14 years had declined in all regions except sub-Saharan Africa (ILO 2006, 8). Liebel, however, raises serious doubts regarding the accuracy of the content of the report, both in relation to the statistics presented and lack of empirical proof that the 'end of child labour is within reach' (Liebel 2007).

The ILO report is at pains to stress that it is premature to speculate on the reasons for the global decline. It is unclear what the cause of the increase in economically active children in sub-Saharan Africa is, especially in light of the fact that, just as in the other world regions, African countries have ratified Convention 182, have a number of IPEC programmes operating to eliminate child labour and receive international assistance to combat the worst forms of child labour. In light of this, what makes Africa different? Given the reality of the situation is it really possible to eliminate worst forms of child labour in Africa or at all? This chapter cannot answer these questions, but will raise these and other issues for discussion as they lie at the heart of the challenges facing the continent in its efforts to create a safe environment for children.

International Legal Instruments

The CRC and the ACRWC

The CRC and the African Charter on the Rights and Welfare of the Child (ACRWC) deal with child labour and the worst forms of child labour in articles 32 and 15 respectively. Neither make express reference to the 'worst forms of child labour', but this is not surprising as both were adopted prior to Convention 182.

Article 32 of the CRC essentially deals with the child's right to be protected from economic exploitation, hazardous and harmful work, regulation of work for children and establishing a minimum age for admission to employment (without setting a specific age). Detrick (1999, 563) notes that the use of the word 'and' between the term 'economic exploitation' and the words 'from performing any work' in article 32(1) indicates that the CRC's drafters did not regard all work performed by children as economic exploitation. Van Bueren (1995, 264) argues that this approach illustrates the fundamental difference between the right to work and being obliged to work: economic exploitation amounts to work at the expense of development, and child labour is exploitative when it threatens the physical, mental, emotional or social development of the child. This obviously accords with the provisions of article 3 of Convention 138 (discussed later in this chapter), which allows children to perform work above the minimum age of employment (as well as certain light work, again above a minimum age for such work), provided such work, by its nature or the circumstances in which it is carried out, is not likely to jeopardize the health, safety or morals of young persons.

It has been noted that the CRC Committee has given particular attention to economic exploitation by holding a Day of General Discussion on 'Economic exploitation of the child' in 1993 when, *inter alia*, the Committee invited financial institutions, including the World Bank and International Monetary Fund, to discuss the need to protect the rights of children in economic reform programmes (Hodgkin and Newell 2002, 486). In addition, the Committee has expressed concern at countries who have made reservations or declarations in relation to article 32 – whether the reservation be related to the progressive implementation of the provisions of the article, as in the case of India, or because the rights contained in article 32 are already adequately protected in domestic law, as in the case of New Zealand (Hodgkin and Newell 2002, 485). These observations of the Committee illustrate its concern regarding compliance by states, but the need to comply with the CRC has been strengthened by the provisions of Convention 182, which ensures a richer content for article 32 by its reference to the need for states to have regard to 'the relevant provisions of other international instruments'.

On the other hand, the Committee has exhibited careful reflection on issues attendant to child labour by its concern regarding factors external to states, such as macro-economic policies on a global scale which can affect the realization of children's rights. This is bolstered by Convention no. 182's call for international co-operation regarding economic development and poverty eradication. It is highly unfortunate, however, that the provisions of the CRC and Convention no. 182 do not bind international financial institutions.

However, the implications of the CRC on the issue of child labour do not stop at article 32. Article 33 deals with the protection of children from the illicit use of narcotic drugs and psychotropic substances and the prevention of the use of children in the production and trafficking of such drugs and substances; article 34 deals with the protection of children from all forms of sexual exploitation and sexual abuse; article 35 deals with the protection of children from being abducted, sold or trafficked; and article 36 constitutes a 'catch-all' provision protecting children from 'all other forms of exploitation prejudicial to any aspects of the child's welfare'.

Article 15 of the African Children's Charter (ACRWC) seems to be based on the wording of article 32, with some notable exceptions. On a positive note, article 15 seems to broaden the scope of the CRC's protections by referring to 'all forms of exploitation' as opposed to 'exploitation' alone (Gose 2002, 61). However, it omits reference to work that is prone to 'interfere with the child's education' and 'or to be harmful'. The result is a much narrower protection being afforded to African children. Gose (2002, 62) argues that these are accidental omissions; however, it could be argued that the inclination to protect cultural practices and identities played a role in the drafting of this provision, especially if one has regard to the realities of African children, who in the name of household chores and cultural obligations, are denied full access to education.

Nonetheless, article 15 introduces a provision that is designed to ensure more effective and widespread implementation of the ACRWC, namely, the obligation on states to disseminate information on the dangers of child labour (Gose 2002, 64). In so doing, the ACRWC creates a precursor to the supplementing Recommendation (no. 190) to Convention 182, which expressly calls for wide social mobilization.

The International Labour Organization Conventions 138 and 182

The ILO Minimum Age Convention (no. 138) was the first universal child labour treaty dealing with standards applicable to working children. Right at the outset, article 1 requires states to 'pursue a national policy designed to ensure the effective abolition of child labour and to raise progressively the minimum age for admission to employment or work to a level consistent with the fullest physical and mental development of young persons'. This not only places the goal of eliminating child labour at the vanguard, but also intimates that despite the Convention setting a minimum age, it is just that: a minimum, which states are required to progressively raise.

Convention 138 provides the standard relating to setting the minimum permissible age at which children can work: this age must not be below 15 years (for developed countries) and 14 years (for developing countries). It also provides that such minimum age excludes 'light work' in which the minimum ages of 12 and 13 are applicable for developed and developing countries respectively. Boyden, Ling and Myers (1998, 195; see also Hanson and Vandaele 2003, 120) provide an interesting insight into the application and implementation of minimum age standards. They begin by noting that the minimum age standard represents the ideal of childhood as being a time of privilege, dedicated solely to education and play, a time in which children are dependants and protected from having to engage in economic activity. They proceed to explain that where this model of childhood exists, it seems natural and is assumed to represent the universal norm of how children should be raised, yet there is no evidence that this type of childhood produced children who are happier and more adjusted for adult life than other models. In truth, they point to the fact that there is evidence that children thrive in a variety of childhood situations, including those in which they become economically active at an earlier age. Accordingly, they argue that the minimum age standard in Convention no. 138 is such that it restricts the freedom or choice of children to work below a certain age for any reason.

Expanding this argument, Bourdillon, Myers and White (forthcoming 2008) contend that a universalized standard excluding children below a particular age from employment or work as set in article 2 of Convention no. 138 is unjustified. The reasons they give are that insufficient attempts have been made to determine the impact of setting a minimum age for admission to employment or work on children; there is existing evidence that the policy often harms the children it claims to protect; and the effort of enforcing 'blanket prohibitions' affecting all work (even safe work) diverts attention away from the need to intervene in forms and conditions of work that are harmful to children.

From an African perspective this is especially true. Sloth-Nielsen and Mezmur (2007) have noted the widespread disregard for Convention 138 because of the fact that it limits the child's ability to become economically and individually empowered and fulfil his or her duties under article 31 of the African Children's Charter, which provides for, *inter alia*, the child's duty to work for the cohesion of the family, the child's duty to assist the family in times of need and the child's duty to serve his or her national community by placing his or her physical and intellectual abilities at its service.

The protective mantel for children initiated by Convention 138 was given further substance by ILO Convention no. 182 on the elimination of the worst forms of child labour. In the 86th session of the International Labour Conference in 1998, the ILO proposed the adoption of a new international instrument to combat the worst forms of child labour, supplemented by recommendations for practical action and assistance. The ILO circulated Report VI(1) *Child Labour: Targeting the Intolerable*, chronicling the exploitation and abuse of working children, surveying international and national law and practice and, through an accompanying questionnaire, seeking the views of governments, employers' and workers' organizations on the possible scope and content of a new international instrument. As motivation, ILO Report VI(1) noted that the climate at the time provided 'unknown opportunities and possibilities that should enable us to make a directive assault on child labour' (1998, 57). It argued that the new convention would fill the gaps in current international legal instruments, set clear priorities for national and international action, and build on Convention no. 138. It noted that an obstacle to the greater ratification of Convention no. 138 was the fact that many states viewed its provisions as too complex and difficult to apply in its entirety and therefore there was a need to complement the minimum age Convention and focus on the most intolerable forms of child labour. The Report (1998, 57) pointed also to the fact that there was economic development in developing countries in Asia and Latin America and that such development was predicted for Africa as well. This was seen as an indication that countries were able to put in place time-bound programmes to combat and eliminate child labour, much as they had achieved rapid growth rates and increased *per capita* income (amongst other socio-economic objectives) within time-bound development programmes. Furthermore, special attention was necessary for children who are subjected to even greater exploitation and abuse on account of their particular vulnerabilities, such as the very young and girls. Importantly, it was recognized that there was a pressing need for prevention. The Report acknowledged that worst forms of child labour 'can be attacked on a lasting basis only if short-term action is conceived within the framework of a national policy that gives primacy to preventive measures, including the provision of free, universal, compulsory education ...'.

On 17 June 1999, ILO Convention no. 182 on the worst forms of child labour was unanimously adopted by the ILO member states together with its supplementing recommendation (no. 190) and it came into force on 19 November 2000. In article 3, Convention no. 182 defines the worst forms of child labour as comprising all forms of slavery or practices similar to slavery, such as the sale and trafficking of children, debt bondage and serfdom, and forced or compulsory labour including the forced or compulsory recruitment of children for use in armed conflict; the use, procuring or offering of a child for prostitution, for the production of pornography or for pornographic performances; the use, procuring or offering of a child for illicit activities, in particular for the production and trafficking of drugs, and work which by its nature or the circumstances in which it is carried out, is likely to harm the health, safety or morals of children.

The Convention requires states parties to define worst forms of child labour accordingly, and requires them to adopt various measures to ensure compliance with its provisions. Thus, states are required to prohibit through both employment and criminal law any of the worst forms of child labour. They also have to provide for the right of child victims of worst forms of child labour (when this happens) to appropriate direct assistance and removal from the worst forms of labour, as well as for their rehabilitation and social integration. This should include the right to access free basic education and, wherever possible, appropriate vocational training.

Some of the unique features of the Convention have been its call for 'immediate and effective measures' to combat and eliminate worst forms of child labour, the requirement for states to design and implement programmes of action, and for the establishment of monitoring mechanisms (Noguchi 2002, 355). In particular, the obligation to design and implement programmes of action together with effective and time-bound measures has been argued to take states' obligations beyond simple prohibitions (Noguchi 2002, 360). What makes the Convention stand out against other ILO conventions that require their provisions to be applied in law and practice is the fact that Convention 182 sets out the requirements for action in substantive provisions, thereby allowing for inaction by governments to be highlighted and consequent pressure placed on them to comply with their undertakings (Noguchi 2002, 360).

Other commentators have highlighted the fact that Convention 182 has taken the debate about child labour further by extending the scope of the minimum age Convention to activities that are clearly criminal in nature, as well as addressing various 'Achilles heels' of Convention 138 such as the non-specificities of what measures states should take to enforce the provisions of the Convention (Davidson 2001, 217). Convention no. 182 has been hailed as 'important because it identifies the illegal activities that endanger children's safety and welfare, and it sets realistic goals for Member States' (Davidson 2001, 224).

While all the above is true, the complexity of the issue almost appears to have been lost sight of. Although Convention no. 182 adopts a far more targeted approach to child labour by recognizing that more concrete obligations may be needed for states and that a clear focus on issues such as prevention, education and rehabilitation of victims is needed, there is reason for caution in regarding the Convention as a significant development in the child rights arena and elimination as a goal that is ultimately achievable. This is because of the difficulties of eliminating crimes such as child prostitution, child trafficking, drug trafficking and so on, which does not seem to have been adequately acknowledged. Is it therefore true that the elimination of certain *crimes* (as opposed to worst forms of child labour) within time-bound measures is a 'realistic goal'? Obviously the worst forms of child labour and these crimes against children should be addressed with the full force of action that states can muster, but I am posing the question that if one examines the true nature of worst forms of child labour, can states reasonably be expected to 'eliminate' within a 'time-bound' programme actions that their and international criminal justice systems have been grappling with for centuries? Conceptually, 'elimination' is not the only hurdle that needs to be overcome. Given the use of the terms 'urgency', 'time-bound' and 'immediate' in the Convention, by ratifying it states have obliged themselves to undertake such action. But against what are those terms to be measured? Six months, one year, three years or a decade? Likewise, the decision to adopt time-bound measures could also back-fire on states. In light of potential criticism ensuing from inaction or failure to meet deadlines, are states prepared to set deadlines for action and results that could result in international and domestic censure?

From the African perspective, it is unfortunate that the drafting process of the Convention did not give full cognizance to the challenges facing the continent – such as dire poverty, civil strife and the ever increasing threat that HIV/Aids and other dread diseases pose for African children. Had these challenges been addressed at the outset, the 'elimination approach' to the worst forms of child labour may not have been as directly and unequivocally stated, and a more strategic approach adopted. Some of these challenges were eventually acknowledged in the ILO 2006 Report, discussed in more detail below. However, the challenges noted here do not trump the need to protect child victims, and therefore the adoption of Convention no. 182 was useful in calling attention to actions constituting worst forms of child labour, albeit that the ultimate goal of Convention no. 182 is possibly unattainable.

Convention No. 182 Put Into Action

There have certainly been concerted efforts made to apply the Convention in order to combat the worst forms of child labour. The Infocus Programme on the Elimination of Child Labour (IPEC) within the ILO was created to enhance the ILO's response to its core goal of eliminating child labour. It has been noted that while a substantial number of countries that have ratified Convention no. 182 have indeed adopted time-bound measures against one or more worst forms of child labour, this has usually happened in countries where there is an IPEC project to support such-time bound programmes (ILO 2006, 18; see further White 2005 and Lansky 1997).

Tanzania

In the United Republic of Tanzania, for example, the government has committed itself to the elimination of worst forms of child labour in the country by 2010 (ILO 2006, 38). The ILO 2006 Report documents the steps that the Tanzanian government has undertaken in support of this time-bound programme, and these include a child labour strategies document which was developed to become the Strategic Programme Framework (SPF) for the programme, linked to the National Strategy for Growth and Reduction of Poverty (NSGRP). The second phase of the NSGRP for 2005–2010 has been developed and includes child labour indicators as well as addressing several important goals directly related to the elimination of child labour. The aim is to reduce the number of children engaged in the worst forms of child labour by 75 per cent by 2005 and the child labour participation rate from the current 25 per cent to less than 10 per cent in 2010. In addition, there has been an effort to reduce the number of out-of-school children through the Ministry of Education's Complementary Basic Education in Tanzania programme. The government has also produced a list of hazardous tasks for children as set out in Convention 182, and this has been translated into local languages to promote community awareness.

It has been said that the implementation of the child labour interventions in Tanzania, under the auspices of IPEC, has demonstrated the critical role of awareness-raising and advocacy campaigns, which is also vital to the process of building a solid social foundation to address the problem (Mallya 2006, 1 and Mmari 2005, 169). The IPEC programme has revolved around 'a strategically focused, systematic, comprehensive and sustainable media-driven public awareness and community mobilization action' (Mallya 2006, 1). This awareness-raising programme is comprised of a number of strategies. The first is capacity building – this has focused on media practitioners in each of the districts in Tanzania, with a view to make an in-depth analysis of their individual, as well as collective, capacity needs for effective and sustainable advocacy work on the worst forms of child labour generally, as well as specifically within the individual districts. The media's capacity needs have then formed the basis for a support package that has included training workshops on media advocacy on the worst forms of child labour. Second, there has been the promotion and establishment of local/folk media – this has involved the identification of existing local/folk media groups or institutions in the districts in order to enlist their involvement in the public mobilization and information campaign against the worst forms of child labour. Once identified, they have been provided with sensitization and orientation on child labour, been assisted to formulate themes on worst forms of child labour with strategic messages on the child's right to education, and encouraged to undertake drama and singing performances to targeted audiences such as community leaders, parents, teachers, pupils and local government officials.

The establishment of, facilitation and support to media coalitions has also played a critical role. These coalitions comprise information officers, journalists and other media practitioners in each district and have taken the form of consultative fora to define jointly priority areas for worst forms of child labour and share information and ideas on the promotion of media campaigns on child labour. Finally, there have been public mobilization campaigns through various print and electronic mass media, such as posters, leaflets and video shows. Journalists, television and radio producers have been consulted to produce and publish case studies, news briefs and feature articles on child labour as well as to broadcast strategic television and radio programmes.

Collectively, these strategies have produced a social mobilization campaign that is community driven, imbued with a sense of local ownership and responsibility towards the monitoring of the child labour media campaigns, the formulation of community by-laws on child labour and the generation of political will to combat child labour through targeting political leaders in all levels of government (Mallya 2006, 5). However, again it must be noted that although results in raising awareness on worst forms of child labour have been achieved, the goal of elimination remains. It is encouraging that Tanzania's National Strategy for Growth and Reduction of Poverty deals with the issue of child labour, but amongst the many challenges facing Africa, are crimes such as those constituted by the worst forms of child labour, so that the issue needs to be addressed within that context as well.

Madagascar

Madagascar has developed an action plan entitled 'Institutional Support for the Abolition of Child Labour in Madagascar', financed by IPEC and the ILO and carried out by the Ministry of Labour and Social Laws (African Child Policy Forum 2007). The programme has a number of aims that cut across various issues.

The first relates to the prevention of child labour, *inter alia*, by creating awareness with a focus on convincing public opinion that work performed at an early age has harmful consequences for the health and development of the child; and improving relations between the various institutions and organizations that seek to protect and realize the rights of working children.

The second aim relates to the immediate withdrawal of children exposed to the worst forms of child labour (such as those defined under article 3 of Convention no. 182), and the need for steps to eliminate these worst forms of child labour in the country. The final goal is aimed at the improvement of the living and working conditions of children who are not exposed to the worst forms of child labour, but are still involved in work, through awareness raising and other measures. These measures are to be established by a working group that has been created for the development and follow-up of the programme.

In addition, the Ministry of Justice has initiated a programme with the ILO and IPEC entitled 'Reform of the legal framework for the elimination of the worst forms of child labour', scheduled to run over 29 months and aimed at supporting the Ministry in its law reform efforts, popularization, awareness raising, and education of the population, especially parents, on the rights of children in relation to work. It will develop information, education and communication materials such as booklets and enlist the assistance of the media to print articles in the daily newspapers. This programme seems to have a good balance between awareness raising, law enforcement measures and prevention. In addition, the spread of obligations across departments and ministries also ensures more inter-departmental co-operation and attention to worst forms of child labour as the issue does not just fall within the ambit of one arm of government. This action plan needs to be commended for its attention to prevention and how prevention initiatives can complement the usual law enforcement measures.

Southern Africa

In Southern Africa, the ILO has a strong presence through the Towards the Elimination of the worst forms of Child Labour (TECL) programme located within the IPEC office. TECL is running programmes aimed at eliminating the worst forms of child labour in South Africa, Botswana, Namibia, Swaziland and Lesotho (the latter four known as the BLNS countries).

In the BLNS countries, comprehensive time-bound strategies focusing on child labour, such as the Child Labour Action Programme in South Africa, have not yet been developed. For that reason the focus of the TECL programme in these four countries is on laying the foundations for concerted action against the worst forms of child labour as well as child labour more generally. Although the review and development of policies and legislation, public awareness raising and actual interventions to address worst forms of child labour are important elements of a comprehensive time-bound child labour action programme, TECL support to the BLNS countries focuses mainly on contributing to knowledge on the worst forms of child labour and the drafting of a country action plan or framework for such a plan to address them (TECL 2005). In these four countries, poverty and HIV/Aids were identified as the primary circumstances that increase the risk of child labour. The initial focus in the BLNS countries is to gather information on the prevalence, nature and extent of the key priority areas of concern identified for each country, insofar as rapid assessments have not already been done. The TECL programme will also focus on the policy and economic environment by assessing key legislation, policies and programmes to identify any need for legislative reform and capacity development. Together with awareness raising, the two streams will lay the foundation for a consultative process with key government departments, the social partners of the ILO as well as the broader civil society aimed at the drafting of an action plan for each country to address the matter of child labour including its worst forms. The final aim is to draft action plans for the individual countries to address child labour including its worst forms as identified for that country. These activities began in 2005 in all four countries and are ongoing. Programme Advisory Committees on Child Labour representing government departments, organized labour, business and civil society guide the development and implementation of the programmes in each country.

South Africa

The first draft South African Child Labour Programme of Action (CLPA) was provisionally approved by representatives from various government departments on 4 September 2003, subject to certain amendments and the costing of the various recommended action steps to be implemented by the key government departments, and was submitted to the South African cabinet for noting in July 2005. In 2007 the National Child Labour Programme for South Africa: Phase 2, to run from 2008 to 2012, was adopted by the government. In drafting the CLPA, certain principles were adhered to and these included the prioritization and identification of the worst forms of child labour for South Africa, the examination of best practices elsewhere, sustainability and the avoidance of duplication (South African Department of Labour 2003, 3). The CLPA identified a wide range of activities that fall under the mandate of various government departments and agencies, some of which were already contained in existing policy, and others that are new and require expenditure and budgets. Annexure A of the 2003 CLPA sets out the actual action steps that have to be undertaken by designated stakeholders including the Departments of Justice, Social Development, Education, Labour, Correctional Services and South African Police Service (SAPS) as well as employers and NGOs. These steps included policy development, public awareness campaigns, collection of data and statistics, and training, amongst many others. It is important to note that the criminal justice sector departments play a critical role in the policy document – thereby recognizing the nexus between worst forms of child labour and crime.

The key elements of the CLPA are the rollout of programmes on poverty alleviation, employment, labour, and social matters in areas that involve work that is harmful to children; the promotion of new legislative measures aimed at prohibiting the worst forms of child labour; the strengthening of national capacity to enforce legislative measures; and increasing public awareness and social mobilization against the worst forms of child labour (South African Department of Labour 2003, 4). However, although these key elements meet the requirement of criminalizing worst forms of child labour as set out in Convention no. 182, the question remains as to whether this law enforcement-type approach is sufficient.

Having noted existing South African law and policy on child labour, including constitutional provisions, provisions in labour laws – such as the Basic Conditions of Employment Act and the Occupational Health and Safety Act – provisions in the South African Schools Act providing for compulsory education, and the existence of grants for children as well as provisions for welfare proceedings to be initiated where children are in need of care and protection, the CLPA deals with the development of policy specifically aimed at addressing child labour. It highlights the fact that any policy on child labour must address poverty and impoverishment. Further, it reviews the likely impact of HIV/Aids on child labour policy; the need for prevention strategies to combat child labour; and links the CLPA with other policies addressing child labour, notably social welfare grants that may impact on the drive to eliminate worst forms of child labour (South African Department of Labour 2003, 25). Again, these policy considerations seem to be cross-cutting and comprehensive in their approach to addressing the worst forms of child labour, but can they address the goal of elimination of worst forms of child labour? Possibly not, as illustrated by an example detailed below.

One of the worst forms of child labour that South Africa has identified as a problem in the country is the illicit use of children in illegal activities. The 2003 CLPA identified four action steps to be taken in eliminating this phenomenon (these action steps were revised in 2007 based on the outcomes of a pilot programme to address the use of children in the commission of crime). On the one hand, it can be argued that the action steps rely too heavily on other policies and laws, particularly those in the criminal justice system. They fail to take into account the possible failures in criminal justice policy that may thwart their implementation. For instance, one action step mentions the promotion of diversion of children away from the criminal justice system.[2] Although diversion happens in practice at present in South Africa, legislation creating legal certainty around the practice is long overdue. Moreover, the original proposals, in the form of the Child Justice Bill 49 of 2002, that diversion would apply to all children irrespective of the offence, seems likely to change at the hand of the South African Parliament (see for instance Ehlers 2006 and Skelton 2006). The possibility has been mooted that the option of diversion will be excluded for certain children who have committed serious (scheduled) offences. This runs contrary to the spirit and intention of the original Child Justice Bill which did not differentiate between children and their eligibility for diversion on the basis of offences committed.[3] Rather, it directed that each child should be assessed individually and that the unique circumstances of such child should be taken into consideration when making a decision about diversion. If the proposed changes become a reality, they could exclude a number of children used to commit crime as a worst form of child labour from the benefits of diversion, if the offences with which they are charged are excluded from diversion (for example, murder or armed robbery).

Second, the action steps create standards that may be impossible to deliver upon. For example, an action step contained in the 2003 CLPA (but removed in the 2007 version) required the investigation and prosecution of adults who use children to commit crime. Although there are various offences available in South African law that perpetrators may be charged with (for instance, incitement or conspiracy), it has emerged that the investigation and prosecution of adults is nigh on impossible without the necessary evidence; and such evidence, in the absence of testimony from the children who may for various reasons, including fear for their safety, not be able to testify, is simply not available to ensure these prosecutions occur (Children's Rights Project, Community Law Centre, 2007). This indicates that the original drafters may not have fully comprehended the implementation requirements for this particular action step. This is an example that bears out the concerns of certain commentators who have noted that prostitution, pornography and the drug trade are vice crimes that are notoriously difficult to eliminate. Law enforcement efforts typically drive these activities underground without actually eliminating them (Smolin 2003; Frank and Muntingh 2005).

Finally, this then leads to the third difficulty with the action steps relating to the illicit use of children to commit crime, namely, they indicate a lack of insight into the extent of the problem outside of the context of child labour. The CLPA, as well as international instruments such as Convention no. 182, extol the value of schooling and vocational training in the fight against child labour. However, when the benefits of education or skills development are outweighed by the presumed financial benefits of the 'second' economy or the 'economy of crime', little can be done to lure children away from adults in the criminal underworld who use them in their

---

2   See Chapter 9 in this volume for a more detailed discussion of diversion and its meaning.

3   The Child Justice Bill of 2002 was passed in a reworked version by the South African House of Assembly in June 2008, and the possibility of children charged with serious offences being diverted has ultimately not been completely excluded.

illicit endeavours. The larger issue of crime prevention, and especially preventing organized crime as opposed to just law enforcement measures against perpetrators, is significantly absent from this section in the CLPA.

Therefore, even though both versions of the CLPA deal with a range of issues thought to be vital in any attempt to eliminate worst forms of child labour, the actual concrete actions that need to be taken may not lead to the desired result. The action steps related to the illicit use of children to commit crime are a prime example. This worst form of child labour reaches across a broad spectrum of criminal activities and a law enforcement approach aimed at individuals alone will not lead to the elimination thereof. In fact, given the high crime rate in South Africa, the solution does not seem to be readily apparent and it is certainly not to be found in the CLPA.

In light of this, it is hoped that the insights developed in the South African process can be used as learning blocks for the action programme development in the BLNS countries, as well as other countries embarking on a time-bound, action programme process.

Legislating Against Child Labour

A recent International Organization for Migration (IOM) study has examined legislation in certain Southern African countries (Malawi, Mozambique, South Africa, Tanzania, Zambia and Zimbabwe) to determine the legal and practical obstacles in prosecuting child labour (Thompson 2006). The findings confirm that most countries have enacted laws to prohibit child labour and that it is an offence to employ a child under a certain age or in hazardous or inappropriate work (Thompson 2006, 1). In addition, certain countries in the region have enacted or are in the process of enacting laws to prohibit worst forms of child labour.

The study found that the Zambian Employment of Children and Young Persons Act (2004) was the 'most promising' for prohibiting serious child labour, including its worst forms. The Act prohibits children under a certain age from working, as well as prohibiting the employment of children in 'hazardous' or 'harmful' labour, thereby also complying with the requirements of the Minimum Age of Employment Convention (Thompson 2006, 4). Over and above this, the statute prohibits the employment of a child under 18 years of age in 'any type of employment or work which by its nature or the circumstances in which it is carried out, constitutes a worst form of [child] labour'. The study notes that the statute, following the precedent set in Convention no. 182, defines worst forms of child labour along the lines of the definition set out in article 3. While lauding the content of the Act, the study notes that the legislation is still relatively new and under-utilized (Thompson 2006, 5).

Thompson also refers to the South African Children's Act 38 of 2005 (partially in force) in the context of child trafficking, noting that the law contains a specific offence of child trafficking. Subsequent to the IOM study, the Children's Amendment Act 41 of 2007 was passed; this now prohibits worst forms of child labour in South African law.

The value of the new children's legislation in South Africa is in the fact that it escalates the issue of worst forms of child labour beyond the criminal justice sphere.

One of the main implications of the Act for children who have been found to be victims of child labour or exploitation relates to their care and protection. Section 150 of the Act sets out the grounds on which a child can be found to be in need of care and protection by a children's court; should such a finding be made, the court is empowered to make a range of orders relating to the child's welfare. One such ground on which a child can be found in need of care and protection is if a child 'has been exploited or lives in circumstances that expose the child to exploitation' (as defined). Such a finding requires the children's court to make an order which can include, *inter alia*, foster care, placement in a child and youth care facility, or an order that the child receives treatment. This aims to ensure that the needs and welfare of children who are in need of care and protection are addressed within a legislative framework. Similar mechanisms are available in the Kenyan Children's Act which provides a non-exhaustive list of circumstances in which children can be found to be in need of care and protection. However, the concern that has been raised is that existing remedial measures are significantly limited in practice, especially for children in need of care and protection on account of them being orphans or lacking parental care (African Child Policy Forum 2007).

Interestingly, section 150(2) of the South African Children's Act states that a child who is a victim of child labour *may* be a child in need of care and protection and must then be referred for investigation by a designated social worker. If after investigation a social worker finds that the child is not in need of care and protection, the social worker must where necessary take measures to assist the child, including counselling, mediation, prevention and early intervention services, family reconstruction and rehabilitation, behaviour modification, problem solving and referral to another suitably qualified person or organization. So in this instance, even though there is no court order finding the child to be in need of care and protection, a social worker must still provide services where needed. It is unclear how this will be monitored as it is merely a statutory obligation and not a court order.

South Africa and Kenya have thus used welfare legislation to address children who may be victims of child labour and certain worst forms of child labour under the protective mantel provided to children in need of care. The provisions of both acts provide a concrete, legal framework that can deliver services to children who are victims of child labour and exploitation. This legislative emphasis on the welfare of children who are victims of child labour is noteworthy, as it moves the focus away from relying only on law enforcement measures aimed at offending 'employers', the effectiveness of which is questionable, to combat the worst forms of child labour.

Overall, the IOM study found that the region's labour statutes are generally adequate (Thompson 2006, 7). However, in respect of worst forms of child labour, the study concludes that there are certain potential legal limitations in the region, which may limit their effectiveness in certain circumstances; singled out are narrow definitions or scope of existing child labour laws, low penalties for offences and lack of extra-territorial jurisdiction (Thompson 2006, 8). However these observations are focused solely on the law enforcement aspects of combating worst forms of child labour in legislation. Such an approach fails to recognize that the law enforcement approach may not be sufficient to eliminate worst forms of child labour within the context of the criminal community. Finally, the study fails to examine and analyse what other legislative measures may be in place for assisting victims of worst forms of child labour – an obligation set by Convention 182.

Challenges in Eliminating Worst Forms of Child Labour in Africa

The ILO 2006 Report devotes a specific section to Africa, pointing out that poverty and HIV/Aids are two of the greatest hardships facing the continent (ILO 2006, 64). However, the Report goes on to note that some sub-Saharan countries have demonstrated economic growth rates, school enrolments have increased in others and the 2005 G8 Summit's Gleneagles Communiqué presents an opportunity for child labour to be strategically dealt with (ILO 2006, 64). In addition, it points out the increase in donor aid being channelled to the sub-continent. The provision of aid, however, can be misleading. What must actually be analysed is the continent's capacity to implement programmes, not only the availability of resources. While there may be enough money available on the one hand, on the other, there may be a lack of suitably qualified persons, poor budgeting, inequitable service delivery and bad expenditure.

A recent report has revealed that by 2010 an estimated 15.7 children in sub-Saharan Africa will have lost at least one parent due to HIV/Aids and even where the disease's prevalence stabilizes or begins to decline, the number of orphans will continue to grow or at least remain high for many years (UNICEF, UNAIDS and PEPFAR 2006). Despite also acknowledging the surge in leadership and resources for the fight against the disease, this report argues that there is insufficient understanding of the scourge and that knowledge of the conditions of orphans and vulnerable children on the sub-continent needs to increase, amongst others through ensuring more systematic data-collection (UNICEF, UNAIDS and PEPFAR 2006, v). Aside from orphanhood and all its costs, the report also notes systemic consequences of HIV/Aids that impacts upon the lives of children, such as disrupted health and education systems due to the infection of health workers and teachers (UNICEF, UNAIDS and PEPFAR 2006, 10).

Without being defeatist, the link between child labour, poverty, education and HIV/Aids in Africa appears to present a far greater challenge than seems to be acknowledged in the ILO 2006 Report. What is, however, encouraging are the efforts of IPEC to significantly strengthen its work, including increasing the knowledge base on child labour, mainstreaming child labour concerns, studies on education and child labour, and building capacity for action (ILO 2006, 65).

Conclusion

The rhetoric, the political outrage, the enactment of domestic laws and implementation strategies are all aimed at eliminating the worst forms of child labour and countering the nefarious actions of adults who enslave children and use them in commercial sex work and illicit activities. These criminal actions that ultimately result in economic exploitation of children are slowly being seen in a context beyond the sphere of the ordinary criminal justice system, as actions that rob children of their childhood as well as their autonomy. The ILO's efforts to eradicate these social harms that beset children are well thought out and crafted to ensure that governments expeditiously address issues of social justice within the context of child labour. Ultimately, however, the enemies are not only the criminals who target children but also dread disease, poverty and civil strife, not to mention the complications introduced by globalization and the world trade system. Africa, as a continent hardest hit by adversity, will have to embrace the issues and develop comprehensive, committed strategies that recognize the inter-linkages that exist in combating worst forms of child labour in order to try to determine workable responses.

Resources

Articles, Books and Chapters in Books

Bass, L.E. (2004), *Child Labor in Sub-Saharan Africa* (London: Lynne Rienner Publishers).

Bequele, A. and Boyden, J. (eds) (1988), *Combating Child Labour* (Geneva: International Labour Office).

Bourdillon, M., Myers, W. and White, B. (2008 forthcoming), 'Re-assessing Minimum Age Standards for Children's Work', *The International Journal of Sociology and Social Policy*, special issue on children and work (copy on file with the author cited with the permission of William Myers).

Boyden, J., Ling, B. and Myers, W. (1998), *What Works for Working Children* (New York: UNICEF and Save the Children Sweden).

Davidson, M. (2001), 'The International Labour Organisation's Latest Campaign to End Child Labor: Will it Succeed Where Others Have Failed?', *Transnational law and Contemporary Problems* 203.

Detrick, S. (1999), *A Commentary on the United Nations Convention on the Rights of the Child* (The Hague: Kluwer Law International).

Gomango, S.P. (2001), *Child Labour: A Precarious Future* (Delhi: Authors Press).

Hanson, K. and Vandaele, A. (2003), 'Working Children and International Labour Law: A Critical Analysis', *The International Journal of Children's Rights* 11, 73.

Hodgkin, R. and Newell, P. (2002), *Implementation Handbook for the Convention on the Rights of the Child* (Geneva: UNICEF).

Isaacman, A. and Allman, J. (eds) (2006), *Invisible Hands: Child Labor and the State in Colonial Zimbabwe* (London: Heinemann).

Kielland, A. and Tovo, M. (2006), *Children at Work: Child Labour Practices in Africa* (London: Lynne Rienner Publishers).

Lansky, M. (1997), 'Perspectives: Child Labour: How the Challenge is Being Met', *International Labour Review* 136, 2.

Liebel, M. (2007), 'The New ILO Report on Child Labour: A Success Story, or the ILO Still at a Loss?', *Childhood: A Journal of Global Child Research* 14:2, 279–84.

Mendelievich, E. (1979), *Children at Work* (Geneva: International Labour Office).

Mmari, D. (2005), 'Combating Child Labor in Tanzania: A Beginning', in Weston, B.H. (ed.).

Myers, W. (ed.) (1991), *Protecting Working Children* (London and New Jersey: Zed Books Ltd in association with UNICEF).

Ncube, W. (1992), 'The African Cultural Fingerprint', in Ncube, W. (ed.) *Law, Culture, Tradition and Children's Rights in Eastern and Southern Africa* (Aldershot and Brookfield, VT: Ashgate).

Noguchi, Y. (2002), 'ILO Convention No. 182 on the Worst Forms of Child Labour and the Convention on the Rights of the Child', *The International Journal of Children's Rights* 10, 355.

Smolin, D. (2003), 'A Tale of Two Treaties: Furthering Social Myths through the Redemptive Myths of Childhood', *Emory International Law Review* 17, 967.

Van Bueren, G. (1995), *The International Law on the Rights of the Child* (The Hague: Martinus Nijhoff).

Weston, B.H. (ed.) (2005), *Child Labor and Human Rights: Making Children Matter* (Boulder, CO: Lynne Rienner Publishers).

White, B. (2005), 'Shifting Positions on Child Labor: The Views and Practice of Intergovernmental Organisations', in Weston, B.H. (ed.).

Reports and Other Documents

African Child Policy Forum (2007), *In the Best Interests of the Child: Harmonising Laws in Eastern and Southern Africa* (Addis Ababa: African Child Policy Forum).

Children's Rights Project (2007), *Children Used by Adults to Commit Crime (CUBAC): Final Report on Pilot Programme Implementation*, ILO, 2007 (Western Cape: Community Law Centre).

Ehlers, L. (2006), *Child Justice: Comparing the South African Child Justice Reform Process and Experiences of Juvenile Justice Reform in the United States of America*, Criminal Justice Initiative Occasional Paper Series 1 (Cape Town: Open Society Foundation for South Africa).

Frank, C. and Muntingh, L. (2005), *Children Used by Adults to Commit Crime (CUBAC): Children's Perceptions* (Pretoria: International Labour Organization and Programme Towards the Elimination of Child Labour).

Gose, M. (2002), *The African Charter on the Rights and Welfare of the Child* (Bellville: Cape: Community Law Centre, University of the Western Cape).

ILO (1998), *Report VI (1) Child Labour: Targeting the Intolerable*, International Labour Conference 86th Session (Geneva: International Labour Office).

ILO (2006), *The End of Child Labour: Within Reach. Global Report under the Follow-up to the ILO Declaration on Fundamental Principles and Rights at Work* (Geneva: International Labour Organization).

IPEC (2003), *IPEC Report on Action against Child Labour 2003–2004: Progress and Future Priorities* (Geneva: International Labour Office).

Mallya, W. (2006), 'Awareness Raising on Child Labour: Experience from Tanzania', unpublished paper delivered at the Regional Child Labour Conference (RECLISA) (Johannesburg).

Ministry of Employment and Labour, Kingdom of Lesotho (2005), *Special Studies on the Worst Forms of Child Labour in Lesotho: Herdboys, Street, Domestic Workers and Child Sex Workers*.

Programme Towards the Elimination of Child Labour (TECL) (2005), *Supporting the Time-Bound Programme to Eliminate the Worst Forms of Child Labour in South Africa's Child Labour Action Programme and Laying the Basis for Concerted Action against Worst Forms of Child Labour in Botswana, Lesotho, Namibia and Swaziland, Annexures 1–4* (Pretoria).

Skelton, A. (2006), 'The Influence of the Theory and Practice of Restorative Justice in South Africa with Special Reference to Child Justice', unpublished LLD thesis (Pretoria: University of Pretoria).

Sloth-Nielsen, J. and Mezmur, B.D. (2007), 'A Dutiful Child: The Implications of Article 31 of the African Children's Charter', paper presented at the 10th ordinary meeting of the African Committee of Experts on the Rights and Welfare of the Child, Cairo, Egypt.

South African Department of Labour (2003), National Child Labour Programme of Action for South Africa, draft 4.10.

South African Department of Labour (2007), National Child Labour Programme for South Africa: Phase 2: 2008–2012, version 4.4.

Thompson, J. (2006), 'Legal and Practical Obstacles to Prosecution of Child Labour Exploitation in Southern Africa', unpublished paper delivered at the Regional Child Labour Conference (RECLISA) (Johannesburg).

UNICEF, UNAIDS and PEPFAR (2006), *Africa's Orphaned and Vulnerable Generation: Children Affected by Aids* (New York: UNICEF).

Internet-based Resources

Report on the Worst Forms of Child Labour, the Global March Against Child Labour accessed at <http://www.globalmarch.org/worstformsreport/world/index.html>.

Survey of Activities of Young People in South Africa: Country report on children's work-related activities, Statistics South Africa, Department of Labour, 2001, <http://www.labour.gov.za/download/9499/Research%20report%20-%20Survey%20of%20Activities%20of%20Young%20People%20in%20South%20Africa%201999%20-%20Country%20Report.pdf> (accessed on 5 October 2007).

Index